Civil Religion & the Presidency

The cover photo is a painting on glass
entitled *Memorial to Washington*.
It was painted in China about 1800.
Courtesy, The Henry Francis du Pont Witherthur Museum.

Civil Religion & the Presidency

Richard V. Pierard & Robert D. Linder

Academie
Books Grand Rapids,
Michigan
Zondervan Publishing House

Civil Religion and the Presidency
Copyright © 1988 by Richard V. Pierard and Robert D. Linder

Academie Books is an imprint of Zondervan Publishing House,
1415 Lake Drive, S.E., Grand Rapids, Michigan 49506.

Library of Congress Cataloging in Publication Data

Pierard, Richard V., 1934–
    Civil religion and the presidency.

    Bibliography: p.
    Includes index.
    1. Civil religion—United States.   2.Presidents—
United States—Religion.   1. Linder, Robert Dean.
II. Title.
BR517.P54   1988   322'.1'0973   88-6217.

ISBN 0-310-28331-0

Edited by Susan E. McShane and Eileen Roesler

Printed in the United States of America

88 89 90 91 92 93 / CH / 10 9 8 7 6 5 4 3 2 1

CONTENTS

FOREWORD

In 1969 Clifton F. Brown spoke of a process of "religio-cification."

In 1940 Justice Felix Frankfurter wrote that "the ultimate foundation of a society is the binding tie of cohesive sentiment."

In 1955 Will Herberg spoke of "civic faith," during the 1950s and 1960s Sidney Mead kept talking about "the religion of the republic," and in 1967 Robert N. Bellah took a word from Rousseau and began to point to America's "civil religion."

In 1974 I distinguished between "prophetic" and "priestly" civil religion.

In 1974 Michael Novak talked about "choosing our king" and showed how the president of the United States fulfilled royal and sacerdotal roles.

Finally, in 1988 Richard Pierard and Robert Linder have put together the notions of religiocified cohesive sentiment in the form of civil religion that finds its priestly fulfillment in the president of the United States.

To begin in this way to point to the focus of this book may make it seem simply derivative. It is so only in the sense that historians must always build on each other's work. We follow traces others have left, walk trails they have blazed, study road maps and topographic surveys they have devised—but the goal is always to work back to the sources and see what these reveal about a phenomenon.

The sources for these two historians are the writings of and about presidents of the United States in their most priestly moments. The cast of characters is in part predictable. In the case of all movements, one goes back to beginnings, revisits the founders. In the American case, the "father of his country," George Washington, was an obvious choice. The respectful people of his generation produced children who venerated him and grandchildren who made him an icon and adored him.

Abraham Lincoln? He was and remains at the spiritual center of national life. A highly ambiguous and flawed individual, he used his rhetorical gifts and reflective powers to reach almost transcendent levels as he grasped for meaning in the midst of the worst bloodshed the citizens of this continent ever visited upon themselves. Lincoln spoke of his own "political religion," and made decisive contributions to ironic and tragic interpretations of national life even as he imparted hope to this "last, best hope of earth." He became an icon even as he smashed icons.

In no one's list of great presidents would you find William McKinley. Yet, in an imperial hour he somehow managed to give voice to a people's (often base) yearnings and to get assassinated. The mix of his words and that sad event helped place him in the pantheon of those who were priests of civil religion, and our two authors must deal with him.

Woodrow Wilson? Easily, he belongs to this gallery. One of the most learned and theologically informed of all the presidents, he served in wartime as a crusader and again as an ambiguous figure. He was cocksure about his purposes as he led the nation into World War I, and he spoke of the American cause as a service not to the generalized God of civil religion but to Christ himself, yet he is remembered as a failure in his own most nobly intended cause. A priest he was, at a strange altar.

Franklin D. Roosevelt? A giant among twentieth century presidents and, again, a wartime figure, he used his charisma and rhetorical gifts to project priestly roles as a civil religionist, and he belongs.

Dwight D. Eisenhower brought credentials associated with war and helped end one war during his presidency. He also consciously embarked on a crusade againt "atheistic communism" and summoned religious symbols to support his peacetime presidency during a "religious revival."

Richard M. Nixon "used" civil religion, and assigned to the people the attributes that once belonged to God, as he set out to convince and for a time did convince many that he stood in the great tradition of civil religionists.

Jimmy Carter added a new twist, because his image was

less identified with generalized faith in the Enlightenment God most presidents evoked; he was born again, devoted to Jesus. Yet, he displeased the fellow born-again people and had his finest moments dealing on an interfaith basis with a Jewish and a Muslim people's leader.

And then came Ronald Reagan, who, as we shall see, politicized and exalted civil religion to its highest point in American history.

I have run down the gallery, taking care not to give away the plot as Pierard and Linder tell it, but only to prepare the reader for the sequence and, I hope, to build up some suspense as to what it was these leaders evoked, how they did it, and what the legacy was.

Why bother? Why disturb the peace of those who think of presidents as presidents, priests as priests, patriotism as something done in the public sphere and religion as something done in church? I believe these authors are convincing when they imply and when they explicitly contend and show that the outcomes of presidential priestly civil religion are fateful. They have to do with the deepest definitions of a people, the highest points they reach, the most idolatrous depths in which they wallow. Dissection and analysis are important and useful tools, and this is what we get here.

To their credit, these historians make some important discriminations. Civil religion is not always religious nationalism or self-idolatry. There is usually some ambiguity in the employment of religious symbols, and they know it and show it in respect to the civil religion of the presidents and the people who elect them.

I believe they also keep pointing to a theme that can rescue American civic faith from idolatry. In the spirit of Robert Bellah, they keep pointing to the motif of "transcendent justice" which Americans inherited from the Hebrew prophets and the more profound of the enlightened founders. Transcendent justice calls forth a God beyond the gods of the nation to judge it. Utterances in support of it usually come from the prophetic elements in a religion, but at its best, the presidency has seen some of its priests turn prophetic. One sometimes goes for decades watching for that motif. When it appears, the office of the presidency and the people who look to it are indeed well-served.

Could it be that in a modest way this book will contribute to the thoughts of a readership whose members can play some part in assuring that transcendent justice, not national idolatry, might issue in moments of crisis? It is an immodest hope, but we must begin somewhere, and the pages which follow offer some valid and noteworthy clues. We are in Pierard's and Linder's debt.

MARTIN E. MARTY
The University of Chicago

PREFACE

For over two decades, we have been thinking, speaking, and writing about the relationship between religion and politics in Western society. Naturally the times in which we lived affected our deliberations. We reached adulthood in the tranquil Eisenhower era with its consensus religiosity and general feeling of well-being, but the resurgence of emotionally charged and often ill-informed Christian anticommunism in the late 1950s amd early 1960s was a matter which caused us some concern. Then, we shared in the excitement of a new vision for the United States that was the fruit of the Kennedy years and the Civil Rights Movement, and we saw these dreams shattered in the deepening Vietnam imbroglio and increasing tempo of violence at home. After the tragic death of John F. Kennedy, we watched the rise and fall of presidents Lyndon B. Johnson, Richard M. Nixon, Gerald R. Ford, and Jimmy Carter—all of whom associated with ecclesiastical dignitaries and professed some type of Christian faith, and we observed that religion was introduced into each of the election races in one way or another. Many had said that the election of the Roman Catholic Kennedy in 1960 brought an end to religion as a presidential campaign issue; subsequent events proved them incorrect. In fact, Ronald Reagan in 1980 and 1984 appealed openly to people of religious commitment for their support with the argument that his worldview and program corresponded to theirs. What transpired during the 1988 race simply confirmed that religion has become a matter which no presidential candidate can ignore.

Also, two parallel developments occurred during our lifetime. One was the growth of religious pluralism. The United States continued to be by far the most religious of all the industrialized countries in spite of the advance of secularization, but this religiosity was reflected in a proliferation of Christian denominations and sects and non-Christian religions which had taken place under the benevolent eye of a constitutional system that practiced separation of church and state and guaranteed religious liberty to its citizens. The second was the revival of a form of evangelical Christianity which stressed the faith that had been common to the nation during its golden years of growth in the nineteenth century. As increasing numbers turned to the "old-time religion," their spiritual leaders began to evoke the vision of an earlier America—a "Christian nation, under God." They called for a return to this "Christian America" which they believed had once existed—a nation founded on Christian principles and honoring Christ and the Bible. Moreover, they became actively involved in politics in order to make their presence felt and wishes known. Their goal was to bring the country back to its Christian foundations in order that God could once again bless his "chosen nation."

But, how could both of these things take place at once? How could the nation become more religiously pluralistic (and some would argue more pluralistic in every respect) and at the same time return to its "Christian" origins, that is, be a nation basically evangelical in orientation? How could the vast number of Americans who believed in God in a general sense or who practiced non-Christian religions be integrated into the same country with those who firmly believed that Jesus Christ was "the Way, the Truth, and the Life," and the integration be carried out in such a fashion that would allow all parties to feel they belonged to the same political community? This, in fact, appeared to be happening in the America of the late 1960s, 1970s, and 1980s–but how?

To come to grips with this seemingly paradoxical situation, some scholars in the 1960s began employing the term "civil religion" to conceptualize and describe the religio-political developments of recent American history.[1] They pointed out that nearly all organized societies, including the United States, have a religious base which might be called civil or public religion. This civil faith had varied in America over the years, but its strength was that in the final analysis, it was elastic and protean. Civil religion served as the overarching faith of the American nation in such a manner that evangelicals and non-evangelicals alike could accept presidential leadership under the Almighty in accomplishing the nation's sacred mission to spread freedom throughout the world while at the same time maintaining the "nation under God" at home.

We, like most other commentators on religion and politics, have found the concept of civil religion useful in helping to explain the American phenomenon to people both in the United States and elsewhere. Supreme Court Justice William O. Douglas once aptly observed, "We are a religious people whose institutions presuppose a Supreme Being,"[2] but how that is actualized has been the source of never-ending controversy.

In the following pages, we will examine one facet of the problem—the interrelationship of civil religion and the presidency—with the goal in mind of promoting civilized behavior, democratic values, and political dialogue among Christians and non-Christians alike. The survival of the American experiment in religious and political freedom depends on our ability to practice these things. Thus, the matters we will discuss are both timely and enduring, not only for those in the United States, but also for individuals everywhere who wish to understand the role of public religion in American life.

1

CIVIL RELIGION AND THE PRESIDENCY

"New York Like a Vast Church," proclaimed the headline on page one of the November 26, 1963, issue of the *New York Times* which reported the funeral of President Kennedy held the day before in Washington, D.C. There, in language appropriate for the civil religion setting, were recorded the final respects the nation paid its fallen leader, an event which almost every American living at the time remembers.[1]

AN INAUGURAL AND A FUNERAL

Only two years and ten months before, John Fitzgerald Kennedy, the youngest person ever elected to the highest office in the land and first American president born in the twentieth century, had taken his sacred oath of office: "I do solemnly swear that I will faithfully execute the office of the President of the United States, and will to the best of my ability preserve, protect, and defend the Constitution of the United States"—to which he added the traditional words, "so help me God!" He took this oath with his hand resting on a family Bible, the Douay version, the English translation made for Roman Catholics in the sixteenth century. Nearly one million people were in Washington for the inaugural parade and some twenty thousand looked on in person as he took the oath, while another eighty million watched the first inauguration festivities to be shown on color television.

Under a cold but sunny sky, the Kennedy inaugural ceremony on January 20, 1961, unfolded with prayers offered by Protestant, Catholic, and Eastern Orthodox clergy and a Jewish rabbi—given, as a *New York Times* reporter put it, "to bolster him in his pledges."[2] In the invocation, Richard Cardinal Cushing from Kennedy's own Roman Catholic archdiocese of Boston asked the Almighty to give the young chief executive strength "to implement with personal sacrifice the objectives of our national purpose." Later in the program, Archbishop Iakovos of the Greek Orthodox Church of North and South America implored the Lord to have mercy on his "faithful servant our beloved President John F. Kennedy" and asked God to "exalt the prestige of our country and the office of our President, and send down upon him Thy rich mercies." At another point in the ceremony, Dr. John Barclay, pastor of the Central Christian Church in Austin, Texas, thanked Eternal God "for our country, for the manner in which Thou didst lead our fathers to establish this nation in which all men have equal rights to life, liberty, and the pursuit of happiness." With respect to the new president and vice president, he prayed, "Help them to lead us to return to the virtues of our fathers: industry, honesty, and frugality. Under their leadership may we recapture the faith of our fathers and their spiritual optimism." Finally, Rabbi Nelson Glueck, president of the Hebrew Union College of Cincinnati, pronounced the benediction: "We turn to thee, O God, in deepest gratitude on this exalting day of reaffirmation of our nation's ideals and unity, and of personal avowal of sacred obligation to our President." None prayed in Jesus' name.[3]

Interestingly enough, the religious highlight of the day was Kennedy's own inaugural address. The new president, heretofore not known as a man of great religious piety, began his speech:

> We observe today not a victory of party but a celebration
> of freedom—symbolizing an end as well as a beginning—
> signifying renewal as well as change. For I have sworn
> before you and Almighty God the same solemn oath our

forebears prescribed nearly a century and three quarters ago.

He continued:

> The world is very different now. For man holds in his mortal hands the power to abolish all forms of human poverty and to abolish all forms of human life. And yet the same revolutionary beliefs for which our forefathers fought are still at issue around the globe—the belief that the rights of man come not from the generosity of the state but from the hand of God.

Then, he concluded:

> Finally, whether you are citizens of America or of the world, ask of us the same high standards of strength and sacrifice that we shall ask of you. With a good conscience our only sure reward, with history the final judge of our deeds, let us go forth to lead the land we love, asking His blessing and His help, but knowing that here on earth God's work must truly be our own.[4]

The three places in his brief address where Kennedy mentioned the Deity identify three important religious themes. First, he confessed the existence of God and the nation's accountability to him. Second, he acknowledged the existence of rights that are bestowed by God rather than the state and with which the state may not rightfully interfere. Third, he pointed out the responsibility of all, especially Americans, to strive to do God's work here on earth. The speech was widely hailed by friend and foe, Democrats and Republicans, Americans and those from other countries, as rich in content and graceful in style. It was a promising beginning for an attractive, articulate, idealistic young leader.

However, on November 22, 1963, Kennedy's mission and dreams for the country were smashed by an assassin's bullet in Dallas, Texas—and the nation mourned. In his analysis of the public reaction to Kennedy's death, political scientist Sidney Verba discovered a religious commitment to the nation and its symbols, a close meshing of the sacred and the secular in the top institutions of the American political system. Further, as he probed more deeply, he found evidence of this primordial religious commitment at the deeper levels of political involvement as well. In the weekend following the murder, the overwhelming majority of Americans engaged in prayer or took part in special church services, or both. Moreover, public religious ceremonies abounded in response to the assassination. As previously indicated, New York and the entire nation seemed to react in a religious fashion.[5]

The funeral itself was the occasion for a great outpouring of national grief. Over a million people jammed the capital for the event, while nearly one out of every two adults in the nation watched on television. After a distinctly Christian service in St. Matthew's Roman Catholic Cathedral, the public ceremonial began as the coffin containing the president's body was borne through the streets of Washington to its final resting place in Arlington National Cemetery. Reporters noted that people who seldom cried, even at the funerals of their own loved ones, shed tears on that day, while bands played hymns like "Onward Christian Soldiers," "America the Beautiful," and "The Cross and the Flag." Several onlookers acknowledged that they had not brought a camera with them because to do so would have been "touristy and sacrilegious."

The procession finally wound its way across the Potomac to Arlington. There, at the head of the slain president's grave, an eternal flame was lit. The final resting place looked down onto the Lincoln Memorial, and behind it, like a great religious shrine itself, lay the gleaming white domes and spires of the city of Washington.[6]

Clearly, all of this activity associated with the Kennedy inaugural and funeral represented a great religio-political drama which the people involved in it seemed to take for granted. It was, in fact, an example of American civil religion in action, with the president of the United States its focal point.

THE PRESIDENCY AND RELIGION

From the beginning of the nation, the presidency has been of great importance to the American people. In the early days of the republic eminent men like George Washington, John Adams, Thomas Jefferson, Andrew Jackson, James Polk, and Abraham Lincoln lent their prestige to the institution. Later, once America had became a great world power, the process reversed, and the office now bestows its prestige upon the individual who occupies it.

The presidency today has much the same general configuration as in 1789, but the contours are a hundred times magnified. The president is still all the things that the Founders intended him to be (an independent chief executive with considerable power but coequal with the legislature and judiciary), but he is more. In comparing the presidency under Washington with the office after 1945, one finds several remarkable changes in character to be evident. First, the office is infinitely more powerful. Second, the president is much more heavily involved in making national policy. Third, he is a far more highly political figure than the framers of the Constitution intended him to be. Fourth, through the expansion of voting rights and the increased role of public opinion in electoral politics, the presidency has been converted into a democratic office in a manner unforeseen at the outset of the republic. Finally, the institution has acquired an enormous prestige in its own right. In summary, most historians agree that the outstanding feature of American constitutional development has been the gradual growth of the power and prestige of the presidency. The upshot of this is that a president, unlike a citizen in private life, occupies a position of power from which he can affect, for better or for worse, the lives of the great mass of people who reside in the United States as well as those in the remainder of the world.[7]

Concomitant with the growth in the power and prestige of the office is the manner in which the American chief executive functions in the dual role of head of state and head of government. Only the Constitution limits the vast potential inherent in this arrangement. Consequently, the president historically has been looked upon as a one-person distillation of the American people, just as surely as the monarch is of the British people. As President William Howard Taft observed about this special relationship between the chief executive and his constituency, he is "the personal embodiment and representative of their dignity and majesty."[8]

Part of the role of embodying and representing the people has been a religious one. This religious role has been accentuated during the periodic spiritual awakenings in American history, and the years since the late 1960s have been such a time. Beginning during the era of student upheaval and the drop-out, tune-in drug counterculture, a revival of major proportions swept across the American religious landscape. The Jesus People, a resurgent fundamentalism, the charismatic movement (a rejuvenated evangelical Christianity of many stripes in several denominations)—all these combined to produce a new religious force to be reckoned with in national life.

By the mid-1970s, the evangelical (theologically conservative) wing of Protestantism had drawn the attention of the news media and acquired a reputation for influence and growth. In 1976, Jimmy Carter became the first presidential nominee since Woodrow Wilson to talk openly and freely about his personal faith and even confessed to having been "born again." In the same year, the Gallup organization reported it had detected signs of a national religious revival. Conservative denominations were growing and many well-known people in public life testified to having been converted to Jesus Christ. National polls revealed that 46 percent of American Protestants claimed to have had some kind of born-again experience, as did a third of the population at large. Moreover, 48 percent of all Protestants reported that they interpreted the Bible "literally." In the late 1970s, a host of television evangelists appeared in prime time and the first Christian TV network was launched. By the end of the decade, Rev. Jerry Falwell's Moral Majority and a number of similar organizations were busily enlisting theologically conservative Christians for right-wing political action. Feeling that they had been left out of everyone else's liberation, a variety of biblical Christians (fundamentalists, charismatics, evangelicals in mainline denominations) began pressing for a place in the national sun.[9]

In 1980, this reemergence of a dynamic evangelical Christianity penetrated the race for the highest office in the land. For the first time in history, American voters had the choice of three major candidates who claimed to be born again—Carter, Ronald Reagan, and John Anderson. Religion and politics intersected in a way that had not been seen for years. More and more religious issues appeared on the political agenda of the nation, generated by the new religious climate and the concerns of people of faith.

In reality, religion has long been an element in presidential politics, even in recent times. In 1952 and 1956, for example, many people expressed concern about Adlai Stevenson's divorced status and his inclination toward Unitarianism. In 1960, Kennedy's Roman Catholic faith was a major but not necessarily a decisive factor in the choice of many Protestant voters. In 1964 and 1968, the threat of war and the drive for civil rights overshadowed the elections, leading many religious people to back the candidate they perceived would most likely promote peace and the expansion of civil liberties. In 1972, both candidates, Richard M. Nixon and George McGovern, used religious language and imagery to woo the American voters. In 1976, born-again Baptist Jimmy Carter burst upon the scene, only to be confronted by a Republican rival, Gerald R. Ford, who also purported to be a Bible-believing evangelical Christian.

In the 1980 and 1984 elections, the aspirants spoke a great deal about religion, and groups like the Moral Majority brought religious questions to the fore. In 1980, Carter, Reagan, and Anderson were forced to discuss not only their personal faith, but also abortion, school prayer, and federal aid to parochial schools. Considerable fundamentalist support flowed to Reagan, who soundly defeated the incumbent Carter. Moreover, the forces of the religious right claimed to have been the decisive factor in the defeat of several so-called liberal members of Congress.

In 1984, after a vigorous primary campaign between former Yale Divinity School student Gary Hart, Baptist preacher Jesse Jackson, and Methodist minister's son Walter Mondale, the Democrats settled upon the latter as their standard-bearer. Once again, with strong support from the religious right, President Reagan emerged victorious. Ignorance of religious matters and terminology, especially of evangelical Christianity, clouded the reporting of these recent presidential races. Nevertheless, it was clear that religion was a hot topic, that people of faith were beginning once again to flex their political muscles on the national scene, and that much of the action was swirling around the office of the president.[10] The foregoing illustrates how intimately the presidency and religion have been connected. All thirty-nine presidents have been friendly toward organized religion. Twenty-eight were church members, while the other eleven publicly professed belief in God. All of them attended church on various occasions and considered themselves in some sense to be Christians. Most importantly, they used traditional "God words" in their public speeches, especially inaugural addresses—like President Kennedy did in his 1961 inaugural.

However, the connection between religion and the presidency has intensified in recent times, beginning with the Eisenhower administration. Piety returned to the Potomac under the immensely popular general from Kansas. Presidential visits with such noted evangelical leaders as Billy Graham became commonplace in the Eisenhower years and continued through the Kennedy and Johnson terms. Graham was such a good friend of Lyndon Johnson that the president designated him as the minister to preach his funeral.

The relationship was just as warm an issue during the Nixon era. Many evangelical Christians gave their full support to Nixon in 1968 because they felt that the man from California with the Quaker background and solid friendship with Billy Graham surely was God's choice for the job. Most of them supported Nixon to the bitter end in the deepening Watergate scandal in 1973–74. During 1976, labeled by George Gallup, Jr., as the "Year of the Evangelical," both major candidates were identified as evangelical Protestants— Carter, the Southern Baptist, and Ford, an Episcopalian who in the 1960s had renewed his faith thanks to the ministrations of Evangelist Billy Zeoli. The contenders in 1980 and 1984 were friendly to voters with religious concerns and either professed some kind of personal religious experience or had a substantial background in the church.[11]

However, it was Ronald Reagan who brought a new, highly charged religio-political climate to the White House. Backed with fervor and passion by many of the most devout people in the country, he responded by adopting a religiously conservative social agenda for his regime. In so doing, he became the darling of the New Religious Right, and an intimate relationship developed between the two.

Some of this intimacy resulted from the fact that the New Religious Right and the New Political Right shared the same political goals. But a great portion of it also was based on the perception that Reagan was "one of them"—spiritually, politically, and socially. This, in turn, was largely because the religious rightists believed that the president spoke their language. And he did. Still, that language, that common meeting ground of the adherents of the religious right and the political right, was essentially the language of civil religion, not Christianity. In fact, Reagan has been one of the most astute practitioners of civil religion to occupy the White House in the twentieth century.

CIVIL RELIGION AND THE PRESIDENCY

Historically speaking, the presidency has been intimately linked to civil religion, and this has bonded the presidency to religious Americans. The very uniqueness of the American political arrangement demands this. The First Amendment to the Constitution guarantees religious freedom and forbids the establishment of any church or religion in the United States. The result is a strict separation of the institutions of church and state but not of religion and politics as such. Americans have always been a fundamentally religious people and this extends to every level of life, including politics.

As noted previously, the president occupies a special place in American life—a place that is at once political and religious. The president of the United States is no faceless corporate executive. The way he lives affects the self-image of the people, and his lifestyle and tastes greatly influence those of Americans at large. For example, Eisenhower encouraged a "relaxed" generation, Kennedy an "activist" decade. Nixon tended to divide people into those who felt good about America and were appreciative of its blessings and those who were uneasy about the country and unsure about its policies.

Especially in the modern era of instantaneous communications and intimate press coverage of the White House, individual citizens have perceived their destinies to be bound up with that of their president. That is why most people during the course of a week react personally and intimately to the actions of the president—with hatred, rage, contempt, bitterness, love, approval, admiration, pride. Moreover, since most citizens regard America with religious feeling, scorn for political opponents often becomes theological, as, for example, the experience of Senator Mark Hatfield sadly revealed.[12] All of this quasi-religious political devotion and emotion is then channeled through many religious and political tributaries into the ocean of the presidency. This office is the single object of their flow.

Few students of politics would dispute that there is a

religious component to the presidency, though determining whether the man influences the office in this way or vice versa is beyond the purposes of this book. The truth is that most Americans regard the office with a measure of religious awe and that certain presidents down through history have used the position with great success in playing the role of prophet and/or priest in America's public religion.

In any event, scholars generally agree that whether he is religiously active or passive, the foremost representative of civil religion in America is the president. He not only serves as head of state and chief executive, but he also functions as the symbolic representative of the whole of the American people. He affirms that God exists and that America's destiny and the nation's policies must be interpreted in the light of the Almighty's will. The rituals that the president celebrates and the speeches he makes reflect the basic themes of American civil religion.[13]

WHAT IS CIVIL RELIGION?

What exactly is civil religion and how does it work? An essay published in 1967 by sociologist Robert N. Bellah entitled "Civil Religion in America" stimulated a public awareness of the topic and a spirited debate in the scholarly community that continues to this day.[14] In this he maintains that civil religion must be approached sympathetically because it possesses its own seriousness and integrity and that scholars need to try to understand it as they would any bona fide religion. His article suggests what terms might be suitable for such an analysis.

Bellah argues that American civil religion arose from germinal national events such as the Declaration of Independence as well as subsequent words and deeds of the Founders, and he traces the manner in which these have been utilized. He offers a favorable evaluation of the phenomena of American civil religion as constitutive of a genuine religion, over and against those who have criticized or undervalued it, and expresses wonder that "something so obvious should have escaped serious analytical attention." He concludes that since modern Westerners usually compartmentalize religion and differentiate it from secular activities, it has not been easy for them to see that "every group has a religious dimension." Religious elements are integral to the social system of the United States, and Americans can discover a "positive institutionalization" of civil religion in their national past and present.[15]

Not all scholars have accepted Bellah's thesis at face value. Some modify it by arguing that, rather being than a highly institutionalized civil religion with an established creed and clear-cut practices, there exists a religious state ritual which has a far more fluid reality. They maintain that in every generation a new civil religion is constructed by the national mood, the international balance of power, and especially the strength of presidential personalities. In other words, the observable religious practices of the state can be construed as products of particular national figures in their expression of religious attitudes.[16]

In light of the foregoing, can a working definition of civil religion be constructed for the purposes of this book? The answer is yes. Anthropologists, sociologists, and historians have pointed out for a long time that, although Americans have managed to a large degree to keep church and state separate, they have not traditionally segregated religion from politics. Even if the separation of the institutions of church and state is possible and desirable,[17] an attempt to divorce religion from politics in any society, American or otherwise, is unrealistic.

In any case, anthropologist Clifford Geertz and sociologist Peter Berger contend that all organized societies operate from what is essentially a religious base and that political leadership has a religious dimension. They believe that humans instinctively impose order upon reality and that to implement this they posit a "sacred cosmos" which locates their lives in an ultimately meaningful order. But this process serves another vital function as well because society, like the individual, requires a cosmic frame of reference. Sociologist Robin Williams argues that every functioning society needs a common religion which will provide an overarching unity capable of overcoming conflicts and cleavages within society. There is considerable evidence of an intimate relationship between religion and social solidarity. Societies need common goals and values validated through some cosmic frame of reference which their members recognize as defining their collective existence.[18]

In ancient societies, religion pervaded all aspects of life. An offense against society was the same as an offense against the gods. In medieval and early modern times, the institutional church often served as the provider of common goals and values, many times in the form of an officially established faith. However, in modern America the church has been relegated to the status of one of many interests within society, and it is not the institution which ordinarily furnishes the sacred symbols to bring together all the components of society. Michael Novak insists that precisely because there is no official state church in America to provide the sacred symbols of transcendence for society, a vacuum exists which the state itself inexorably fills. Meanwhile, Bellah maintains that the beliefs, values, rites, and ceremonies which constitute the basic symbols of transcendence in any given society unify the members of a political community and give meaning to their collective life. For him, this is a nation's civil religion. Some would add that the national leader is the one who pulls all of this together and makes it work—in the case of the United States, the president.[19]

There is definitely substance behind this concept. According to Bellah, the reality of civil religion "depends less on the existence of certain things out there than on a consensus that it is a useful way of talking about things that indubitably are out there."[20] In other words, it is like what the famous baseball umpire Bill Klem used to say about the placement of a pitched ball: "They ain't nothin 'till I call 'em!" In a similar fashion, careful students of American society can find abundant evidence of civil religion if they "call 'em"—that is, identify the numerous manifestations as they appear before their discerning eyes.[21]

Therefore, this study accepts the reality of civil religion, even though it is only a scholar's term. This concept sometimes goes by other names—public, political, or societal religion; public piety; civic faith; the common faith; theistic humanism; or in the case of the United States, secularized Puritanism, the religion of the republic, the American Way, American Shinto, and often "the American Democratic Faith." Whatever one calls it—and here, for historical purposes, the preferred term is civil religion—it refers to the widespread acceptance by a people of perceived religio-political traits regarding their nation's history and destiny. It relates their society to the realm of ultimate meaning, enables them to look at their political community in a special sense, and provides the vision which ties the nation together as an integrated whole. It is the "operative religion" of a society—the collection of beliefs, values, rites, ceremonies, and symbols which together give sacred meaning to the ongoing political life of the community and provide it with an overarching sense of unity above and beyond all internal conflicts and differences. Civil religion is unique in that it has reference to power within the state, but because it focuses on ultimate conditions, it surpasses and is independent of that power.[22]

Moreover, a civil faith must be independent of the institutional church as such or it will merely be an ecclesiastical endorsement of the state, and it must be genuinely a religion or it will only be secular nationalism. Thus, the public faith is not particular religion or expressions thereof, but its nature is such that those who hold specific beliefs can read into it whatever meaning they choose. Because of its protean and transdenominational exterior, it also requires a core civil theology—a religious way of thinking about politics—which supplies the society with meaning and a sense of destiny, interprets the historical experience of the people, and provides a sense of dynamism, uniqueness, and identity.

Even though, in the words of Bellah, there exists "an elaborate and well-institutionalized civil religion in America," this same civil religion can be utilized by shrewd and skillful politicians such as the president for purposes of state. In other cases, the state itself reaps the benefit of the instinctive desire on the part of its citizens to give their country a semireligious devotion. Be that as it may—institutionalized, manipulated, or instinctive—the practice of civil religion involves the mixing of traditional religion with national life until it is impossible to distinguish between the two. It is a general faith, one that stands in contrast to the particular faith of denominational groups which claim the allegiance of only a segment of the population. In the United States, civil religion has become a rather elaborate mixture of beliefs and practices born of the nation's historic experience. As such, it constitutes the only real faith of millions of its citizens.[23]

Nevertheless, unlike being Presbyterian or Jewish, adhering to the national faith does not mean belonging to an organization or breaking ties with an organized religious group or church to which one belongs. A civil religionist might also be a Roman Catholic, or a Methodist, or a Mormon, or even an agnostic, since a goodly part of its symbolism requires no belief in God. Whether an agnostic or atheist could become president is another question. There is no constitutional prohibition against a nonbeliever holding the highest office in the land, but it certainly would be a radical break with tradition and a violation of American civil religion if an elected chief magistrate could not use the word "God" the way all previous presidents have.[24] Thus far, through thirty-nine chief executives, this has not happened.

Despite its many limitations, civil religion has been the American answer to the radical pluralism encouraged by the First Amendment and by the historic stand of Baptists, Mennonites, and Quakers against any fusion of church and state. It has provided an overarching religious arrangement under which most of the denominations and sects can thrive while at the same time participating or not participating in the public rituals with their religious and not-so-religious fellow Americans, each according to their choice or eccentricities.

Some forms of civil religion emphasize the Deity while others see the nation itself as the reference point of highest loyalty and final judgment. It also exists in at least two varieties which may be labeled as "prophetic" and "priestly" civil religion. In a functional sense, the prophet stands before the people and speaks to them the necessary (and sometimes unpleasant) words from God, but the priest stands before God and speaks on behalf of the people. The prophet focuses on judgment and repentance while the priest pronounces words of comfort, praise, and celebration.

Both forms of public religion have been present in American history—with the prophetic dominating the scene from the foundation of the republic until the mid-twentieth century and the priestly prevailing through the latter half of this century. In prophetic civil religion, the president seeks to conform the nation's actions to the will of the Almighty, thus countering idolatrous religious nationalism and calling the nation to repent of its corporate political sins. In the priestly variety, however, the president's prophetic role is muted. Instead of the Deity, he tends to make the nation itself (or national goals or security) the ultimate reference point for evaluating the deeds of his country. As the high priest of the civil faith, he leads the people in affirming and celebrating the nation, and at the same time he glorifies the national culture and strokes his political flock.[25]

Whatever its emphasis, prophetic or priestly, American civil religion represents an alliance between politics and religion at the national level, resting on a politicized ideological base: (1) there is a God; (2) his will can be known and fulfilled through democratic procedures; (3) America has been God's primary agent in modern history; and (4) the nation is the chief source of identity for Americans in both a political and religious sense. According to this outlook, Americans are God's chosen people, a New Israel which made the exodus to the Promised Land across the sea and became a "city on a hill," a light to the nations, proclaiming the message of democracy as the salvific doctrine that will lead the human race to freedom, prosperity, and happiness. Evidence of the civil faith includes the biblical imagery and references to Almighty God and Providence that have pervaded the speeches and public documents of the nation's leaders from the earliest times, the religio-political symbolism of much of the architecture of the nation's capital, patriotic songs in church hymnals, the display of the nation's flag in church sanctuaries, the celebration of national holidays in which themes of "God and country" are skillfully blended (e.g., Memorial Day, Independence Day, and Thanksgiving), the inclusion of "under God" in the Pledge of Allegiance, and above all, the national motto "In God We Trust." That is civil religion.[26]

THE PRESIDENT'S ROLE IN THE CIVIL FAITH

The president's role in the expression of such a faith should be rather obvious. He is in effect the "pontifex maximus" of American civil religion—principal prophet, high priest, first preacher, and chief pastor of the American nation. It all began in 1789 with George Washington, who declared in his first inaugural address:

> It would be peculiarly improper to omit in this first official act my fervent supplications to that Almighty Being who rules over the universe, who presides in the councils of nations, and whose providential aids can supply every human defect, that His benediction may consecrate to the liberties and happiness of the people of the United States a Government instituted by themselves for these essential

purposes, and may enable every instrument employed in its administration to execute with success the functions allotted to his charge. In tendering this homage to the Great Author of every public and private good, I assure myself that it expresses your sentiments not less than my own, nor those of my fellow citizens at large less than either.[27]

Forty-one inaugurals later, Dwight D. Eisenhower launched a presidential administration by "assuring himself" that he and his fellow citizens were in agreement that homage should be paid to the Deity and by offering a prayer of his own in which he invited the watching and listening millions to join with him in an act of worship.[28] Commenting on these two speeches, historian Paul Carter observes:

> From the standpoint of a conservative eighteenth-century critic of republican governments, which were expected to pull down religion along with law, property, and respect for one's betters, the conduct of both Presidents would have been quite unexpected, as if the first magistrate should also act as *pontifex maximus*. The Constitution, to be sure, provided that no religious test should ever be required of anyone holding office or public trust under the United States; the prescribed inauguration oath itself had been given a carefully nonsectarian wording: "I do solemnly swear." But the Constitution began to be interpreted and transformed in the moment of its execution, and George Washington acted from the first as high priest of a national Establishment, using stately diction which somehow compounded the spirit of deistic Freemasonry with that of the *Book of Common Prayer*.[29]

Thus, when at the close of his acceptance speech at the Republican National Convention in 1980 Ronald Reagan invited the audience to join with him in "a moment of silent prayer" which was terminated by his benedictory of "God bless America," he was engaging in a hallowed civil religion tradition.[30]

Most presidents have been a mixture of prophet, priest, preacher, and pastor, and any president can be any or all of these, if he chooses. For example, Abraham Lincoln, usually regarded as a leading prophet of civil religion, could also be priestly on occasion; and his second inaugural address is considered the greatest presidential pastoral of all time. One of the most noted White House "preachers" was Theodore

Roosevelt, who labeled the presidential podium a "bully pulpit,"[31] and his pontifical moral judgments echoed throughout the land. In fact, most presidents were excellent public speakers, and several of them preached, moralized, and exhorted as they addressed their concerns and pastoral wisdom either to Congress or the American people. Eisenhower had a pastor's heart but he had his priestly moments as well, as when he intoned, "America is the mightiest power which God has yet seen fit to put upon his footstool. America is great because she is good."[32]

More recently, Jimmy Carter engaged in prophetic type exhortation while Ronald Reagan was perhaps the greatest high priestly president ever to occupy the office. Reagan also was quite effective in his role as presidential pastor and preacher, but his administration was almost barren of prophetic content. Overall, the trend during the last half of the twentieth century has been toward a more priestly and a less prophetic presidency.[33]

In the hands of dynamic presidents, civil religion has been a potent tool for the governance of the nation. Under their guidance, the civil faith has been a far more fluid reality than Bellah would appear to allow. On the other hand, less active presidents simply acquiesced in the performance of their sacred duties as a part of an institutional civil religion, guided by its already established code and traditions. Much like any other religion in the past, it is the personality of the leader that has made the difference.[34]

ASSESSING PRESIDENTIAL CIVIL RELIGION

Space limitations preclude a treatment of the powers, roles, and duties of the presidency itself or of the activities of all thirty-nine individuals who have served as chief executive. More importantly, no analysis of the presidential role in civil religion could explain the totality of its impact on America and its citizens. As historian Clinton Rossiter correctly points out:

> It is a whole greater than and different from the sum of its parts, an office whose power and prestige are something more than the arithmetical total of all its functions. The President is not one kind of official during one part of the day, another kind during another part—administrator in

the morning, legislator at lunch, king in the afternoon, commander before dinner, and politician at odd moments that come his weary way. He is all these things all the time, and any one of his functions feeds upon and into all the others.[35]

That includes his duties as pontifex maximus of the American civil religion, and these will be the primary concern of the study.

Moreover, although knowledge about the personal faith of the presidents is essential for an understanding of their public religious roles, this is not another book on "God in the White House." Much more significant is how civil religion is mediated to the American people through the presidential office and the impact it has on those citizens who take their own personal faith seriously. One must not forget that American society contains a significant religious component and civil religion plays a key role in establishing national unity by promoting a common religious faith.

The underlying reality is that presidential leadership has a crucial religious dimension. All chief executives have consciously or unconsciously sought to relate their understanding of the nation and its needs to a sacred cosmos. Just as the role of the president in national and world affairs has increased over the years, so it has in the realm of civil religion as well. The result is that the concept of civil religion contributes to evaluating the nature and effectiveness of presidential leadership itself.

In the succeeding chapters, nine landmark presidencies will be selected to illuminate the changing pattern of the office's involvement in civil religion over the past two centuries. The role of the individual chief executive in civil religion will be assessed, including how each one used it and how it used him. At the same time, the work will trace the development of American civil religion from a general Protestant faith at the beginning of the republic to the present-day general theistic civil faith, and examine its progression from a predominantly prophetic to a predominantly priestly type of civil religion. It will explain why recent presidents have relied so heavily on religious rites and ceremonies to direct what many currently regard as a secular society. Moreover, it will raise the question of whether presidential involvement in civil religion poses a threat to religious liberty or the personal faith of individuals who participate in the civic rites. In the process, the meaning of all this for the future of religion in general and for Christianity in particular will be weighed.

To appreciate properly the meaning of civil religion and the role of the presidency in it, one must see it as a phenomenon which evolved in Western society over a long period of time. Although the history of civil religion in the West is a highly complex topic, a brief survey of its development will provide the necessary understanding of the religio-political context in which American national leaders function today and thereby supply a historical framework in which the preceding theoretical discussion may be placed.

2

FROM ROME TO THE REAGAN ERA: CIVIL RELIGION IN THE WESTERN WORLD

"God almighty does not hear the prayer of a Jew!" With these ten little words uttered at the National Affairs Briefing of the Religious Roundtable in Dallas, Texas, on August 22, l980, the Reverend Dr. Bailey Smith of Oklahoma City, president of the Southern Baptist Convention, raised a furor that took many months to calm. At the same time, he provided his hearers with an unexpected but valuable insight into the nature of civil religion.

DR. SMITH, THE PRESS, AND CIVIL BLASPHEMY

Newspeople at the gathering picked up on the statement and reported it widely. Ironically, neither they nor Smith himself understood its meaning in the context in which it had been made, the reporters were largely uneducated in the language and folkways of evangelical religion, and Pastor Smith did not grasp the nature of the meeting he was addressing. The incident reflected just how ill-equipped the American press was to deal with the religious bombs that had been bursting about their ears in ever-increasing numbers since the mid-1970s and which reached full intensity during the election campaign of Ronald Reagan in 1980. Most newspeople lacked the stock of cultural knowledge about conservative religious traditions necessary to realize what was happening. Further, few of them were informed about history and religion or had any prior experience in reporting religion.[1]

As for Smith, he had committed "civil blasphemy" by being too Christian and too specific in a civil religion setting. Certainly, as he later pointed out, his words were reported sensationally and out of context. Still, even in context he was speaking as a revivalistic Baptist preacher to a crowd whom he thought would be sympathetic to his remarks. In the main, it probably was; but his audience had come not to a revival meeting but to a political rally. The National Affairs Briefing was intended to be a leadership forum for people who shared conservative theology and a right-of-center political orientation. As Jerry Falwell and James Robison, two of the prime movers of the Dallas meeting, affirmed time and again, the New Religious Right was a coalition not only of evangelical Christians but also of political conservatives within the Roman Catholic, Mormon, and "mainline" Protestant denominations.[2] In fact, two of the luminaries at the event were Paul Weyrich, a Catholic, and Howard Phillips, a Jew.

Smith admitted in a backstage interview: "I don't even know what I'm doing here."[3] It was little wonder, then, that in one fell swoop he managed not only to provide reporters with a sensational headline but also to embarrass his hosts as he thundered from the podium:

> And if America is going to know revival, there must be the preaching of the supremacy of Christ. I'm telling you, all other gods beside Jehovah and his son Jesus Christ are strange gods. It's interesting to me at great political rallies how you have a Protestant to pray, and a Catholic to pray, and then you have a Jew to pray. With all due respect for those dear people, my friend, God almighty does not hear the prayer of a Jew, for how in the world can God hear the prayer of a man who says Jesus Christ is not the true Messiah? It is blasphemous.[4]

These words were offensive, not only in the ears of religiously plural America but especially in the context of a political meeting that was based squarely on American civil religion and dedicated to rallying the conservative religious forces of the country behind the candidates of the New

Right. At such gatherings it was permissible to talk about God in general but not Jesus Christ in particular. Civil religion, even as the focal point of a modern conservative political crusade designed to restore America to righteousness and world respect, could not function as the nation's public faith in the last half of the twentieth century except under a generally theistic umbrella.[5]

ROUSSEAU AND CIVIL RELIGION

Bailey Smith's gaffe illustrates how civil religion had relegated particular religion to a secondary role in public life. But, to see how the overarching, generalized civic faith had submerged the specific faiths and harnessed them to the political order, one must trace the evolution of the phenomenon in the Western world. Although it is probably as old as civilization itself, the phrase "civil religion" was coined in the eighteenth century.[6] Accordingly, the starting point for this historical survey will be the conceptualization of the term.

The thinker credited with inventing it was Jean-Jacques Rousseau, the tormented Enlightenment genius who began life as a Calvinist, converted to Roman Catholicism as a teenager, and ended up as a dazed deist. In 1762, this self-educated wanderer and plebeian misfit wrote the most radical political work of the century, *The Social Contract*. Here he developed the theme he had first advanced in 1751, that humans were naturally good and it was their social institutions which rendered them evil. *The Social Contract* elaborated on this and thereby attempted to resolve the most persistent problem in Western political thought, that of the reconciliation of freedom and authority.[7]

It is Rousseau's religious thought which is of prime interest to the historian of civil religion. On the one hand, he substituted a sentimental faith for revealed religion and removed Christian doctrines from their supernatural context, thus paving the way for humanistic liberalism. On the other hand, to replace orthodox Christianity, he posited a rationalistic public faith, one which ironically has been embraced with considerable zeal by many modern-day Christians. In any event, those who study the history of civil religion have to deal with his terminology and conceptualization.

Rousseau no more invented civil religion than Karl Marx

invented communism. The two simply described something which presently or previous existed, each adding his own particular interpretation of or variation to the phenomenon he identified. Marx attempted to place socialism on a scientific base, while Rousseau struggled to create enlightened civil religion.

Rousseau was above all a cosmopolitan individualist committed to the ideals of the Enlightenment. This intellectual movement was closely identified with him and his fellow *philosophes* (French men of letters like Voltaire, Diderot, and Montesquieu) and the English thinker John Locke, all of whom believed firmly in reason, natural law, and progress. They held that human reason would free people from their ills and lead them infallibly to perpetual peace, utopian government, and a perfect society. Reason would facilitate the discovery of the natural laws regulating existence, thereby insuring human progress. Their thought was colored by a belief in fundamental human goodness and the ability of people to improve themselves through their own efforts.

Rousseau apparently obtained from Locke the idea for a civil religion based on a minimum creed that would instill civic spirit and discipline in the citizenry. Locke's list of basic beliefs necessary for the maintenance of a viable civil society included the existence of God, the messiahship of Jesus, and adherence to biblical ethics. In his own *Social Contract*, Rousseau used a number of Locke's assumptions, particularly the social contract and to some extent the notion of natural law. Drawing upon Lockean concepts, he expounded his own doctrine of popular sovereignty and the right of revolution. But his effort to harmonize individual freedom with membership in a social group ruled by law was incomplete, often puzzling, and open to a variety of interpretations. These inadequacies aside, many of Rousseau's ideas found their way into modern constitutional thought. In addition, he also tried to resolve the proper relationship between society and religion in an enlightened, pluralistic state, following the broad outline for a general civic faith set forth by Locke.[8]

Rousseau began his exposition of civil religion by acknowledging that "no state was ever founded without having religion as its basis." Some form of religion was necessary for social solidarity, since it generated common sentiments which served as the social glue of the nation-state. However, although it was the most pervasive religion in the West, Christianity was unsuited to be a civil faith for the new nation-states because it required a dual allegiance from its adherents, thereby weakening the state's claim to full political power over its subjects. The Christians' highest loyalty was to God (or, during the Middle Ages, to God via his vicar on earth, the pope) rather than to any political entity, even though it was evident that they could live at peace in a state which allowed them freedom of worship.

Civil religion was the device Rousseau hit upon to solve the problem of religious allegiance and dual loyalty. It also provided a larger moral context by which the behavior of the body politic might be measured in order to restrain the tendencies for selfish expression by the political whole. And it was also a way to achieve and ensure social peace after the disruptive religiously inspired wars of the previous two centuries. This thinking lay behind an important chapter in *The Social Contract* entitled "Civil Religion":

> There is therefore a pure civil profession of faith of which the Sovereign [the political ruler] should fix the articles, not exactly as religious dogmas, but as social sentiments without which a man cannot be a good citizen or a faithful subject. . . .The dogmas of civil religion ought to be few, simple, and exactly worded, without explanation or comment. The existence of a mighty, intelligent, and beneficent Divinity, possessed of foresight and providence; the life to come, the happiness of the just, the punishment of the wicked; the sanctity of the social contract and the laws: these are its positive dogmas.[9]

In short, Rousseau's civil religion would provide the moral glue for the political order created by the social contract. Or, to put it another way, it would be the general will of the people expressed religiously in the life of the state with a benign but watchful Supreme Being to preside over the keeping of the public faith.[10]

In many ways, Christianity in medieval Europe and religion in general in other earlier societies served as the social cement which Rousseau envisioned as the main purpose of his enlightened civil faith. However, in his scheme civil religion assumed a much more vital role because the context was more than political. Civil society became the focus of the Deity's work on earth, the ark of social salvation, the way to the new heaven and earth. It was the center of humankind's religious as well as political loyalty. In this context, people found security and freedom and expressed themselves morally and rationally. In short, civil religion was the vehicle that provided the members of Rousseau's body politic with identity and meaning. It was the focal point of one's civic life, while conventional religions (such as Christianity) were relegated to the sphere of private conscience alone. As he saw it, innumerable gods and their cults could exist as long as they did not interfere with the overarching devotion to the state.[11]

Further, Rousseau's civil religion had no transcendental referent. Although he did refer in *The Social Contract* to "the gods" as the only infallible source of true law, yet his stress on the contract and the central role of the body politic essentially upheld the sovereignty of the general will. In a society lacking the Christian emphasis on a transcendent personal God, civil faith stood under no higher law. Human reason was the key to discerning the general will and, though not infallible, it certainly assumed the character of transcendence. Reason enabled each individual member of Rousseau's civil society to read the revelation of Nature's God in the creation. For many practitioners of civil religion before and since, the state encompassed everything that mattered; there was no law or loyalty higher than the state. To Christians specifically, this also meant that in a religiously plural state where evangelical Christianity was merely one of several faiths, it was ever in danger of losing its witness to the political institutions by melting into the larger, all-encompassing civil faith. The likelihood of idolatrous subservience to the state lurked in Rousseau's earthbound public religion because it had no fixed transcendental referent by which the nation could and would be judged.[12]

ROMAN CIVIL RELIGION

Thus, Rousseau conceptualized but did not invent the practice of civil religion. It existed in the earliest organized human communities, usually based upon some form of pagan or folk religion which gave the society meaning through certain symbols and structures. To be sure, Rousseau rejected ancient paganism along with the Roman

Catholic Church and evangelical Christianity as models for civil religion. In his opinion, paganism was founded on error, Catholicism produced divided loyalties (two codes of legislation, two rulers, two countries), and evangelical Christianity was too otherworldly and failed to bind the hearts of the citizens to the state.[13] Still, an examination of the pagan state religions of ancient Greece and Rome reveals that in most respects they were closer to his criteria than he realized.

Sociologist Emile Durkheim agreed with Rousseau's contention that a common, overarching civil religion was constitutive of the unity and character of every society. The vast majority of the people could identify with the general public faith and affirm it at regular intervals by means of collective ideas and sentiments. Durkheim called attention to the existence in antiquity of what Rousseau and others would call civil religion—a societal faith sustained by common beliefs and ceremonials.[14] In Greece, for example, official paganism was the handmaiden of the state, giving it moral coherence and serving as social cement in the manner that Rousseau expected civil religion to do.

Moreover, Durkheim discovered that ancient expressions of civil faith were generally tolerant of all except those who would not accept its simple dogmas or who pretended to accept them but really did not. Rousseau later agreed, but in his ideal state, antisocials were to be banished and hypocrites punished by death, as happened to Socrates in 399 B.C. Appropriate to Rousseau's paradigm, Socrates was condemned by an Athenian jury on the charge of introducing strange gods and corrupting the youth of the city-state. Whether these were trumped-up charges against a man who had professed reverence for the laws of Athens is beside the point. What matters is that he had tampered with the religio-political order of the day.[15]

His pupil Plato examined the order of being and its relation to civil theology in *The Republic*. Like Rousseau, Plato outlined a minimum body of creedal truths which must be maintained in a viable state. These closely resembled the general beliefs of the *The Social Contract*. For instance, Plato posited belief in a beneficent deity, argued that achieving a just political order required the citizens to honor their parents and the gods, and advocated that all should be required to accept this simple religio-political creed. In short, his civil theology stressed the need for a fundamental consensus through a minimal dogma that lay beyond public debate and maintained that this elementary civic faith would serve as the social glue of his ideal state.[16]

Although similar in some ways to that of the Greeks, Roman civil religion was more highly developed and like its modern counterparts. As their civilization spread, the Romans evolved a religiously sanctioned "Roman Way of Life" which served as a substructure for coexistent faiths in their emerging empire. They developed a quasi-religious society, cemented by a common allegiance to the emperor himself. Eventually his subjects revered him as a manifest god and savior in the imperial state cult which doubled as the civil religion of the realm. Alongside it existed the other religions whose adherents could practice their faith as enthusiastically as they wished, so long as they nominally accepted the official one, an action which was absolutely obligatory. The emperor occupied a peculiar position in the state cult in that he served as *pontifex maximus* (chief priest) while increasingly becoming an object of worship.[17]

As the crises of the empire intensified in the third and fourth centuries after Christ, a strong civil faith that would unify its peoples and sanctify the state's claim to authority became more and more necessary. From Decius (249–251) and Diocletian (284–305) to Theodosius the Great (379–395), the emperors increasingly used the device of civil religion to strengthen the spiritual foundations of the state. Historian Edward Gibbon commented concerning this, "The various modes of worship which prevailed in the Roman world were all considered by the people as equally true; by the philosophers as equally false; and by the magistrates as equally useful."[18]

The early Christians were persecuted because they stubbornly refused to cooperate with those rulers who wanted to establish a viable public faith by grafting their dynamic and growing movement onto the tree of Roman civil religion. The Christians believed that their God was a jealous one who would brook no rivals, certainly no mere earthly emperor, and they refused to sacrifice to Caesar as the state cult required. Hence they were adjudged seditious enemies of the state and treated accordingly.[19]

The emperors found their efforts to strengthen and expand civil religion and later to co-opt Christianity for state purposes to be frustrating. Imperial civil religion never worked as well as they had hoped, especially after the early fourth century when they began to link it to Christianity. The intermingling of civil religion with the Christian faith began after Emperor Constantine I (312–337) embraced Christ, sometime around 312. Historians have long debated the nature and genuineness of his conversion. Some argue that he was nothing more than a shrewd political schemer bent on harnessing the vitality of Christianity to the faltering Roman state, while others insist his conversion was sincere albeit superficial. Of course, it might be that he did not make a thoughtful commitment and simply did not understand the implications of accepting Christ.[20]

In any case, as time passed, Constantine increasingly spoke in favor of Christianity and gradually granted its adherents a favored position in the state. The impact of his conversion and preference for the way of Christ was immediate and widespread. The populace recognized that their ruler approved of Christianity and intended to give it a special place among the religions of the realm; thus it became the wave of the future. There was a great influx of people into the churches, many of whom were concerned with imperial favor and not the cause of Christ. The disease of widespread nominalism infected Christianity—a curse which has been with it ever since. Moreover, after Constantine's conversion, the Christian faith began to supplant the state cult of emperor worship, and the fourth century saw the emergence of "Christianity as civil religion" in the Roman Empire.

Historian W. H. C. Frend speculates that for twelve years after his conversion, Constantine held his two allegiances in uneasy tension—one to the old ways of the Roman gods and the emperor cult, the other to the new Way of Christ—until he became sole ruler of the divided empire in 324. Then he resolved the issue in favor of the Christian God, personal religion was transformed into official policy, and he laid plans for his great Christian city of Constantinople, where he finally moved the imperial capital in 330.[21]

During the period when he was evolving his personal and somewhat superstitious brand of Christianity, Constantine also wrestled with relating his new faith to the state. Quite revealing is the concluding sentence in a letter written in 313 to Aelafius, a Christian official in North Africa:

Since I am informed that you too are a worshipper of *the Highest God*, I will confess to your gravity that I consider it absolutely contrary to divine law that we should overlook such quarrels and dissensions [he means between rival parties in the North African church], whereby *the Highest Divinity* may be moved to wrath not only against the human race, but against me myself, to whose care he has by his heavenly will committed the government of all earthly things.[22]

The civil religion language stands out; the "immortal gods" had now been displaced as the protectors of the empire by "the Highest God." The use of this term for the deity was not customary in traditional Roman religion, so it signaled a shift in thinking. Yet it was general enough to serve as an appellation for the god of civil religion while being sufficiently different from the old terminology to be understood as referring to the sovereign God of Christianity. Thus, the genius of the new civil religion had been established in the religious language of the political rulers—a reference to God which could mean all things to all people. Ironically, the Christian God could not be assimilated into the Roman pantheon, but he was co-opted by Roman civil religion.

Constantine's personal ardor for Christianity steadily grew while he used the faith as the central and solidifying focus of his reunited empire. The Christian clergy now were recognized as civic as well as religious leaders, with a corresponding elevation in status, and the church-state boundaries were increasingly blurred as Christianity took on the role of an official state religion and the civil religion of the entire realm. Paradoxically, this did not bring about the imperial unity for which the fourth-century rulers longed. The emergence of a Christian emperor like Constantine actually fanned the flames of division, since many Christians resisted the encroachment of the state. They insisted that their first allegiance was to the "City of God" rather than to the "City of Man." Gibbon may have been wrong in placing primary responsibility upon Christianity for the collapse of the Roman Empire; nevertheless, it did not provide the hoped-for support for the tottering system by serving as a viable civil religion. Thus, Rome eventually staggered off into historical oblivion while the Christian faith remained to form the basis of a new civilization.[23]

In the course of its struggle with the state and emer-

gence as the majority faith, Christianity had lost its original
dynamism and prophetic quality, and its position in relation
to the world had become compromised. During this era,
more and more Christians accepted the imperial idea of a
universal society based upon quasi-religious assumptions.
The emperor was stripped of his status as a god but retained
his position as a religio-political figure under the Highest
God, who now presided over Rome's fortunes. A fateful
liaison had been forged between the City of God and the City
of Man which bore tasteless if not bitter fruit during the
Middle Ages.[24]

MEDIEVAL AND RENAISSANCE CIVIL RELIGION

The Christian commonwealth which emerged out of the
ruins of the Roman Empire dominated Western culture for
nearly a thousand years. There was little evidence of a
Rousseauistic civil religion until the latter part of the period,
since an institutionalized Christian church possessing a
much more particularistic set of dogmas than those Rousseau
envisioned served as the unifying worldview for most
medieval states. The Western mind at this time was reluctant
to accept the classical emphasis on civic virtues in conjunc-
tion with a civil religion, and the very nature of the feudal
system sanctioned by a strong church militated against this.
Further, the concept of fatherland, so common in the ancient
world, had lost its religious flavor and connotations in the
medieval era, and in terms of ultimate loyalties, Christians
were increasingly called upon to choose between pope and
king. The story of medieval church-state relations is too
complex to recount here, but the struggle for religious and
political supremacy consumed the energies of popes and
princes for hundreds of years. Not until the twelfth or
thirteenth century was there any hint of a return to civil
religion as a broad, state-oriented common faith.

In an instructive study entitled *"Pro Patria Mori* in
Medieval Thought," historian Ernst Kantorowicz examines
the emergence of civil religion in Western Europe in the late
Middle Ages. After dealing with motifs flowing from the
concept of "death for the fatherland" in political and
religious thought in this period, he finds that something
closely resembling modern-day civil religion had begun to
develop then.[25] He points out that during much of the

Middle Ages the *patria* (fatherland) of the Christians was not any earthly place but heaven, the celestial city of the blessed. However, with the appearance of national monarchies in the twelfth and thirteenth centuries, a gradual shift from heaven back to earth began as the *patria* came to refer to a kingdom or to the crown as the visible symbol of a national, territorial community. Developments facilitating this shift included taxation for the defense of the realm (the realm was eventually fused with the *patria*); the politicizing of the Crusades (taxation that was good for the realm of Christ in the Holy Land was also good for the realms of England and France); the transfer of the concept of the "holy soil" overseas to the sacred soil of the French or English fatherland; the association of those martyred on a crusade with those killed in the defense of the earthly fatherland; and the custom of sanctifying actions on behalf of the realm with the slogan, "For God and crown."[26]

Most important for the history of civil religion was the emergence of the organic concept of the state, a mode of thinking which developed out of the experiences of the Crusades and wars of the time. Thus, the king was the head and his subjects the members of the body politic. Reason and nature demanded that all members of the body serve the head as well as be controlled by it. Likewise, the king's peace was not only that of the realm, but also of the church, of learning, virtue, and justice, which permitted the concentration of forces for the reconquest of the Holy Land. Before long, the French saw war for France as war for "the Holy Land of France." In this context, Joan of Arc cried, "Those who wage war against the holy realm of France, wage war against King Jesus!"[27] That remarkable fifteenth-century peasant girl articulated a concept held in common with her better-educated contemporaries—that the French were a peculiar people chosen by God to carry out the orders of heaven.

The organic view of the state was linked with another major change in political and religious thought. The term *corpus mysticum*, which originally referred to the Eucharist, was gradually transferred to the church as an organized body to reinforce its institutional unity. After decades of debate, Pope Boniface VIII in his bull *Unam Sanctam* (1302) proclaimed as official doctrine that the church was "one mystical body the head of which is Christ." The use of *corpus mysticum* to designate the church in its sociological and ecclesiological aspects occurred at a critical point in church history.[28]

This usage linked the rapidly developing structural organization of the church with the liturgical sphere, but at the same time it placed the church as an ecclesiastical organism on a level with secular polities which were starting to assert themselves as self-sufficient communities. The terminological change also coincided with the period when corporative and organic doctrines began to pervade Western political thought. Secular political communities borrowed the term *corpus mysticum* from the church and applied it to themselves, using it for their own ends. During the four-teenth century, it came to mean any *corpus morale et politicum* (political and moral body), whether church or state, and every person was regarded as belonging to some "mystical body." A few interpreted this to mean humanity in general, others as Holy Mother Church, but still others as *patria*, the fatherland.

The upshot was that more and more Europeans came to see themselves as citizens of a state in a religious and moral sense. As the national monarchies grew in size and strength, they utilized every means at their disposal to secure their subjects' loyalty. When popes and kings clashed, people increasingly gave their fundamental allegiance to the mon-archs. Eventually, the state distanced itself from the church and appropriated the ethical values and emotions which had been largely absent from early medieval political institutions but had been common to civil religion in antiquity.

Kantorowicz emphasizes that this politicized idea of the *corpus mysticum* was widely accepted by the fifteenth-century humanists of Renaissance Italy. The growth of city-states there and nation-states elsewhere in Europe was accompa-nied by an upsurge of civil piety or "civic humanism." The older theme of "the mystical body of the church the head of which is Christ" was transformed into "the mystical body of the state the head of which was the prince." Kantorowicz then concludes:

> Here the parallelism of spiritual corpus mysticum and secular corpus mysticum, of the mystical body's divine head and its princely head, of self-sacrifice for the heavenly transcendental community and self-sacrifice for the terrestrial metaphysical community has reached a

certain point of culmination. And from this high-point onward the historian will find it easy to coast down that road which ultimately leads to early modern, modern, and ultra-modern statisms.[29]

The sixteenth century marked the end of the medieval synthesis and the beginning of cultural and religious pluralism in the West. It was a time of religious turmoil and change flowing out of the Protestant, Catholic, and Radical Reformations. Renaissance intellectual trends, the rise of nation-states, the exploration and exploitation of the New World, and raging inflation helped to make this a most tumultuous century. The great age of revolutions and civil wars had begun, and the future lay with those states which created a secular base for the maintenance of public peace. As the "wars of religion" subsided and the new national states stabilized, civil religion appeared all over Europe. It developed most fully in countries where "enlightened despots" nursed a public faith that coincided with Rousseau's model.[30]

CIVIL RELIGION IN MODERN EUROPE

The exact character of civil religion in Europe during the past two centuries is not entirely clear. Existing studies are tentative and inconclusive, and the distinctions between it and particularistic state churches are often fuzzy. The pluralistic element which fostered civil religion in some European nations was based on the adoption of religious liberty and separation of church and state, while elsewhere it was the presence of what might be called secularism (or secular humanism), liberalism, socialism, or fascism rather than a rival religion that challenged the established churches and constituted the main ingredient in the development of a civil religion.

In many instances, state churches served the purposes of civil religion and some still do, especially in multiethnic countries like Belgium or Switzerland. Further, nationalism took on features of religion, including the claim to ultimate and universal reality, but nationalism is not by itself civil religion. To be sure, both secularism and nationalism substituted earthly, utilitarian values and ends for transcendent ones, but historian Ronald VanderMolen insists that neither biblical Christianity nor anything like modern American civil religion was a major configuration on the religio-political map of post-Napoleonic Europe. What actually existed were secularized societies which contained a residue of Christian ideals and values.[31]

On the other hand, a recent study of modern Italy by Robert Bellah reveals a variety of civil religions existing side-by-side in that country: pre-Christian pagan survivals, traditional Italian Catholicism, liberalism, socialism, and activism (or renewed fascism). By pre-Christian pagan survivals, he means the religion of the basic social structure itself, that which is embedded in the family, village, and work group and which closely resembles Japanese Shinto. Italian Catholicism is and always has been a civil religion, because of the very nature of the Catholic faith and because the papacy with its inherent political implications has been an Italian institution for centuries. Until fairly recently, it was impossible to defy the Catholic political system without challenging Catholicism as a religion. Thus, liberalism, socialism, and activism (fascism) were forced to be civil religions (that is, religio-political organisms) in order to compete with the Catholic civil faith. Bellah sees some signs that an eclectic civil religion based on all of these elements is now emerging as a response to pluralism.[32]

Another manifestation of civil religion in modern Europe was found in Nazi Germany. Historian David Diephouse calls attention to this:

> For the Nazi true believer, Hitler's order inspired loyalty through its apocalyptic political gospel and the charismatic personal appeal of the Fuhrer. For a much broader range of Germans, however, the regime's legitimacy rested upon its ability to exploit the troubled reservoir of historic German attitudes towards the state and nation.[33]

He maintains the Third Reich had a public faith that was simultaneously a folk religion, the transcendent universal religion of the nation, and religious nationalism. But, he adds, it was more than this. The Third Reich was a "synthetic barbarism," as Reinhold Niebuhr put it, where the state became fused with an explicit religion of the state. For Jacques Ellul, the essence of Nazi Germany was secularism come full circle: the Hitler regime was civil religion carried to its logical conclusion, that is, all conventional distinctions between the sacred and secular disappeared, religious fervor was effectively transferred from the realm of faith to that of politics, and there was no transcendental reference point other than the state itself. Hitler may have fulfilled Rousseau's ideal of civil religion better than he knew.[34]

ANGLO-AMERICAN CIVIL RELIGION

Civil religion developed in a more advanced form in England than elsewhere in the sixteenth and seventeenth centuries because of the paradox of a state church (the Church of England) existing amidst religious diversity (the Puritans and their sectarian offspring). In fact, the Anglican Church existed as the *via media* (middle way) between Roman Catholicism and continental Protestantism. Technically, it was a state church and not a civil religion, but its diversity and latitude gave the appearance of civil faith. Certainly after the death of Elizabeth I in 1603, some English thinkers saw the need for an overarching public faith, as sectarians multiplied and began expressing themselves denomination- ally. The relatively early emergence of civil religion in England was crucial for American religious history. Just as the majority of the basic political and social ideas which molded America originated in Britain, so New World civil piety did also.

The most noticeable ingredient of the developing civil religion was the conviction that England was "God's New Israel" and the English were his "covenanted people." This feeling was expressed as early as 1559 by Bishop John Aylmer, who asserted that "God is English" and put these words in the mouth of England, speaking to her beloved subjects:

> Besides this, God hath brought forth in me the greatest and most excellent treasure that he hath for your comfort and all the world's. He would that out of my womb should come that servant of his, your brother John Wycliffe, who begat Luther, who begat truth.[35]

John Foxe popularized the "chosen nation" theme in his highly influential *Book of Martyrs* (first published in 1563), the classic providential tale of England's unique role in history. The cosmic struggle between God and Satan underlay all of human history, and England was the divinely chosen instrument of victory. According to Foxe, God was steadfastly leading the English nation to its rendezvous with destiny, and from Wycliffe to Henry VIII and his break with Rome to the first Elizabeth, God's hand guided England in defying the antichrist, that is, the papacy. The day was coming when England would fulfill its divine commission to free the world from papal bondage and usher in the millennium. The specific way God would accomplish his plan was not always clear during this stormy period, but one thing was certain— England was his anointed vessel.[36]

As it turned out, Parliament was the instrument God used to carry out his sacred purposes; or at least that was the prevailing view in 1641 when the *Book of Martyrs* underwent its eighth printing and the country teetered on the brink of civil war. The English, particularly the Puritans, likened themselves to ancient Israel, and just as God's covenant with Israel was conditional, so too was his covenant with England. They were both a chosen nation and a covenant people and each stood under God's judgment and ultimately were accountable to him.

These impressions of England's special relation to God were strengthened during the Civil War (1642–49) and Commonwealth (1649–60) periods, but the understanding of covenant status was modified during the 1650s when the country developed a full-blown civil religion with its emphasis on transcendence. The Puritans, especially Lord Protector Oliver Cromwell, adopted a stance linking politics, morality, and religion which allowed Christian truth to transcend and control the world of politics. Not even the elect nation lay beyond the normal canons of civic morality.[37]

Nevertheless, there was a gap between theory and practice in the Commonwealth. Although in theory the Puritans distinguished between the state as God's agent of salvation and the protector of societal stability, in practice they did not always observe this distinction. In short, English civil religion was a mixed bag. Many events of the Cromwell years contradicted such stated ideals of the Commonwealth as religious toleration and the separation of church and state. There was also an ominous tendency to substitute the state for the church and to substitute peace, freedom, and material prosperity for the gospel's emphasis on the world of the spirit.[38] Thus, many evangelicals became disenchanted with the great republican experiment, the Puritan movement was torn by internal disputes, and more and more "saints" withdrew their support from Cromwell, who had become a benevolent dictator.

As disillusionment set in, a crisis engulfed the Commonwealth from which it never recovered. In 1658, Cromwell died and two years later the monarchy was restored. Dr. John Owen, an Oxford don and Puritan intellectual, originally had been full of millennial hope and staunchly supported the new order in England; but as early as 1652 he had grown frustrated and disillusioned. He lamented:

> What now, by the lusts of men, is the state of things? Say some, there is no gospel at all; some others, if there be, you have nothing to do with it. . . .Some make religion a colour for one thing; some for another;—say some, the magistrate must not support the gospel; say others, the gospel must subvert the magistrate. . . .Now, those that ponder these things, their spirits are grieved in the midst of their bodies;—the visions of their heads trouble them. They looked for other things from them that professed Christ; but the summer is ended and the harvest is past, and we are not refreshed.[39]

Although Cromwell and the Puritans failed in their effort to complete the Reformation and establish a semisectarian state church, the imagery of England as a chosen vessel lingered long after their demise.

A portion of the Puritan ethos and worldview was assimilated by John Locke and funneled into the Enlightenment. Locke's work on civil theology drew from both common sense and revelation as found in the Holy Scriptures. He embraced and broadened the Puritan ideal of limited toleration within the framework of a required minimum body of civil and religious dogma, and he added a certain rationality based on natural law and reason. Much of this later found its way into the thinking of Rousseau.[40]

The Puritan experience also had a profound impact upon America. It was religious people—the Pilgrims and Puritans of Massachusetts, the Quakers of Pennsylvania, the Presbyterian and Reformed churches of New Jersey, and the Anglicans of Virginia—who gave America its original identity. Yet, even though they all possessed an essentially Reformation worldview, they did not bring with them a fully developed civil faith that fit the American situation. Instead, Puritan and Lockean thought and the wilderness environment shaped the public faith of the colonists and contributed to its unique character. Five components went into the formulation of the American civil religion.

THE CHOSEN NATION

The first of these was the chosen nation theme, which the Puritans brought from the mother country. They saw themselves as a New Israel, a light to the nations. Such imagery implied responsibility to the transcendent God of the universe and provided a theological foundation for a theological people and a degree of self-awareness seldom equaled in political societies before or after. On this foundation was established the central core of beliefs which in 1982 led President Ronald Reagan to declare, "Be proud of the red, white, and blue, and believe in her mission. In a world wracked by hatred, economic crisis, and political tension, America remains mankind's best hope. The eyes of mankind are on us."[41]

These early Americans, especially the ones who settled in New England, knew what they wanted to do, and as a result the Pilgrims of Plymouth occupied a special place in the hearts and minds of colonial America. (Sam Adams and "the boys" during the Revolutionary War often referred to "Mother Plymouth.") The Mayflower Compact of 1620 demonstrated that the Pilgrims envisioned the establishment of a godly, moral, and just society based on biblical principles. This was true even though the passengers on the tiny ship included both "saints and strangers," as William Bradford, the first governor of Plymouth Plantation described the religious mix of Pilgrims and non-Pilgrims in the original Massachusetts settlement.[42]

When this resolute little band of Separatists (Nonconformist English Protestants) sighted the Cape Cod coast, they realized that they were far north of the site to which the Virginia Company had granted patent privileges. The absence of valid rights to the area caused considerable uneasiness among those on the *Mayflower*, especially the non-Separatists. In an effort to hold the group together, the leaders persuaded forty-one male passengers to sign a solemn pledge. Not only did this serve as the constitution of the new colony, but also more than any other piece of literature in the colonial period, it provided an ideological cornerstone for American civil religion.

The Mayflower Compact declared that the purpose of the Plymouth colony was to establish a "civil body politic" which would honor God and advance the Christian faith:

> In the name of God, amen. We whose names are underwritten, the loyal subjects of our dread sovereign lord, King James, by the grace of God, of Great Britain, France, and Ireland King, Defender of the Faith, etc., having undertaken, for the glory of God, and advancement of the Christian faith, and honor of our King and country, a voyage to plant the first colony in the northern parts of Virginia, do by these presents solemnly and mutually, in the presence of God and one another, covenant and combine ourselves together into a civil body politic, for our better ordering and preservation and furtherance of the ends aforesaid; and equal laws, ordinances, acts, constitutions, and offices, from time to time, as shall be thought most meet and convenient for the general good of the colony, unto which we promise all due submission and obedience.[43]

This document and Governor Bradford's history of the colony's early years reflect a theological awareness and sense of identity and destiny which set the tone for New England and in many ways for America itself.[44]

Even more than the Pilgrims, the Calvinistic Puritans who settled in Massachusetts a decade later stressed the theological-political concept of divine chosenness. The Cambridge-educated lawyer John Winthrop, a person described by contemporaries as intelligent, self-sacrificing, and devoutly Christian, was elected the first governor of the Massachusetts Bay colony, and it was he who endowed America with the imagery of the "city upon a hill." While at sea on the *Arbella*, Winthrop composed his famous tract, *A Modell of Christian Charity*. It outlined the purpose and polity of the civil order which the shipload of Puritans hoped to establish in the New World. He applied a theory of the organic community to the enterprise, emphasized the special covenant relationship that those who knew God through Jesus Christ enjoyed, and stressed that God expected unique behavior from his people. Only when the inhabitants of the colony realized that God had covenanted with the community and that the welfare of each person depended on the welfare of the body politic would they comprehend the love of neighbor which was the cohesive element of the corporation. If they would covenant with each other to form a polity based on true godliness and biblical principles, then they would enjoy peace and prosperity. The result would be:

> Wee shall find that the God of Israell is among us, when ten of us shall be able to resist a thousand of our enemies, when he shall make us a prays and glory, that men shall say of succeeding plantacions: the lord make it like that of New England: for wee must Consider that wee shall be a City upon a Hill, the eyes of all people are upon us.[45]

According to Winthrop, they were involved in a mission of cosmic significance. They were the test case which would determine whether people could live on earth in a civil state according to the will of God. In old England the Puritans were being frustrated in their effort to bring the Reformation to a logical and successful conclusion, but now they had the opportunity to do so in New England. Their outpost in the wilderness could be a "city upon a hill," a moral and political example to the entire world. Their Zion would be the hub of the universe, whose light and wisdom would radiate in all directions for the good of humanity and the glory of God. This belief became a part of the ideology of Puritan New England and eventually of most Americans. In fact, people belonging to the other Protestant denominations in the colonies also possessed a political outlook which contained a strong sense of transcendent responsibility to the God of the universe. The religious refugees, even more than those who came for economic and political reasons, gave America its first and most lasting identity.

The chosen people theme fit naturally with the Revolution. The colonists' success in throwing off British rule confirmed the uniqueness of the American experience and simply added more stones to the structure of civil theology. The way in which the Founding Fathers, such as John Adams, reminded the younger generation that the "real revolution" had been accomplished in people's hearts before 1776 revealed that they saw the Revolution as a stage in American development.[46] The Calvinist ideal of "a new people" permeated almost every aspect of political thought, and when it was fused with rational elements from deism, the doctrines, themes, and ceremonies of a distinctively American civil religion emerged.

The Declaration of Independence, the Constitution, and later, Lincoln's Gettysburg Address became the sacred scriptures of the new public faith. Just as the colonists saw their own church covenants as vehicles of God's participation in history, so these public documents became the covenants which bound the people of the nation together in a political and religious union and secured for them God's blessing, protection, and summons to fulfill their historic mission.

A leadership imagery developed that paralleled the biblical account of Israel and led to the Founding Fathers mythology. Such revolutionary leaders as Benjamin Franklin, George Washington, John Adams, and Thomas Jefferson were lionized. Before long, Washington had become the Moses-liberator figure, Jefferson the prophet, and Lincoln the theologian of the national faith. The words and acts of the Founders, especially the presidents, shaped the civil religion. In their statements the early chief executives reinforced the chosen nation theme. Jefferson, for example, in his second inaugural address (1805) tied together the chosen people and their leaders:

> I shall need, too, the favor of that Being in whose hands we are, who led our fathers, as Israel of old, from their native land and planted them in a country flowing with all the necessaries and comforts of life; who has covered our infancy with His providence and our riper years with His wisdom and power, and to whose goodness I ask you to join in supplications with me that He will so enlighten the minds of your servants, guide their councils, and prosper their measures that whatsoever they do shall result in your good, and shall secure to you the peace, friendship, and approbation of all nations.[47]

The imagery was complete: Europe is Egypt, America the Promised Land, and God has led his people to establish a new order which will be a "city upon a hill."[48]

In addition, during the first hundred years of nationhood, American civil religion developed its own cultus, that is, a system of worship. These ceremonies, holidays, and symbols fused patriotism with piety and, to some extent, melded God and country. Memorial Day, for example, could be seen as the high holy day. As Conrad Cherry notes:

> The Memorial Day celebration is an American sacred ceremony, a religious ritual, a modern cult of the dead. Although it shares the theme of redemptive sacrifice with Christianity and other religions, and although the devotees would insist that the God invoked is the God of Judaism and Christianity, the Memorial Day rite is a national service that unites Protestants, Catholics, and Jews beyond their differences.[49]

The same generalization holds for Thanksgiving Day and the Fourth of July. The ritual and language used in their celebration is not that of any particular denomination or even a broadly defined evangelical Christianity but of a larger national faith. This permits the participants to read into it what they want. They can unite with their fellows to confront mutual enemies and satisfy their need for a common identity and sense of destiny. In the case of Memorial Day, the sentiment of a threefold unity can be seen—a unity of the living among themselves, of all the living to the dead, and of all the living and dead as a group to the Deity.

As Memorial Day integrates the local community into the civil religion, so Thanksgiving Day ties in the family. Moreover, the Fourth of July is a time to eulogize the faith of the Founding Fathers and to celebrate the events connected with the establishment of the chosen nation. All three provide occasions for fusing piety and patriotism and expressing the belief that the United States has a providential assignment to act as the guardian and promoter of freedom and democracy throughout the world. These holidays, along with lesser ones like Veterans Day and the birthdays of Washington, Lincoln, and Martin Luther King, Jr., serve as a ritual calendar for American civil religion. And, the public schools—up to the mid-twentieth century at least—provided a place for the cultic celebration of the civil rituals.[50] Other expressions of the faith of the chosen nation include singing "God Bless America" in church, the inclusion of patriotic songs in hymn books, the "God-talk" that punctuates the speeches of politicians, and the repeated acts of religiosity by presidents.

A final component was added to the chosen nation motif

during the Civil War, when the themes of death, sacrifice, and rebirth were introduced. This was symbolized by the life and death of Abraham Lincoln and expressed vividly in the martyred president's Gettysburg Address. In the same vein, the Lincoln Memorial in Washington has become a national temple before which more recent ceremonies of civil religion have been performed.[51]

The connection between political piety and sacrifice is clearly illustrated in the prominent place of the flag in civil religion symbolism. Foreign observers often call attention to how America gives a much larger role to its flag than other nations do. At the outset this was a response to the young republic's need for unifying symbols, but the flag soon became a virtual end in itself and evoked from the citizenry a form of religious devotion. The linkage of religious sentiments with reverence culminated in the Civil War period when the national banner became a rallying point for patriotic Americans. In 1865 Oliver Wendell Holmes penned a poem entitled *God Save the Flag!* This bit of verse, often cited by civil religionists on the Fourth of July, shows clearly how the biblical concepts of sacrifice and the shedding of blood for redemptive purposes could be tied together with loyalty to the nation and its ideals:

> Washed in the blood of the brave and the blooming,
>> Snatched from the altars of insolent foes,
>> Burning with star-fires, but never consuming,
>> Flash its broad ribbons of lily and rose.
> Vainly the prophets of Baal would rend it,
>> Vainly his worshippers pray for its fall;
>> Thousands have died for it, millions defend it,
>> Emblem of justice and mercy to all.
> Borne on the deluge of old usurpations,
>> Drifting our Ark o'er the desolate seas,
>> Bearing the rainbow of hope to the nations,
>> Torn from the storm-cloud and flung to the breeze!
> God bless the Flag and its loyal defenders,
>> While its broad folds o'er the battle-field wave,
>> Till the dim star-wreath rekindle its splendors,
>> Washed from its stains in the blood of the brave![52]

More recently, Justice Felix Frankfurter asserted in a famous Supreme Court decision allowing schools to compel pupils to participate in the flag salute ritual:

The flag is the symbol of our national unity, transcending all internal differences, however large, within the framework of the Constitution. This Court has had occasion to say that ". . .the flag is the symbol of the Nation's power, the emblem of freedom in its truest, best sense. . . .[I]t signifies government resting on the consent of the governed; liberty regulated by law; the protection of the weak against the strong; security against the exercise of arbitrary power; and absolute safety for free institutions against foreign aggression."[53]

CIVIL MILLENNIALISM

The second factor in the formulation of American civil religion was civil millennialism, a secularizing of themes which flowed out of the First Great Awakening of the 1730s and 1740s. The chosen nation idea lent itself to this development because national purpose was part and parcel of why Americans saw themselves as an elect people. Holmes was referring to millennial expectations when he spoke of America as "bearing the rainbow of hope to the nations."

The recasting of the theistically oriented chosen nation theme into a civil millennial mode occurred in the period between the end of the Great Awakening and the outbreak of the Revolution in 1775. The Awakening had raised expectations that the millennial kingdom of Christ was about to dawn, but as revival fires cooled and routine religion prevailed once again, some clerics saw hope for the future only in the activity of God's people, wherever they might be. Others, however, clung to the millennial vision and spoke about events in America as if they were directly related to God's plan for the end of the age.

The result was a subtle but profound shift in religious values whereby the clergy of the post-Awakening era redefined the ultimate goal of apocalyptic hope. The old expectation that all nations would be converted to Christianity was diluted with the commitment to America as the new seat of liberty. First France and then England were portrayed as the archenemies of liberty, both civil and religious. In an insightful study of this trend, historian Nathan Hatch observes:

The civil millennialism of the Revolutionary era, expressed by rationalists as well as pietists, grew directly out of the politicizing of Puritan millennial history in the two decades before the Stamp Act crisis. . . .Civil millennialism advanced freedom as the cause of God, defined the primary enemy as the antichrist of civil oppression rather than that of formal religion, traced the myths of its past through political developments rather than through the vital religion of the forefathers, and turned its vision toward the privileges of Britons rather than to a heritage exclusive to New England.[54]

Thus, the First Great Awakening was a popular movement that laid the groundwork for an emotional, future-oriented American civil religion. The revolutionary generation built an American nation on the religious foundations of evangelical revivalism. The Awakening was America's first truly national event. It fostered intercolonial relations, made respectable the use of terms like "liberty," "virtue," and "tyranny" in public discussions, and created a model of leadership calling for a direct response from the people. Most importantly, the latter-day New England Puritans were joined by many Anglicans, Presbyterians, and Dutch Reformed of equally evangelical persuasion in seeing themselves as commissioned to awaken and guide the nation into the coming age of millennial fulfillment. In the process, Calvinist ideology underwent secularization without losing its moral force.[55]

However, as the churches moved out, the nation moved in. Speaking of this development, church historian John E. Smylie notes:

Gradually in America the nation emerged as the primary agent of God's meaningful activity in history. Hence Americans bestowed on it a catholicity of destiny similar to that which theology attributes to the universal church.[56]

As mentioned earlier, the colonial evangelicals who believed that their own church covenants were vehicles of God's action in history came to see the founding documents as new covenants which bound together the people of the nation and secured for them God's blessing and call to historic mission.

In the nineteenth century, this secularization of the millennial ideal became the fateful linkage of religious and political sentiments known as "Manifest Destiny." The term was first used by journalist John L. O'Sullivan in 1845: "Our manifest destiny [is] to overspread and possess the whole of the continent which Providence has given us for the development of the great experiment of liberty and federative self government entrusted to us."[57] For countless people this meant that Almighty God had destined them to spread over all of North America, and, as they did, they were to take their uplifting and ennobling democratic and religious institutions with them.

Most nineteenth-century American Protestants embraced this outlook and regarded their country as a "redeemer nation" which had a mission to save the world by creating a new humanity based on evangelical religion and democratic institutions. In an address to the Indiana Methodist Conference in 1861, which was colored by the crisis of the Civil War, Bishop Matthew Simpson bluntly articulated this viewpoint:

> God has given us a peculiar position before the nations of the earth. . . .A nation that has in itself the power to elevate its own citizens, and to exert good influence upon nations abroad, has the especial favor of God. . . .It is certainly not in God's plan that we should pass away. Then how could the world do without us? The people of all nations look to us. If our country goes down, one-half of the world would raise a wail of woe, and sink lower. God. . .cannot afford to lose the United States.[58]

Thus, a secularized evangelical millennialism had become a part of the civil religion of the land.

THE EVANGELICAL CONSENSUS

A third formative element was a national religious consensus that, broadly speaking, was provided by the evangelicals. The First Great Awakening instilled evangelical values in national life, but Americans at the time of the Revolution were not particularly religious in the conventional sense. In fact, formal church membership sharply declined during the conflict. In the Second Great Awakening at the turn of the nineteenth century, the revivalists triumphed and gave the United States its basically evangelical cast. Historian William G. McLoughlin calls attention to this:

> The story of American evangelicalism is the story of America itself in the years 1800 to 1900, for it was evangelical religion which made Americans the most religious people in the world, molded them into a unified, pietistic-perfectionist nation, and spurred them on to those heights of social reform, missionary endeavor, and imperialistic expansionism which constitute the moving forces of our history in that century.[59]

Of course, this was not the civil religion which Rousseau had in mind, but evangelical Christianity did provide the religious glue for the republic. It established the ethical norms that stood above parties, denominations, sects, and creeds as it informed the consciences and molded the lifestyles of three generations of Americans.

At this juncture, it is important to recall that civil religion is not merely a form of nationalism.[60] The latter is a state of mind in which individuals render their highest loyalty to their nationality, thus placing all other allegiances on a secondary level. It demands that the members of a nation give allegiance to their nation-state or work to create such an entity if it does not already exist. Nationalism can be an element in civil religion and becomes very dangerous if the nation itself is the highest reference point in the exercise of civil faith. If such is the case, religious commitment is given to the state rather than to the Deity who is supposed to stand in judgment over the state and its actions. In America, nationalism was integrated into civil religion through a happy marriage between evangelical Christianity and liberal democracy which in turn was presided over by a smiling Creator. Nineteenth-century American Christians felt they could wholeheartedly give allegiance to the nation because it was God's chosen instrument to spread *both* Christianity and democracy. They saw the two concepts as branches of the same evangelical tree. There was no conflict in loyalty to God and to his chosen nation. And if it strayed from its calling, there were prophetic leaders (such as presidents) and founding documents (like the Declaration of Independence and Constitution) to call it back to its appointed tasks.

Ralph H. Gabriel in his classic study, *The Course of American Democratic Thought*, labeled this fusion of evangelical religion and national interests and worldviews the "American Democratic Faith." Pietists, Calvinists, and Dissenters all contributed to the evangelical religion of the land which flowed in the same channel as romantic democracy. The parallels between their doctrines were remarkable: common assent to a basic moral law, agreement with the Calvinist insistence that constitutional government was necessary for the restraint of evil, the shared doctrine of the free individual, common adherence to the philosophy of progress, and accord in the conviction that America's mission was to save the world from both autocracy and satanic governance.[61]

This interpenetration of evangelical Christianity and democratic ideals was illustrated by the universally used *McGuffey's Eclectic Readers*. William H. McGuffey was a Presbyterian clergyman, professor of ancient languages and philosophy, college president, and advocate of public education who deliberately set out to "shape the rising generation to our model." To accomplish this, he developed a civil catechism/elementary school reader which sold an estimated 120 million copies between 1836 and 1920. The books not only taught children how to read but also inculcated in them the American civil faith.[62] According to the *McGuffey Readers*, there were three essential elements in the life of a "public." They were the common story of the people of the nation, a vehicle for a set of symbolic acts which the public could use to celebrate the nation's history and future, and ethical directives regarding its common work and destiny. To fulfill the first essential, McGuffey held up the Puritans as the creators of the civil faith and moral heroes of the republic. As for the second, the speaker's platform—solidly embedded in the traditions of the orator and revival preacher—was the chosen vehicle. The ethical dimension was provided by evangelical Christianity. Its norms were those of the republic—individual responsibility and rectitude, sound literary tastes based on the Bible, the glorification of hard work, piety (love of God), kindness (love of neighbor), and patriotism (love of country). These three elements reinforced the conviction that the United States was God's New Israel and the hope of the world. These values and their secularized counterparts were accepted by evangelicals and non-evangelicals alike in nineteenth-century America.

THE DEIST CONTRIBUTION

The fourth component was provided by the intellectual and political elite whose rationalist outlook proved to be compatible with the general evangelical tone of the civil faith. This was due to the fact they possessed social ideals that were in harmony with the prevailing religious temper of the nation, while the Protestant leaders identified with the political philosophy of the ruling elite. For example, two Founding Fathers, Thomas Jefferson (convinced deist) and John Witherspoon (staunch Calvinist) agreed that humans possessed a natural, innate ability to grasp the truth about the world and morality without need of divine grace or revelation. Thus, political thought in Revolutionary America was based on the assumption that the light of natural reason could reveal the eternal principles of God's law to any unprejudiced, right-thinking individual. To be sure, orthodox Christians like Witherspoon believed that depravity touched the wills of humans but did not necessarily blind their intellects. This is why the deist Jefferson and near-atheist Thomas Paine could share with the evangelical Christian patriots a single political orthodoxy.[63]

Moreover, as the Second Great Awakening spread across the land, the common religious faith increasingly became evangelical and the common political faith popular democracy. As a result, biblical religion and liberal democracy merged in the evangelical mind. The common social values like those propagated by the *McGuffey Readers* rested on this fact. Since the intellectual and political elite, though mostly deists, shared these values, they joined in a united front with their fellow-citizens. Moreover, studies of the American Enlightenment reveal the existence of far more flexibility in its attitude toward organized religion than was the case with its European counterpart, precisely because there was no established church upheld by or upholding a monarchy. Even if the American deists did not enter into the fullness of the evangelical faith, they did imbibe much of its political and social expression.[64]

Historians have long debated whether the deists influenced the evangelicals more than the evangelicals influenced the deists, or vice versa. The truth is that the two streams—evangelical Christianity and deism—were twin tributaries which merged to form the river of civil faith in the fledgling republic. However, in the nineteenth century the evangelicals—especially the Dissenters of the colonial period— gained the upper hand, and the deistic element faded into the shadows from whence it would be summoned in the more pluralistic twentieth century.

Numerous scholars point out how this cluster of evangelical-deistic ideals made up the early national faith. America was the meeting ground of these compatible but different forms of thought. For the intellectuals, the natural law of the *philosophes* was the expression of the will of God, while Christians regarded the moral law as the primary expression of the divine will. However, both perceived the Creator God as the source either of natural or moral law, as the case might be. The key theme of evangelical Christianity was that true liberty came to the person who had been released by Christ from the fetters of sin, while central to the democratic faith was the doctrine of the free individual. Thus, freedom under God was a common value shared by evangelicals and non-evangelicals alike in the early republic. The civil religion was based on the interlocking piety of two devoutly held ideologies—deistic politics and evangelical faith—and it rested on a heartfelt belief in the twin concepts of freedom and democracy in the context of a New Israel with a sense of divine mission.[65]

A SELF-AUTHENTICATING HISTORY

Fifth, there had to be a measure of self-authenticating history in the American experience. In other words, the course of human events seemed to bear out that the United States was indeed God's elect nation and was ordained to spread civil and religious liberty to the farther regions. After all, the nation came into being and expanded by an unprecedented series of events that gave it fundamentally transcendent properties which secular social contract theories could not explain. Sober rationalists like Jefferson and others of his generation recognized the transcendent quality in the birth of the nation. He in effect became the first prophet of American civil religion when he wrote in the Declaration of Independence: "With a firm reliance on the protection of Divine Providence, we mutually pledge to each other our lives, our fortunes, and our sacred honor." Later, in the second inaugural address, he declared:

I shall need, too, the favor of that Being in whose hands we are, who led our fathers, as Israel of old, from their native land and planted them in a country flowing with all the necessaries and comforts of life; who has covered our infancy with His providence and our riper years with His wisdom and power.[66]

Jefferson genuinely acknowledged divine transcendence: it fit so well with the ideal of chosen nationhood, manifest destiny, evangelical values, and deistic civil piety.

For most people the facts were clear. America was born in unusual historical circumstances and was blessed with extraordinarily talented leaders in its formative years. It was a land with vast natural resources and a temperate climate, one which enjoyed a splendid isolation from the Old World while it experimented with republican ideas and institutions. It successfully endured the fiery furnace of civil war and came through the time of testing stronger than before. In short, there was substance to the half-grudging, half-admiring remark allegedly made by Otto von Bismarck in 1898 when he received news of the American romp in Cuba in the war with Spain. The retired German chancellor growled that there seemed to be a special Providence which looked after drunkards, fools, and the United States of America.[67]

To oversimplify, being an American in the nineteenth century was to vote for causes that advanced democracy and to behave in accordance with evangelical values. This was the essence of civil religion in that era. At the same time, however, an element of deistic civil religion lingered in the wings, always willing to play a supportive role, but perhaps also waiting for an opportunity to steal the show.

INTO THE TWENTIETH CENTURY

Unfortunately for evangelical Christianity's spiritual vitality, toward the end of the century it entered into a period of cultural captivity. For reasons too complex to examine here, it became identified with the prosperity and sentimentality of Victorian America. Then, in the wake of the new immigration, theological liberalism, and the stresses of urbanization and industrialization, the evangelical consensus gradually hardened into the Protestant Establishment. The change from consensus to establishment was both an expression of satisfaction with the status quo and a signal that the old mainline Protestant denominations were determined to defend their prerogatives. At the same time, they braced themselves for the threat from without—foreigners, anarchists, Catholics, Jews, and German rationalists (the last-named bringing with them higher criticism and liberal theology). Also, the new ideologies of Marxism and Darwinism began challenging the Christian faith and putting Protestants on the defensive. Most importantly, during the years 1890 to 1914, the Protestant Establishment cohabited with corporate capitalism, and their miscegenetic offspring was materialism, militant nationalism, and a much more broadly based and less evangelically influenced civil religion.

For their part, many evangelicals found it difficult to harmonize the historic Christian faith with their old outlook toward American society, now that it was becoming so pluralistic. Whereas in previous generations to be an American had meant to hold evangelical values, this was increasingly less true after 1890. The massive influx of immigrants who did not share the evangelical Protestant worldview of the older population forced a redefinition of what it was to be an American. To complicate matters further, most of the recent arrivals did not push on to the frontier where they would be more easily assimilated into the new life, but instead settled in the cities and retained their old ethnic religions, which often were quite different from the evangelical faith prevalent among native Americans.

These developments were beyond the control and perhaps even the comprehension of the religious leaders, and the old, confident evangelical consensus rapidly turned into a worried, defensive Protestant Establishment. The chosen nation theme now smacked of superiority and condescension, the mission of American democracy turned into strident nationalism and even imperialism, and the philosophy of progress was transformed into blatant materialism. In the process, civil religion became more and more an expression of American tribal identity, while pressures were mounting to enlarge the umbrella of civil faith to accommodate the many non-Protestant newcomers.

Of course, a more deistic civil faith existed alongside and in some ways was a functional part of the evangelical civil religion consensus all through the nineteenth century. This preference for the civic theology of the Enlightenment was most obvious in the intellectual community before the turn of the century. Then, when the bitter Fundamentalist-Modernist controversy of the 1920s shattered the Protestant Establishment, a new and more latitudinarian civic piety moved to the forefront. During World War I and even more in World War II, this broader Judeo-Christian brand of civil religion helped to mobilize an increasingly pluralistic nation against foreign enemies.

The key figure in the interwar period who urged such a revival and expansion of the civil faith was none other than John Dewey. Whereas in the early years of the republic the evangelical consensus swept the intellectuals along in the formation of the first American civil religion, after World War I the intellectuals proposed that the churches join them in revising civil religion to meet the needs of the post-Protestant era. Dewey and others argued that the new values of liberal humanism—based on secular materialism and the common good of an increasingly pluralistic society—should replace those of the old *McGuffey Readers* and be inculcated in the nation's school children. In fact, his ideas of "progressive education" dominated American schools in the middle decades of the twentieth century.[68]

After 1945, civil religion experienced another upsurge as American political leaders struggled with the threat of Soviet aggression. National unity also was endangered by a multitude of new problems that went beyond religious and cultural pluralism, such as racial and political unrest, the assertion of ethnic particularism, the alienation of youth from the system, and the widespread repudiation of traditional personal values and sexual mores. In trying to meet the need for unity in a country with a steadily decreasing amount of religious and cultural cohesion, the base of civil religion was further expanded. During the course of American history, its umbrella had grown from evangelical consensus to Protestantism-in-general, to Christianity-in-general, to the Judeo-Christian-tradition-in-general, and finally to deism-in-general.[69]

It is little wonder that over the years the president's role in civil religion has changed in response to the challenges involved in governing the country. New peoples and increased power have brought new problems and prospects for the future, and presidential leadership, both in politics and civil religion, reflects the changing character of the nation and needs of its public faith. The president is still the foremost representative of civil religion in the United States, and much of the public mythology which now surrounds the office had its origin with the first chief executive, George Washington. His role in the development of early civil religion is examined in the next chapter.

3

GEORGE WASHINGTON AND THE FOUNDATION OF AMERICAN CIVIL RELIGION

There is no better evidence for the presence of a dynamic civil religion in early American history and no better example of the desperate need Americans felt for a dignified and worshipful national hero than their passionate haste in elevating George Washington to civil sainthood following his death in 1799. That Washington quickly became a national saint there can be no doubt. This is best illustrated by the struggle over the possession of his sacred remains which began soon after he had drawn his last breath. The question at once became: where is the proper final resting place for the holy relic? As historian Daniel J. Boorstin notes, "The struggle over the possession and proper location of the bodily remains of the Hero, if not equaling that over the Holy Grail, expressed a not dissimilar cultic spirit."[1]

WHERE SHOULD THE BODY LIE?

Interest in the location of the tomb was present from the moment when, shortly before her own passing in 1802, Martha Washington reluctantly gave her consent to Congress for the removal of her late husband's body from Mount Vernon to a place of honor in the nation's capital. Because no crypt had been prepared to receive the remains and there was a division of opinion over where they should reside, nothing further was done about the matter during the generation following Washington's death. However, as the centennial of his birth in 1832 approached, a lively debate occurred over the site of the final resting place in an atmosphere of heightened tension between Congress, on the one hand, and the Washington family, the state of Virginia, and the rest of the South, on the other. A House committee early in 1830 called for an appropriation to finance the construction of a magnificent mausoleum in the Capitol rotunda to house the remains of both George and Martha Washington. In the ensuing debate, one southern congressman objected to the transfer of "our venerated Washington" from Virginia soil while another spoke against the desecratory removal of the "the sacred bones" to the capital. A Vermont representative responded that the very presence of Washington's "sacred dust" would somehow sanctify the deliberations of Congress, and the eminent Henry Clay urged the action because "he would himself discriminate between Washington and any man who had lived, from Adam down."[2]

The controversy was abruptly terminated on February 16, when, less than a week before the proposed ceremony, John Augustine Washington, then the occupant of Mount Vernon, flatly refused to allow removal of the body. After a mysterious attempt a few years later to steal the remains from the family home, a new vault was constructed and locked, and the key thrown into the Potomac.

The political skirmishing over the civil saint's tomb was a manifestation of a deep religious instinct which had gripped the American people. It was important where the divine man lay because, wherever the site might be, it would inevitably become a center of sacred power. The controversy over the final resting place of the first leader of the young nation illustrates the nature and extent of early civil religion. The quasi-religious devotion of a nation to a long-dead Washington is indicative of the new civil faith and parallels other mythological developments surrounding the personage of the Great Founder.[3]

THE LIFE OF THE AMERICAN MOSES

Washington towered like a giant among the Founding Fathers. In commanding the patriot army during the American Revolution, he risked his reputation, fortune, and life. As the leading rebel, the incarnation of the patriot cause, he almost literally thrust his head into the hangman's noose. Without his inspirational influence, the endeavor he led could hardly have triumphed. In short, there was good reason why this remarkable person became a revered figure in the mythology of early American civil religion.[4]

He was born in Westmoreland County, Virginia, on February 22, 1732. His first American ancestor, John Washington, came to Virginia from England in 1657. This immigrant's descendants remained in the colony and gained a respected place in society. Involvement in farming, land speculation, trading, milling, and the iron industry were the means by which the family rose in the world. George's father, Augustine, had four children by his first wife and six by his second, Mary Ball, who was the mother of the future president.

Washington's early life included the conventional experiences of a young man growing up in the American wilderness—the practical skills one learned in the fields and forests and on the rivers. Surveying for land development purposes and soldiering in the French and Indian War were his main activities as a youth. In that conflict, he witnessed the humiliating defeat of British General Edward Braddock, who tried to fight Indians as if he were engaging the French at Blenheim. After it was over, he returned to Mount Vernon, which he had inherited in 1752 upon the death of his half-brother Lawrence. He had no plans or desires except to grow tobacco and enjoy the planter's pleasant life.

In 1762, he was elected a vestryman of Truro Parish of the Church of England, a position which in that period traditionally fell to gentlemen of Washington's class. Vestrymen had many duties, ranging from building roads and operating ferries to caring for orphans and helping supervise the work of the parish church. For him the position was a training ground for later political activities. Also, one had to be a vestryman before he could become a member of the House of Burgesses, Virginia's colonial legislature. Washington soon was elected to that body as his father and grandfather before him had been.

By the time formal hostilities between the mother country and her American subjects had begun, Washington's leadership abilities were widely known throughout the colonies. As a member of the Burgesses he had opposed the Stamp Act, and later he was named a delegate to the First Continental Congress which met at Philadelphia in 1774. The next year a second congress convened, and with the outbreak of war, the body on June 15, 1775, appointed the forty-three-year-old Virginian commander-in-chief of its virtually nonexistent army.

He soon proved to be more than just a military commander; he was the embodiment of everything positive in the American character. He had no illusions of grandeur and gave no thought to the future except to express an intense longing to return to Mount Vernon, but he assumed and fulfilled every responsibility thrust upon him. He not only led the army but also constantly wrote letters to Congress, state leaders, and state governments, begging them for the wherewithal to maintain his forces. He had to mediate quarrels among his officers and placate the cold, hungry, and unpaid troops. He ignored intrigues against his authority, and the intriguers came to grief. In his relations with the French, he proved to be a first-rate diplomat. Refusing to accept a salary, he frequently dipped into his own modest fortune to buy comforts for his fighting men and to help their destitute families.

Thus, Washington brought something more important to the cause than military ability and statesmanship, namely, the priceless gift of character. Although he was scrupulous in his respect for the civil power, some in Congress and state governments were jealous of him and feared that he would be too successful and assume dictatorial power. However, he had no such intentions and was regarded by his soldiers and by the people in general with respect and affection. He did not have a Napoleonic personality and did not arouse a fanatical loyalty among his troops; but the common soldiers knew that they could depend on his bravery, wisdom, and sense of justice.

Furthermore, Washington had been a powerful force in maintaining unity among the colonies. He had retained the confidence of all factions by refusing to use the army for selfish ends and by insisting on order, discipline, and respect for leadership. He was so successful in this regard that the American Revolution is unique among political upheavals for its absence of bloody purges, reigns of terror, and any mass liquidation of opponents.

When it became evident that the Articles of Confederation were not doing the job of providing unity for the new political entity, Washington was one of the half-dozen leaders instrumental in calling a convention to revise the document. The body convened in Philadelphia in May, 1787, and Washington, who was a delegate from Virginia, was elected its presiding officer. It proceeded to scrap the existing Articles of Confederation and replace it with a new Constitution. The leading light in the convention was his close associate, James Madison, and the document written there embodied Washington's essential ideas.

The Federal Constitution provided for an electoral college to choose the chief executive for the United States, and it twice unanimously selected Washington. He neither sought nor wanted the presidency of the new nation, but his compelling sense of duty prevailed over his innermost wishes, just as it had during his eight years as commander of the American colonial army.

On April 30, 1789, he was sworn in as the first president at a ceremony in New York City. With his right hand resting on a Bible, he repeated the brief oath prescribed in Article 2 of the Constitution:

> I do solemnly swear (or affirm) that I will faithfully execute the office of President of the United States, and will to the best of my ability, preserve, protect, and defend the Constitution of the United States.

It said nothing about what followed, which was a precedent-setting, voluntary choice on the part of Washington. He added the words, "So help me, God," and bent down and kissed the Bible which was held by the secretary of the Senate.

WASHINGTON'S RELIGION

Every president since Washington has appended the phrase to the oath and sworn it upon a Bible, but what were the religious beliefs of the man who initiated this pious practice at the inaugural ceremony? Myths cluster quickly around heroes, even in their lifetimes, and Washington was no exception. Many of these myths had to do with his religious life; they have been related in a host of books and articles published since his death. He was, according to these accounts, "a Christian hero and statesman," "Christ's faithful soldier and servant," "the founder of a Christian republic," "the great high-priest of the nation," and "a man of abiding faith."[5] In the 1930s it was suggested that Washington should be duly canonized as the first official saint of the Protestant Episcopal Church to which he belonged; while more recently the claim was made that "not once during his distinguished service to the nation did he minimize or shelve his deeply felt commitment to God, to the Bible, or to his Lord and Savior, Jesus Christ."[6]

In light of all these testimonies to his personal religious devotion, Paul F. Boller, Jr., the leading authority on Washington's faith, commented rather sarcastically:

> Indeed, judging from the many instances of Washington's preoccupation with devout observances which were accumulated over the years by such enthusiasts as Mason Locke Weems, Edward C. McGuire, William Meade, William J. Johnstone, Joseph Buffington, and W. Herbert Burk, to name only the most influential, it would appear that Washington had time for little else but the ritual of piety. He attended church regularly, said grace at mealtime, was active in church work, went out of his way to receive the sacrament of the Lord's Supper when away from home, filled his utterances, both official and unofficial, with religious exhortations, and observed private devotions with almost relentless regularity wherever he happened to be—in his library, in his army tent, at the homes of friends and strangers, and in the woods, thickets, groves, and bushes, if no shelter was at hand. He seems, in fact, to have been perpetually at prayer.[7]

Boller went on to show in his book, *George Washington and Religion*, that most of these stories of religiosity were based on hearsay and popular legend and were lacking in the kind of evidence that would hold up in a court of law.[8]

The most widely told legend about Washington's piety—one which exemplifies all the rest—is that of his kneeling at prayer in the snow at Valley Forge during the desperate winter of 1777–78. The story was first purveyed by the greatest Washington mythmaker of all times, Mason Locke "Parson" Weems, in his best-seller, *The Life and Memorable Actions of George Washington*, the first edition of which appeared in 1800, a few months after the first president's death. Born in Maryland in 1759, Weems was one of the first two Americans ordained in England to the Episcopal priesthood of the United States shortly after independence had been won. By the time of his death in l825, his life of Washington had gone through about thirty editions, each a little longer than the previous version. He was the first to tell the story of Washington's "Gethsemane," as some call the Valley Forge episode.[9]

According to Weems, Washington had his headquarters in the house of Isaac Potts, a Quaker who, as a Christian pacifist, opposed the war. One day, when the prospects, morale, and physical state of the Continental Army were at their lowest, Potts was passing through the woods and found Washington kneeling in the snow, hat off, in prayer, his horse tethered to a nearby sapling. Potts, motionless with surprise, "continued on the place till the general, having ended his devotions, arose; and, with a countenance of angelic serenity, retired to headquarters." Potts then rushed home to tell his wife what he had seen and to affirm that he had been converted to the view that the war was just after all and that Washington would prevail.[10]

This tradition has been celebrated in verse, bronzed on a plaque on the base of Washington's statue at the building on Wall Street in New York where he took the oath as president in 1789, commemorated on a two-cent United States postage stamp in 1928, and memorialized in the private chapel for the use of Congress constructed in the Capitol in 1955, whose prominent feature is a stained-glass window above an oak altar depicting the kneeling figure of Washington at Valley Forge. In fact, a national iconography has grown up around it. In a 1976 survey of Revolutionary War events depicted in stained glass, Esther Harris and Doris Bowman found no fewer than ten versions of the Valley Forge prayer, including one in a Massachusetts church in which the Virgin Mary appears to Washington on the occasion. Unfortunately, as Boller points out, the story "is utterly without foundation in fact."[11]

If popular legends of Washington's piety like this "Gethsemane scene" are not true, then what *were* his religious beliefs and practices? His upbringing centered on a simple belief in God and compliance with the ritual of the Church of England, the established religion of colonial Virginia, but it was not marked by special zeal or active faith. His older half-brother Lawrence, generally regarded as young George's role model, practiced the Anglican faith without bigotry, pious ostentation, or notable fervor, and as a result the future president grew up feeling that a person's religious beliefs were strictly his own business. The Protestant Episcopal Church, as it was called after the separation from Britain, was Washington's lifelong public affiliation. Whatever he thought about it privately, it was a part of the world which he took for granted. He was baptized, married, and buried according to its rites and ministrations. As in most Virginia families of that day, it supplied the grace at meals ("God bless us in what we are about to receive") and afterward ("God make us thankful for his mercies"), and taught him reverence for the Bible. Even though as an adult in pre-Revolutionary Virginia he attended the fox hunt much more frequently and with greater commitment than he did the parish church, he maintained a consistent if somewhat desultory relationship with his denomination to the end of his life.[12]

In addition to the influence of his half-brother and parish church, Washington was affected in matters of religion by the ideas of the Enlightenment. Although the evidence for this is not conclusive, it is substantial. In his maturity, before the Revolution, he read such key Enlightenment figures as John Locke, Voltaire, Alexander Pope, and Thomas Paine. He also spoke with feeling of the justice, power, wisdom, and goodness of Providence, and in typical Enlightenment deistic terminology, insisted that people who respected "the eternal rules of order and right, which Heaven itself has ordained" could look forward with confidence to "the propitious smiles of Heaven" on their endeavors. He wrote to Joseph Reed in 1776: "I will not lament or repine at any acts of Providence because I am in a great measure a convert to Mr. Pope's opinion that whatever is, is right."[13]

Clearly, Washington had an unquestioning faith in Providence and voiced that faith on numerous occasions. That this was no mere rhetorical flourish designed for public consumption is apparent from the constant allusions to

Providence in his personal letters. His reliance upon a Grand Designer along deist lines was a meaningful, but not necessarily complex or subtle, part of his life. Echoing Rousseau, he wrote to James Anderson in 1795 that "in politics, as in religion, my tenets are few and simple."[14] It was also during the years before the Revolution that he joined the Masonic Lodge, an organization in which he would become well-acquainted with nature's law and Nature's God.[15]

Washington's experiences in the war and later in the presidency apparently deepened his religious faith. Although references to Jesus Christ and the basic tenets of the Christian faith are virtually nonexistent in his wartime and presidential correspondence, it is evident that his belief in a beneficent Providence had grown more profound. A good example of this was his farewell speech to Congress in December 1783 when he resigned his commission. His address before the dignitaries who then were meeting at the state house in Annapolis was a profoundly emotional one for this usually reserved man. As he praised his officers, his hands trembled and he used both of them to hold the paper from which he read. His voice choked:

> I consider it an indispensable duty to close this last solemn act of my Official life, by commending the Interests of our dearest Country to the protection of Almighty God, and those who have the superintendence of them, to his holy keeping.[16]

And with that, he took his leave.

It was this genuine but generalized faith in God as the Creator and Ruler of the universe that Washington took with him into the presidency. Most American unitarian-deists regarded God as standing apart from his creation, not communicating directly with humanity, but somehow taking a hand in human affairs in the guise of fate, destiny, or Providence—terms often used by Washington. Some unitarian-deists were privately skeptical, others belligerently argumentative, and still others simply philosophically curious about theology, revealed religion, creeds, and the sacraments, but at least in America, they believed in God and generally in a life after death. Jesus was revered, but his deity either rejected or doubted. The Bible was regarded as a great source of moral teaching but not necessarily as the final authority for one's worldview or lifestyle. In short, eighteenth-century American unitarian-deism provided the kind of outlook which Rousseau and other Enlightenment thinkers considered best suited for civil religion.[17]

Washington's own religious pronouncements as president were basically unitarian with deistic overtones and in keeping with civil religion beliefs. The Rev. Dr. James Abercrombie, rector of St. Peter's Church in Philadelphia where Washington often worshipped when the seat of government was located there, went so far as to affirm that the chief executive was a deist and lax in his attention to the Eucharist. To be sure, Washington was not antireligious or disrespectful toward the church, but according to testimony from both Abercrombie and Rev. William White, the first Episcopal bishop of Pennsylvania, Washington was not a zealous churchgoer nor was he in the habit of partaking of the sacrament. Moreover, he was notorious for not kneeling to pray in public worship. At the church in Philadelphia, he often attended the pulpit service but left before the observance of the Eucharist, usually leaving the more devout Mrs. Washington behind with the other communicants. When Dr. Abercrombie in a sermon scolded those in places of public trust who set bad examples by turning their backs on the sacrament, Washington was so irked that he never appeared at St. Peter's on Communion Sunday again. This ambivalence toward orthodoxy characterized Washington's churchgoing habits and his attitude toward organized religion in general during his years as president. He attended sporadically, listened courteously, but participated little in the life of the local church. He never spoke of any personal belief in Christ but rather reserved his affirmations of faith in the Supreme Ruler of the Nations for his personal letters or civil religion occasions of the government such as the presidential inaugural.[18]

Washington's profound belief in Almighty God and his public piety were buttressed by a stern moral code, a kind of secular puritanism which involved self-discipline but not necessarily self-denial. His strong character, his physical stature (over six feet tall), and his stately bearing lent him an aura which could be translated into religious devotion by the masses. His taciturnity complemented his physique in generating that sense of awe and regard which Americans felt in his presence and gave weight to his public pronouncements on religion. At the same time, Washington himself seemed to possess the political intuition to cultivate those attributes which fostered the legend already growing around him. His protestations of modesty and renunciations of pay, his public attitude of putting his country ahead of himself, his slow and deliberate pace, his affirmations of belief in the guidance of Divine Providence, his sterling personal character—all combined to produced the popular image of the divine political man. This set the stage for Washington's unique contributions as president to the initial development of America's civil religion. He would become both its first major spokesman and first practitioner, and after his death a leading figure in its unfolding civil theology.[19]

WASHINGTON THE CIVIL RELIGIONIST

Washington's civil religion flowed naturally out of his unitarianism and desire for tolerance and national unity. Above all, he wanted the new nation to succeed. With this in mind, he crafted an inaugural address that would set the tone for all those which followed. It was his great "Invisible Hand" speech which Christians, Jews, deists, and all other who held a belief in God—something which nearly everyone in those days did—could apprehend in his or her own way.

As historian Catherine Albanese points out, the creed, code, and cultus (system of worship) of the first American civil religion were firmly in place by the time of the first inauguration. Through these, the ordinary history of the country was linked to extraordinary religion. The creed proclaimed the United States as a chosen and millennial nation, charged with providing an example and fulfilling a mission to raise up others to republican institutions. The code emphasized right and patriotic behavior by citizens and government, thus setting an example which would be instrumental in accomplishing the American mission. At the same time, the code institutionalized the jeremiad, the public lament about the sins of America and its station under God's judgment, which presumably preceded any action to correct problems. Interlinked with creed and code, the cultus of the civil faith designated sacred space and time in national shrines and patriotic holy days. It offered a series of national saints (beginning with Washington), holy objects, and ritual practices to help people keep in touch with creed and code.

Although there were ambiguities in the meaning of the creed, code, and cultus, their central affirmation was the messianic destiny of America as the chosen nation.[20]

There is no better example of the transcendent nature of the early civil religion than Washington's first inaugural address, in which he both acknowledged and sought divine favor. Standing before the assembled Congress and various government officials in New York City's Federal Hall, the chief executive outlined his hopes for the new nation and institutionalized its civil religion. After protesting his inadequacy for the office, he proceeded to link "the Invisible Hand" with the political fortunes of the American people:

> It would be peculiarly improper to omit in this first official act my fervent supplications to that Almighty Being who rules over the universe, who presides in the councils of nations, and whose providential aids can supply every human defect, that His benediction may consecrate to the liberties and happiness of the people of the United States a Government instituted by themselves for these essential purposes, and may enable every instrument employed in its administration to execute with success the functions allotted to his charge. In tendering this homage to the Great Author of every public and private good, I assure myself that it expresses your sentiments not less than my own, nor those of my fellow-citizens at large less than either. No people can be bound to acknowledge and adore the Invisible Hand which conducts the affairs of men more than those of the United States. Every step by which they have advanced to the character of an independent nation seems to have been distinguished by some token of providential agency; and in the important revolution just accomplished in the system of their united government the tranquil deliberations and voluntary consent of so many distinct communities from which the event has resulted can not be compared with the means by which most governments have been established without some return of pious gratitude, along with an humble anticipation of the future blessings which the past seem to presage.[21]

Then, he expressed his hopes for the government and the American republic and concluded by saying:

> I shall take my present leave; but not without resorting once more to the benign Parent of the Human Race in

humble supplication that, since He has been pleased to favor the American people with opportunities for deliberating in perfect tranquillity, and dispositions for deciding with unparalleled unanimity on a form of government for the security of their union and the advancement of their happiness, so His divine blessing may be equally conspicuous in the enlarged views, the temperate consultations, and the wise measures on which the success of this Government must depend.[22]

During both terms in office, President Washington in his public pronouncements repeatedly connected piety and patriotism, God and country, and divine benevolence with the well-being of the nation. One theme pervading these speeches was the seeking of divine favor. In his annual message to Congress in 1794, Washington declared in what amounted to an American psalm:

Let us unite . . . in imploring the Supreme Ruler of nations, to spread his holy protection over these United States: to turn the machinations of the wicked to the confirming of our constitution: to enable us at all times to root out internal sedition, and put invasion to flight: to perpetuate and to verify the anticipations of this government being a safe guard to human rights.[23]

Nor was he reticent to acknowledge divine favor, and in the vein of prophetic civil religion, to link it to divine forgiveness for national sins. Thus, he proclaimed Thursday, November 26, 1789, as a day for national thanksgiving. In that historic act, he urged all Americans to "unite in most humbly offering our prayers and supplications to the great Lord and Ruler of Nations, and beseech him to pardon our national and other transgressions."[24] Again, in his annual address to Congress in 1796, the president paid tribute to divine favor and expressed hope that it would continue to the benefit of the people and government of the American nation:

The situation in which I now stand, for the last time. . . . naturally recalls the period when the Administration of the present form of Government commenced; and I cannot omit the occasion. . .to repeat my fervent supplications to the Supreme Ruler of the Universe, and Sovereign Arbiter of Nations, that his Providential care may still be extended to the United States; that the virtue

and happiness of the People may be preserved; and that
the Government which they have instituted, for the protection of their liberties, may be perpetual.[25]

Finally, Washington molded and shaped the civil faith
by repeatedly stressing the value of religion in public life and
by linking religion with public morality, republican institutions, and national happiness. Nowhere is this more evident
than in his celebrated Farewell Address, actually an essay
which he published in the September 17, 1796, issue of the
American Daily Advertiser. For the last time, the retiring
president assumed his role as civil pastor of the nation and
taught his people, saying:

> Of all the dispositions and habits which lead to political
> prosperity, Religion and Morality are indispensable sup-
> ports. In vain would that man claim the tribute of
> Patriotism, who should labour to subvert these great
> pillars of human happiness, these firmest props of the
> duties of Men and citizens. The mere politician, equally
> with the pious man ought to respect and to cherish
> them. . . .Whatever may be conceded to the influence of
> refined education on minds of peculiar structure, reason
> and experience both forbid us to expect that National
> morality can prevail in exclusion of religious principle. It
> is substantially true, that virtue or morality is a necessary
> spring of popular government.[26]

WASHINGTON THE OBJECT OF CIVIL RELIGION

The Father of His Country was not only a molder and
practitioner of civil religion, but he also became a part of its
cultus, its system of worship. This apotheosis began even
before his death. The Revolution was fought in an atmosphere of disagreement, dissension, bitterness, and rancor—
all manifestations of the party spirit which Washington
would later so strongly condemn. Confronted with the
paradox of their oneness and manyness, the patriots perceived the need for unity in their common task. This in turn
generated an unconscious demand for a collective faith and
collective symbols to express their union; that faith was a
civil one which transcended party and denominational
differences.

One of the first unifying symbols was George Washington himself, who met their requirements for someone who

could bind their founding faith and its growing civil theology to a human center. In Washington, the mysterious chemistry of body and spirit provided the raw material out of which a collective representation of American personhood could be formed. He was a kind of superbeing who epitomized the ideals of character and consciousness which patriots understood as "best" in the ancient classical sense. In retrospect, they knew that in Washington they had discovered the highest, the strongest, the most excellent way; and they were heartened in the pursuit of the goals of independence, since they could contemplate the realization of these in the person of one of their own. Despite minority opposition to him as commander-in-chief and as president—and there was sometimes bitter opposition—almost overnight Washington became a living tribal totem for the emerging nation.[27]

In the figure of Washington, the Americans found a person, larger than life, who could help to make them one, and so while he lived, the veneration began. Locks of his hair were treasured, babies were baptized with his name, and legends circulated about his miraculous abilities as a war leader. Actors read speeches in his honor from the stage, and birthday celebrations for him were elaborate, even during his lifetime. In 1779, a German-language almanac called him "the Father of his country," while orators everywhere praised him in the most dramatic terms. When he traveled to New York for his first inauguration in 1789, the route became the scene for elaborate rituals expressing his greatness. In Philadelphia a new bridge was constructed that spanned the river like a triumphal arch, and a small child crowned him. At Trenton, New Jersey, several hundred girls dressed in white serenaded him, and tens of thousands gathered to welcome him when he arrived in New York. It is little wonder that scholars of all persuasions find it exceedingly difficult to characterize the historical Washington; and some agree with Marcus Cunliffe, who in 1958 concluded in exasperation that it was "useless for his biographers to try to separate Washington from the myths and images surrounding him."[28]

Contemporaries even compared Washington to Jewish and Roman heroes. He was the Moses who freed his people from bondage and the Joshua who led them into the Promised Land. At the same time he was Cincinnatus, the Roman general who had left his plow to fight for his country, and then when the task was done, laid down the sword and returned to his farm. This double identification with themes from Jewish and Roman history revealed the complex nature of American civil religion. Like that of Israel, it grew out of the dominant national culture, which at the time was Protestantism. Like that of Rome, it summed up the cosmopolitan spirit of the intellectuals of the nation, which reflected the ideals of the Enlightenment.

As mentioned above, the place of Washington in American civil religion developed following his death, and his physical remains were venerated. In addition, annual rites and a declamatory liturgy grew up around the observance of his birthday. Until recently, the only birth anniversary (other than that of Jesus Christ on December 25) celebrated as a legal holiday in every state of the union was that of George Washington. Speakers used the occasion to declare the grandeur of the first president. Most noteworthy was Edward Everett's oration which he delivered around the country from 1856 to 1860 to assist the Mount Vernon Association in raising funds to acquire Washington's home as a public shrine. He gave the same two-hour oration, "The Character of Washington," some 129 times and secured about $90,000 for his patrons. It immediately became a classic in the national liturgy.

Moreover, Washington's name was honored uniquely. Not only was the nation's capital named after him, but also the state of Washington (admitted 1889), thus making him the only person after the colonial era whose name was given to a state. Likewise, Washington is the most common placename of towns, townships, and counties in the United States. His countenance became a national icon, as his portrait was to be found in public halls and private homes around the country. A European traveler, Paul Suinin, observed in 1815 that it seemed as if "every American considers it his sacred duty to have a likeness of Washington in his home, just as we have the images of God's saints."[29] In the twentieth century, his face was placed on the one dollar note and the quarter dollar coin. And his saintly qualities were praised in song, verse, and the written word. William Bryan, a scholar who has examined the vast corpus of Washingtonian literature, comments:

If one were to read only the biographies written before 1855, he would think Washington a demigod who descended to earth (his character already fully developed and flawless even in childhood), freed his people from oppression, steered their government for a few years, and then returned to heaven.[30]

Even more important for the development of American civil religion was the compelling Moses analogy.[31] Probably no aspect of Washington's life was so well articulated as that of "the American Moses," the man who led his people from tyranny to freedom. This was especially seen in the eulogies delivered at his death. The noted Boston preacher Thaddeus Fiske proclaimed in a memorial service the already widely held idea: "As the deliverer and political saviour of our nation, he has been the same to us, as Moses was to the Children of Israel."[32] The imagery was almost irresistible. After all, the Puritans had fervently believed and the young country eagerly accepted the concept that America was "God's New Israel," his chosen nation. Therefore, the Washington as Moses imagery was easily and naturally grafted onto the Puritan tree of civil religion, for just as Moses of old had led God's elect people from the bondage of Egypt, so Washington was able, as one preacher put it, "to carry his American Israel through the waves and wilderness of revolution and to place them in the Canaan of peace and independence."[33]

Early in the Revolutionary War, patriots began to see the conflict as their escape from something worse than the Egyptian bondage of the Israelites. "The deliverer of America" was one of Washington's popular postwar titles.[34] It became commonplace to refer to the Revolution as "our miraculous deliverance from a second Egypt—another house of bondage," to liken the Fourth of July to the day the Hebrews "came up out of Egypt," and to insist that "God had raised up a Washington" just as he had earlier "qualified and raised up Moses."[35]

In the ten weeks following his death occurred the most sustained effort to compare the first president to the ancient Hebrew lawgiver. In the hundreds of eulogies delivered across the land, especially in New England, Washington was favorably compared to a wide range of biblical, classical, and modern heroes, but nothing was so persistent and well-developed as the contention that the departed leader had truly been a Moses for America. Among the most frequently used texts for these sermons was the thirty-fourth chapter of Deuteronomy, which describes the death of the deliverer and relates that the children of Israel mourned him on the plains of Moab for thirty days. Eulogists like Fiske declared: "Scarcely less sorrowful is the occasion, or less afflictive the death now felt and deplored by this American Israel. . . . The children of Columbia now weep for Washington in the plains of America."[36]

However, the mourning scenes were not the most arresting analogies. Americans were enjoined to weep for Washington as the Hebrews had done for Moses because the lives of the two men seemed to parallel each other so closely.[37] The most striking thing was that God had commissioned each of them to fulfill some great work in the divine plan. Just as the Lord had raised up Moses to lead Israel, so in the words of Massachusetts minister Isaac Braman, he pitied "the abject and servile condition of our American Israel, gave us a second Moses, who should (under God) be our future deliverer from the bondage and tyranny of haughty Britain."[38] The spiritual origins of the two were the same.

Some found similarities in the physical circumstance surrounding their births. Both came from good families and were descendants of immigrants who came to a new land seeking opportunity but instead experienced oppression and tyranny. Early in their lives, the two had been providentially rescued from lesser fates—Moses by his mother in an ark of bulrushes and Washington by his mother who allegedly secured her son's release from being a teenage midshipman aboard a British warship.[39] During their youth, both leaders obtained exactly the kind of education they needed and were prepared for their future roles as deliverers of their respective nations.

The most important part of each savior's story was the end for which they were predestined, namely, to free their peoples. At this point, patriotic orators stressed some even more profound similarities. The most obvious one was that at the outset of resistance neither oppressed nation seemed to have much hope of victory. However, the seeming futility of their cause simply forced the two oppressed peoples to recognize that their deliverers were agents of the Almighty.

After noting the initial misgivings on the part of both "Israels," patriotic preachers turned to the parallels in the liberation process. One New England minister put it succinctly: "Moses led the Israelites through the Red Sea; has not Washington conducted the Americans through seas of blood?"[40] Yet, the orators maintained, both Moses and Washington were more than warriors who led armies. During the conflicts, the two conducted the civilian as well as the military concerns of their nations. As one clergyman stated: "It is abundantly evident, from the sacred history, that Moses was, under God, almost the sole director in both these departments, to the Israelites." Similarly, Washington, while commanding the American military, had also "by epistolary communication, afforded, unto Congress, much light and assistance, especially in cases of difficulty and perplexity; and in considerable measure guided our councils while he led our armies."[41]

Moreover, not only did the liberators have to deal with the foe; they also were faced with domestic detractors. Moses had his "murmurers" and Washington his "tories and traitors." But, declared one preacher, Washington's critics had as little chance of success as Moses's, for "Providence had designed him as the deliverer of his country, and the divine purposes were not be be frustrated."[42] Then, after having served ably in both military and civilian capacities, the two men in their old age left their peoples sage advice by bequeathing their wisdom to posterity in farewell addresses.[43]

From the civil religion standpoint, other parallels were even more important. As New England minister Ebenezer Gay noted, the two men had brought their nations within sight of permanent capitals: "A few steps more, & the israelitish nation would have pitched their Government in Canaan. A few steps more, and the American nation would have pitched their Government in the City of Washington." Both died "at a few hours warning, when their eyes were not dim nor their natural force abated."[44]

They possessed similar "personal virtues," in that they ardently loved their people "and served them with equal zeal, fidelity and disinterestedness."[45] Both were strangers to ambition and diffident as they accepted the roles of leadership which were thrust upon them. In assuming their duties, they demonstrated great self-denial. For a higher cause, Moses gave up the luxuries of the Pharaoh's court and Washington the pleasant life of Mount Vernon. They displayed self-discipline in performing their tasks. Although Moses had slain the Egyptian oppressor of his fellow Hebrews and Washington was said to be "naturally passionate," both learned to control their emotions. They had their extraordinary patience severely tested by the unfounded charges of some of their countrymen. Washington pursued wise policies, and though sometimes reproached as "traitorous, cowardly, and deficient in martial skill," he bore it all. Like Moses, he seemed to know that the detractors would eventually see that his course was best for the nation.[46] Further, both deliverers were preeminently courageous. Finally, they knew the importance of religion and profoundly trusted in God. Thus, the outward behavior of the two had been so remarkably similar precisely because their souls were alike.[47]

Clearly implicit in some comparisons was the idea that Washington may even have been superior to Moses. Since he was not divinely inspired, as was the Hebrew lawgiver, Washington constantly had to depend upon his own physical, mental, and spiritual resources. Moreover, he had entered the Promised Land with his people. After delineating the usual parallels between the two leaders, one zealous pulpiteer even reversed the analogy and proclaimed that Moses was "the Washington of Israel"![48]

The Washington-as-Moses analogy was developed most fully by New Englanders with a Puritan heritage, and it reflected the legacy they bestowed upon American civil religion, namely, the chosen nation theme. Like their Puritan forebears, these people—and, indeed, an increasing number of nineteenth-century Americans—really thought that they were the covenant people whom God had raised up to be his New Israel, appointed to be the example to all humanity. George Washington's life and death were fitted naturally into the civil religion motif which enabled millions of Americans to understand their own politics and history. In keeping with their self-picture as the new covenant people of God, the veneration of the American Moses persisted as a vital element of their belief in the providential guidance of the country well into the twentieth century.

In light of the foregoing, it should be no surprise that Parson Weems described Washington's "death and ascen-

sion" in Mosaic terms. According to Weems: "Feeling that
the hour of his departure out of this world was at hand, he
desired that every body should quit the room. There, by
himself, like Moses alone on the top of Pisgah, he seeks the
face of God."[49] Alone with God, the Moses-Savior of his
generation remembered his country and its "beloved children" he had "so often sought to gather, even as a hen
gathereth her chickens under her wings." The dying hero
saw them "now spread abroad like flocks in goodly pastures;
like favored Israel in the land of promise." At last, the
moment of death came. Washington having closed his eyes
and folded his arms "decently on his breast," exclaimed,
"Father of mercies! take me to thyself," and fell asleep.
Weems then shared the final scene with his readers, though
he soberly admitted that he had heard it only "in Fancy's
ear." It was civil religion heaven:

> His glorious coming was seen far off, and myriads of
> mighty angels hastened forth, with golden harps, to
> welcome the honored stranger. High in front of the
> shouting hosts, were seen the beauteous forms of
> FRANKLIN, WARREN, MERCER, SCAMMEL, and of him who fell at
> Quebec, with all the virtuous patriots, who, on the side of
> Columbia, toiled or bled for *liberty* and *truth*.[50]

So powerful was the sacred memory of the first president that nearly one hundred years later, thirteen-year-old
Mary Antin experienced its impact when she attended public
school in a Boston slum. Born in a Russian ghetto in 1881 and
the descendant of generations of persecuted Jews, she
described her joyous odyssey from immigrant to American:

> How long would you say, wise reader, it takes to make an
> American? By the middle of my second year in school I
> had reached the sixth grade. When, after the Christmas
> holidays, we began to study the life of Washington,
> running through a summary of the Revolution, and the
> early days of the Republic, it seemed to me that all my
> reading and study had been idle until then. The reader,
> the arithmetic, the song book, that had so fascinated me
> until now, became suddenly sober exercise books. . . .I
> could not pronounce the name of George Washington
> without pause. Never had I prayed, never had I chanted
> the songs of David, never had I called up the Most Holy,
> in such utter reverence and worship as I repeated the
> simple sentences of my child's story of the patriot. I gazed

with adoration at the portraits of George and Martha Washington, till I could see them with my eyes shut.[51]

Mary Antin, without realizing it, had begun to partake of American civil religion.

THE PRESIDENT AS THE SPIRITUAL FATHER OF HIS PEOPLE

Thus, the first president of the United States occupies a special place in the development of American civil religion. He gave it a voice and served as the focal point for its formation. He encased the presidency in religion by his words and example, and through his powerful personality he bestowed upon the office a sacred aura. Quickly elevated to civil sainthood following his death, he also became the Moses figure who reminded the people that they enjoyed a common heritage and that God had chosen them as his New Israel for a new era. Since God had blessed his chosen people in their hour of greatest need with the proper figure to lead them, would not the Almighty in other perilous times continue to safeguard his American Israel? That remembrance would give Americans a large measure of assurance and hope as well as a foundation upon which to continue building their nation. In addition, something of Washington's sacred-leader, father-figure role was transferred to each of the presidents. In short, the words and deeds of the Founding Fathers, but especially those of the first president, profoundly shaped the future form and tone of American civil religion.

Washington's life reminded people of the element of self-sacrifice in the political development of their land. Sacrifice is an important theme in most religions, and civil faith is no exception. However, this would become a much more potent aspect of the public religion with the Civil War presidency of Abraham Lincoln and his eventual martyrdom. Whereas the first chief executive firmly established civil religion in the life of the nation through the good offices of his presidency and his myth-inspiring personality, the sixteenth president would lead in the next major step in the elaboration of the national faith, namely, its sacralization.

4

ABRAHAM LINCOLN AND THE SACRALIZATION OF AMERICAN CIVIL RELIGION

On a bright Sunday afternoon in October, 1862, the Congregational church in the village of Fitzwilliam, New Hampshire, was packed with blue-coated men. A company of Union voluteers heard the Rev. William Gaylord explain the cosmic significance of the struggle then under way:

> Oh! what a day will that be for our beloved land, when carried through a baptism of fire and blood, struggling through this birth-night of terror and darkness, it shall experience a resurrection to a new life, and to a future whose coming glory already gilds the mountain tops. That day of future glory is hastening on. That day of a truer and deeper loyalty to God and to country—that day when the oppressor's rod shall be broken, when the sigh of no captive spirit shall be heard throughout all our fair land.[1]

Gaylord was claiming a profound theological significance for the Civil War, and similar sermons were preached in churches all over the North during these trying years. Although no denomination formally altered its confessional statement, it was an unofficial article of faith, at least in Protestant churches, that the conflict would prove to be the decisive point of American, indeed, of world history. As they sang the stirring cadences of Julia Ward Howe's "Battle

Hymn of the Republic," thousands of Northerners actually believed that their eyes were seeing "the glory of the coming of the Lord." A hundred years later, long after the passions of the struggle had cooled, Robert Penn Warren affirmed its importance: "The Civil War is for the American imagination the great single event of our history."[2] Even as the twentieth century draws to a close, the "American imagination" continues to cling to the memory of the War Between the States.

THE LINCOLN LEGEND

At the center of this apocalyptic event in the national experience was Abraham Lincoln, a man whom scholars characterize as "unquestionably our most religious president" and the "theologian of American anguish."[3] He more than anyone else wrestled mightily with the meaning of the conflict, and his role in the development of American civil religion is of paramount importance. According to historian Richard Hofstadter, the Lincoln legend has "a hold on the American imagination that defies comparison with anything else in political mythology."[4] However, separating the real from the mythical Lincoln is complicated by the fact that he produced a body of printed work totaling 2,078,365 words, an amount greater than the Bible or all of Shakespeare's plays. From his words and deeds have arisen images which live on in American memory: the common man, the self-made man, the rail-splitter, the great democrat, the prairie politician, honest Abe, the Great Emancipator, and the beloved Father Abraham.

But most importantly, Lincoln is honored as the religio-political leader who guided the Union to victory through four perilous years of civil war and fostered a national rebirth. In an epic of biblical proportions, this heroic figure shouldered the torments and moral burdens of a blundering and sinful people, suffered on their behalf, infused them with hallowed Judeo-Christian virtues, and then was struck down by an assassin's bullet. He was the martyred savior of the Union.[5]

It is little wonder that a Lincoln cult sprang to life at the moment of his death. In typical hero-worship fashion, enterprising capitalists produced souvenir handkerchiefs, paperweights, and dinner plates with the fallen president's image on them. As the funeral train wound its way from

Washington to the Illinois heartland, seven million people paid their final respects to the beloved one. When the train approached Springfield, the tracks were so slippery from crushed flowers thrown by mourners that it was delayed for three hours plowing through the thick floral carpet. After the interment, souvenir seekers ripped apart the presidential hearse for momentos and had to be dispersed by troops with bayonets. Relic hunters even tore to shreds the blue blanket on "Old Bob," Lincoln's horse.

The caretakers of the Lincoln home in Springfield reported that the adulation continued for decades afterward. Visitors to his bedroom who viewed the one wall that had its original paper were so overcome by the realization Lincoln had slept next to this paper that they kissed it and explained they just had to do so. Others would come in the middle of the night and kiss the doorknob, and some even rang the bell at 4:00 o'clock in the morning and begged to be allowed in to look around. One man knelt and prayed so long in the parlor that the hostess, Mary Edwards Brown, thought he was never going to leave. She also told of two women who asked if they could sign their brother Ezra's name in the guest book even though he had been dead ten years—because, they said, it would mean so much to him.[6]

For many years Lincoln's personal secretary, John Hay, kept a small bit of hair that had been clipped from the president's head on the night of his assassination. He had it mounted in a ring which he presented to Theodore Roosevelt to wear on the occasion of his inauguration on March 4, 1905, because "you are one of the men who most thoroughly understand and appreciate Lincoln."[7]

Scholarly interest has kept pace with the popular enthusiasm. More has been written about Lincoln, including commentaries on his religious faith, than about any other president. Even though he was never baptized and did not join a church, he is widely regarded as America's most genuinely religious president. As Albert Menendez points out: "The anomaly of an unbaptized saint in the White House has long intrigued scholars and religious writers." In good civil religion language, Earl Kubicek sums up the situation well:

> With the exception of the Poet of Galilee, there has been no single individual of any race or culture of all the many

millions of people who have lived and died on this earth,
who have had more consideration paid to his life and
character than has Abraham Lincoln.⁸

FROM THE PRAIRIE TO THE PRESIDENCY

Ironically, the background of America's greatest hero
was most humble, and his modest origins and lofty place in
American esteem are a paradox. Indeed, Lincoln never lost
touch with the common folk even though he became one of
the most accomplished politicians of the age. Although he
was a man of extreme simplicity, he captured the ideals of
America by the artistic use of words. He was one of the few
individuals in public life who could satisfy his political
aspirations but not allow his drive for power to seem callous
or immoral.

He was born on February 12, 1809, in Hardin County,
Kentucky, the son of Thomas and Nancy Hanks Lincoln.⁹
Young Abraham migrated with his parents, first to Spencer
County, Indiana in 1816, and then to southern Illinois in
1830, where he worked as a surveyor, farmhand, ferryman,
and storekeeper. He served as a captain in the Illinois militia
during the Black Hawk War of 1832 but saw no action. He
was the postmaster at New Salem from 1833 to 1836 while he
studied law. He moved to Springfield in 1837, opened a law
office, and gained a reputation as a trial lawyer. Also, he
became involved politically. He sat in the Illinois legislature
from 1834 to 1842 and served a term in the U.S. House of
Representatives from 1847 to 1849 but did not seek reelection.

In 1856, Lincoln joined the newly formed Republican
party and two years later stood for the U. S. Senate. The
debates with his chief rival for the position, Stephen A.
Douglas, drew national attention to him. The most famous of
these was his "House Divided Speech" on June 16, 1858,
where he used the biblical allusion "a house divided against
itself shall not stand" (Matt. 12:25) to argue against the
Kansas-Nebraska Act of 1854. He maintained that the policy
embodied in the measure only intensified the slavery
controversy, there was no middle ground between pro-
slavery and Republican principles, the doctrine of popular
sovereignty reinforced the ominous tendency toward the
national acceptance of slavery, and "this government cannot

endure, permanently half slave and half free." At that time, senators were still chosen by state legislatures (direct election was eventually mandated in 1913 by the Seventeenth Amendment), and the balloting in the State House went against him. Still, he had earned a prominent place in the Republican party, and it nominated him for president in 1860.

Judged by its consequences, the election of 1860 was the most momentous in American history. The issues were so important that the losing side felt it could not abide by the results. After a bitter campaign in which he repeatedly issued assurances that the Republicans did not intend to interfere with slavery in the South, Lincoln emerged victorious. However, many southerners recognized that the Republicans, including Lincoln, disliked slavery and opposed its expansion into new states, and they concluded that abolition could not be far behind. During the campaign, various southern leaders threatened secession if the Republicans won, and true to their word, seven states left the Union even before Lincoln had taken the oath of office. Four more followed after Confederate forces in Charleston, South Carolina, opened fire on Fort Sumter on April 12. Having pledged to preserve the Union, the new president now faced the greatest crisis in American history.

LINCOLN'S PERSONAL RELIGION

Fortunately for the nation, Lincoln brought with him to the presidency five qualities that historian Allan Nevins calls the "conditions of statesmanship," namely, moral strength, intellectual power, an instinct for the spirit and needs of the time, an understanding of the masses, and, in order to mold public opinion, some kind of passion—in Lincoln's case, a passion for democracy.[10] It is clear that his religion integrated these qualities into his personality, thus enabling him to communicate the meaning and goals of the Civil War to the American people. But what was his religion? The answer to that question is not so simple. Although most scholars agree that he was a profoundly religious man, what this actually means is a matter of contention. Further complicating the picture is the way in which various religious communities through the years have tried to claim him as one of their own.

Historians find it difficult to pinpoint the sources of Lincoln's deep spirituality. His parents were God-fearing Baptists in the manner of frontier people, and they associated freely with the evangelical denominations of the day. In later life, Lincoln had tangential relationships with the Presbyterian and Episcopal churches, while his two closest ministerial associates during the White House years were a Methodist bishop and a Presbyterian clergyman, Matthew Simpson and Phineas D. Gurley. In the main, however, he could not assent to much of what passed for orthodox Christianity. Creeds and theological quarrels were not to the liking of this church nonmember; yet he possessed a biblically-rooted faith which gradually matured with the pace of his own experiences. Like so much of his life, Lincoln's religion was complex and paradoxical.[11]

Nevertheless, an analysis of Lincoln's personal faith is crucial to an understanding of his civil religion.[12] One thing is certain: it does not fit into modern categories. For most of his life it was not what people today label "orthodox" or "evangelical"; but on the other hand, Lincoln was not a skeptical "modernist" who had doubts about the supernatural or the Bible. In short, his faith was not static but dynamic in its development.[13] As a young man, Lincoln read the freethinkers Thomas Paine and Constantin de Volney and adopted an Enlightenment style of reasoning; yet he never was the "infidel" which some have claimed he was. At the same time, he was a kind of homespun "spiritualist" who believed that signs, dreams, and portents foretold the future. He spoke often about God but rarely referred directly to Jesus. As a young man, he most likely was a Universalist, one who believed in the eventual salvation of all people.[14]

Lincoln's personal faith grew and deepened during the late 1830s and the 1840s, as he came to sense God's guidance in the events of his life. His marriage to Mary Todd in 1842 was especially significant in his religious development because it brought him closer to conventional church relationships. His occasional attendance at worship with her during their early years together became much more frequent after the death of their son Edward in 1850. Further, the marriage which at first was blessed with mutual affection and comfort came increasingly to have a dark side. Mary grew more and more difficult to live with as the symptoms of mental instability manifested themselves, and after her husband's death, she had to be institutionalized. At times, Lincoln had to leave the house when Mary's anger or hysteria became too sharp. In any case, he learned to cope, and it led to a serenity of faith and a heightened understanding far beyond that of most people.[15]

The 1846 contest for a seat in the House of Representatives also honed Lincoln's spiritual perspectives. His opponent was the leading circuit-riding Methodist preacher of the day, Peter Cartwright, and his supporters waged a rough campaign. They attacked the prairie lawyer on religious grounds, alleging that he was an "infidel" and that his "high-toned Episcopalian" wife was not much better. Against the warnings of his friends, Lincoln decided to beard the Methodist lion on his own turf by going to one of the evangelist's meetings. As Carl Sandburg tells the story:

> In due time Cartwright said, "All who desire to lead a new life, to give their hearts to God, and go to heaven, will stand," and a sprinkling of men, women, and children stood up. Then the preacher exhorted, "All who do not wish to go to hell will stand." All stood up— except Lincoln. Then said Cartwright in his gravest voice, "I observe that many responded to the first invitation to give their hearts to God and go to heaven. And I further observe that all of you save one indicated that you did not desire to go to hell. The sole exception is Mr. Lincoln, who did not respond to either invitation. May I inquire of you, Mr. Lincoln, where are you going?"
>
> And Lincoln slowly rose and slowly spoke. "I came here as a respectful listener. I did not know that I was to be singled out by Brother Cartwright. I believe in treating religious matters with due solemnity. I admit that the questions propounded by Brother Cartwright are of great importance. I did not feel called upon to answer as the rest did. Brother Cartwright asks me directly where I am going. I desire to reply with equal directness: I am going to Congress."[16]

Although Lincoln was victorious, the campaign had grown so scurrilous that he felt compelled to publish a handbill defending himself against the accusation of religious infidelity:

> A charge having got into circulation in some of the neighborhoods of this District, in substance that I am an open scoffer at Christianity, I have by the advice of some

friends concluded to notice the subject in this form. That I am not a member of any Christian Church, is true; but I have never denied the truth of the Scriptures; and I have never spoken with intentional disrespect of religion in general, or of any denomination of Christians in particular.[17]

The death of four-year-old Edward caused him to think more deeply about suffering and mortality. The Lincolns were unable to locate the Episcopal clergyman who had married them and whose church they occasionally attended, so they turned to the Rev. James Smith, the evangelical minister of Springfield's First Presbyterian Church, to conduct the funeral. He provided the spiritual solace the bereaved parents needed, and consequently the Lincolns rented a pew at his church and attended regularly, Mrs. Lincoln eventually becoming a member. Still other events during the period helped to quicken his interest in the Bible, theological concerns, and moral awareness. This, in turn, reinforced his growing aversion to slavery and taught him that God dealt with people both as isolated individuals with the capacity for piety and as collective groups answerable to the Almighty.

Most of the elements of Lincoln's religious evolution during the Springfield years were summed up in the Farewell Address, delivered to his hometown friends as he departed for the capital in February, 1861:

I now leave, not knowing when, or whether ever, I may return, with a task before me greater than that which rested upon Washington. Without the assistance of that Divine Being who ever attended him, I cannot succeed. With that assistance, I cannot fail. Trusting in Him who can go with me, and remain with you, and be everywhere for good, let us confidently hope that all will yet be well. To His care commending you, as I hope in your prayers you will commend me, I bid you an affectionate farewell.[18]

Lincoln's personal faith, though not orthodox in the evangelical sense, had by then become distinctly biblical in its orientation.

The centerpiece of Lincoln's religious commitment was his attachment to the Bible. A reverence for the Scriptures was implanted in him by his Baptist parents and by the revivalism that shaped nineteenth-century culture, and his knowledge of Holy Writ increased steadily over the years. He may have studied it at first to refute it; but in any case, he encountered several devout and knowledgeable Bible students who helped him to become an avid reader of the sacred text. After early doubts, Lincoln was convinced that the Bible truly communicated the will and way of God. By the time he was forty, the Scriptures were solidly integrated into his personal and political vocabulary, and in the debates with Douglas, he repeatedly corrected his opponent's inaccurate use of the Bible.

It even was so much a part of him that his humor flowed naturally from its stories. Senator John B. Henderson of Missouri related one incident in connection with the Emancipation Proclamation. One day in 1862, Lincoln was chatting with the Missourian at the White House when he noticed three congressional zealots for abolition—Charles Sumner, Henry Wilson, and Thaddeus Stevens—coming across the lawn to complain once again to the president about his inaction. Turning to Henderson with a mischievous smile, the president said:

> I attended. . .school. . .in Indiana where we had no reading books or grammars, and all our reading was done from the Bible. One day our lesson was the story of the three Hebrew children and their escape from the fiery furnace. It fell to a little towheaded fellow who stood next to me to read for the first time the verse with the unpronouceable names. He made a sorry mess of Shadrach and Meschach, and went all to pieces on Abednego. Whereupon the master boxed his ears until he sobbed aloud. Then the lesson went on, each boy in the class reading a verse in turn. Finally the towheaded boy stopped crying, but only to fix his gaze on the verses ahead, and set up a yell of surprise and alarm. The master demanded the reason for this unexpected outbreak. "Look there, master," said the boy, pointing his finger at the verse which in a few moments he would be expected to read, and at the three proper names which it contained, "there come them same damn three fellows again!" Just then, the three abolitionists were ushered into the room.[19]

According to William Wolf, Lincoln's knowledge of the Bible "far exceeded the content-grasp of most present-day clergymen." No president had ever had such a grasp of the detail of Scripture, nor had any of them "ever woven its thoughts and its rhythms into the warp and woof of his state papers as he did." Lincoln's confidence in the Bible was eloquently expressed in a response to the "Loyal Colored People of Baltimore," who had just presented him with a magnificently bound copy:

> In regard to this Great Book, I have but to say, it is the best gift God has given to man. All the good the Saviour gave to the world was communicated through this book. But for it we could not know right from wrong. All things most desirable for man's welfare, here and hereafter, are to be found portrayed in it.[20]

The Bible was the foundation and death the catalyst for his further growth in personal faith during the White House years. Several close friends died in the early days of the war and, as historian Mark Noll notes, the heart-wrenching casualty lists from the battlefields increasingly "left him no taste for easy believism, no escape from the mysteries of God and the universe."[21] The death of his twelve-year-old son Willie in 1862 added the sorrow for a lost child to the constant strain and sense of national tragedy of the Civil War, and Lincoln was torn by the deepest personal grief in his life. Since the unhappy Mary Lincoln never recovered from her loss, she became an even heavier care to her already over-burdened husband.

However, the president emerged from the experience with "new moral energy" to lead the Union to a successful conclusion of the terrible conflict.[22] A spiritual awakening which drove him closer to personal faith in Christ brought him out of the pit of despair. No one knows precisely what went on in Lincoln's inner being during the agonizing winter of 1861–62, but many noticed that he was seen more frequently with a Bible in his hand and that he spent more time in prayer. As Ida Tarbell comments about this crucial point in his life:

> There is ample evidence that in this crushing grief the President sought earnestly to find what consolation the Christian religion might have for him. It was the first experience of his life, so far as we know, which drove him to look outside of his own mind and heart for help to

endure a personal grief. It was the first time in his life
when he had not been sufficient for his own experience.[23]

From this time on, Lincoln regularly attended the New York
Avenue Presbyterian Church on Sundays—often even going
to the Wednesday evening prayer meeting—until his un-
timely death three years later.[24]

Sidney Mead thus concludes that Lincoln was "the
spiritual center of American history"; but his nomination
rests essentially on the frontier lawyer's public rather than
his personal faith. Although the former grew out of the
latter, the public faith more deeply affected American
history. Mead also calls the man from Illinois "the most
profound and representative theologian of the religion of the
Republic," while Wolf and Elton Trueblood cite him as the
theologian of American national destiny. Bellah goes even
further to say that he represented "civil religion at its best"
and was "the man who not only formulated but in his own
person embodied its meaning for America."[25]

LINCOLN: THEOLOGIAN OF "THE AMERICAN DEMOCRATIC FAITH"

What, then, constituted Abraham Lincoln's civil theology? How did he embody American civil religion? He began
by returning to Jonathan Edwards and Thomas Jefferson and
insisting that the nation existed not simply as an end in itself
but to serve some higher purpose. It had been "conceived in
liberty and dedicated to the proposition that all men are
created equal." President Lincoln accomplished this fusion of
organic union with transcendent purpose by utilizing the
religious symbolism of the Christian tradition. He drew on
his personal spiritual insights and firm grasp of Scripture to
demonstrate that if the United States were to be "one
nation," it must be "under God."[26]

Lincoln assumed the mantle of leadership of American
civil religion as had the other chief executives before him. He
brought to the office his great reverence for the Bible, the
laws (which he once called "the political religion of the
nation"), and the Declaration of Independence (which he
regarded as both a formal theory of rights and an instrument
of democracy). Like most Americans, he accepted the latter
along with the Constitution as part of the canon of American

civil religion. And, even as he cited the Declaration as civil holy writ, he added his own compositions, much as the New Testament writers built on the Old Testament and filled out the canon of Holy Scripture.[27]

No one ever articulated the beliefs of American public religion so clearly as this master of English prose. He utilized the power of the spoken word, duly recorded and reported in the press, to formulate a civil theology which encompassed American mission, emphasized the necessity of the bonds of religious faith for nationhood, and affirmed a transcendental reference point external to the nation. He sought meaning in the Civil War and concluded that the conflict was a divine judgment upon both North and South for the sin of tolerating slavery.

THE ALMOST CHOSEN NATION

First, Lincoln embraced and clarified the American sense of mission. Like the New England Puritans, he was convinced that God had chosen this people to carry out his plan for humankind. This was something more profound and potent than nationalism, for it presumed that God had work for America to perform that would benefit the entire world.[28] In this respect, Lincoln was the heir to the Puritan concept of a covenanted, chosen people—only now the "New Israel" was the American Elect—and was extreme at times in his expression of the idea. He declared in a speech on February 11, 1861: "When the people rise in masses on behalf of the Union and the liberties of their country, truly may it be said, 'The gates of hell shall not prevail against them.'" The reference was to Jesus' statement in Matthew 16:18, "I will build my church; and the gates of hell shall not prevail against it." Lincoln had gone beyond G. K. Chesterton's definition of America as "a nation with the soul of a church" to make the nation in effect "the church."[29]

But, he qualified this doctrine of divine election ten days later when he referred to America as "his almost chosen people." With this provocative phrase he cast the American vision in a prophetic mold. A gap existed between the ideals and realities of American life, and the occasional foolish behavior of the people as well as their more serious sins always were subject to the judgment of a just God. To be "the chosen people" was not a reward for meritorious behavior or some extraordinary achievement but a responsibility to pursue the high calling of doing the Lord's work in his world. The burden of this was that it was possible to fail as well as to succeed. Even to believe that the nation had closed the gap between the realities and the ideal, that is, to enshrine the status quo, was in itself a failure.

The Puritan heritage, filtered through the eighteenth-century patriots while retaining most of its original strength, profoundly influenced Lincoln's thought. It was the background for his belief in the power of Providence, the necessity for seeking and finding the will of God, the moral dimensions of public life, and corporate and individual responsibility. It was also the foundation for his view of democracy as the political way for the "almost chosen people" as well as his confidence in the wisdom of the electorate, the possibility of making a solemn covenant with God and observing its historical results, the importance of "discerning the signs of the times," and even for his Gettysburg notion of "testing" the nation's vocation. Lincoln worked out the meaning of chosenness and the other implications of the Puritan heritage as he presided over four long years of fratricidal bloodshed.[30]

In so doing, he linked divine destiny with democratic government. Numerous parallels existed between the doctrines of the Puritans and their evangelical heirs and those of political democracy, including the belief in a basic moral law, the need for constitutional government to restrain evil, individual freedom, the desirability of progress, and the mission of America. Lincoln was the person most responsible for fusing the dominant evangelical-biblical religion with democratic ideals and for creating a civil religion version of the "city upon a hill."

He best expressed this doctrine in his annual message to Congress on December 1, 1862. After pleading for a fresh approach to the slavery issue, he declared that "we cannot escape history" and concluded:

> The fiery trial through which we pass, will light us down, in honor or dishonor, to the last generation. We say we are for the Union. The world will not forget that we say this. We know how to save the Union. The world knows we do know how to save it. We—even we here—hold the power, and bear the responsibility. In giving freedom to the slave, we assure freedom to the free—honorable

alike in what we give, and what we preserve. We shall
nobly save, or meanly lose, the last, best hope of earth.
Other means may succeed; this could not fail. The way is
plain, peaceful, generous, just—a way which, if followed,
the world will forever applaud, and God must forever
bless.[31]

Here, Lincoln tied the dynamic concept of America's destiny
under God to the equally forceful idea of a constitutional
republic or democracy, a government by the people. It would
fulfill its destiny by working out in practice and demonstrat-
ing to the world the true possibilities of such a government.
In Lincoln's mind, *the ideal* and *the way* were inseparable.
Thus, the "American Democratic Faith" emerged as the
major ideological component of nineteenth-century civil
religion.[32]

In his study of the Bible and the founding documents,
President Lincoln discovered the essence of the democratic
faith, and he came to feel that "the way" would be revealed
gradually through the ebb and flow of the daily life of God's
chosen people. Although not especially original, these
insights served as the basis for his civil theologizing. First
was a belief in God. It would be impossible for either the
deist or Christian founders to imagine a constitutional
republic without a theistic base. Next was confidence in "the
people"—that difficult-to-define, massive, unbroken stream
of human life with its tremendous inertia and momentum,
through which the Spirit of God worked in effecting his
infinite purposes. In addition was a belief in the voice of the
people as the surest clue to the divine will, but God's will
could be made known in history only if all the channels of
communication and expression were kept open. Finally was
the conviction that truth emerges out of the conflict of
opinions. Both "conflict" and "opinions" must be present if
the democratic faith were to function properly.[33]

Since the concepts of destiny and democracy were both
based on a dynamic, experimental idea of human existence
under God, the important thing was not where the society
and government now are but the sureness of the people's
sense of direction. That is, they must believe firmly in the
essential rightness of the country's general tendency or
movement. So long as the people were confident they were
moving in the right direction, the system was sound and

could function even in adversity. It was essentially a matter of faith both in divine guidance and that the democratic way with all its tortuous ambiguities and disappointments was the best yet devised. This was not necessarily an endorsement of the present state of affairs but rather an expression of confidence that the principle "all men are created equal" would triumph and that government could and ought to be by the consent of the governed.

In the "Last, Best Hope Speech," Lincoln was arguing that the Union should be preserved because it was a republic based on propositions which championed human freedom. To be sure, there were still slaves, but the free had the power to extend liberty to those who did not yet enjoy it. Moreover, the presence of millions of slaves mocked the claim in the sacred founding document that "all men are created equal." Therefore, in order to preserve the chosen nation, the main purveyor of democratic belief in the world, Lincoln called for removing this inconsistency between belief and practice by freeing the slaves.

In the first inaugural address, he eloquently defended government by consent. For it to work properly, the regime must always be sensitive to changes in the will of the governed but yet not be subject to the people's immediate, whimsical desires. Further, rules must exist which define the fundamental law under which the free live and give their common consent. The majority principle was basic to this arrangement. Insofar as possible, the will of the majority must be supreme, and all minorities must accept this. Hence, the government of free people might invoke its coercive power against minorities that deny and flout the majority principle. Not to do so would be to court anarchy and tyranny.

Still, the majority might at times be wrong and it could exercise tyranny just like the minority. What happened then? He reasoned that the only safeguard against this was the conviction that "under God" truth and right were not matters of majority vote. Thus, a democracy without faith in God was likely to degenerate into demagogic mob rule or elective dictatorship. The idea that majority opinion did not determine truth obligated the regime to guarantee to all minorities the right of free expression so that the contention for truth could go on:

> A majority held in restraint by constitutional checks and limitations and always changing easily with deliberate changes of popular opinions and sentiments, is the only true sovereign of a free people. Whoever rejects it does of necessity fly to anarchy or to despotism. Unanimity is impossible. The rule of a minority, as a permanent arrangement, is wholly inadmissible; so that, rejecting the majority principle, anarchy or despotism in some form is all that is left.[34]

The advocates of such a government always labor under the handicap that it is a way of political life conceived as an experiment, one worth trying both in good and bad times. The great apologists of the democratic faith have not defended it in doctrinaire fashion, but when pressed they often say, "Where can we find a better alternative?" Lincoln echoed this sentiment in the first inaugural: "Why should there not be a patient confidence in the ultimate justice of the people? Is there any better or equal hope in the world?" Even under the pressure of the Civil War, he never defended the Union cause in doctrinaire terms. Instead, he presented the conflict as part of the democratic experiment which "embraces more than the fate of these United States."[35]

Thus, at Gettysburg in 1863, instead of celebrating victory, as one of less mature faith would have done, Lincoln reminded Americans that the war was testing whether any nation so conceived and dedicated could long endure. The struggle was a real one, and he recognized that the "almost chosen people" might indeed "nobly save or meanly lose the last, best hope of earth." In short, the war was an effort to preserve both the Union and the American experiment in democracy in order that the nation's God-given mission in the world might continue. This was its theological meaning, as Edmund Wilson acknowledges in an essay entitled "The Union as Religious Mysticism:"

> Lincoln's conception of the progress and meaning of the Civil War was indeed an interpretation that he partly took over from others but that he partly made others accept. . . .Like most of the important products of the American mind at that time, it grew out of the religious tradition of the New England theology of Puritanism.[36]

BONDS OF RELIGIOUS FAITH

Lincoln argued that the bonds of religious faith were needed to hold the nation together. Although most Americans in 1861 agreed with this, it was Lincoln who affirmed and canonized it in his Gettysburg Address on November 19, 1863. The dedication of a national cemetery seemed an unlikely occasion for the most memorable speech in American history. The featured speaker was the leading orator of the day, Edward Everett, who delivered a two-hour address, and the president was simply expected to add some brief remarks in tribute to the fifty thousand on both sides who were killed or wounded in the great battle four months earlier. However, his speech proved to be a theological exposition of the meaning of the conflict and a summons to a higher dedication:

> Four score and seven years ago our fathers brought forth on this continent, a new nation, conceived in Liberty, and dedicated to the proposition that all men are created equal.
>
> Now we are engaged in a great civil war, testing whether that nation, or any nation so conceived and so dedicated, can long endure. We are met on a great battlefield of that war. We have come to dedicate a portion of that field, as a final resting place for those who here gave their lives that that nation might live. It is altogether fitting and proper that we should do this.
>
> But, in a larger sense, we can not dedicate—we can not consecrate—we can not hallow—this ground. The brave men, living and dead, who struggled here, have consecrated it, far above our poor power to add or detract. The world will little note, nor long remember what we say here, but it can never forget what they did here. It is for us the living, rather, to be dedicated here to the unfinished work which they who fought here have thus far so nobly advanced. It is for us the living, rather, to be here dedicated to the great task remaining before us—that from these honored dead we take increased devotion to that cause for which they gave the last full measure of devotion—that we here highly resolve that these dead shall not have died in vain—that this nation, under God, shall have a new birth of freedom—and that government of the people, by the people, for the people, shall not perish from the earth.[37]

Although no Scripture texts are cited in the Gettysburg Address, the language has a biblical ring, and the solemn style echoes the cadences of the King James Version the president knew so well. Wolf points out in his analysis that "Four score and seven years ago" is an inspired adaptation of Old Testament counting, the birth of the nation figure is borrowed from the common biblical phrase "she brought forth a son," and the "new birth" is the imagery of regeneration and the controlling concept behind the picture of purposeful sacrifice. The phrase "under God" was added while he spoke. Thus, the address fused together the grand Christian themes of human life in natural birth, spiritual renewal and rising to newness of life with the experience of the nation.[38]

But, just as the Christian life was a constant battle to bring the realities of life into conformity with scriptural norms, so the nation had been and still was struggling to live up to its ideal in the Declaration of Independence. For eighty-seven years, America had denied its purpose by narrowing the "all" of "all men are created equal" to whites only. At Gettysburg, "the old man of sin" died so that the nation might be "reborn" in the truth of democracy for all people everywhere.[39] As Lincoln scholar Roy Basler observes about the spiritual nature of the speech:

> To it he brought the fervor of devoutly religious belief. Democracy was to Lincoln a religion, and he wanted it to be in a real sense the religion of his audience. Thus he combined an elegiac theme with a patriotic theme, skillfully blending the hope of eternal life with the hope of eternal democracy.[40]

The word *proposition* is significant, since for Jefferson the idea that all men were created equal was "self-evident." It was axiomatic and required no proof. But Lincoln, the interpreter of Jefferson, chose the more precise term proposition. This was borrowed from Euclidean geometry (of which he was fond), and it involved both the requirement of proof and a continual process of being demonstrated. The verb *testing* further depicts this process, although it carries overtones of a trial of faith such as that of Abraham or Job in the Old Testament. Lincoln's theological insight consisted in rooting democracy in the will of God, thus making it a dynamic, living faith. The Civil War, therefore, was a "test" of the "American Democratic Faith." In the background of this language of testing, one can see as well the evangelical theme of justification by faith.[41]

Another sign of Lincoln's visceral conviction that nationhood required the bonds of religious faith was the phrase "under God" in the last sentence.[42] This was not in general use at the time, and it grew out of his meditation on the "almost chosen people" and "last, best hope of people on earth" themes. It was the next logical step in the construction of his civil theology. The chosen nation could easily get out of hand if it failed to realize that it stood at all times under the judgment of God. Yet, the context of Lincoln's theological development and sense of consecration makes it clear that the phrase meant "under judgment" and not "under God's banner." His civil religion was not some kind of idolatrous tribalism in which God became an American totem.

THE TRANSCENDENT REFERENCE POINT

An important part of Lincoln's civil theology was his affirmation of a transcendent reference point which was external to the nation. He adopted a prophetic stance by alerting the chosen people to the judgments of the Almighty, and he steered the public faith away from an idolatrous priestly civil religion which made the nation itself transcendent. In Lincoln's view, God both shaped and judged the nation, and he expressed this repeatedly during his presidency. In 1862, for example, he met with some clergymen, one of whom expressed the hope that "the Lord was on our side." Lincoln shocked the patriotic parsons by responding: "I don't agree with you. I am not at all concerned about that, for I know that the Lord is *always* on the side of the *right*. But it is my constant anxiety and prayer that I and the *nation* should be on the Lord's side."[43] A similar sensitivity to divine judgment was present in his Thanksgiving and National Fast Day proclamations, such as on April 30, 1863, when he summoned the people "to confess our national sins, and to pray for clemency and forgiveness." Although Lincoln believed in Divine Providence, Reinhold Niebuhr perceptively observed that he understood "the error of identifying providence with the cause to which the agent is committed."[44]

By far his most important statement of transcendence

was the second inaugural address which he delivered on March 4, 1865. After commenting on the evils of slavery and secession and acknowledging that four years earlier the country faced a civil war which neither side expected to be lengthy or bloody, he went on to give a theological explanation for the conflict that actually resulted:

> Both read the same Bible and pray to the same God, and each invokes His aid against the other. It may seem strange that any men should dare to ask a just God's assistance in wringing their bread from the sweat of other men's faces, but let us judge not, that we be not judged. The prayers of both could not be answered. That of neither has been answered fully.The Almighty has His own purposes.

> "Woe unto the world because of offenses; for it must needs be that offenses come, but woe to that man by whom the offense cometh." If we shall suppose that American slavery is one of those offenses which, in the providence of God, must needs come, but which, having continued through His appointed time, He now wills to remove, and that He give to both North and South this terrible war as the woe due to those by whom the offense came, shall we discern therein any departure from those divine attributes which the believers in a living God always ascribe to Him?

> Fondly do we hope, fervently do we pray, that this mighty scourge of war may speedily pass away. Yet, if God wills that it continue until all the wealth piled by the bondsman's two hundred and fifty years of unrequited toil shall be sunk, and until every drop of blood drawn with the lash shall be paid by another drawn with the sword, as was said three thousand years ago, so still it must be said "the judgments of the Lord are true and righteous altogether."

> With malice toward none, with charity for all, with firmness in the right as God gives us to see the right, let us strive on to finish the work we are in, to bind up the nation's wounds, to care for him who shall have borne the battle and for his widow and his orphan, to do all which may achieve and cherish a just and lasting peace among ourselves and with all nations.[45]

This document, firmly rooted in a biblical understanding of God, humanity, and history, was both a charter of Christian statesmanship and the most lofty expression of prophetic civil religion in the English language.[46] Although it contained a pastoral element and a call for repentance, the highlight was Lincoln's theological explanation for the war. He defined the American democratic hope with incisive logic and at the same time sustained that vision in its original religious rootage. Moreover, in a manner reminiscent of mystic intuition, he tackled the slavery issue like an Old Testament prophet. His Puritan forebears would have called it a "discerning of the signs of the times," a feeling for "particular providences."

Appropriating the language of the nation's founders and explaining God's intention as that of leading men into freedom, Lincoln showed that slavery contradicted God's will. Since this defiance of divine justice was built into the life of the nation, it was subject to judgment from above. In fact, for some time Lincoln had seen the tragedy and suffering of the war as God's punishment for rejecting his will by not eliminating slavery, and it fell upon both sides because slavery was a national, not merely a sectional evil. He appealed to the country in the stern language of Scripture, "The judgments of the Lord are true and righteous altogether," but showed God's actions were intended to bring about a reformation on the part of his chosen people.

A Christian element was also evident in the speech. Lincoln referred to Jesus' warning about passing judgment on others and alluded to Jesus' summary of the law and Paul's hymn in praise of love when he used the phrase "with malice toward none, with charity for all." However, this disclaimer concerning human judgments on the nearly vanquished opponent did not lead to irresolution in action. Rather, understanding the perspective of two antagonists standing together before the judgment seat of God freed one from self-righteous fanaticism. One could draw on the resource of "firmness in the right as God gives us to see the right." The speech's final line went beyond American public religion and contained a global implication. Achieving a lasting peace with all nations reflected God's purposes for all humankind, and what happened in and to America, the chosen nation, would surely benefit all other peoples.

The second inaugural address marks the culmination of the development of both Lincoln's private and public faith. His personal faith was Christian, while his public faith was pietistic, pastoral, prophetic, evangelical, and enlightened.[47]

What is more, he created yet another document for the canon of civil scripture. Not surprisingly, Charles Woodall attests to that fact:

> It is from this mature stage of his spiritual pilgrimage that come the Gettysburg Address and the Second Inaugural Address. Both as literature and theology, these master-pieces warrant comparison with those of the eighth century prophets of the Old Testament.[48]

By 1862, America's greatest civil theologian had transformed the war to preserve the Union into one which established the Union's reason for existence on the principle of upholding freedom for all persons in the land. Through the Emancipation Proclamation and in his later speeches, Lincoln tied the American dream of democracy to the nation's destiny as the "last, best hope of earth." A people who freed its slaves would be used of God to advance liberty around the world. At Gettysburg, he suggested that the nation was dying to past sins and would rise to a new birth of freedom. Only days before his own death, he led thousands in swearing a solemn oath to finish the appointed task of ending secession and slavery and to bind up the wounds with charity toward all. Lincoln's public theology marked the zenith of nineteenth-century civil religion.

THE MARTYRED LEADER

Like Washington, Lincoln was both a participant in the formulation of civil religion and, after his death, its object. Following his shooting on the evening of Good Friday, April 14, 1865, and death the following morning, he became a part of the cultus of the civil faith. That the first presidential murder occurred at the end of a struggle which Lincoln and most Americans saw in millennial terms simply served to magnify its meaning.

As psychologist Donald Capps points out, the death of a president is of great religious signficance. When it results from natural causes, it may be seen as in line with divine purpose and thus not necessarily at odds with the nation's appointed task. But:

> to view assassination as consistent with divine will would violate one of the deepest convictions of civil religion in

America, that is, that divinely appointed ends cannot be achieved through means inimical to the inalienable rights of individual citizens. Assassination, an act of murder, clearly violates those rights. Thus, the assassination of a President arbitrarily terminates his accomplishment of the divinely appointed acts he promised to carry out to the best of his ability at the time of his inauguration.[49]

Lincoln's death profoundly affected the religious consciousness of the American people. Since he presided during a time of bitter civil war, some mythicization was inevitable; but in his case, the outpouring of grief was spontaneous and overwhelming. The apotheosis of the fallen leader from prairie politician to "Savior of the Union" began at once. Historian David Donald captures the emotional state of a prostrate country:

> The times and events of the Civil War had made a great popular leader necessary. There had been the emotional strain of war, the taut period of defeat, the thrill of battles won, the release of peace. Then had come the calamitous, disastrous assassination. . . .Mourning intensified grief. The trappings of death—the black-draped catafalque, the silent train that moved by a circuitous route over the land, the white-robed choirs that wailed a dirge, the crepe-veiled women, the stone-faced men—made Lincoln's passing seem even more calamitous. Over a million persons took a last sad look at the face in the casket and went away treasuring an unforgettable memory.[50]

Almost at once, comparisons were made with the great figures of Jewish and Christian history. The mourning nation was consoled by the image of "Father Abraham." With a name suggestive of the Old Testament patriarch, he was remembered as the personal saint who symbolized the ideals of American democratic humility.[51] Even more compelling were the images of "the Suffering Servant," the shedding of blood, and the redeeming sacrifice. John Hay reported that Lincoln "bore the sorrows of the nation in his own heart" and that "the cry of the widow and orphan was always in his ears." Others declared that Lincoln's blood, shed for his country, now mingled in the ground with the blood of the countless soldiers who had laid down their lives in the sacred cause. And, as Jesus had made the supreme sacrifice to enable people someday to enjoy heaven, so Lincoln had given his life in order that they could experience a better earth. The story circulated among the humble freedmen in the South that the great man was now in heaven: "No man see Linkum. Linkum walk as Jesus as walk."[52]

Throughout the Union in 1865, preachers and orators portrayed the tragedy in christological terms. Typical was the memorial sermon of Methodist Bishop Gilbert Haven, a staunch northern abolitionist, who drew a parallel between Lincoln's final days and Holy Week. Just as Jesus made his triumphal entry into Jerusalem on a humble donkey, so Lincoln entered Richmond in an unostentatious manner only ten days before his death. Without ceremony or pomp, the president walked the streets of the Confederate capital virtually unattended; while the newly freed slaves "danced around him in an uncontrollable ecstasy of delight." Yet, even while he experienced this moment of triumph, enemies lurked in the shadows, waiting for the opportunity to destroy him. When the appointed hour came, these depraved and jealous men, working through John Wilkes Booth, struck him down. "Without revenge, without malice, without hardness or bitterness of heart," Lincoln met death, secure in the knowledge that he had saved the republic and that his work was finished. Haven then proposed that Lincoln's death be memorialized on the same day that Christians celebrated the atonement of Christ:

> The great day of the church has become yet more solemn in the annals of America. Let not the 15th of April be considered the day of his death, but let Good Friday be its anniversary. . . .We should make it a moveable fast and ever keep it beside the cross and the grave of our blessed Lord, in whose service and for whose gospel he became a victim and a martyr.[53]

From this kind of thinking emerged the image of Lincoln as "the Savior of the Union." Joel Bingham, a prominent Presbyterian minister in Buffalo, New York, asserted that Lincoln, "after having wrought out the painful salvation of the Republic, has been offered a bloody sacrifice upon the altar of human freedom."[54] The element of truth in such rhetoric made it all the more powerful and compelling. In his own suffering he personified the agony of a nation locked in a fratricidal war. Compassion, humility, and integrity had seldom been so evident in a man who wielded such power.

But power is accompanied by awesome responsibilities, and these often will accentuate emotional stress in a religiously sensitive soul. Edmund Wilson points out that whenever possible, Lincoln pardoned soldiers who had been sentenced to death, but still in his position as commander-in-chief he had to approve the executions of 267 men. Thus, he:

> must have suffered far more than he ever expressed from the agonies and griefs of the war, and it was morally and dramatically inevitable that this prophet who had crushed opposition and sent thousands of men to their deaths should finally attest his good faith by laying down his own life with theirs.[55]

The image of Lincoln as a suffering and redemptive Christ-figure has been an enduring one. John Hay called him "the greatest character since Christ," while the Russian author, Leo Tolstoy, referred to him as "a Christ in miniature." Poet Vachel Lindsay projected the image of the "risen" Lincoln: "He cannot sleep upon the hillside now. He is among us:—as in times before!" A popular evangelical contribution to the American Revolution Bicentennial observance affirmed: "In a very real sense he is the 'Savior of the Union.' "[56] Although somewhat exaggerated, there is much truth in W. Lloyd Warner's lyric assessment:

> Through the passing generations of our Christian culture the Man of the Prairies, formed in the mold of the God-man of Galilee and apotheosized into the man-god of the American people, each year less profane and more sacred, moves securely toward identification with deity and ultimate godhead.[57]

In this manner, Lincoln became the redeemer-savior-martyr figure and the new focus of civic piety. Much of this "deification" of Lincoln was metaphorical, but the legend was based on a reasonable body of fact. Political and religious feeling were blended in one majestic figure who might be either admired as a hero or invoked as a god. With the war ended and the question of slavery resolved, the civil religion of Abraham Lincoln—with malice toward none, with charity for all—provided a shared outlook which facilitated national reunion and reconciliation. It assured a war-weary people that they had not fought in vain and promised that the new society could be qualitatively better than what had existed before.

LINCOLN AND CIVIL RELIGION

Lincoln thus joined Washington as the second great hero of the public faith. Washington was recognized as the saintly Father Figure and the American Moses, and Lincoln as the Christ Figure and first great martyr. After another president was assassinated 98 years later, some even suggested that civil religion now had its Trinity—Washington symbolizing the Father, Lincoln the Son, and John F. Kennedy, upon whose grave in Arlington Cemetery an eternal flame blazed, the Holy Spirit.[58] In any event, the ongoing esteem for the two giants is illustrated by a twentieth-century Memorial Day orator in an obscure New England town:

> No character except the Carpenter of Nazareth has ever been honored the way Washington and Lincoln have been in New England. Virtue, freedom from sin, and righteousness were qualities possessed by Washington and Lincoln, and in possessing these characteristics both were true Americans, and we would do well to emulate them.[59]

Lincoln also left behind two civil religion texts. Added to such sacred American documents as the Mayflower Compact, Declaration of Independence, and Constitution were his Gettysburg Address and Second Inaugural. Moreover, the public faith was expanded to include blacks, who now could partake in the blessings of the political system established by the founders and presumably enjoy a share in the destiny of the chosen nation. Consequently, most blacks find it easier to regard Lincoln as the "Father of the Country" than either the Pilgrims of 1620 or George Washington.

Most importantly, the theme of sacrifice had been added to American civil religion. The chosen nation was now the sacred nation baptized in blood. Since all who fought and died in the conflict had been Americans, this shedding of blood was "something special." The idea that sacrifice was "sacred" because it furthered America's God-given purpose as a model of human liberty and equality was integrated into the belief system of the country's faith. The national cemeteries, especially Gettysburg and Arlington which contain so many Civil War dead, furthered this development and served as outdoor cathedrals for the litany of the civil faith. The sacred ceremonies recalled the martyred Lincoln and those who fell in the Civil War so that the American nation could enjoy a new birth of freedom. This, in turn, fostered civil pride, a sense of continuity with the sacred past, and a commitment to future greatness.[60]

In the Lincoln years, the prophetic civil faith "under God" reached its zenith, a sacramental dimension was added, and the sacralization of national life was completed. The office sanctified by the life of Washington and the death of Lincoln then passed to lesser men, but the sacred memory of the two great leaders lingered even as the nation increased in wealth and might. Unfortunately, those who followed often channeled civil religion in directions more closely associated with "national interest" than with "national ideals." Then, a generation after the end of the Civil War, the sacred nation with a mission began to act on the world stage under the leadership of a "born-again" president named William McKinley.

5

WILLIAM McKINLEY AND THE CHOSEN NATION IN ACTION

A group of Methodist ministers called on President William McKinley at the White House on a bright November day in 1898, and they were treated to an remarkable tale about his decision to annex the Philippine Islands. Earlier that year, American forces had seized control from the Spanish authorities, and the president was in a quandary as to what to do next. He spent many sleepless nights pondering the alternatives and even prayed for divine guidance. Finally, the answer came. The United States should take the islands and educate, civilize, and Christianize the Filipinos, who were "our fellow-men for whom Christ also died." With that message from above securely in hand, he retired and slept soundly that night.[1]

FROM SMALL-TOWN LAWYER TO NATIONAL POLITICIAN

This incident excellently reveals the new turn that American civil religion was taking. The chosen nation now moved onto the glittering stage of world politics, led by a devout Christian who harnessed his faith to that of the masses. The twenty-fifth president of the United States took office in 1897, just as the country was emerging from a severe depression to enter upon a period of sustained economic growth. Under his administration it became not only a major industrial state but also an imperial power. He was the "first modern president," a transitional figure between the nineteenth-century concept of a chief executive with carefully circumscribed powers and duties and the twentieth-century idea of an activist and expanding presidency. Many of the present institutions of the executive branch took shape under his aegis, he dealt skillfully with the Congress, and he effectively gauged and responded to public opinion. As a political leader, he confirmed the Republicans as the majority party in the nation and was responsible for the transformation of American foreign policy.[2]

William McKinley, Jr., was born on January 29, 1843, in Niles, Ohio, the seventh of nine children, and was a life-long resident of the Buckeye State. William, Sr., was an ironmaster of modest means, and in 1852 he relocated in nearby Poland so that his children could attend a secondary school there. His wife, Nancy Allison McKinley, was a fervent Methodist, and she did much to inculcate an evangelical faith in her children. She took young William to prayer and class meetings and enrolled him in Sunday school even before he was old enough to attend primary school. At age ten he went forward at a camp meeting to "profess conversion" and united with the church "on probation." Six years later he became a full-fledged member of the Methodist Episcopal Church and at various times served as a Sunday school superintendent, YMCA worker, and trustee in his local congregation. He was a lifelong communicant of the church and attended services regularly, both in Canton where he settled after the Civil War and in the nation's capital. Although the strong-willed Mother McKinley hoped her son would become a minister, another calling awaited him.

McKinley spent a semester at Allegheny College in Meadville, Pennsylvania and returned home to work as a teacher and postal clerk. Then he was caught up in the enthusiasm of the Civil War, and with many hometown chums he joined the 23d Ohio Volunteer Infantry Regiment in June 1861. The regimental commander, Rutherford B. Hayes, took an interest in the unassuming but precocious young man, and the connection had important implications for his later public career. The eighteen-year-old soldier was a devout Christian who attended prayer meetings and eschewed the vices which attracted many of his comrades. He wrote in his diary on August 16, 1861, shortly before the first encounter with the enemy, about the possibility that he might not return:

> I fall in a good cause and hope to fall in the arms of my blessed redeemer. This record I want left behind, that I not only fell as a soldier for my Country, but also as a Soldier of Jesus. [His friends and relatives could be comforted with the solace] that if we never meet again on earth, we will meet around God's throne in Heaven. Let my fate be what it may, I want to be ready and prepared.[3]

He was a conscientious soldier who received a battlefield commission at Antietam the following year, served with distinction throughout the war, and was mustered out at the rank of major in 1865. Since he was a sensitive individual who detested strife, the horrors of the struggle made a deep impression on him. In subsequent years he did not glamorize the Civil War, although he was regularly referred to in political gatherings as "Major McKinley;" as president he somewhat reluctantly committed American forces to combat.

McKinley's principal biographer notes that most of the personality traits of the mature man were already evident in the youth. He was charming, compassionate, dignified, courteous, patient, and deliberate when it came to decision-making. He was oriented toward deeds rather than words, sincere almost to the point of transparency in his dealings with others, and even sympathetic to the concerns of societal outsiders like Roman Catholics and labor unionists. Caution, fortitude, determination, and a sense of destiny undergirded by a deep Christian faith were the hallmarks of his character.[4]

After returning from the war, he read law and in 1867 opened a practice in the county seat of Canton. Before long he had become a successful lawyer and pillar of the community. In 1871, he married Ida Saxton, a banker's daughter, Presbyterian Sunday school teacher, and temperance worker. After the deaths of their two small children, she fell victim to a nervous disorder that left her a semi-invalid for the rest of her life. Yet he remained ever a faithful husband and made her the object of such solicitous care that it seemed for him to take on the character of lifelong martyrdom.

McKinley became involved in local Republican politics and was named chairman of the county central committee in 1868. The next year he was elected to a term as county prosecuting attorney. He labored diligently in Hayes's three gubernatorial campaigns and presidential effort in 1876, while Hayes in return backed his bid for a seat in Congress. Although the underdog, the thirty-four-year-old barrister was victorious and thus embarked on a national career that would culminate two decades later in election to the highest office in the land. He served six terms in the House of Representatives, during one of which he was chairman of the Ways and Means Committee and established a solid reputation as an energetic lawmaker and advocate of tariff protectionism. In 1884, 1888, and 1892, McKinley was a delegate to the Republican national convention and held leadership roles there. The casualty of an off-year Democratic landslide in 1890, he then turned to state politics and served four years as governor of Ohio. His winsome personality, position in a key state, and extensive legislative and administrative experience made him presidential timber in 1896.

McKinley's close friend, the high-rolling Cleveland industrialist Mark Hanna, set out to secure the prize for him. Hanna intended to engineer the nomination by a calculated series of deals and promises to party moguls, but McKinley rejected the scheme. He allegedly said to him: "Mark, some things come too high. If I were to accept the nomination on those terms, the place would be worth nothing to me and less to the people. If those are the terms, I am out of it." For him this was a moral issue, but it also reflected political shrewdness. McKinley realized that if he carried public opinion with him in the campaign, he would be in a position to command loyalty from the party bosses without incurring the political debts that surely would cause him difficulty and embarrassment when the time came to collect on them.[5]

Still, Hanna's intensive organizational efforts and McKinley's own work during the previous months paid off in a first-ballot victory at the convention in June. The Democrats nominated the brilliant young orator from Nebraska, William Jennings Bryan, on a Populist and free silver platform, and the stage was set for a heated struggle for the White House. The Republicans' eventual victory was partially the result of their unrelenting propaganda assault on Bryan as a madman and social revolutionary, and of Hanna's superbly orchestrated "front porch campaign" which brought delegations from around the country, some three quarters of a million people, to McKinley's home in Canton to meet and hear the candidate. But equally as important was the latter's own personal stance. McKinley's vision was one of uniting the geographical sections and the disparate socioeconomic forces of business, labor, and agriculture in a common quest for material wealth, which in turn would be the key to national power. He recognized that to distribute prosperity somewhat evenly was the essence of the American dream, and he presented this as the central goal of the Republican party. This vision, along with an easing of the economic crisis, doomed Bryan's attempt to unite the discontented farmers and miners against the entrenched "money power" of the eastern cities.

A "BORN-AGAIN" OCCUPANT OF THE WHITE HOUSE?

To be sure, McKinley was not the first confessing evangelical to take up residence at 1600 Pennsylvania Avenue. For example, Hayes had held Sunday night hymn sings in the White House, and his teetotaling wife was affectionately referred to as "Lemonade Lucy" because of her practice of serving nonalcoholic drinks at state functions. James A. Garfield had been converted in the Disciples of Christ (Christian Church) and had even been a preacher in his youth. Benjamin Harrison had made a commitment to Christ in a revival during his student days, and was active as a Sunday school teacher and elder in his Presbyterian church in Indianapolis. As a public figure, McKinley followed in this tradition and made no effort to hide his faith. He testified about his Christian experience to a delegation of officials from his denomination who called on him at the White House, telling them that: "Whatever men may think of me or not think, I am a Methodist and nothing but a Methodist—a Christian and nothing but a Christian."[6] When in Washington, he regularly worshiped at the Metropolitan Methodist Church, and like Hayes, often entertained guests with Sunday evening hymn sings in the executive mansion.

During his term as governor of Ohio, McKinley reflected in a speech about the role of religion in the nation's life:

The men who established this Government had faith in God and sublimely trusted in Him. They besought His counsel and advice in every step of their progress. And so it has been ever since; American history abounds in instances of this trait of piety, this sincere reliance on a Higher Power in all great trials in our National affairs. Our rulers may not always be observers of the outward forms of religion, but we have never had a president, from Washington to Harrison, who publicly avowed infidelity, or scoffed at the faith of the masses of our people.[7]

After taking the oath of office at the inauguration ceremony on March 4, 1897, McKinley kissed the Bible which was opened to the text of Solomon's prayer: "Give me now wisdom and knowledge, that I may go out and come in before this people: for who can judge this thy people, that is so great?" (2 Chron. 1:10). Then he proceeded to the customary address and declared that he was assuming the duties of president.

. . .relying upon the support of my countrymen and invoking the guidance of Almighty God. Our faith teaches that there is no safer reliance than upon the God of our fathers, who has so singularly favored the American people in every national trial, and who will not forsake us so long as we obey His commandments and walk humbly in His footsteps.

The bulk of the speech dealt with the specific problems facing his administration—the monetary question, public debt, tariff changes, agriculture, recovery from the depression, trust regulation, civil service reform, naval expansion, immigration, and foreign relations. He concluded by praising the manner in which the nation was now coming together and affirming that he would "permit nothing to be done, that will arrest or disturb this growing sentiment of unity and cooperation," but rather "cheerfully do everything possible to promote and increase it." He had "reverently taken before the Lord Most High" the obligation to carry out the tasks of president and was relying "upon the forbearance and assistance of all the people in the discharge of my solemn responsibilities." However, in his second inaugural four years later McKinley only mentioned the Deity in passing. He promised devotion to the discharge of his presidential duties, "reverently invoking for my guidance the direction and favor of Almighty God," and said the nation would "in the fear of God" expand the bounds of freedom in the new territories that the country recently had obtained.[8]

He had utilized civil religion categories in both speeches, and the views expressed were fully consonant with what he deeply believed and had been saying throughout his life. Interestingly enough, although McKinley spoke from an evangelical perspective, any of his non-evangelical predecessors could have used the same language in their inaugural messages. He had invoked God's guidance, acknowledged his blessings, and proclaimed the need to walk in his ways of righteousness. In these addresses the president pledged before God to do the very best job he could, while the people, energized by the divine force, would assist him in carrying out his duties.

That McKinley was optimistic about the progress of his administration and the abiding presence of divine favor upon the nation was evident from his first annual message to Congress on December 6, 1897. He acknowledged the "beneficent Providence which has so signally blessed and prospered us as a nation." He then referred with satisfaction to "the growing feeling of fraternal regard and unification of all sections of our country" and "the spirit of patriotism" which was universal and ever increasing in fervor.[9] The same outlook was evident in his first Thanksgiving Day proclamation which called attention to the abundance of "God's goodness to us during the past year," the prosperity that has occurred under "His watchful providence," and preservation of peace through "His mighty hand." It then urged people to observe the national thanksgiving and prayer "with appropriate religious services in their respective places of worship," and expressed the wish that prayers should "ascend to the Giver of every good and perfect gift for the continuance of His love and favor to us, that our hearts may be filled with charity and good will, and we may be ever worthy of His beneficent concern."[10]

THE CUBAN CRISIS AND CIVIL RELIGION

Nevertheless, a problem immediately offshore was coming more and more to occupy McKinley's attention, and dealing with this put new and unexpected demands upon the resources of the civil religion. In February 1895, Cuban insurgents had launched a revolt against colonial rule which utilized hit-and-run strikes to pin down thousands of Spanish soldiers and wreck the island's fragile economy.[11] Their goal was independence, and they received considerable financial assistance and arms from private sources in the United States, where public opinion was overwhelmingly favorable to their cause. The odious policy of "reconcentration" (moving people out of the countryside into fortified areas and thereby undercutting the popular base of the uprising) which General Valeriano Weyler adopted in 1896, only led to more misery in Cuba and stirring of passions in the United States. The government in Madrid regarded its sovereignty over the island as non-negotiable, while Washington believed that reforms leading to autonomy, if not outright independence, were required.

McKinley inherited this knotty problem and tried in various ways to alleviate the situation. He approached the Spanish about the possibility of selling their possession but this tactic achieved nothing, so he sent a high-level fact-finding commission to investigate conditions in Cuba. With its report in hand, the president informed the Spanish that warfare "shall at least be conducted according to the military codes of civilization" and that he would monitor their conduct on the island. Accordingly, Spain made some concessions to the United States which seemed to indicate that an amicable peace settlement with the rebels was in the offing, and McKinley resisted the mounting pressures for intervention. However, the insurgents rejected the measures granting more autonomy, the Spanish stance toward the United States' demands hardened, and matters so deteriorated that a battleship, the USS *Maine*, was sent on a "courtesy call" to Cuba in January 1898.

The president's moderation was put to a severe test by a dramatic event on February 15. The *Maine* exploded and sank in Havana harbor with heavy casualties, and a wave of outrage swept across the United States. A naval court of inquiry concluded that a mine or external explosive device had caused the disaster but did not place the blame on any specific person or group. (A new study fifty years later found that it actually had resulted from spontaneous combustion in the ship's coal bunkers.) Nevertheless, newspapers and orators alike called for immediate Spanish withdrawal or the dispatch of American troops to the island. The Spanish stalled and sought to marshal European diplomatic pressure against American designs on Cuba, while the business community and general public came increasingly to feel that something had to be to root out this "tyranny on our doorstep." After failing to win Spanish agreement for an armistice and the eventual granting of independence to Cuba, McKinley sent a message to Congress on April 11 that held open the possibility of a negotiated settlement through nonrecognition of the Cuban insurgency, but at the same time suggesting that the United States might intervene as an impartial neutral party to halt the conflict. It was not a war message as such, but things moved so quickly that within two weeks the two countries had declared war on each other.

Civil religion ideas were much in evidence during the crisis weeks prior to the outbreak of hostilities. For example, in his message to Congress McKinley declared: "In the name of humanity, in the name of civilization, in behalf of endangered American interests which give us the right and the duty to speak and to act, the war in Cuba must stop." He then requested congressional authorization to use military and naval forces if needed to end the hostilities between the government of Spain and the Cuban people and to secure a stable and tranquil regime on the island. If this threat of armed intervention achieved the desired result, "then our aspirations as a Christian, peace-loving people will be realized."[12]

For months McKinley had been under pressure from a bellicose Congress and the so-called "yellow press" (most notably William Randolph Hearst's *New York Journal* and Joseph Pulitzer's *New York World* which were vying with each other in sensationalistic reporting about conditions in Cuba) to take some sort of action. At the same time, it is important to remember that for many years the president, a devout churchman, had been exposed to sermons portraying America as a nation chosen by God for a peculiar destiny and the fulfillment of that vocation as the country's highest moral obligation. Many clerics taught that the United States as a Christian nation should stand aggressively for Christianity and the uplifting of humanity throughout the world. Publicists in the foreign missionary movement were arguing that the time was ripe for a great, worldwide Christian advance.

Thus, religious people found it easy to view the Cuban problem as a moral one and to urge forthright measures by the United States to resolve it.[13]

Accordingly, the religious press saw the nation in moral and missionary terms and insisted that if it went to war, it must do so only for righteous causes. In September 1897, for example, the Episcopalian *Churchman* declared about another issue stirring passions in Christian circles, the genocidal massacres that were taking place in Turkish Armenia:

> Great peoples have great responsibiltities. They can have no wars for self-aggrandizement. They must—or be recreant to all that makes them grand or free or worth dying for—stand by the weak and defend the helpless, and advance the banner of mercy and justice over the world.[14]

McKinley was present in the Sunday service at the influential Metropolitan Methodist Church on March 13 when Pastor Hugh Johnson told his congregation that war would not take place unless there was "absolute justification" for it. He was confident that the chief executive would uphold national dignity and honor but at the same time not rush into war because of popular passion or hysteria. Johnson maintained that the United States with its inexhaustible wealth and resources had nothing to fear from a weak and bankrupt Spain, even if it had France and the Latin nations as allies. If all "three corners of the world" came against us in arms, we would shock them:

> But this power is controlled by intelligence, patriotism, and Christian principle, and only stern duty to humanity and civilization, just relations with our fellow-men, and National honor will lead us to let loose the dogs of war. Desiring and praying for peace, let us hope that the extent and vigor of these war preparations will avert the conflict and assist the cause of peace.[15]

Dr. Robert S. MacArthur of Calvary Baptist Church in New York City criticized the "unseemly" behavior of Congress in the debate currently raging over McKinley's message of April 11, and he insisted that "at this critical juncture in our Nation's history. . . , it is the duty of the Church to urge the Nation to stand by our patriotic, brave, and sagacious President, who has earned for himself the admiration of all true Americans." MacArthur lamented the sinking of the *Maine* as the "blackest crime of the century," condemned Spain as a nation of bullfighters who became a nation of butchers in Cuba, and suggested "the Great God" might "use the American people as His instrument in driving this tyrant from the Western Hemisphere." If war should come, "it ought to be in a very true sense a holy war," that is, one "for the preservation of honor and in the interest of humanity."[16]

A SPLENDID LITTLE WAR FOR THE GLORY OF GOD

The American ambassador in Great Britain, John Hay, wrote to his friend Theodore Roosevelt on July 27, 1898, to convey congratulations for the quick victory that the American forces had achieved over the outclassed Spanish: "It has been a splendid little war; begun with the highest motives, carried on with magnificent intelligence and spirit, favored by that Fortune which loves the brave."[17] Senator Redfield Proctor of Vermont asked Secretary of War Russell A. Alger three days after the cessation of hostilities: "Was there ever before such a war with such great results, so short in duration, such wonderful successes, with no reverses?"[18] These comments epitomize well the attitude of most contemporaries about the brief conflict which cost little in money and lives and transformed their country into an imperial power.[19]

No longer reticent about resorting to arms, President McKinley took personal charge of war planning and mobilization. The navy was already poised for action, and in accordance with predetermined plans, the Asiatic squadron was ordered to sail from Hong Kong to the Philippine Islands and attack the Spanish fleet based there. On May 1, George Dewey's force of seven modern ships confronted ten obsolete vessels anchored in Manila Bay, destroyed them without encountering significant resistance, and then awaited further instructions. Three months later when 10,900 American troops had arrived, the Philippine capital was taken with a minimum of bloodshed.

The army, however, was anything but prepared. Its strength numbered about 30,000, but it lacked reserves and a general staff to plan and direct strategy. To conduct the war,

Congress authorized a volunteer force of 200,000 and an increase in the regular army, so that the total army strength reached 274,000. Those who enlisted were poorly trained, provisioned, and equipped. Although the navy slapped a blockade on the Cuban ports and bottled up the Spanish squadron in Santiago Bay, it neglected to provide sufficient transportation for the army which was to attack the city of Santiago.

As a result, many soldiers languished for weeks in the hot sun of Tampa, Florida, awaiting travel to the combat zone. Among the volunteers was Theodore Roosevelt, who had resigned his position as assistant secretary of the navy and organized a cavalry unit known as the Rough Riders. He and others commandeered a motley collection of boats to bring much of the amateur army to Cuba. Around 16,900 soldiers eventually reached the island, and on July 1 they attacked the heavily fortified village of El Caney and the heights known as San Juan Hill and then marched on Santiago. Four days later the Spanish squadron suffered a crushing defeat at the hands of a fleet commanded by William T. Sampson, and within two weeks the American forces completely controlled Cuba. On July 25, troops landed in Puerto Rico and encountered little opposition.

On July 30, the United States outlined its terms of peace. These included Cuban independence (the Teller Amendment rashly adopted by Congress at the outbreak of the war had declared Cuba would be given to the Cubans), the cession of Puerto Rico and Guam to the U.S., and the right to occupy and dispose of the Philippines as it saw fit. An armistice was concluded on August 12 incorporating these provisions, and the final peace treaty was signed in Paris on December 10, 1898. Only 365 Americans were killed in battle and 1,600 wounded—but 2,220 succumbed to disease because of the inadequate sanitary conditions in the camps.[20] Still, most people saw that as a small price to pay for the national glory which had come from this "splendid little war."

During May and June, McKinley's time was tied up with managing the war and he said little about it publicly, but according to the summaries of sermons contained in John Smylie's study of Protestant support for American nationalism in this era, many clergymen readily portrayed it as a holy war. David Gregg of the Lafayette Avenue Presbyterian

Church in Brooklyn declared on April 24 that the war was motivated by higher goals:

> It is out and out altruistic. There is no revenge in it. There is no enrichment in it. It is not mercenary in the least atom. It is principle from Alpha to Omega. If there were no Christ and Christianity it could never be. It partakes of the brotherhood of man.

Wayland Hoyt of the Epiphany Baptist Church in Philadelphia asserted that there had never been a war:

> more righteous than that which we have undertaken, nor one closer to the law of the self-sacrificing Christ that we bear one another's burdens. If there ever was a war simply for the sake of humanity with no desire or purpose of national greed of any sort, it is the one that now is upon us, calling our soldiers and navy to arms.

The noted pulpit orator T. Dewitt Talmage said it was "the most unselfish war of the ages." It was one "inspired by mercy, which is an attribute in man imitative of the same attribute of God." Unlike most other conflicts which were wars of ambition or conquest, this was one of mercy. Everyone who died in it, fell "in the cause of mercy" and became "a martyr for God and his country."[21]

Not only evangelical ministers signaled their unqualified approval of the American triumph. The liberal Henry Van Dyke of New York's Brick Presbyterian Church asserted that war was something both historically and ethically necessary. It was sent by "God's providence" to test and bring out the best or the worst in the heart of a nation. It was neither a blessing nor a curse, but rather a sacrifice, "the heaviest cross that a nation is ever called upon to bear." War was certainly necessary when an oppressor nation trampled out the life of a weaker people. The "noble and patriotic president" had done everything possible to avert war except:

> to abandon entirely the duty of the strong to protect the weak, to say at once, and finally, that so long as Cuba belongs to a foreign power it is none of our business what horrors happen there. But to say such a thing as that would involve more than a change in National policy. It would mean a change in National character. We have prayed for peace. The prayer has been denied. Now we must pray for victory.[22]

These are not isolated examples. Many sermons of the time, published as pamphlets or quoted in newspapers, supported American involvement in the conflict by utilizing civil religion categories like higher principles, self-sacrifice, divine mandate, and altruism. But nothing better exemplified the use of civil religion in this era than President McKinley's eloquent call for national thanksgiving issued on July 6, 1898. This went far beyond the ordinary Thanksgiving Day proclamations which he (like most presidents) issued annually,[23] and it must be seen as the premier civil religion document of the McKinley administration:

> At this time, when to the yet fresh remembrance of the unprecedented success which attended the operations of the United States fleet in the Bay of Manila on the 1st day of May last, are added the tidings of the no less glorious achievements of the naval and military arms of our beloved country at Santiago de Cuba, it is fitting that we should pause, and, staying the feeling of exultation that too naturally attends great deeds wrought by our countrymen in our country's cause, should reverently bow before the throne of Divine Grace and give devout praise to God, who holdeth the nations in the hollow of His hands and worketh upon them the marvels of His high will, and who has thus far vouchsafed to us the light of His face and led our brave soldiers and seamen to victory.

> I therefore ask the people of the United States upon next assembling for Divine worship in their respective places of meeting, to offer thanksgiving to Almighty God, who, in his inscrutable ways, now leading our hosts upon the waters to unscathed triumph, now guiding them in a strange land through the dread shadows of death to success, even though at a fearful cost, now bearing them without accident or loss to far distant climes, has watched over our cause and brought nearer the success of the right and the attainment of just and honorable peace.

McKinley then requested prayers for those on the battlefields and at sea and national sympathy for those who died or were suffering from wounds and disease, and he asked "the Dispenser of all good" to restore peace to our land and tranquility to the war-ravaged areas.[24]

In the proclamation, the president had called for national humility in a time of glorious achievements and the giving of praise to God who was responsible for the victories.

On the following Sunday, churches across the land, Protestant and Catholic alike, held thanksgiving services in response to McKinley's appeal. According to press reports, there was "a concert of patriotic utterances" in which thanks were given for the glorious American victories and prayers offered for the early consummation of peace. One minister in New York, Rev. John P. Peters of St. Michael's Episcopal Church, commented that the remarkable feature of the war was that no one seemed "to have entered into it for sordid reasons." He went on to say:

> Our war is waged not for mere conquest and the acquirement of territory, but for the advancement of genuine civilization and the equal rights of men. Such being the case, we can feel assured that God is on our side and that victory will continue to abide with our army and navy.[25]

Perhaps the most remarkable sermon preached on that festive day was by Bishop Frank Bristol in the Metropolitian Methodist Church in Washington with McKinley in the congregation. The crowd was so animated by his eloquence that they frequently broke out in spontaneous applause, so the reporter noted. Bristol's theme was the providence of God in history, and his text was Psalm 98:1, "O Sing unto the Lord a new song; for he hath done marvelous things: his right hand, and his holy arm, hath gotten him the victory." He argued that the nineteenth century had shown the advance of Providence because it was more scientific than earlier ages. Whereas ancient peoples had trusted in luck, chance, and miracles, modern society depended upon law, and Providence lay behind law. Science and knowledge brought modern peoples in touch with Providence because God worked his will by the agency of nature's laws and human thoughts. Hence, Americans were in league with the mighty laws that govern things, and "God is on the side of good farming, good financiering, good politics, good guns, good battleships, good discipline, good generalship, and good causes." He then turned to biblical figures and asked boldly:

> Is this then a less providential age than the age of Moses? Is the electric light less providential than the pillar of fire? Is a Dakota wheat harvest less providential than a shower of manna? Is a South Carolina cotton crop less providen-

tial than the quails of the Wilderness? Are the orange groves of California less providential than the vineyards of Old Eshol? Was the discovery of America less providential than the exodus of the children of Israel? Was the Declaration of Independence less providential than the decalog of Sinai? Were the guns of Dewey and Sampson less providential than the ram's horns of Joshua, the lamps and pitchers of Gideon, or the rod of Moses? Were Manila and Santiago less providential in the history of human freedom than Jericho and Ai? Is Christian civilization less providential than was Jewish barbarism?

What could explain the victories at Manila and Santiago? Was it superior guns? Bristol intoned: "I say superior men stood behind the guns, superior schools stood behind the men, the superior religion stood behind the schools, and God, the Supreme, stood behind the religion." There, he said, was our lesson of Providence. "If God ever had a peculiar people He has them now." The men who stood before Santiago were not the product of a day or century but the consummate flower of the ages, the highest evolution of history. They had climbed century by century up the steeps of light and liberty and now stood in sight of the glorified summits of the universal freedom and brotherhood. As such, they were the heirs of the Civil War, the American Revolution, the Pilgrims, the Reformers, the martyrs, and the apostles, and these last had touched the Christ. "There is our Providence in history."[26] Rarely will one find such a bold affirmation of civil religion as this.

President McKinley once again expressed a word of appreciation for the help of God in his annual message to Congress on December 5, 1898. In the middle of a lengthy, triumphalist account of the conflict, he paused to give recognition to the Deity:

> In tracing these events we are constantly reminded of our obligations to the Divine Master for His watchful care over us and His safe guidance, for which the nation makes reverent acknowledgment and offers humble prayer for the continuance of his favor.[27]

CIVIL RELIGION AND IMPERIAL EXPANSION

To liberate Cuba from the Spanish yoke was one thing; to acquire an empire was something else. McKinley's decision to demand the cession of Puerto Rico and Guam could be seen as reaping the spoils of victory, but when the Philippine Islands were added to the package, the peace settlement took on a whole new dimension. There a revolt against the Spanish had been underway since 1896, but the Filipino rebels and their leader Emilio Aguinaldo were largely shut out of the capture of Manila on August 13, actually one day after the official cessation of hostilities. They had anticipated gaining independence in the same fashion as Cuba had, but they were to be disappointed. In the Treaty of Paris, the United States agreed to pay Spain $20,000,000 and take possession of the archipelago, although the Senate did not ratify the treaty until February 6, 1899.

McKinley on December 21 ordered American sovereignty to be extended throughout the islands.[28] This action, together with the annexation of Hawaii and Wake Island in July, the partition agreement in Samoa the following year, and promotion of the Open Door policy and intervention in the Boxer Rebellion in China, meant that the United States had become an imperial power in the Pacific. Aguinaldo's people would not accept the transfer of the Philippines from Spanish to American rule, and a bloody insurrection ensued that took three years to suppress, cost far more in lives and money than the brief war with Spain, discredited the trusteeship justification for the takeover, and so divided the country that expansionism was an election issue in 1900.[29]

The evidence is clear that McKinley had decided early in the conflict to acquire at least part of the Philippines; less certain is when he opted to demand the entire archipelago.[30] That decision apparently was made between September 16 and October 28, 1898. The aforementioned explanation of his action to the delegation of five Methodist dignitaries who visited him at the White House on November 21, 1899, has the ring of truth because the comments were made after the Philippine insurrection was underway, and he had had time to reflect on the implications of his decision. Also, none of the others at the meeting ever contradicted the report which General James F. Rusling published in the *Christian Advocate*. As it is an important indication of the impact which the president's religious faith had on his public actions, it deserves some attention.

The group represented the General Missionary Committee of their denomination which at the time was in session in

Washington, and they presented a resolution of thanks to the president for the courtesy he had shown the convention. As they started to leave, McKinley said:

> Hold a moment longer! Not quite yet, gentlemen! Before you go I would like to say just a word about the Philippine business. I have been criticized a good deal about the Philippines, but don't deserve it. The truth is I didn't want the Philippines, and when they came to us, as a gift from the gods, I did not know what to do with them. [He then explained how he sent Dewey there to destroy the Spanish fleet so it could not attack the West Coast.]

> When next I realized that the Philippines had dropped into our laps I confess I did not know what to do with them. I sought counsel from all sides—Democrats as well as Republicans—but got little help. I thought first we would take only Manila; then Luzon; then other islands, perhaps, also. I walked the floor of the White House night after night until midnight; and I am not ashamed to tell you, gentlemen, that I went down on my knees and prayed Almighty God for light and guidance more than one night. And one night late it came to me this—don't know how it was, but it came.

He described the alternatives open to him. He could give them back to Spain—but that would be cowardly and dishonorable; turn them over to France or Germany, America's commercial rivals in the Orient—but that would be bad business and discreditable; leave them to themselves—but they were unfit for self-government and soon the anarchy and misrule would be worse than Spain's; or consider a fourth option:

> There was nothing left for us to do but to take them all, and to educate the Filipinos, and uplift and civilize and Christianize them, and by God's Grace do the very best we could by them, as our fellow-men for whom Christ also died. And then I went to bed, and went to sleep, and slept soundly, and next morning I sent for the chief of the War Department (our map-maker), and I told him to put the Philippines on the map of the United States [pointing to a large map on the wall of his office], and there they are, and there they will stay while I am President![31]

At the same time, many in Christian circles were talking about the possible benefits that could accrue from the Philippine acquisition. A report presented to the Presbyterian Board of Foreign Missions on May 25, 1898, referred to the "peace-speaking guns of Admiral Dewey" and the "startling providence of God" which was opening this field to missionary work. "We cannot ignore the fact" that God has given these islands "into the hands of American Christians. . .and has by the very guns of our battleships summoned us to go up and possess the land." Methodist Bishop John F. Hurst said a month later that "American heroism" opened the way for Protestantism to enter the islands. "The fact that the bonds between Spain and the Philippines have been severed by American valor brings the appeal home to American Christians. Who should enter a door first, if not he who breaks its bolts?" In fact, John Smylie points out that the pulpits and religious press of the nation ran the same kind of interference preceding the Philippine annexation decision that they had prior to the outbreak of war itself.[32]

McKinley traveled around the Midwest in October defending his record and helping Republican candidates in the off-year election, and he repeatedly introduced civil religion themes into his discussion of the Spanish conflict and its results:

- *Arcola, Illinois, October 16*: We have had great glory in the war and in its settlement we must be guided only by the demands of right and conscience and duty.
- *Chicago, Illinois, October 19*: With no feeling of exultation, but with profound thanksgiving we contemplate the events of the last five months. They have been too serious to admit of boasting or vain-glorification. . . .Almighty God has His plans and methods for human progress and not infrequently they are shrouded for the time being in impenetrable mystery. Looking backward we can see how that hand of destiny builded for us and assigned us tasks whose full meaning was not apprehended even by the wisest statesmen of their times. [With the territorial expansion must come] a constant movement toward a higher and nobler civilization.
- *Logansport, Indiana, October 21*: The war has made us a united people. We present a spectacle of 75,000,000 people, representing every race and nationality and section, united in one faith and under one flag.
- *Noblesville, Indiana, October 21*: [Regarding the territorial arrangements in the peace,] I pray God that wisdom may

be given all of us to so settle this vexed and vast problem as to bring honor to our country, justice to humanity, and the general good of all.

• *Columbus, Ohio, October 22*: Whatever obligations shall justly come from this strife for humanity, we must take up and as free, strong, brave people, accept the trust which civilization puts upon us.[33]

Speaking in Atlanta later in the year, the president praised the war for bringing the nation together and celebrated the victory and peace as presaging good to humanity. The domains came to us "not as the result of a crusade of conquest, but as the reward of temperate, faithful, and fearless response to the call of conscience, which could not be disregarded by a liberty-loving and Christian people." Our armies at Manila and Santiago "fought not for gain or revenge but for human rights [and] the freedom of the oppressed." Our strength "has been employed solely for humanity and always tempered with justice and mercy. . . , confident that our course is one of duty and our cause that of right."[34]

McKinley addressed the Philippine question in particular in Boston on February 16, 1899, just ten days after the Senate had ratified the Treaty of Paris by a mere one-vote margin. He maintained the islands "were intrusted to our hands by the war, and to that great trust, under providence of God and in the name of civilization, we are committed. It is a trust we have not sought; it is a trust from which we will not flinch." Then he explored the alternatives to taking them, which he insisted could not have been justified either in the sight of God or man, and evoked a rousing ovation from the crowd with this assertion:

> We were obeying a higher moral obligation which rested upon us. We were doing our duty by them [the Filipinos] as God gave us the light to see our duty, with the consent of our own consciences, and with the approval of civilization.

These people are now committed into the guiding hand, liberalizing influences, generous sympathies, and uplifting education "not of their American masters, but of their American emancipators." They will be given peace, order, and beneficent government and will "bless the American republic because it emancipated and redeemed their fatherland and set them in the pathway of the world's best civilization."[35]

NATIONAL MISSION AND CIVIL RELIGION

William McKinley's use of civil religion categories was a vital element of the national mission rationale for American overseas expansion.[36] The "manifest destiny" argument of the 1840s was dusted off and refurbished for the world of the 1890s, so that people came to feel it was "inevitable" that America would carry the message of Christian civilization to the benighted and barbaric peoples in the "uncivilized" quarters of the world. As one writer in 1899 flatly stated, it was "the duty and the manifest destiny of the United States to civilize and Christianize" the Filipinos.[37] This, of course, harmonized perfectly with the "white man's burden" or "trusteeship" view that many advocates of imperialism were proclaiming, namely, that the vigorous white races were responsible for bringing liberty, good government, education, economic development, and Christianity to their "little brown brothers."

The civil religion dimension of trusteeship was the belief that Providence had chosen America to carry out this awesome assignment, which was one of pure altruism. Throughout its existence the American nation was God's elect, the apple of his eye, and it had done great deeds thanks to the strength of his mighty arm and the faithfulness of the people. Such a belief in divine election was expressed not only in innumerable sermons but also in a popular book of the day, *The Hand of God in American History*.[38]

In the light of this situation, it would be unfair to regard McKinley's actions during the Spanish-American War simply as hypocrisy, as Reinhold Niebuhr seems to suggest in his influential *Moral Man and Immoral Society*.[39] Rather, the president was both a patriot who believed in the rightness of his country's actions and a devout Christian. In fact, he remained committed to his faith right to the very end in September 1901, when he was struck down by an assassin's bullet. As McKinley lay dying of his wound, he asked those around him to pray and in a feeble voice recited the Lord's Prayer and murmured: "It is God's way. His will, not ours be done."[40] This reflected well the situation that prevailed throughout his life, namely, that his personal faith and the civil one were two sides of the same coin. Thus, he was patently sincere in his belief that America was a divinely chosen nation and as president he was God's instrument to do his bidding on earth.

McKinley's life and work epitomize the Protestant civil religion consensus that held sway in the last decade of the nineteenth century and which provided the spiritual underpinning for the nation to become a world power. The chosen nation theme, which was so fundamental to civil religion throughout the century, now experienced a shift in focus from the North American continent to the world stage. As the United States emerged from isolation, it would have to take on broader responsibilities and exercise international leadership. The president who drew on the resources of civil religion for this task was Woodrow Wilson.

6

WOODROW WILSON AND THE MORALIZATION OF AMERICA'S SPECIAL MISSION

The Senate chamber was packed on the afternoon of July 10, 1919, as President Woodrow Wilson, who only two days earlier had returned from the peace conference in Paris, strode vigorously past the assembled members of the Senate, House of Representatives, and his cabinet, mounted the rostrum, and in a thirty-seven minute speech presented the treaty with Germany ending World War I. He told the lawmakers that the United States entered the struggle:

> only because we saw the supremacy, and even the validity, of right everywhere put in jeopardy and free government likely to be everywhere imperiled by the intolerable aggression of a power which respected neither right nor obligation and whose very system of government flouted the rights of the citizen as against the autocratic authority of his governors. And in the settlements of the peace we have sought no special reparation for ourselves, but only the restoration of right and the assurance of liberty everywhere. . . .

He challenged his audience to accept the treaty with its controversial League of Nations, because the only question:

> is whether we can refuse the moral leadership that is offered us, whether we shall accept or reject the confidence of the world. . . .

It was our duty to go in [to the war], if we were indeed the champions of liberty and of right. We answered to the call of duty in a way so spirited, so utterly without thought of what we spent of blood or treasure, so effective, so worthy of the admiration of true men everywhere, so wrought out of the stuff of all that was heroic, that the world saw at last, in the flesh, in noble action, a great ideal asserted and vindicated, by a Nation they had deemed material and now found to be compact of the spiritual forces that must free men of every nation from every unworthy bondage. . . .

The stage is set, the destiny disclosed. It has come about by no plan of our conceiving, but by the hand of God who led us into this way. We cannot turn back. We can only go forward, with lifted eyes and freshened spirit, to follow the vision. It was of this that we dreamed at our birth. America shall in truth show the way. The light streams upon the path ahead, and nowhere else.[1]

Upon this eloquent note he ended his address. Cheers and applause reverberated through the chamber, but some Senators stared into space and were strangely quiet. With moralizing phrases drawn from civil religion, Wilson had appealed to the country over their heads, but they remained unconvinced. The treaty would never be ratified.

AN ACADEMICIAN IN POLITICS

What sort of man was this president, who punctuated his speeches with words like right, liberty, moral leadership, duty, ideal, destiny, spiritual forces, and God? Wilson was of Scottish Presbyterian stock, as his maternal grandfather, Thomas Woodrow, was from a long line of Presbyterian churchmen.[2] The elder Woodrow had emigrated from Carlisle, England, to North America in 1835, occupying pulpits in Canada, Ohio, and Kentucky. His daughter, Jessie (1830–88), married Joseph Ruggles Wilson in 1849. The latter was the son of a Scots-Irish printer, James Wilson, who came to America in 1787 and became a successful newspaperman and legislator in Ohio. Joseph was born in 1822 and was educated for the ministry. A pastor at churches in Ohio, Virginia, Georgia, and North Carolina, he also was one of the founders of the Southern Presbyterian Church, serving as its Stated Clerk from 1861 to 1898 and as its Moderator in 1879.

The recipient of an honorary doctorate, he taught on occasion at two Presbyterian theological seminaries, Columbia (South Carolina) and Clarksville (Tennessee), and edited a church newspaper. Retiring in 1893, he died ten years later.

Thomas Woodrow Wilson was born in the manse (parsonage) at Staunton, Virginia, on December 28, 1856, the third of four children. (He discontinued using his first name when he reached adulthood.) A year later, Joseph Ruggles Wilson received a call to a congregation in Augusta, Georgia, which meant the youth would be raised in the South. As a result, the future president acquired many southern traits, among them a paternalistic outlook on the racial issue and a patronizing attitude toward women, but he did not identify with the "lost cause" of the Confederacy and as an adult thought in "national" terms. The Civil War made a deep impression on young Woodrow but did not cause the family severe hardships. He also received a religious upbringing from his parents which included daily devotions, Bible reading, hymn singing, Sunday school, and the Rev. Dr. Wilson's sermons.[3] In 1870, the family moved to Columbia, South Carolina, where Joseph had accepted a position at the seminary. There young Woodrow was taken into the membership of the Presbyterian church.

The elder Wilson, hoping his boy would enter the ministry, enrolled him in the church-related Davidson College in North Carolina. However, the son found that he preferred the vocation of politics to that of the church and dropped out after two terms. Then, he entered the College of New Jersey (renamed Princeton University in 1896), where he compiled a good record as a student and excelled in debating and literary endeavors. After graduating in 1879, he went to law school at the University of Virginia and in 1882 was admitted to the bar in Georgia.

Wilson joined a practice in Atlanta but soon lost interest in law and opted for a teaching career. He enrolled in the graduate program at Johns Hopkins University in 1883, where he studied American constitutional development and theory with some of the foremost scholars of the day and received a Ph.D. in 1886. His first book, *Congressional Government*, was accepted as his dissertation. (Wilson would be the only United States president who had an earned doctorate and who came from the academic world.)[4] In 1885, he embarked on a career in higher education as a professor of history at Bryn Mawr College. In the same year he married the twenty-five-year-old Ellen Louise Axson, the daughter and granddaughter of distinguished Southern Presbyterian ministers. Their relationship was warm and intimate, and they had three daughters. As a scholar, Wilson was quite productive, and in the next seventeen years he turned out five books, a multi-volume popular history of the American people, and untold numbers of articles. His interest lay mainly in the interrelationship between law, politics, and administration. In 1888, he moved to Wesleyan University in Connecticut and two years later returned to his alma mater to become a professor of jurisprudence. Popular with the students, he had the reputation of being a superb lecturer, one who combined the talents of a preacher and a professor.

At the same time, Wilson was highly ambitious and longed for a leadership role. His opportunity came in June 1902 when the Princeton board of trustees decided to replace the president of the university. A ground swell of support from students, alumni, and faculty led to his selection as the man who could lead the institution out of the morass of financial and academic decline and into the twentieth century. In one of his initial statements, Wilson made the kind of comment that would be repeated time and again in his later life as a public servant:

> The objects that we seek in a university are not selfish objects. There is here no interest served which is a personal interest. We are here to serve our country and mankind, and we know that we can put selfishness behind us.[5]

The pattern of leadership which Wilson displayed during his eight years at the helm of Princeton University was essentially the same as that during his time in Trenton and Washington. The early years in each position were characterized by achievement and the later period by conflict and even defeat. His significance for Princeton lay in his demanding high standards of academic integrity, stressing the university's role in perpetuating the cultural tradition on which Western civilization rested, and upholding the college as a laboratory for a democratic society, a place where ability would obliterate the distinctions created by material gain. As Wilson put it, if the educational institutions were to be enlisted in the nation's service, they could not serve a particular social stratum. Education in its true terms had to be seen as "a public, not a private instrumentality."[6]

Wilson had considerable success in his early years in curricular reform and putting the institution on a sound financial footing. But the strain of trying to convince the trustees to accept a radical restructuring of student life at Princeton resulted in a stroke in 1906 that permanently impaired his vision in one eye. He lost the battle over his reorganization plan and then was embroiled in a bitter conflict about the establishment of a graduate college. As the power struggle intensified, the prospect of public life grew ever more appealing.

Although he had never held any elective office, Wilson was an astute political thinker who had gained a national reputation through his writings and work at the university. It was not clear where he stood politically (for some years he had been a conservative Cleveland Democrat), but now he seemed to be somewhat of a progressive, and insiders in the New Jersey Democratic party approached him about the gubernatorial nomination. Although the ambitious but beleaguered university administrator had some qualms about jumping into the fray, he was enticed by the possibility that winning this election would make him a logical contender for president of the United States. When the party convention in September 1910 named him as the candidate, he resigned from the university and went on to victory in November. Cut loose from his academic moorings, he now launched his political career.

During his first year as governor, he secured the passage of a respectable package of progressive legislation—a tightening up of the election laws, direct primary elections, regulation of public utilities, inspection of factories and food storage facilities, regulation of hours and working conditions for women and children, and authorization for cities to adopt a commission form of government—and he circumvented the spoils system by appointing able people to state offices. In his speeches he regularly talked about the power of the ordinary people and about fighting greed and corruption. In the second year, the Republicans regained control of the legislature and thwarted much of his program, while increasingly he traveled around the country promoting his presidential hopes.

A deadlock developed between Wilson and Speaker of

the House Champ Clark at the 1912 Democratic convention,
but Wilson won out on the forty-sixth ballot. A hard-fought
campaign followed, as the opposition split between the
incumbent William Howard Taft and former President
Theodore Roosevelt who, after failing to secure the nomination, bolted the G.O.P. for the Progressive party. Wilson
countered Roosevelt's appeal to progressive sentiment by
announcing his own "New Freedom" program which called
for greater popular control of the state and national governments, elimination of monopolies in the industrial and
financial world, and a low tariff. He showed himself to the
people, as Arthur Walworth puts it, to be a "compassionate
pastor, philosopher, historian, and orator, a man of intellect
who could be depended on to act in the national interest."[7]

WILSON AS PRESIDENT

After winning a plurality of the popular vote, Wilson
entered the White House where he quickly asserted forceful
leadership and thereby contributed significantly to the
strengthening and extension of presidential power. During
the first term, he acted as the responsible head of his party
and worked closely with its congressional leaders to develop
and obtain passage of his legislative program. He also was
the first president since John Adams to address the Congress
in person. The first two years saw a string of successes in the
implementation of his progressive platform; a tariff reduction, the Clayton Antitrust Act, creation of the Federal Trade
Commission, and banking and currency reform (the Federal
Reserve System). Still, he was not a doctrinaire social
reformer, as evidenced by his appointment of cautious
people to the new agencies and reluctance to act on the so-
called "social justice" questions like assistance to farmers
and organized labor, child labor protection, woman suffrage,
and racial integration. In fact, his administration's prosegre-
gationist stance was one of the worst blots on its record.[8]

By 1916, however, Wilson moved away from this
"conservatism" and courted the supporters of the former
Progressive party with a decidedly more reformist stance. He
defied big business interests by appointing Louis D. Brandeis
to the Supreme Court, who was backed by progressives and
labor leaders and was the first Jew to be seated on the
highest bench; and he secured passage of significant farm

and labor legislation and a measure granting autonomy in the Philippines.

Moreover, Wilson had to deal with foreign policy problems of greater magnitude than any that had confronted the country since the War of 1812. He and Secretary of State William Jennings Bryan had largely been ignorant of foreign affairs, were moralists who thought of foreign policy in terms of eternal truths rather than expediency, and had a "missionary" approach to international questions; that is, they believed they understood what contributed to the peace and well-being of other countries better than the leaders of these lands. Their desire was to promote justice and international peace and give all peoples the blessings of democracy and Christianity, even if that meant interference in the internal affairs of other nations.[9]

This outlook was reflected in the conclusion of conciliation ("cooling off") treaties between the United States and thirty other countries in 1913–14, the adoption of a benevolent policy toward the Chinese Republic,[10] pressuring Japan to scale down its demands on China in 1915, the move to equalize the Panama Canal tolls and apologize to Colombia for American misdeeds a decade earlier, military intervention in Haiti (1915) and the Dominican Republic (1916), coercing Nicaragua to accept a treaty permitting intervention in the future, and the purchase of the Danish Virgin Islands (1917). The worst side of "missionary diplomacy" was seen in Mexico, where Wilson refused to recognize the revolutionary regime and interfered repeatedly in the country's domestic politics, including a brief occupation of Veracruz in 1914. The "punitive" expedition against Francisco "Pancho" Villa in 1916 brought the two countries dangerously close to war; but then a Joint High Commission was formed to investigate the causes of tension, and in early 1917 he withdrew the troops from northern Mexico and reestablished diplomatic relations.

The most important problem facing the president was the crisis that erupted in far-away Europe in August 1914. Because he seriously underestimated the nationalistic tensions and considerations of power politics that motivated the warring powers, Wilson appealed to his people to "be neutral in fact as well as in name. . .impartial in thought as well as in action."[11] Nevertheless, Americans took up sides, often on the basis of ethnic loyalties, though sentiment tilted toward the Allies from the beginning because of the background of German-American rivalry in the Caribbean and Pacific and the German violation of Belgian neutrality. During the next two years, further bias in favor of the Allies was secured not only by British and French propaganda with its skillful exploitation of German mistakes (especially submarine warfare), but also by the stimulating effect which Allied munitions purchases had on the American economy. Wilson himself was convinced that a basic reform of international relations was required, one that would put an end to conquests, guarantee equal rights to all nations regardless of their size, prevent the private manufacture of munitions, and provide through an association of nations the means whereby all would work together to prevent conflict. He also favored a compromise peace and believed both sides shared the responsibility for the war.[12]

It was a critical time in his personal life as well. His wife Ellen died in August 1914; and the grief-stricken chief executive buried himself in work and became more dependent on his intimate adviser, Colonel Edward M. House, who strongly favored intervening on the Allied side. However, a new love soon entered Wilson's life, a strong-minded widow named Edith Bolling Galt, whom he married in December 1915. Unlike the president's first wife, Edith took a great interest in the affairs of state and became familiar with his work. Then in June 1915, Bryan resigned in protest against Wilson's "unneutral response" to German submarine warfare, and many peace activists turned against him. At the same time, he faced mounting pressure on the right flank from Roosevelt and other promoters of "preparedness."

Since the progressives viewed the rearmament campaign as fostering militarism and a sell-out to big business, Wilson in 1916 only very cautiously increased defense spending and was judicious in his criticism of German U-boat activity. By portraying himself as the one who kept America out of the war and supporting government assistance to advance the interests of less-favored groups and regions, he gained a narrow victory over his able Republican opponent, Charles Evans Hughes, in the 1916 presidential contest.

Wilson made an all-out push to secure a peace without victory with his famous speech of January 22, 1917, which also contained many of the elements of his later Fourteen Points.[13] However, his efforts were negated by the actions of advisers like House and Secretary of State Robert Lansing who worked to steel British resistance,[14] by public indignation over the alleged German offer of an alliance to Mexico, and by the resumption of unrestricted submarine warfare designed to bring Britain to its knees. Wilson promptly broke relations with Germany, and following the sinking of three American merchant vessels on March 18, he reluctantly asked Congress for a war resolution.[15] Since most Americans were still clinging to their "double wish" to uphold national honor and stay out of the war, it was uncertain up to the last minute whether Congress would agree to intervention in the conflict.[16]

After the vote on April 6 to enter the World War, the president took far-reaching steps to mobilize the country's military, economic, and emotional resources. A dizzying array of boards and regulations involved the government in every sector of the economy, an army was raised, equipped, and transported across the Atlantic, and conformity to the war effort was vigorously promoted. In numerous speeches, most notably the message to Congress where he spelled out the Fourteen Points, Wilson proclaimed America's objective to be that of a liberal peace; and in the fall of 1918 the exhausted Germans agreed to an armistice on what they thought would be the Wilson peace program.

After having won the war, however, Wilson lost the peace. He unwisely urged voters to give a blanket endorsement to the Democratic party in the 1918 congressional election, thereby making foreign policy the basis of his appeal.[17] This enraged the Republicans who regained control of Congress and in effect repudiated Wilson. He also had difficulty in persuading the Allies to accept his peace principles, and he traded some of them away in the Paris negotiations in order to obtain the inclusion of the League of Nations covenant in the final treaties. Although he attended the talks in person, he neglected to include any senator or leading Republican on the team accompanying him. His health was failing, a situation which was obvious at the conference and which seriously affected his dealings with the Senate after the signing of the Treaty of Versailles in 1919. Wilson locked horns with the equally strong-minded chairman of the Foreign Relations Committee, Henry Cabot Lodge, and refused to consider any compromise qualifying the United States involvement in the League of Nations.

After fruitless discussions with the committee about membership in the League, he took his case to the people in an exhausting speaking tour through the Middle West and West. When he fell ill in Pueblo, Colorado, on September 25, his doctor ordered him back to Washington immediately. A week later, at a critical point in the Senate's consideration of the treaty, Wilson suffered a massive stroke.

Although he was fully disabled for two months and did not meet with the cabinet for six months, his wife controlling all access to him, he did experience a partial recovery. When the ratification vote took place on November 19, he instructed the Democratic senators to reject any reservations, and the treaty was defeated. On March 19, 1920, it came up for a second vote with the reservations modified, but the president refused any compromise and it was turned down again.

He hoped to see the 1920 election serve as a "solemn referendum" on the League of Nations, but a landslide of hostile votes buried the Democratic candidate James M. Cox and Wilson's dream. Still, he was awarded the Nobel Peace Prize for his efforts. In July 1921, Congress declared the war with Germany to be ended, and the Harding administration signed a separate peace agreement without the League of Nations. Wilson spent his last years in relative seclusion as an invalid at his residence in Washington and died peacefully on February 3, 1924.

WILSON'S RELIGIOUS FAITH

It is one of the great ironies of American religious history that the two most "evangelical" presidents in the twentieth century, Woodrow Wilson and Jimmy Carter, were in large part rejected by those Protestant evangelicals who possessed the same deep faith in Jesus Christ that they did. Certainly, it is no exaggeration to say that religion was the central factor of Wilson's entire being.[18] It was, as he told an audience in 1914, something he had learned in his home but was not taught to him "dogmatically." His parents believed that Christianity was "catching," and if the atmosphere of the home did not make a Christian of the child, nothing they could say would penetrate him.[19]

In his youth, Wilson had a steady diet of family worship, Bible reading, study of the *Shorter Catechism*, and stories of the Scottish Covenanters. In fact, he so proudly identified with this heritage that he declared in a speech in London on December 28, 1918: "The stern Covenanter tradition that is behind me sends many an echo down the years."[20] Thus, he acquired a Presbyterian faith that centered around covenant theology, one which involved divine sovereignty linked with love for the world. This theology held that God exhibited both love and authority toward his children. The individual was his agent in the world and God blessed human activity. "Success" was measured by how close one came to total obedience to the divine will and law. The world was a battlefield of good and evil, and one must not compromise principles in the struggle. God's law was the constitution for the world and the Bible the guide for a person's life. Hard work was a fulfillment of one's duty to God and would result in divine favor.

The young Wilson gained the confidence that even though the world might be against him, God was with him and would bless his efforts when they were done in accordance with the principles of his certain and unchanging law. One's ambitions were correct if they were defined in terms of serving God, not self. When conflicts arose, he rested securely on his commitment to God's moral law and rejected compromise as half-hearted obedience. As biographer Arthur Link points out, he tended to identify his own fixed opinions and prejudices with divine principle, and in disputes he was absolutely convinced that he was defending the right.[21] This moralistic and legalistic character distinguished Wilson's religious faith throughout his life.

At the age of sixteen, Wilson had a crisis conversion experience in a service at the Columbia Seminary chapel (an event which he still fondly recalled even after becoming president), and on July 5, 1873, he applied for membership in the First Presbyterian Church of Columbia. The minutes record that he and two other "young men out of the Sunday School and well-known to us all" gave "a free confession" in which they "exhibited evidences of a work of grace begun in their hearts;" they then were "unanimously admitted" into the church.[22] That he was less than satisfied with his spiritual development was poignantly reflected by a notation in his journal the following year: "Although I professed Christ's name some time ago, I have increased very little in grace and have done almost nothing for the Saviour's cause here below." He then resolved to rededicate himself to God's service and "to endeavor to attain nearer and nearer to perfection."[23]

Numerous writers point out that he read the Bible daily—his official biographer Ray S. Baker claims he wore out two or three of them—and that he prayed on his knees daily, said grace before meals, and had family worship. He regarded prayer as "the only spring" at which one could "renew his spirit and purify his motive."[24] He also was a lifelong churchgoer, in that he joined a congregation in each of the cities where he resided, was ordained a ruling elder in the Princeton Presbyterian church, and moved his membership to Central Presbyterian Church in Washington when he became president. He regularly attended the latter until his illness in 1919, had a warm relationship with its pastor, spoke at the cornerstone laying for its new building, and occasionally took part in presbytery meetings. He loved the "simple service" of the small church, whose members permitted him to worship quietly, and he referred to it as "a dear old-fashioned church such as I used to go to when I was a boy" and "a congregation of simple and genuine people to whom it is a matter of utter indifference whether there is a [social] season or not."[25]

He had no problem with doubt, for as he commented to his physician, Dr. Cary Grayson, "so far as religion is concerned, argument is adjourned." In a conversation with a friend during the second year of his presidency, he affirmed:

> My life would not be worth living, if it were not for the driving power of religion, for *faith*, pure and simple. I have seen all my life the arguments against it without ever having been moved by them. . . .Never for a moment have I had one doubt about my religious beliefs. There are people who *believe* only as they *understand*—that seems to me presumptuous and sets their understanding as the standard of the universe.[26]

On another occasion he wrote to an acquaintance about his "faith in God's providence that sustains more than anything else can," and he told Grayson, "If I were not a Christian, I think I should go mad, but my faith in God holds me to the belief that He is in some way working out His own plans through human perversities and mistakes."[27]

In his academic career, religion occupied a prominent position. At Princeton he was, as Walworth puts it, the university pastor. He wrote in 1896 that religion was central to its existence, the "steadying torch which has made her a school of duty." In his judgment, religion if adequately conceived, was "the true salt wherewith to keep both duty and learning sweet against the taint of time." President Wilson believed Princeton's mission was to offer a general education infused with moral ideals and imperatives, and no university could do this "if its teachings be not informed with the spirit of religion, and that the religion of Christ, and with the energy of a positive faith." In another speech, he called Princeton "a place of sound religion."[28] He was a regular speaker in the chapel and for the campus religious organization, the Philadelphian Society, and between 1904 and 1910 he regularly delivered the baccalaureate sermon to the graduating class.[29]

Moreover, Wilson taught that a good statesman should have a faith in Jesus Christ which was based on the Bible as a standard. Thus, he linked morals to actions and principles to deeds, but he had little grasp of the moral ambiguity in most political actions. One always did right by opposing that which was wrong, as most conflicts were battles over principles, not personalities.[30] Eventually, he adopted a more flexible, relativistic, and reformist political theory; but he still stressed absolutes and ideals in his religious talks. This indicates the great difficulty he had in integrating his political and religious thought, but he resolved the problem by identifying patriotism, social and political involvement, and religion in what John Mulder calls the "Wilsonian synthesis of personal religion and political power." He saw the Christian faith as driving people toward serving others, which in turn required some to be leaders and possess power. The limitation and justification for such power was its exercise on the behalf of others.[31]

Gradually, Wilson came to see that the church's duty was not only to save souls, as vitally important as that was, but also to save the world. He said in 1904 that people were not drawn into heaven for fear they would go to hell, but because the Scriptures taught a gospel of love which drew them. In 1906 he declared "Christ was not a reformer," but he supplied the "motive force" for people to "reconstruct and better human life." In a speech in 1908, he averred that Christianity did not come into the world to set crooked things straight, purify social nature, or elevate our lives, but rather its object "is the individual, and the individual is the vehicle of Christianity." In 1910 he labeled "Christian Socialism" a contradiction in terms, in that while its motives were Christian, when it was translated into a definite program involving social compulsion, it ceased to be a spiritual one.[32]

The transition in his thinking was revealed in an address on May 26, 1909, at Hartford Theological Seminary. Early in his message he reiterated the old individualistic theme that the business of the church was not to "pity men" or rescue people from suffering "by the mere means of material relief, or even by the means of spiritual reassurance." Rather, it stood at the center of thinking life and showed "the spiritual relations of men to the great world processes. . . , to the plan of life." Then, he declared it was "a very significant matter" that the gospel was to save the world as well as individuals:

> If men cannot lift their fellow-men in the process of saving themselves, I do not see that it is very important that they should save themselves, because they reduce Christianity by that means to the essence of selfishness, and anything that is touched with selfishness is very far removed from the spirit of Christianity. Christianity came into the world to save the world as well as to save individual men and individual men can afford in conscience to be saved only as part of the process by which the world itself is regenerated. . . .You are setting afoot a process which will lift the whole level of the world and of modern life.[33]

Speaking at General Theological Seminary in New York on April 6, 1910, he insisted that the church had "an extraordinary opportunity" to supply society with a "clear standard of moral measurement," one that could reevaluate and reassess men and affairs. The church could contribute enlightenment and guidance to our bewildered society, and it "ought to expound the difference between individual responsibility and corporate responsibility."[34]

By the time he reached the White House, his thinking had matured. As he explained to the Pittsburgh YMCA on October 24, 1914, he was "not fond of thinking of Christianity as the means of saving individual souls." Rather, it taught that character development was a by-product of acting outside the circle of one's narrow selfish interests:

> Christ came into the world to save others, not to save himself; and no man is a true Christian who does not think constantly of how he can lift his brother, how he can assist his friend, how he can enlighten mankind, how he can make virtue the rule of conduct in the circle in which he lives. . . .

> Since the world—the world of affairs, the world of society—is nothing less and nothing more than all of us put together, it is a great enterprise for the salvation of the soul in this world as well as in the next. . . .Your measurements, your directions, your whole momentum, have to be established before you reach the next world. And this world is intended as the place in which we shall show that we know how to grow in the stature of manliness and of righteousness.[35]

It should be mentioned that Wilson was not a pietist in the sense of being overly concerned about securing and keeping his own salvation. As a Calvinist, he understood this had been settled with his election by God. Although he took the Bible seriously, he avoided theological disputes on his campus. The Darwinian hypothesis did not disturb him, as indicated by the support he gave his uncle, Dr. James Woodrow, who was fired by Columbia Theological Seminary in the 1880s for publicly acknowledging acceptance of the new scientific doctrine. During his presidency, Princeton was formally declared to be a nonsectarian institution, and he appointed the first Jew and Roman Catholic to the faculty. Although Wilson was suspicious of Catholic immigration from Europe and the temporal claims of the papacy, he was tolerant of Catholics in general. In fact, upon becoming governor of New Jersey, he chose a young Catholic lawyer, Joseph P. Tumulty, to be his private secretary, and despite some criticism in Protestant circles, Tumulty remained at Wilson's side until he left office in 1921. Wilson also had cordial relations with James Cardinal Gibbons, Archbishop of Baltimore and the leader of American Catholics, even though there were some tensions between Washington and the Holy See during the war.[36]

A MORALIZED CIVIL RELIGION

Wilson's religious concerns were moral, not theological in character. He saw the world in synthetic, holistic terms and tended to reduce all issues to well-defined moral categories. As he declared in a baccalaureate sermon on June 12, 1910:

> There are definite comprehensible practices, immutable principles of government and of right conduct in the dealings of men with one another. . . .There is such a thing as justice and a noble force in men who are righteous and love the truth.[37]

That same year, he explained that America's task was to translate its material force into moral force, its power into intellectual and spiritual liberty. By doing this, Americans would recover the traditions and glories of their history.[38] In the first inaugural address he challenged his people to recognize that:

> our duty is to cleanse, to reconsider, to restore, to correct the evil without impairing the good, to purify and humanize every process of our common life without weakening or sentimentalizing it.[39]

Christianity was the instrumentality that could accomplish these intentions. He said "our wills have to be regenerated and our purposes rectified" before we could enact the legislation that would record our society's "moral achievement." By transforming lives, Christianity enabled people "to erect great spiritual standards" in place of the little personal ones they had before. In the long run, the verdict of God was what counted, and "the moral judgment would be the last judgment, the final judgment, in the minds of men as well as the tribunal of God."[40]

The most important aspect of religion was not worship, piety, or contemplation, but rather service, as Wilson declared in various speeches. Religion "is the energy of character" which "concentrates upon a service. . .greater than the man himself." The "spirit of religious service is the chief and crowning spirit of service for all men" (1902). The true Christian was the person who thought constantly how he could assist others and "make virtue the rule of conduct" where he lived (1914). The church was put into the world "not only to serve the individual soul, but to serve society also" (1915). At the signing of the tariff bill in 1913, the president remarked that through this "we have served our fellow men and have, thereby, tried to serve God." On the contrary, sin "in almost all its forms" was selfishness (1910).[41]

This emphasis on service related directly to his understanding of America. In 1915 he asserted that patriotism was like Christianity, in that it was the devotion of the spirit to something greater than itself. Both were "transforming influences" and were the "embodiment of the things that are entirely unselfish—the principles of self-sacrifice and devotion." America's only reason for existence "was to show men the paths of liberty and mutual serviceability." The nation provided "the common man" with freedom, justice, and an equal opportunity to succeed. Thus, America was "great in the world" since it was the "successful embodiment of a great ideal of unselfish citizenship."[42] He looked forward to the day when "we shall be blessed among the nations, because we succored the nations of the world in their time of distress and of dismay." From the beginning, America was destined to be "the servant of mankind."[43]

In carrying out its mission to show the world the incalculable benefits of free institutions, America received guidance from two sources, the church and the Bible. The church was a model of mutual self-sacrifice and thereby constituted a standard for society. It revealed that the "spirit of Christianity" was one of assistance, counsel, vitalization, and interest in everything that affected the lives of people.[44]

In his famous address, "The Bible and Progress," given in Denver on May 7, 1911, Wilson said the Scriptures revealed that each person was a distinct moral agent, all would be judged by a "fixed and eternal standard," everyone must engage in a "spiritual warfare" against sin and wrong in the world, and liberty was a "spiritual conception" which was worth fighting for. The Bible stripped life of its disguises and pretenses, elevated those standards by which alone true greatness and strength were assessed, and demonstrated what had made America great.

Reform was nothing more than trying to conform actual conditions and laws "with the right judgments" of human conduct and liberty. Reform always came from the people, "out of the hearts of those who never exercised authority and never organized parties." He prayed that they would never cease to be inspired by the Scriptures, the "charter of liberty." It would abash the "statesman sunk in the practices that debase a nation," because "the finger of God" was against anyone who "plots the nation's downfall or the people's deceit." In conclusion:

> There will be no halt to the great movement of the armies of reform until men forget their God, until they forget this charter of their liberty. Let no man suppose that progress can be divorced from religion, or that there is any other platform for the ministers of reform than the platform written in the utterances of our Lord and Savior.

> America was born a Christian nation. America was born to exemplify that devotion to the elements of righteousness which are derived from the revelations of Holy Scripture.[45]

In a speech at a Sunday school convention on October 1, 1911, Wilson reiterated his high regard for the Bible and applied it to American life. By now a serious presidential contender, he reminded his audience of the great problems facing the country and affirmed in classic civil religion language the nation's spiritual heritage:

> I should be afraid to go forward if I did not believe that there lay at the foundation of all our schooling and of all our thought this incomparable and unimpeachable Word of God. If we cannot derive our strength thence, there is no source from which we can derive it. . . .The providence of God is the foundation of affairs, and. . .only those can guide, and only those can follow, who take this providence of God from the sources where it is authentically interpreted.[46]

AMERICA'S WORLD MISSION

Wilson thus brought to his presidency a moralized public faith that stressed obligation, duty, and service. America had a mission to fulfill, and as its spiritual leader he sought to bring the nation into conformity with divine standards. Also, he was convinced of his own calling, for as he told a party mogul just before the inauguration, "God ordained that I should be the next President of the United States," and no mortal "could have prevented that."[47] He set the tone of earnestness at the outset of his administration by refusing to permit an inaugural ball, feeling that the solemnity of the occasion should suggest dedication rather than festivity. His public image was one of seriousness and distance from people, yet he stirred the masses with his oratory and expressions of high principles, as his inaugural address revealed:

> The feelings with which we face this new age of right and opportunity sweep across our heartstrings like some air out of God's own presence, where justice and mercy are reconciled and the judge and the brother are one.[48]

Wilson was at heart a "political missionary." He believed that "men" could improve the world in which they lived and that America, due to its unique history and place in divine plan, could serve as the vehicle of global reform. Following the American lead and example, nations could eliminate oppression and war, live together in peace, prosperity, and harmony, and thereby fulfill God's will for an orderly world. There was, of course, an implicit national chauvinism in this program, since it assumed the moral and historical excellence of Anglo-Saxon culture and particularly its constitutional arrangements. He was, in effect, a "secular evangelist" for American political ideals—institutions and attitudes which were more or less already on the scene when he entered the White House—such as democracy, capitalism, and American superiority (in a moral and universalistic sense, not selfish territorial aggrandizement or European-style imperialism).[49]

These were the components of the "idealism" that marked Wilsonian foreign policy. He believed that all peoples were capable of democracy, for "when properly directed, there is no people not fitted for self-government," and, referring to Mexico, he intimated that this country "shall have just as much freedom in her own affairs as we have."[50] Thus, he saw the Six-Power Consortium created in 1911 to provide capital for railroad construction in China as an imperialistic scheme to gain control over the country's internal affairs, and he withdrew American support from it in order to support "democracy" there. In 1913, he refused to recognize the Huerta government in Mexico since he did not regard it as a legitimate constitutional regime, and the ensuing meddling in Mexican affairs betrayed Wilson's ideals and left a legacy of bitterness. The same was true when he applied this standard of the establishment of enlightened, responsible governments through free elections to revolutionary Russia in 1917. The denial of recognition to the

Bolshevik regime contributed to Soviet alienation from the West and helped fuel anticommunist hysteria in the United States. Wilson tried to apply constitutional and democratic criteria to several unstable Central American and Caribbean states, and the result was military intervention or diplomatic pressures that seemed very much at odds with his ideas of democracy and self-determination.

When war broke out in Europe, Wilson, like most Americans, opted for neutrality. He assumed the conflict was rooted in traditional rivalries which needed to be removed if lasting peace were ever to come. Still, he did not seriously try to break the British naval blockade and in 1915 began allowing the Allies to purchase goods on credit. However, he roundly condemned the German submarine counterblockade as immoral and a violation of international law and the rights of neutrals. During 1916 he tried in vain to mediate a compromise peace which would involve a return to the status quo of 1914, an agreement by all warring parties to forego annexations and indemnities, and the creation of a new international order.[51]

Addressing the Senate on January 22, 1917, the president called for immediate cessation of hostilities, a "peace without victory," a "peace between equals." It must be one that would recognize the principle of government by consent, free access to the seas, limitation of armaments, national self-determination, and elimination of "entangling alliances." He said, "These are American principles, American policies," but they were also "the principles of mankind and must prevail."[52] However, neither side assumed the war had stalemated, and neither would accept such a peace. Then, Germany decided to force a quick end to the conflict by resuming all-out submarine warfare.

When Wilson's subsequent policy of "armed neutrality" proved to be of no avail, he reluctantly convened Congress on April 2 and delivered his "war message." He insisted that America's quarrel was with the German government, not its people, which had "selfish designs" and "did what it pleased and told its people nothing." He asserted that a partnership of democratic nations was needed to keep the peace for which the United States would fight, because "the world must be made safe for democracy." In ringing words that epitomized Wilsonian idealism, he intoned:

We have no selfish ends to serve. We desire no conquest, no dominion. We seek no indemnities for ourselves, no material compensation for the sacrifices we shall freely make. We are but one of the champions of the rights of mankind. We shall be satisfied when those rights have been made as secure as the faith and the freedom of nations can make them.

Just because we fight without rancour and without selfish object, seeking nothing for ourselves but what we shall wish to share with all free peoples, we shall, I feel confident, conduct our operations as belligerents without passion and ourselves observe with proud punctilio the principles of right and of fair play we profess to be fighting for.

America would not act with animus or enmity toward the Germans but only against "an irresponsible government which has thrown aside all considerations of humanity and of right and is running amuck." Concluding with an appeal to civil religion and an allusion to Martin Luther's speech at the Diet of Worms, Wilson dedicated the nation to upholding the right:

America is privileged to spend her blood and·her might for the principles that gave her birth and happiness and the peace which she has treasured. God helping her, she can do no other.[53]

Although Wilson said America would conduct its operations "without passion" and "in a high spirit of right and fairness," the country rushed into the war with exuberance.[54] One of the victims was civil liberties, as conscientious objectors were harassed, opposing voices of any kind silenced, and irrational hatred against all things German unleashed. For the most part, the churches enthusiastically backed the war effort, but at the same time their involvement in wartime ministries fostered the growth of ecumenical endeavor.[55] The war also contributed immensely to the integration of Roman Catholics and Jews into American life and paved the way for the expansion of the civil religion consensus into that of the "three great faiths."

Wilson expressed his peace aims repeatedly, from the inaugural address to the major speeches of 1918—Fourteen Points (January 8), Four Principles (February 11), and Five Particulars (September 27).[56] They were summed up in one sentence in a Fourth of July address: "What we seek is the reign of law, based on the consent of the governed and sustained by the organized opinion of mankind."[57] In adopting the liberal peace program, Wilson recognized that his country was fighting for different reasons than the others, and he made clear that the United States was not an "allied" but an "associated" power in the war. By offering Germany "a place of equality among the peoples of the world" in the Fourteen Points address, Wilson called for peace in the name of all that was high and holy in the Western democratic and Christian traditions, and thereby countering the appeal of international communism which offered the universal class struggle as the alternative to decadent Western civilization.[58] But Germany's imposition of a victorious peace on Russia excluded all hope of a negotiated settlement.

When the war ended, Wilson gave full credit to God and moral force for the victory. He said in Carlisle, England, on December 29: "The knowledge that wrong was being attempted has aroused the nations. They have gone out like men upon a crusade," and they defeated the "outlaw" that was abroad. Now we were trying to place "the conscience of the world" on the throne. In his Thanksgiving proclamation on November 18, Wilson mixed civil religion terminology with his moralizing:

> God has in His good pleasure given us peace. . . .It has come as a great triumph of right. Complete victory has brought us, not peace alone, but the confident promise of a new day as well in which justice shall replace force and jealous intrigue among the nations. Our gallant armies have participated in a triumph which is not marred or stained by any purpose of selfish aggression. In a righteous cause they have won immortal glory and have nobly served their nation in serving mankind. God has indeed been gracious. . . .A new day shines about us, in which our hearts take new courage and look forward with open hope to new and greater duties.[59]

However, by the time the peace conference opened in January, Wilson had lost his strategic advantage. American power was no longer needed to defeat Germany, while his support at home was uncertain. He had gone forth on an apostolic mission to preach the new political gospel to the decadent continent, but the statesmen were not listening. He told the plenary session on February 14, 1919, "Wrong has been defeated, but the rest of the world is more conscious than it ever was before of the majesty of right." The French leader Clemenceau more accurately gauged the situation when he quipped: "God gave us his Ten Commandments, and we broke them. Wilson gave us his Fourteen Points— we shall see."[60] Although his position gradually eroded, Wilson still was able to get most of his points into the treaty, while the necessary machinery for its later revision was provided by the League of Nations.

Unfortunately, Wilson failed to carry the day with the Senate opposition when he brought the treaty home, and to generate public support, he barnstormed the country in September. Speech after speech was laced with religious imagery:

- *San Francisco, California, September 18*: "I believe in Divine Providence. If I did not, I would go crazy. . . .I do not believe there is any body of men that can defeat this great enterprise."
- *Berkeley, California, September 18*: The "halo" or glory of the American Army was that it "made conquest of peace for the world." This "noble army of Americans who saved the world" was greater than the armies which sought the Holy Grail or tried to redeem the Holy Sepulchre.
- *San Diego, California, September 19*: The American forces seemed to people over there "like bodies of crusaders come out of a free nation" to sacrifice their lives for an idea, namely, "the spiritual purpose of redemption that rests in the heart of mankind."
- *Los Angeles, California, September 20*: "We desired to offer ourselves as a sacrifice for humanity."
- *Pueblo, Colorado, September 25*: Americans have accepted the truth of justice, liberty, and peace, and it would lead us "into pastures such as the world never dreamed of before."[61]

At that point, Wilson became ill and was rushed back to Washington. The treaty was not ratified, his work was repudiated, and his people rejected the special mission which he conceived for them. However, the public did not reject civil religion as such but only Wilson's formulation of what their international obligations ought to be.

THE ROOTS OF FAILURE

The obstinacy that so often manifested itself in self-righteous moralism, especially during the later stages of Wilson's presidency, is not easy to explain. Some have turned to psychological theory for help, and of all the presidents only Richard Nixon has been the object of more psychohistorical investigations.[62] Most writers call attention to the rigid religious beliefs that were inculcated in his youth, and a few even attribute Wilson's unusual actions to his Christian faith, a judgment which reflects more the bias of those who make the charge than it does the available evidence. However, at least one commentator suggests that the source of his problems was physiological. Bert Edward Park, M.D., maintains that Wilson suffered from "progressive dementia" resulting from multiple, small-vessel lacunar infarctions (strokes) that were related to high blood pressure. He believes Wilson had a number of small strokes beginning in 1896, a chronic condition that was exacerbated in fall 1919 by an atherosclerotic blockage of a large blood vessel supplying the right side of his brain while he was in Colorado, followed by a second and more devastating stroke that occurred after his return to the capital.

He concludes that hypertension and atherosclerosis contributed to Wilson's dementia, the technical term now used by physicians to denote a deterioration in intellectual powers. That is not the same thing as "insanity."[63] The symptoms of such a condition are memory loss, errors in judgment, irritableness, and quarrelsomeness, all traits which Wilson manifested during his second term. According to Park, this progressive deterioration of his mental functions explains the president's hard-nosed attitudes toward congressional opponents during and after the war, the disastrous attempt to make the 1918 midterm election a referendum on his policies, and his decision to go to Paris and grapple personally with forces that he poorly understood, while not utilizing the assistance of the team of experts who had been assembled to study the war aims of the belligerents.[64] At the talks he was forgetful, inflexible, impervious to arguments and facts that went against his presuppositions, and obsessed with the League of Nations scheme. As the weeks passed, he turned against his close advisers and became more and more a loner. The man who had talked about "open covenants, openly arrived at" became increasingly secretive and participated in deals made behind closed doors. Thus, intellectual decline had already set in before the catastrophic stroke in the fall permanently disabled him, and these "recognizable seeds of discord" restricted any meaningful progress in the negotiations with the Senate.[65]

The point of this medical discussion is that Wilson's illness very much affected the manner in which he expressed his public faith. Nevertheless, he brought to it an emphasis on moral accountability and a prophetic style of civil religion which summoned the nation to exercise a higher sense of responsibility. Wilson believed his country was obliged to work to create a better world in which all people could live in peace and under governments of their own choosing.

The darker side was that neither the majority of Americans nor most people elsewhere shared his sense of providential mission. His fellow citizens were anxious to return to what Warren G. Harding inelegantly labeled "normalcy," and they retreated into isolationism and smug self-satisfaction. Although at the end of 1918 the European masses welcomed him as the "savior" who would lead humanity out of the wasteland, disillusionment soon set in. Partially, this was a reaction to America's inability to comprehend their own national aspirations, but many became resentful of his naive effort to "evangelize" the world—to bring the dubious benefits of American democracy, capitalism, and culture to all people. His moralism and messianic vision were not acceptable to an "unregenerate" world, while the Protestant piety on which it was predicated was steadily losing its hold at home.

A more expansive vision of national purpose was needed, one that emphasized the positive values of the American experience without moralizing them and that was based on a much broader religious consensus. After a decade of hedonistic excess, international isolationism, and then bitter depression, the nation was ready for this kind of civil religion. The president who would usher in the new era was Franklin Delano Roosevelt.

7

FRANKLIN D. ROOSEVELT
AND THE EXPANSION OF
AMERICAN CIVIL RELIGION

The news rang out through millions of radio receivers on the morning of June 6, 1944, that the D-Day invasion had begun. For two years, people had eagerly awaited the Allied landing in France which would drive out the Germans and bring an end to World War II. Month after month, troops and supplies poured into Britain but there was no action, and the Soviets grew so impatient with their British and American counterparts that they began thinking of making a separate peace. But now, the troops were storming the beaches of Normandy.

A SIMPLE PRAYER

President Franklin D. Roosevelt went on the radio that day to announce the invasion was underway; but instead of delivering an emotional speech, he called on his fellow Americans to join with him as he recited the following prayer:

> Almighty God: Our sons, pride of our Nation, this day have set upon a mighty endeavor, a struggle to preserve our Republic, our religion, and our civilization, and to set free a suffering humanity.

Lead them straight and true; give strength to their arms, stoutness to their hearts, steadfastness in their faith.

They will need Thy blessings. Their road will be long and hard. For the enemy is strong. He may hurl back our forces. Success may not come with rushing speed, but we shall return again and again; and we know that by Thy grace, and by the righteousness of our cause, our sons will triumph.

They will be sore tried, by night and by day, without rest—until the victory is won. The darkness will be rent by noise and flame. Men's souls will be shaken with the violences of war.

For these men are lately drawn from the ways of peace. They fight not for the lust of conquest. They fight to end conquest. They fight to liberate. They fight to let justice arise, and tolerance and good will among all Thy people. They yearn but for the end of battle, for their return to the haven of home.

Some will never return. Embrace these, Father, and receive them, Thy heroic servants, into Thy kingdom.

And for us at home—fathers, mothers, children, wives, sisters, and brothers of brave men overseas—whose thoughts and prayers are ever with them—help us, Almighty God, to rededicate ourselves in renewed faith in Thee in this hour of great sacrifice.

Many people have urged that I call the Nation into a single day of special prayer. But because the road is long and the desire is great, I ask that our people devote themselves in a continuance of prayer. As we rise to each new day, and again when each day is spent, let words of prayer be on our lips invoking Thy help to our efforts. . . .

And, O Lord, give us Faith. Give us Faith in Thee; Faith in our sons; Faith in each other; Faith in our united crusade. Let not the impacts of temporary events, of temporal matters of but fleeting moment—let not these deter us in our unconquerable purpose.

With Thy blessing, we shall prevail over the unholy forces of our enemy. Help us to conquer the apostles of greed and racial arrogancies. Lead us to the saving of our country, and with our sister Nations into a world unity that will spell a sure peace—a peace invulnerable to the schemings of unworthy men. And a peace that will let all of men live in freedom, reaping the just rewards of their honest toil.

Thy will be done, Almighty God. Amen.[1]

This unique action revealed the enormous change that had taken place in only three decades. The United States was no longer culturally a Protestant, let alone an evangelical nation, but one in which all faiths were to have a part, and President Roosevelt personified the new era of cultural, ethnic, and religious heterogeneity. Although of upper-class origins, he identified with the concerns of the masses and affirmed the virtues of the new pluralism. In the dark days of the Great Depression and World War II, he drew on the resources of the civil religion to offer a discouraged nation the hope of a new beginning and to rally his people for the difficult struggle. The civil religion thus was expanded to include everyone in the Judeo-Christian tradition to mobilize the American nation in a "holy war" against the ungodly Axis tyranny.

FROM COUNTRY SQUIRE TO THE WHITE HOUSE

Franklin Delano Roosevelt came from solid patrician stock.[2] His distant ancestor Claes Martenssen van Roosevelt had migrated to New Amsterdam from Holland in the 1640s (Theodore was descended from his elder son and Franklin from the younger one), and numerous Roosevelts in the succeeding generations were prominent in commercial or political life in New York. His father James (1828–1900) was a well-to-do businessman (coal and railroads), speculator, and country squire who purchased and lived on an expensive but unostentatious estate at Hyde Park in the Hudson valley. James's first wife died in 1876, and four years later he married a woman half his age, Sara Delano, whose father had garnered great wealth in the China trade and also owned an estate along the Hudson. Franklin was born on January 30, 1882, the only child of their union. Although he had been baptized in the Dutch Reformed church, James was a vestryman at the St. James Episcopal Church in Hyde Park and young Franklin was baptized there.

All indications are that he had a happy, serene, and secure childhood. His father and mother cared deeply about him, devoted much time to his rearing, and instilled in him a sense of stewardship and noblesse oblige. He possessed every comfort, traveled extensively with his parents (not only to Europe but also to Washington where he met his father's friend, President Cleveland), enjoyed the society of

New York City in the winter, and spent summers at the family cottage on Campobello Island, New Brunswick. He was educated by tutors until age fourteen, when he was sent to an elite boarding school in Groton, Massachusetts. His fellow students were all from the same social class, and the adjustment was rather easy.

There Franklin came under the influence of the school's founder and headmaster, Endicott Peabody, an Episcopalian rector from one of New England's most prominent families. He maintained a lifelong relationship with Peabody, who performed his wedding and officiated at two inaugural church services while he was president. The clergyman not only became a substitute for Franklin's father, but also did more to shape his character than anyone else besides his parents.[3] Peabody regarded the boys entrusted to his care at Groton as his own family, and he communicated to them a religious faith characterized by its simplicity. He linked service to faith—"Serve the Lord with gladness" —which meant service to God, country, and mankind, and that included political life as well as concern for the poor. Peabody did not care for outward displays of emotion and had little interest in religious intellectualism. His intention was to cultivate "manly Christian character, having regard to [the] moral and physical as well as intellectual development" of his charges at Groton. He believed in religion, character, athletics, and scholarship, most likely in that order.[4] In short, it was a mixture of messianic idealism and simple pragmatism, which interestingly enough, were the distinctive traits of Roosevelt's religion during his years as president. In fact, he wrote Peabody forty years after leaving Groton: "I count it among the blessings of my life that it was given to me in formative years to have the privilege of your guiding hand and benefit of your inspiring example."[5]

In 1900, Roosevelt entered Harvard where thanks to his social origins he fit in well. He was a relatively indifferent student and inveterate socializer, but he got his first taste of leadership by becoming editor of the Harvard *Crimson*. The sudden elevation of his illustrious cousin to the presidency in 1901 enhanced his interest in politics, and Franklin's ties to Theodore's branch of the family were strengthened by his marriage to the latter's niece, Anna Eleanor Roosevelt in 1905. From their union came five children. Eleanor would eventually prove to be more than just the wife of a famous man, for she developed her own career as a lecturer, writer, and social activist.

After graduating with a degree in political history and government, Franklin entered law school at Columbia University, passed the New York bar exam in 1907, and joined a law firm. Unlike the other Roosevelts, James had been a Democrat, and after some early flirtations with the Republican party, Franklin followed his father's path. To be sure, his decision in 1910 to enter politics by running for the state senate as a Democrat was due more to the fact that the party leaders asked him to run than to inner conviction. Still, he waged a brilliant campaign against difficult odds and won the seat from his home county. As an upstater, he belonged to the reformist faction that challenged the power of Tammany Hall (the New York City machine), and his efforts attracted nationwide attention. He gained considerable legislative experience here and was reelected in 1912 on a platform of agrarian progressivism and antibossism.

Roosevelt recognized that Woodrow Wilson's star was rising in the party, and he defied Tammany power by supporting him for the Democratic presidential nomination. Because of this he was given an appointment in the Wilson administration as assistant secretary of the navy, the same post which his cousin had used as the springboard to political power. This was a most important part of the young man's apprenticeship. As he was in charge of the business affairs of the navy, he developed his executive skills. Although he favored a large navy, he worked on individual situations as they developed and achieved solutions on a piecemeal basis. He learned how to listen, decide, and cut through bureaucratic knots—all the time taking full credit for whatever turned out well. His practice was to experiment, make a move, and see what happened; in other words, he preferred vigorous action with tentative commitment. He took risks, absorbed ideas from all directions, and dealt adroitly with people. Above all, he displayed the trait that was the hallmark of the later New Deal, namely, to adopt any policy or program that looked as if it might have a chance of success, and if it did not work, cover the failure with even bolder new plans.[6]

Because of the intense pressure placed on him by his superiors (including President Wilson) to stay on the job, Franklin was unable to follow Theodore's example and achieve martial glory in World War I, but he did vicariously experience the conflict in a tour of the battlefields in July and August 1918. He enhanced his standing in the party by actively supporting Wilson's League of Nations proposal, which resulted in his nomination for vice president in 1920. However, the ticket was crushed by the Republican steamroller, and then his political career seemed finished when a brutal attack of polio in 1921 left him permanently unable to walk unassisted.

Still, thanks to an indomitable will and driving ambition, Roosevelt was able to overcome his disability. He discovered the curative powers of Warm Springs, Georgia, which became his second home and a treatment center for polio victims. He dabbled in journalism and business ventures, but above all he remained involved in politics. He was a prominent figure at the 1924 party convention and in 1928 was elected governor of New York, succeeding his close friend Alfred E. Smith, who was the Democratic presidential candidate that year. As the leader of the most populous state in the union, Roosevelt gained further administrative experience and showed vigor in confronting the problems of the depression.

From here he was catapulted into the presidency and became the only person ever to be elected to the nation's highest office four times. He had accepted "the need for change, for new departures, for experiments" and "recognized that government was not a bogy but an instrument for meeting the problems of change," as James MacGregor Burns puts it.[7] Roosevelt's New Deal reflected his concern with immediate problems, commitment to action, and aversion to any kind of sweeping theory or eternal absolutes in the economic and political realm. And, as the world edged ever closer to war and finally plunged into the abyss, he manifested the same sense of pragmatism in readying the United States for the conflict and leading his people to the threshold of victory. Under his administrations the country and the office of the presidency were profoundly transformed. The powers of government were vastly expanded, and the nation assumed a central position in global politics from which it could never retreat.

ROOSEVELT'S RELIGION

Like most presidents, Franklin D. Roosevelt possessed a personal faith which was tightly integrated into his public one, and it is no easy task to distinguish between them.[8] For example, in all four of his inaugural addresses he used the "God words" associated with civil religion. In the first one on March 4, 1933 (which because of the Twentieth Amendment was the last inauguration in March), he utilized two biblical images—the plague of locusts and the money changers in the temple—and ended with an appeal to the Deity:

> In this dedication of a Nation we humbly ask the blessing of God. May He protect each and every one of us. May He guide me in the days to come.

Roosevelt made a brief reference in the second address on January 20, 1937, to his determination to do the will of the American people, while "seeking Divine guidance to help us each and every one to give light to them that sit in darkness and to guide our feet into the way of peace." In the third (1941), he spoke of the democratic "spirit" and "faith" of America and said that we would go forward in the service of our country, "by the will of God."[9]

The very short fourth inaugural (1945) contained the most moving civil religion terminology. The president observed that he had taken the solemn oath of office not only before his fellow citizens but also "in the presence of our God," and he knew that it was not America's purpose to fail. He affirmed the necessity for American involvement in keeping the peace in the postwar world and concluded:

> The Almighty God has blessed our land in many ways. He has given our people stout hearts and strong arms with which to strike mighty blows for freedom and truth. He has given to our country a faith which has become the hope of all peoples in an anguished world.
>
> So we pray to Him now for the vision to see our way clearly—to see the way that leads to a better life for ourselves and for all our fellow men—to the achievement of His will, to peace on earth.[10]

The externals of his religious commitment are readily discernible, but their inner meaning is more difficult to assess. As mentioned earlier, he was christened in St. James Episcopal Church, Hyde Park. In 1928, he became a vestry-man and later its senior warden (the highest lay office), as his father before him had been, and he took the job in the small congregation quite seriously. His son James recounts that after he had become president and was responsible for spending billions of dollars, he would in his spare time work to save a few hundred dollars at St. James. He had a close relationship with its rector, Rev. Frank Wilson, and with his Groton teacher, Endicott Peabody; both men were welcome visitors at the White House. He was also a trustee of the Cathedral of St. John the Divine in New York City. He liked the music, ritual, and doctrine of the Episcopal Church and derived an inner peace from participation in its worship services. A prized possession was a family Bible printed in Holland in 1686, and he used it in his two gubernatorial and four presidential inaugurations opened to his favorite pas-sage, 1 Corinthians 13, the famous love chapter. He was especially fond of verse 13: "And now abideth faith, hope, charity, these three; but the greatest of these is charity."[11]

On each inaugural day Roosevelt attended a special prayer service before proceeding to the place where he would take the oath of office. The first three were held at St. John's Episcopal Church on Lafayette Square and the last in the East Room of the White House. Officiating at them were Wilson, the pastors of St. John's (and later St. Thomas's where he usually worshiped in the capital), and Endicott Peabody (1933 and 1937). At the services, patriotic hymns were sung and prayers offered seeking divine guidance for the nation and president.[12] Roosevelt also held a commemo-rative observance on the anniversary of his first inaugura-tion, and Peabody often was invited to participate. In fact, Burns reports that on March 4, 1944, the eighty-six-year-old educator (he died eight months later) was present at the East Room reception and in a full and vibrant voice asked divine help for "thy servant, Franklin" and to "save us from all false choices."[13]

As Roosevelt's spiritual mentor, Peabody viewed the president's religious activities approvingly. A Republican, he had voted for Hoover in 1932, but he quickly became one of his pupil's boosters and even placed a picture of him in his Groton study. In 1935, Peabody wrote Roosevelt about the inaugural service:

I rejoiced in joining with you in prayer for strength which you would need in meeting the solemn responsibilities of your office. This Service, unbeknownst to you no doubt, seems to have made a deep impression upon the minds of people all through the country and many were strengthened in their faith by your example. It is a great thing for our country to have before it the leadership of a man who cares primarily for spiritual things. At a time when the minds of men are distraught and their faith unsteady, a spiritual leader at the head of the nation brings fresh power to the individual and to the cause of Christ and His Church.

I venture to think that your going to Church means more to the people throughout the land than almost anything else that you can do. . . .To the country at large, both to believers and non-believers, it means a lead which a great company will follow as they would not be inclined to do if you had shown indifference to the greatest thing in the world.[14]

Roosevelt in fact had a rather simplistic approach to religion. He was not especially regular in church attendance,[15] and he paid no attention to doctrine or theological questions. His beliefs were a very personal matter, and he seldom talked about them, even with his wife or intimate associates. Nevertheless, these people agree that religion for him was an anchor and a source of strength and direction. That is why he asked for special church services on important public occasions and crisis situations. Because he believed in a loving God who created a good world, his attitude toward the world was profoundly optimistic. No matter how bad things might seem to be at the moment, they would come out right in the end. And if he as God's servant placed his trust in him, the divine purposes would be accomplished. His wife summed up the matter this way: "It was a very simple religion. He believed in God and in His guidance."[16]

This sense of self-assurance and deadly seriousness flowed from Roosevelt's almost childlike belief that he was doing the work of God. It lay behind his tendency to sermonize and moralize, whether in the struggle against moneyed interests, a reactionary Supreme Court, or the enemies of freedom and democracy. It also gave him an unbounded confidence in the rightness of his cause, regardless of the situation in which he found himself. As adviser Rexford Tugwell observes: "The secret of his unassailable serenity and his easy gaiety lay in this sense of oneness with the ongoing processes of the universe and his feeling of being. . .in tune with the infinite."[17]

Those close to Roosevelt stress that he was "a deeply religious man," but at the same time they point out his basic open-mindedness and respect for all religions.[18] He had an almost flippant attitude toward the content of belief. Eleanor mentions that she once asked him whether he felt their children should go to church and have Christianity inculcated in them or be left free to make up their own minds about religion as they grew older. Her husband replied that he thought the children had better attend church and learn what he had learned. It could do them no harm. She then asked him, what if the teachings were not true. He said: "I really never thought about it. I think it is just as well not to think about things like that too much."[19] On another occasion she expressed to him a cynical disbelief in some spiritualist conversations with the dead, summaries of which had been sent to her. He replied very calmly:

> I think it is unwise to say you do not believe in anything when you can't prove that it is either true or untrue. There is so much in the world which is always new in the way of discoveries that it is wiser to say that there may be spiritual things which we are simply unable now to fathom. Therefore I am interested and have respect for whatever people believe, even if I cannot understand their beliefs or share their experiences.[20]

In 1938, Interior Secretary Harold Ickes asked the chief in passing how he had become an Episcopalian. Roosevelt responded by describing his father's and his own involvement in the Hyde Park congregation, but added that his family was "very Low Church" and he personally preferred "a Presbyterian, Methodist, or Baptist sermon" to an Episcopalian one.[21]

RELIGIOUS COOPERATION TO BUILD A BETTER NATION

Franklin D. Roosevelt's indifference to particular religion was an essential element in forging the new civil religion consensus. He supported candidates and selected advisers without regard to their religious affiliation, and he did not pressure his people to attend the church services held on his behalf from time to time. As president, he delivered speeches before or sent greetings to groups belonging to the major faiths and accepted honorary degrees from schools like Catholic University of America and Notre Dame.

In the 1928 election campaign, he strongly denounced religious bigotry, as Samuel Rosenman recounts in his memoirs. A lawyer and former state legislator (who also was Jewish), he joined Roosevelt's staff that year as a speech writer, and one of his first assignments was to help draft an address on the topic. The candidate was indignant at the treatment which Al Smith, the retiring governor and Democratic nominee for president, was receiving because of his Roman Catholic faith, and he dictated a paragraph to Rosenman about seeing wounded American soldiers being carried to the rear on stretchers when he visited the front in World War I. Roosevelt declared that "somehow in those days people were not asking to what church. . .these American boys belonged." If anyone in the audience had seen what he had seen and knew what the country had gone through, and still could "cast his ballot in the interest of intolerance and of a violation of the spirit of the Constitution of the United States, then I say solemnly to that man or woman, 'May God have mercy on your miserable soul.' "[22]

Rosenman became one of Roosevelt's closest advisers, and he was in a good position to observe his behavior. Rosenman appreciated his sincere commitment to tolerance and human brotherhood and his unconcern with distinctions of religious belief. "This was a new kind of man in politics for me: one who did not seem to care—or even know—whether you were a Catholic, Protestant, or Jew."[23]

In 1937, this outlook was excellently reflected in an open letter which President Roosevelt sent to The Calvert Associates, a Catholic organization that promoted religious and civic liberty:

> The lessons of religious toleration—a toleration which recognizes complete liberty of human thought, liberty of conscience—is one which, by precept and example, must be inculcated in the hearts and minds of all Americans if

the institutions of our democracy are to be maintained and perpetuated.

We must recognize the fundamental rights of man. There can be no true national life in our democracy unless we give unqualified recognition to freedom of religious worship and freedom of education.

He ended by expressing the hope that "this nation, under God" would uphold the right of all within its borders "to the free exercise of religion according to the dictates of conscience."[24]

That same year, Roosevelt initiated the practice of having both Protestant and Catholic clergy pray at the presidential inauguration ceremony, and prayers henceforth were always included in the program.[25] The invocation was given by Rev. ZeBarney T. Phillips, chaplain of the Senate, and the benediction by Rt. Rev. Msgr. John A. Ryan of Catholic University, director of the Social Action Department of the National Catholic Welfare Conference. The latter was a good friend of the president. (The first inaugural prayer by a Jewish rabbi occurred in 1949 and by an Orthodox clergyman in 1957.)

The controversial "radio priest," Father Charles E. Coughlin, was an early supporter of the New Deal and tried to worm his way into Roosevelt's inner circle, but the president was suspicious of his demagogic tendencies. The two got along during 1933 and 1934, but a permanent break resulted when Coughlin joined in the effort to block American membership in the World Court. Moderate Catholic activists sided with Roosevelt against the priest and he was effectively isolated. When he trailed off into anti-Semitism in the late 1930s, the administration did everything it could to discredit him.[26]

The Coughlin case revealed both Roosevelt's readiness to work with Catholics when they would back his program and his aversion to anti-Semitism, although recent scholarship shows that he took a cautious and pragmatic approach to the matter of admitting Jewish refugees from Germany, considering the political risks to be too great to allow them unlimited entry.[27] Still, his attitude toward American Jews was quite positive. He regularly issued proclamations for the High Holy Days, sent congratulatory letters to Jewish groups, endorsed the annual Brotherhood Day of the

National Conference of Christians and Jews, and in 1938 was awarded the American Hebrew Medal. In 1937, Roosevelt wrote to the 40th Congress of the Zionist Organization of America, whose president was the distinguished Rabbi Stephen S. Wise, praising the Zionist achievement in Palestine and expressing the hope that the group would find "new inspiration and new light" to achieve a "happy solution" to problems there.[28]

In the 1944 election campaign, the president was outraged when some opponents charged Sidney Hillman, an important labor leader and head of the Office of Production Management, with controlling the Democratic party and called attention to his Jewish origins. He struck back with a fiery speech in Boston where he linked the critics of Hillman to the "bigots" who had been "gunning for Al Smith" in 1928. He insisted that "religious intolerance, social intolerance, and political intolerance have no place in our American life," and after listing some ethnic surnames of "our fine boys" who were "fighting magnificently all over the world" in the war, he affirmed that it was our duty to make sure there was no room in the country for racial or religious intolerance or for snobbery.[29]

Bigots occasionally raised the question of Roosevelt's ancestry, and James once asked his father if he minded being accused of having Jewish blood. He replied that he had searched his genealogy in the futile hope of finding some and added, "I wish I was." Philip Slomovitz, the editor of the *Detroit Jewish Chronicle*, wrote the president in 1935 about the matter, and he responded that he knew only that the Roosevelts had come from Holland but added: "In the dim past they may have been Jews or Catholics or Protestants. What I am more interested in is whether they were good citizens and believers in God. I hope they were both."[30]

For Roosevelt, idealism, patriotism, and faith were inseparable. In the 1936 annual message to Congress, he talked about the necessity to "fear not, view all the tasks of life as sacred, have faith in the triumph of the ideal, give daily all that you have to give, be loyal, and rejoice whenever you find yourselves part of a great ideal enterprise." Thus, he could tell the military and naval chaplains in 1934 that the "supreme values are spiritual" and our task is to build an "exemplary character" which withstands all the storms of life. Religion was essential for the success of democracy, as he pointed out in a letter in February 1935 to a committee representing twenty Jewish and Christian denominations in Washington which was promoting the importance of religion and church attendance in the life of a democracy.

> In a nation like ours, where church and State are and must remain independent, it is highly important that our churches—using the word in the broadest sense—should feel their responsibility for strengthening those spiritual ideals of worship and service so essential to our highest welfare as a nation.[31]

In other words, Roosevelt believed that the public faith with its emphasis on civility provided an indispensable underpinning for the New Deal. He reminded the Federal Council of Churches of Christ in December 1933 that they and the other religious bodies, Gentile and Jewish, stood "ready to lead in a new war of peace—the war for social justice." He alluded to the early churches which, because they were united in a social ideal, had advanced through the centuries. And now:

> we are embarking on another voyage into the realm of human contacts. That human agency which we call government is seeking through social and economic means the same goal which the churches are seeking through social and spiritual means.

> If I were asked to state the great objective which Church and State are both demanding for the sake of every man and woman and child in this country, I would say that that great objective is "a more abundant life."

We "are at one in calling for collective effort on broad lines of social planning," and this "is wholly in accord with the social teachings of Christianity." He acknowledged that the younger generation might not necessarily be committed to the traditional beliefs and practices of the various churches, but they could support the "fundamentals of social betterment." The churches and the government, "while wholly separate in their functioning, can work hand in hand" to promote social justice. At the same time, the public authority would guarantee the churches—Gentile and Jewish—full freedom of worship and not interfere in their inner life, but they still could demand of the regime that it maintain and further a "more abundant life" for all citizens.[32]

Two months earlier, the president had delivered a similar message to the National Conference of Catholic Charities. He mentioned the "practical application of the teachings of Christianity," referred to efforts at alleviating human suffering as evidence that "God is marching on," and affirmed the goal of "giving every man his due." He praised the rekindling of America's pioneering spirit, which he labeled the "spirit of neighborliness." A democracy was bound together by the ties of neighborliness; human beings could not live unto themselves alone. The charitable endeavors of the churches were vital, since government agencies could not do the job themselves. The churches were able to maintain the personal contact between neighbor and neighbor, while the spiritual values they instilled counted for more in the long run than material values. Those in other lands who sought to eliminate the right of people to believe in God and to practice that belief:

> have in every known case, discovered sooner or later that they are tilting in vain against an inherent, essential, undying quality, indeed necessity, of the human race—a quality and a necessity which in every century have proved an essential to permanent progress—and I speak of religion.

He had not doubted for a moment that we would "climb out of the valley of gloom," since the spirit of our people "has not been daunted." The measures of recovery and relief have preserved the best in American history and a new structure was being built on these. We would conquer the depression because "the spirit of America springs from faith—faith in the beloved institutions of our land, and a true and abiding faith in the divine guidance of God."[33] In a radio address on Brotherhood Day, February 23, 1936, the chief executive told the nation that America was not the product of any single race, creed, or class, and that religious understanding was a necessity because the best in the American tradition was the spiritual. The qualities of "faith in God and man" were needed for the fulfillment of the American vision. He welcomed "a revival of the spirit of religion," one that:

> would sweep through the homes of the Nation and stir the hearts of men and women of all faiths to a reassertion of their belief in God and their dedication to His will for themselves and for the world. I doubt if there is any

problem—social, political, or economic—that would not melt away before the fire of such a spiritual awakening.

If people would meet together to "pool our spiritual resources" and thereby discover ways of mutual and neighborly helpfulness, they could find common ground on which all of us could stand and then move forward "as men and women concerned for the things of the spirit."[34]

THE CRISIS OF WORLD WAR II

An expanded civil religion consensus based on brotherhood and harmonious relationships among the faiths contributed to restoring confidence in the national institutions which had been brought low by the depression. But Roosevelt also used it to strengthen public resolve to resist the growing threat to America's security poised by militant, expansionistic regimes in Europe and Asia. It played a key role in arousing awareness to the ever-widening international crisis, uniting a hitherto divided people in the war effort, and bringing the United States through to final victory.

The 1936 Brotherhood Day address contained an ominous note that increasingly was appearing in Roosevelt's statements, that democracy faced a growing threat from "godless" dictatorships. Here he suggested that the chief religious issue was not between the Christian and Jewish faiths but "between belief and unbelief." It was not any of the specific faiths that were being called into question, but all faith. Religion was confronted with irreligion, and because of that threat, "you and I must reach across the lines between our creeds, clasp hands, and make common cause."[35]

On December 1, 1936, at the Inter-American Conference for the Maintenance of Peace in Buenos Aires, Argentina, President Roosevelt made an impassioned speech heralding the democracy found in the Americas as the hope of the world. After enumerating democracy's many benefits, he served notice that it would be incomplete if the nations of the West did not affirm their faith in God. He argued that the human race was distinguished from other forms of life by the existence of religion and all attempts to deny God have and would come to naught. Freedom of religion was in the constitutions and practice of the American states, but this presupposed a belief and trust in God. Thus, the faith of these countries "lies in the spirit" and "the sisterhood of the Americas is impregnable so long as her Nations maintain that spirit. In that faith and spirit we will have peace over the Western Hemisphere."[36]

As the Japanese armies marched into China, the Italians into Ethiopia, and the Germans into Austria, the world edged ever closer to war. Roosevelt tried to move the United States away from its stance of storm-cellar neutrality, but public disillusionment with World War I and the upsurge of isolationism thwarted his efforts.[37] On numerous occasions he sought to convince Congress of the need to put "our own house in order in the face of storm signals from across the seas"—to no avail. The resolution of the Czechoslovakian crisis in the Munich agreement only made him more aware than ever of how dangerous the international situation had become, and so on January 4, 1939, he confronted the matter head-on in his State of the Union Address.

The president pointed out that undeclared wars were raging around the world and that the arms race was growing steadily more deadly. The storms from abroad directly challenged three institutions indispensable to Americans— religion, democracy, and international good faith. Religion, by teaching man his relationship to God, gave the individual a sense of his own dignity and taught him to respect himself by respecting others. Democracy was a covenant among free people to honor the rights and liberties of their fellows. International good faith sprang from the will of civilized nations to respect the rights and liberties of other nations. In a modern civilization all three complemented one other.

But now, freedom of religion was under attack by sources opposed to democracy, and free worship disappeared wherever democracy was overthrown. And when both vanished, good faith and reason in international affairs would give way to strident ambition and brute force. Therefore:

> An ordering of society which relegates religion, democracy, and good faith among nations to the background can find no place within it for the ideals of the Prince of Peace. The United States rejects such an ordering, and retains its ancient faith.

> There comes a time in the affairs of men when they must prepare to defend, not their homes alone, but the tenets

of faith and humanity on which their churches, their governments, and their very civilization are founded. The defense of religion, of democracy, and of good faith among nations is all the same fight. To save one we must now make up our minds to save all. . . .

God-fearing democracies of the world which observe the sanctity of treaties and good faith in their dealings with other nations cannot safely be indifferent to international lawlessness anywhere.[38]

The outbreak of war in Europe in September, the fall of France in the following spring, and the great aerial assault on Britain made this for Roosevelt no mere academic question. In the following months, he instituted military conscription, undertook a massive effort to rearm America, developed an Atlantic defense program, declared the United States to be the "arsenal of democracy" that would assist the beleaguered democracies, and pushed the momentous Lend-Lease program through Congress. His readiness to use civil religion concepts to whip up public support for this in a highly divided country could be seen in three important addresses.

In a campaign speech in Cleveland on November 2, 1940, he talked about the "deeply ethical principles" on which America and its democracy was founded and the necessity for national unity which would make the country prosperous, free, strong, and "a light of the world and a comfort to all people." If such an ethically based national unity were achieved, "all the forces of evil [could] not prevail against it," for so it was "written in the Book" as well as in the moral law. In eloquent terms, he set forth a vision of America, one which would point the road to the future for all the world to see. One element of it would be "an America devoted to our freedom—unified by tolerance and by religious faith—a people consecrated to peace, a people confident in strength because their body and their spirit are secure and unafraid." He ended by affirming: "The spirit of the common man is the spirit of peace and good will. It is the spirit of God. And in His faith is the strength of all America."[39]

Two months later in his State of the Union message, Roosevelt extended his vision of the future to that of a world founded on "four essential human freedoms"—freedom of

speech and expression, freedom to worship God in one's
way, freedom from want (economic well-being), and freedom from fear (reduction of armaments to the point that no
country could commit aggression against its neighbor). This
was no vision of a distant millennium but a kind of world
attainable in our own time through the cooperation of free
countries working together in a civilized society, and it was
the "very antithesis of the so-called new order of tyranny"
which the dictators were seeking to create. Our nation "has
placed its destiny in the hands and heads and hearts of its
millions of free men and women; and its faith in freedom
under the guidance of God," and he pledged that the United
States would support those people everywhere who were
struggling for human rights.[40]

His Navy Day radio speech (October 27, 1941) was
designed to impress upon the American public the peril
which faced civilization if Hitler triumphed. To achieve this,
he revealed a "secret map" which contained Germany's
design for the new order in the Americas and a "detailed
plan" of the Nazis "to abolish all existing religions—Catholic, Protestant, Mohammedan, Hindu, Buddhist, and Jewish
alike." It called for the seizure of all church property,
forbidding the cross and other symbols of religion, liquidation of the clergy, and creation of an "International Nazi
Church" which would be served by orators sent out by the
regime. The Bible as Holy Writ would be replaced by *Mein
Kampf*, and the cross by the swastika and the naked sword.
"The god of Blood and Iron" would take the place of "the
God of Love and Mercy." Roosevelt's listeners were urged to
"well ponder" what he said and to support his efforts "to
end the curse of Hitlerism" and establish a new peace which
would allow "decent people everywhere a better chance to
live and prosper in security and in freedom and in faith."[41]

One action with serious religious ramifications was
Roosevelt's establishment of unofficial diplomatic relations
with the Holy See. The president had met Cardinal Eugenio
Pacelli in 1936 when, as papal secretary of state on a visit to
the United States, the cardinal called on him at Hyde Park. In
1939, Pacelli became Pope Pius XII. On December 23,
Roosevelt informed the new pope that he would like to send
a representative in order that "our parallel endeavors for
peace and the alleviation of suffering might be assisted."
Pius was agreeable and Roosevelt named his "old and good

friend," Myron C. Taylor, the board chairman of U.S. Steel, as his personal envoy. He wrote the pope that Taylor, actually an Episcopalian, would serve as the channel of communications for any views they might wish to exchange "in the interest of concord among the peoples of the world," and it was his "sincere hope that the common ideals of religion and humanity itself can have united expression for the re-establishment of a more permanent peace on the foundations of freedom and an assurance of life and integrity of all nations under God."[42]

Although the primary objective was to secure a listening post in the heart of Fascist Italy, this relationship had civil religion written all over it, but many Protestants, liberals and conservatives alike, criticized it as a threat to the principle of church-state separation. One curious thing that transpired through the Vatican connection was Roosevelt's unsuccessful effort to convince Pius that the religious situation in the Soviet Union was not as bad as that in Germany. He wrote the pope on September 3, 1941, that he had been informed the "churches in Russia are open" and the regime might even recognize freedom of religion there, although no church would be able to intervene in educational or political matters. If this could be accomplished, the possibility of the restoration "of real religious liberty" in Russia would be on a much better footing than in Germany. Moreover, the Soviet dictatorship was less dangerous to the safety of other nations than the German variety, because the only weapon it used outside its borders was communist propaganda while the Germans utilized "every form of military aggression for the purpose of world conquest." Thus, Russia's survival was less dangerous to religion, the church, and humanity in general than the German dictatorship. He wished that church leaders in the United States would recognize these facts clearly,since "by their present attitude on this question" [i.e., anticommunism] they "directly assist Germany in her present objectives."[43]

Once the United States was drawn into the hostilities, the chief executive frequently appealed to his fellow Americans' faith in God and sense of national purpose. In the War Message to Congress after the attack on Pearl Harbor, he eloquently denounced the Japanese treachery and reaffirmed his faith in America's "righteous might," declaring that "with confidence in our armed forces—with the unbounding determination of our people—we will gain the inevitable triumph—so help us God." He asked the nation to set aside New Year's Day, 1942 as a day of prayer for divine guidance, and in his State of the Union address on January 6, he declared the dictators knew that victory for us meant victory for freedom, the institution of democracy, the ideal of the family, the simple principles of common decency and humanity, and religion. They could not tolerate that because "the world is too small to provide adequate 'living room' for both Hitler and God." While the enemy was guided by brutal cynicism and contempt for the human race, Americans were fighting to cleanse the world of ancient ills and were inspired by the faith that "God created man in His own image." Further, they were fighting to defend the doctrine that all are equal in the sight of God against an enemy which attempted to create a world in its own image of tyranny, cruelty, and serfdom. Because this was a conflict between good and evil, no compromise could end it. Only "total victory" could reward the champions of tolerance, decency, freedom, and faith.[44]

Roosevelt also emphasized prayer as a weapon in the struggle. He read a "United Nations" (the World War II alliance) prayer on Flag Day, June 14, 1942, that asked God to grant victory over the tyrants and give us faith, understanding, brotherhood, wisdom, patience, skill, and valor. He also asked God for "a common faith" that people throughout the world would possess bread, peace, justice, righteousness, freedom, security, and an equal opportunity to excel. He proclaimed both Thanksgiving Day, 1942, and New Year's Day, 1943, as days of prayer where we would "solemnly express our dependence on Almighty God."[45]

Then, at the time of the Normandy invasion, Roosevelt recited the prayer quoted at the beginning of the chapter. Although carefully planned, the operation was extremely risky, and to him prayer seemed to be a better way of rallying the nation than presidential oratory. This remarkable action utilized the potential of the public faith to bond Americans together in a holy and righteous cause. It looked forward to victory "in our united crusade," both to save the country from the "apostles of greed and racial arrogance" and to lead the nations into a "world unity" that would spell a sure peace and allow all people to live in freedom and reap the rewards of their honest toil.[46]

THE EXPANDED CIVIL RELIGION

By promoting harmony, tolerance, and brotherhood, Roosevelt did much to break down barriers between Catholics and Protestants, counter the evil of anti-Semitism, and integrate the "three great faiths" into a national consensus. He then drew on the resources of civil religion to rally the public in the struggle against inhuman and allegedly godless dictatorships. Finally, as the following illustrations reveal, the public faith effectively assisted in the war effort.

On February 3, 1943, the *Dorchester*, a troopship bound for Europe,was torpedoed off Greenland. Four army chaplains, two Protestant, one Roman Catholic, and one Jewish, passed out life jackets, and when the supply was exhausted, they gave their own to soldiers who had none. As the ship went down, they were last seen standing on the deck, arms locked, and praying. Hailed as an inspirational example— "men of all faiths can be proud that these men of different faiths died together"—they were posthumously awarded Distinguished Service Crosses in a widely publicized ceremony.[47]

In fact, nothing typified more the civil religion consensus than the army and navy chaplaincy. Edward L. R. Elson, a Presbyterian pastor and high-ranking World War II chaplain, maintained that no other military establishment "in all history" provided for the spiritual needs of servicemen and women like that of the United States. Ministers with qualifications equal to their clerical contemporaries were drawn from "all phases of our religious culture" on a proportional basis, and the government provided them with chapels and "the best field equipment ever developed" and paid their salaries.[48]

On May 21, 1944, a festival of national solidarity called "I Am an American Day" was held in New York's Central Park. Over a million people gathered to watch 150,000 new citizens take the Oath of Allegiance for the first time and to hear speeches by various dignitaries. Representatives of the three faiths delivered prayers calling for victory and peace, including Rabbi Stephen S. Wise, who prayed that American war aims would "prove worthy of Thy blessing" and pleaded for a "spirit of deepened and ennobled loyalty to our country" and a "spirit of brotherliness to one another across all barriers of race and faith." The eminent Judge Learned

Hand of the U.S. Circuit Court of Appeals told the multitude that as Americans they were there to affirm faith in liberty. He stressed that the "spirit of liberty" moved people to seek to understand the minds and interests of others, and it "is the spirit of Him who, nearly two thousand years ago, taught mankind. . .that there may be a kingdom where the least shall be heard and considered side by side with the greatest."[49]

Although he was not noted for his personal piety, President Roosevelt had recognized the importance of a public faith which could join the people together in spiritual solidarity during a critical time of trial. Unfortunately, a fatal stroke on April 12, 1945, denied him the opportunity to see the victory for which he had striven so hard. His successors, Harry S. Truman and especially Dwight D. Eisenhower, would intensify and expand the new civil religion consensus and root it even deeper in American life.

8

DWIGHT D. EISENHOWER
AND THE INTENSIFICATION
OF CIVIL RELIGION

At a glittering luncheon in the luxurious Waldorf-Astoria
Hotel in New York City in December 1952, President-elect
Dwight D. Eisenhower addressed the directors of the
Freedoms Foundation, a conservative patriotic organization.
In the course of his remarks he dropped a memorable
phrase: "Our form of government has no sense unless it is
founded in a deeply felt religious faith, and I don't care what
it is."[1]

His comment was couched in a cold war context, and he
was speaking to a group that upheld patriotism and religion
as weapons to be used in the ideological conflict with
"godless international communism." It illustrated just how
much the Judeo-Christian civil religion consensus was being
enhanced and harnessed in the struggle. In this "golden
age" of the 1950s, a generalized religiosity permeated the
national institutions, and many Americans were convinced
that "belief in God" was what distinguished their country
from Soviet communism with its officially sponsored
atheism.

THE COLD WAR AND PASTORAL CIVIL RELIGION

In the cold war years, the president came to play what
amounted to a pastoral role. He comforted his people, gave

them wise leadership, and served as a spiritual example. Eisenhower seemed ideally suited for the job. Not only was he the great hero of World War II, a military man who stood above politics and was motivated by duty, not personal gain, but also he had claimed, "I am the most intensely religious man I know."[2] He extricated the country from the Korean War, advocated moderate solutions to divisive political problems, and promoted religious values in a way which linked personal and public faith. The pluralism that now dominated the religious landscape insured that only free-thinkers, agnostics, and atheistic humanists who did not acknowledge a Supreme Being would lie outside the civil religion pale. The question of whether adherents of non-Western faiths like Muslims, Hindus, and Buddhists also could be integrated into the civil religion consensus that was being intensified and extended throughout American society in the Eisenhower era was not seriously discussed. Still, the logic of the situation seemed to indicate that sooner or later they would have to be included as well.

THE MAKING OF A SOLDIER PRESIDENT

Dwight David Eisenhower came from a humble back-ground.[3] His parents, David Eisenhower (1863–1942) and Ida Stover (1862–1946), were born into Pennsylvania German families that belonged to a group called the River Brethren;[4] and both of them found their way to colonies founded by the group in Kansas. They were married in 1885 and settled in Abilene where they raised six boys, of which Dwight was the third. The elder Eisenhower lost everything in a business bankruptcy and temporarily worked on the M.K.T. railroad in Denison, Texas, where Dwight was born on October 14, 1890. The following year he returned to Abilene to take a job in a creamery as a mechanic and twenty-five years later switched to the gas company. A frugal, industrious man, he did not particularly distinguish himself in the community.

Religion played a fairly significant role in the home life of the Eisenhower family.[5] Family worship was held twice a day which included Bible readings as a regular feature, and the parents shunned vices like smoking, drinking, swearing, card playing, and gambling. Still, church attendance apparently was not stressed, the devotional activities were purely mechanical in nature, and because of the Anabaptist nature of the River Brethren, the boy Dwight was not baptized. When he was around ten years old, his mother joined the Jehovah's Witnesses, and his father eventually followed her into the sect, but with little enthusiasm. The latter was a harsh disciplinarian but their home was serene and secure, and life in the small community on the Kansas prairie was peaceful and idyllic. The boys were taught to be honest, hard-working, obedient, and self-reliant, with the emphasis placed on accomplishment rather than intellectual effort and contemplation, and on caution rather than creativity. As Stephen Ambrose puts it, they learned to be managers, not artists, scholars, or political thinkers.[6]

In school, Dwight made good grades but at the same time was an enthusiast for sports (baseball and football) and the outdoor life (hunting, fishing, and camping). In fact, it was in the area of sports that he first demonstrated his talents as a leader and organizer. Then, an event occurred that later was much embellished in the literature of popular piety. His leg became infected as the result of a minor knee abrasion, and the doctors decided that only an amputation would save his life. The fourteen-year-old high schooler insisted that he would rather die than allow his leg to be cut off, and he had his older brother stay by the bedside to prevent the operation from taking place. Finally, the infection receded and after a long convalescence he recovered. Later, countless inspirational stories alleged that the whole family had prayed day and night for his recovery, but the Eisenhower boys insisted that prayer was a normal part of the family's life and denied that their parents had done anything out of the ordinary.[7]

After completing high school in 1909, Dwight worked at the creamery and applied for a senatorial appointment to the U.S. Naval Academy. However, he was offered a nomination to the U.S. Military Academy, and he saw the opportunity as too good to turn down. Although his parents were pacifists, neither of them sought to dissuade him, but there are indications that his strong-willed mother never accepted her son's choice of a military career. At West Point he was a good but not brilliant student (he finished 61 in a class of 164), and his main love was football until a knee injury sidelined him. Then he turned to coaching where he demonstrated the traits that were to mark his entire career—

optimism, organizational skill, competitiveness, enthusiasm, hard work, powers of concentration, talent for working with the material available, ability to draw out the best in subordinates, and dedication to team work. There he also picked up the military's prejudice against politicians and self-serving civilians.

In 1915 he graduated, was commissioned, and assigned to Fort Sam Houston, Texas, where he met Mary Geneva (Mamie) Doud, the daughter of a prosperous Denver businessman. Six years his junior, she married Eisenhower in 1916; they had two sons, one of whom died in infancy. Because of the nature of military life, they never lived in any one place for a substantial length of time until he became president. Although Eisenhower avidly sought overseas duty during World War I, he was assigned to various posts in the United States where he gained considerable organizational experience and also worked with tanks, a new weapon with great potential. After the war ended, the army was reduced to a minuscule size which meant he was frozen at the rank of major for the next sixteen years.

The 1920s and 1930s proved a relatively uneventful time of apprenticeship. He served in a number of places, including the Panama Canal Zone, Paris, the Philippines, and Washington, D.C. Although by 1940 he had only risen to lieutenant colonel, he had served under or with several important figures in the American military establishment, above all, Douglas A. MacArthur. In these years he learned how to deal with bureaucracies and politicians and carry out military planning—the very kind of skills that enabled him to coordinate the Allied effort in World War II and to lead the United States as president.

With the coming of war in Europe, Eisenhower rose quickly in the hierarchy and by 1941 was a one-star general. Immediately after Pearl Harbor, the army chief of staff, General George C. Marshall, summoned him to Washington and put him in charge of planning the Far Eastern campaign. Then in early 1942, Marshall made him head of the entire war planning operation. He developed the scheme for a unified Allied command in Western Europe, and in June was named commander of the European Theater of Operations. He directed the attacks on North Africa and Italy, and on Christmas Eve 1943 was appointed Supreme Allied Commander in Europe. Eisenhower's greatest achievement was carrying out Operation Overlord, the invasion of France in 1944. After that, he was elevated to five-star general and steered the Allies to final victory in May 1945. At the same time, he attempted to work out amicable relations with the Soviets and viewed the postwar future with great optimism. Gradually his assessment of the Russians changed, and he soon developed a hard-line anticommunist stance.

The general's career, however, was far from over. Following V-E Day, he directed the American occupation forces in Germany and in November returned home to become army chief of staff. He was increasingly in the public eye, and speculation mounted about the possibility of a presidential candidacy in 1948. Instead, he retired from the army early in the year, wrote his war memoirs, *Crusade in Europe*, which became an instant best-seller, and assumed the presidency of Columbia University in New York City. Although he seems to have enjoyed the position, President Truman persuaded him to accept the command of the newly created North Atlantic Treaty Organization forces. In December 1950 he went on indefinite leave from Columbia (he formally resigned in November 1952) to take up this new challenge.

At his post in Paris, Eisenhower could avoid making comments about domestic and partisan issues in the United States, while at the same time he worked on developing the Atlantic alliance and embellishing his image as a statesman. More and more he was being touted as a presidential candidate, even though it was not altogether certain as to which political party he belonged. After his name had been entered in some early primaries in 1952, he decided in April to give up the NATO job and return to the United States to run as a Republican. He swamped the Robert Taft forces in the party convention to gain the nomination, which necessitated that he resign from the army. (Congress restored his five-star general's commission in 1961.) The campaign took the theme of a moral crusade against governmental corruption and godless communism, although in reality the candidate adopted a middle-of-the-road, conciliatory approach and presented himself as a decent, fair-minded man who was a born and experienced leader. He said he was accepting the challenge of the presidency, not for personal ambition but because it was his duty, and he promised the American people peace with prosperity, a reduction in the size of the federal government, dignity in the White House, and the elimination of communists and crooks in Washington. His decisive victory over Adlai Stevenson in November demonstrated the magnitude of his personal popularity.[8] For most Americans the next eight years were comfortable ones. The frustrating war in Korea was ended, conflict in China and Vietnam was avoided, tensions between the United States and Soviet Union eased somewhat, and the economy did well. The increasing tempo of the civil rights movement and the demands of black Americans for full equality, the anticommunist crusading of Joseph McCarthy and others of his ilk, the Sputnik crisis, and the worsening of East-West relations in the late 1950s cast dark shadows on this otherwise tranquil scene; but Eisenhower showed himself to be an effective manager and retained his popularity to the end. He spent his last years in retirement as a respected elder statesman and died peacefully in 1969.

THE COLD WAR AND RELIGIOSITY

The popularity of preachers like Billy Graham, Norman Vincent Peale, and Fulton Sheen and the rising level of church and synagogue membership were indicators of the postwar religious resurgence which many called a "revival." This flowering of institutional religion was closely linked to the expansion and diffusion of civil religion. Moreover, the latter came to be a prime weapon in the American cold war arsenal, as politicians and preachers alike extolled the virtues of patriotism and religion in the struggle with "godless international communism." Eisenhower made good use of it long before he set foot in the White House, even as Truman had during his administration.[9]

For example, in his 1949 inaugural address, Truman set forth a four-point program for combating the "false philosophy" of communism and offered civil religion as the counterweight to it. He maintained that "the essential principles of the faith by which we live" were the rights to equal justice under the law, equal opportunity to share in the common good, and freedom of thought and expression. All people were equal because they were "created in the image of God." The difference between democracy and communism involved "material well-being, human dignity, and the right to believe in and worship God." He assured his fellow

Americans: "Steadfast in our faith in the Almighty, we will advance toward a world where man's freedom is secure."[10]

In 1950, a few days before the outbreak of the Korean War, Truman told a Lutheran delegation that the United States had become the "leader of the moral forces of the world." Americans believed that the law under which they lived was "God-given," since their "traditions have come from Moses at Sinai, and Jesus on the Mount." However, there were those [he implied the Soviet communists] who "do not believe in a moral code" and "even go so far as to say there is no Supreme Being." The following year, he asserted at the cornerstone laying for the New York Avenue Presbyterian Church in Washington that "religion should establish moral standards for the conduct of our whole Nation, at home and abroad." He insisted that "our religious faith" provided the answer to the "false beliefs of Communism" and that God had brought the nation to its present position of power and strength "for some great purpose." Thus, it was America's duty "to defend the spiritual values—the moral code—against the vast forces of evil that seek to destroy them."[11]

Shortly after his dismissal from the command in Korea and triumphal return home in 1951, General Douglas MacArthur affirmed the need for patriotic fervor and religious devotion. He said there could be "no compromise with atheistic Communism—no half-way in the preservation of freedom and religion. It must be all or nothing." Some were seeking to convert America to a form of socialistic endeavor that would lead directly to communism, but this was counterbalanced by a "deep spiritual urge in the hearts of our people." This spirituality was America's great safeguard and resource, and it served as

> an infallible reminder that our greatest hope and faith rests upon two mighty symbols—the Cross and the Flag; the one based upon those immutable teachings which provide the spiritual strength to persevere along the course which is just and right—the other based upon the invincible will that human freedom shall not perish from the earth. These are the mighty bulwarks against the advance of those atheistic predatory forces which seek to destroy the spirituality of the human mind and to enslave the human body.

To this he added: "Our Christian faith" is the "mighty bulwark of all freedom."[12]

No one in these times was more forceful in affirming religion in general and Christianity in particular as the answer to the communist challenge than the youthful evangelist, Billy Graham. His meteoric rise to stardom in 1949–50 took the country by surprise, and he became not only the central figure in American evangelicalism for the next three decades but also the confidant of presidents in a manner unparalleled in the nation's history. In his path-breaking Los Angeles Crusade in 1949, Graham served notice that the world was divided into two camps. On the one side was Western culture which had its foundations in the Bible and the great revivals; on the other was communism which had declared its opposition to God, Christ, the Bible, and all religion and was "inspired, directed, and motivated by the Devil himself." He publicly prayed for American victory in the Korean War, bitterly condemned the MacArthur firing, and made a Christmas visit to Korea in 1952. He praised the congressional investigating committees who were exposing undercover communists and lamented that America was "rapidly becoming a second-rate power" even as the communists were drawing on the "supernatural powers" provided by the devil. In various sermons in 1951, he declared that "communism is a fanatical religion that has declared war on the Christian God," America "is engaged in a death struggle with it," and "over 20,000 have been slain for the name of Christ in Korea since the war began."[13]

To help show the country's spiritual colors, public and private bodies alike sprang into action. Congress in April 1952, adopted a resolution mandating the president once a year to "set aside and proclaim" a National Day of Prayer in which the citizenry "may turn to God in prayer and meditation at churches in groups, and as individuals;" every chief executive since then has dutifully carried out this charge.[14] At its 1951 national convention the American Legion decided to sponsor an annual "Back to God" observance to commemorate the heroic deaths of the four chaplains on the *Dorchester* in 1943. The Legion intended to increase the awareness of God in people's lives by urging them to seek divine guidance in their everyday activities and to engage in regular church attendance, daily family prayer, and the religious training of youth.[15] One of the Legion's founders and veteran State Department official, Herve J. L'Heureux, proposed a "Prayer-for-Peace" movement to the patriotic group in 1948, and the idea spread widely in the early 1950s.[16]

In 1951, an interfaith committee initiated an annual "Pilgrimage to Washington," a three-day tour of places of artistic, cultural, and historical interest in the capital. The leaders conducted religious observances at these spots and bestowed a "Churchman of the Year" award at a banquet. At the 1952 pilgrimage dinner, six presidential hopefuls appeared and joined in calling for a "moral revival" in the United States. In 1951 and 1953, Senator Ralph E. Flanders of Vermont tried to revive the Christian Amendment, the idea that the Constitution would be changed to include a reference acknowledging the nation's allegiance to Jesus Christ, but this so blatantly flew in the face of the civil religion consensus that his bill never got out of committee.[17]

EISENHOWER'S REDISCOVERY OF RELIGION

There is little indication that Dwight Eisenhower was concerned about religious matters prior to World War II.[18] Commentators often note that during much of his army career he had not attended church regularly, although occasionally he went to the post chapel. Possibly this may have been a reaction to his mother's conversion to the Jehovah's Witnesses; but the evidence is far too sketchy to render a firm judgment. It is clear, however, that his experiences as a commander during the war revived the dormant faith he had acquired as a youth. In the same interview in 1948 where he said he was "the most intensely religious man I know," he added that "nobody goes through six years of war without faith." Then, he qualified this by saying, "that doesn't mean I adhere to any sect." Actually, what he reflected was the "army chapel approach to religion," the transdenominational faith that is propagated through the military chaplaincy.

Already during the war, stories of "Ike's" piety had begun to appear. One was that of his "little service." This held that as the Allied forces were departing from Malta for the assault on Sicily in July 1943, the general went to the top of a high hill with a small group of his staff to watch the operation. Deeply moved by the spectacle, he suddenly snapped to a rigid state of attention, lifted his hand reverently in a formal salute, and then dropped his hand and bowed his head in a short silent prayer. After this, he turned to an aide and said: "There comes a time when you have done all that you can possibly do, when you have used your brains, your training, and your technical skill, when the die is cast, and events are in the hands of God—and there you have to leave them."[19]

Unsubstantiated accounts also circulated about him spending hours on his knees before he gave the final order for the invasion of France, much like the legendary prayer of George Washington at Valley Forge. During the 1952 presidential campaign he probably fed the myth when he spoke of "the most agonizing decision of my life" that was made on the occasion. He had to postpone the landing because of adverse weather conditions, and the consequences of this could have been disastrous. However, his action prevented an almost certain failure from occurring,and Eisenhower concluded from the experience:

> If there were nothing else in my life to prove the existence of an almighty and merciful God, the events of the next twenty-four hours did it. This is what I found out about religion. It gives you courage to make the decisions you must make in a crisis, and then the confidence to leave the result to higher power. Only by trust in one's self and trust in God can a man carrying responsibility find repose.[20]

The necessity to justify his calling as a commander was what impelled Eisenhower to come to terms with the matter of faith. He later confessed that the question which individual soldiers asked him most frequently was: "Why are we here?" He found that the key to the answer was religious:

> I believe that every soldier—every American soldier, at least—seeking to find within his own soul some reason for being on the battlefield, for enduring the things he has to endure there, has in the long run got to fix this relationship [to the service of God] in his own mind if he is to be really a soldier who can carry forward the terrible load that devolves upon him in those circumstances.

His response was that "they were defending a free way of life, and that free way of life was imbedded deeply in the religious faith of their fathers." [21]

Reflecting on his war experiences in a speech to the Military Chaplains Association in 1954, he reiterated that it was important to fix in the minds of his soldiers what they were fighting for—the whole system that provided them a free home, free way to life, free education, free expression—was based on a religious foundation. He went on to praise Cromwell's soldiers—who marched into battle singing hymns while they hewed off heads with a sweep of their swords—because they were "wildly enthusiastic" about the cause for which they were fighting. They believed there was a direct connection between what they were risking their lives to do and "something very deep in their souls." Thus, each individual American fighting man needed to know what his country stood for and that the cause for which he fought was spiritual in its origin and essence.[22]

Eisenhower saw World War II as a "crusade," a fact reflected in the title of his war memoirs. His men were engaged in a life-and-death struggle with Axis tyranny, and freedom was a value derived from their status as children of God. The Allied nations were fighting to uphold democracy, a political concept that made no sense apart from its religious foundations. His stance was illustrated in an oft-cited conversation with the Soviet commander Georgi K. Zhukov shortly after V-E Day, where he tried to explain the American philosophy of government. Marshal Zhukov claimed that the Soviets were having difficulty in promulgating their theory of civilization and government because the appeal was made to the "idealistic" in people, while the Americans did better because theirs appealed to all that was "materialistic and selfish." Eisenhower, however, decided it was "hopeless" to talk to his Russian counterpart about the American form of government, since it was "founded in religion" and the Soviets believed the latter was "the opiate of the people."[23]

EISENHOWER'S CIVIL RELIGION

Eisenhower constructed his civil religion on this premise, and he elaborated upon it in speech after speech in the post-war years and during his presidency. It was articulated most eloquently in the earlier cited address before the Freedoms Foundation on December 22, 1952. After relating the Zhukov anecdote, he argued that the Founding Fathers separated from Britain and formed a new order based, not on accident or birth or color of skin, but on the idea that "all men are endowed by their Creator." He went on to say:

> In other words, our form of Government has no sense unless it is founded in a deeply felt religious faith, and I don't care what it is. With us of course it is the Jud[e]o-Christian concept but it must be a religion that all men are created equal . . . .

> Even those among us who are, in my opinion, so silly as to doubt the existence of an Almighty, are still members of a religious civilization, because the Founding Fathers said it was a religious concept they were trying to translate into the political world.

This was "the basic doctrine to which we must always cling," and he urged his hearers to become familiar with the tenets of that religion as well as the political teachings that have come down to us. He then exhorted his audience:

> Have I done my duty unless, in all my conduct, in my examples with my fellow citizens, I am living this democracy, indeed this religion, the tenets of this religion? Until I have done that I am not doing my best.

If Americans could fulfill that charge, they would win the ideological war with communism, ensure a peaceful and free world, and pass on to their grandchildren the kind of life which would "guarantee them opportunity to live in dignified fashion with their God and their fellow citizens."[24]

In this statement one can identify the three key elements that constituted Eisenhower's public faith. First was the emphasis on the individual as a spiritual being and spiritual matters in general. At a Daughters of the American Revolution convention in 1947, he declared:

> Insistence upon individual freedom springs from unshakeable conviction in the dignity of man, a belief—a religious belief—that through the possession of a soul he is endowed with certain rights that are his not by sufferance of others, but by reason of his very existence.[25]

At the cornerstone laying for the Eisenhower Museum in Abilene in June 1952, he talked about faith, the "real fire" within the builders of America:

> Faith in a Provident God whose hand supported and guided them; faith in themselves as the children of God,

endowed with purposes beyond the mere struggle for survival; faith in their country and its principles that proclaimed man's right to freedom and justice, rights derived from his divine origin. Today, the nation they built stands as the world's mightiest temporal power, with its position still rooted in faith and in spiritual values.[26]

In his acceptance speech at the Republican National Convention a month later, the candidate asserted that "we are now at a moment in history when, under God, this nation of ours has become the mightiest temporal power and the mightiest spiritual force on earth."[27]

From a platform in Boston on the eve of the election, Eisenhower expounded on the didactic function of "faith." According to him, faith taught that we are the children of God, that each person's dignity had a divine origin, that our brotherhood had a sublime meaning only when understood to be under God's fatherhood, and that our ideals of democracy and freedom must be much more than sentimental moods or romantic notions. The latter are not the tender inventions of poets, he maintained, but eternal laws of the human spirit.[28] This did not differ substantially from what he had said two years earlier at Columbia University—that no human being, regardless of his station in life, "merits more respect than any other animal of the woods or fields unless we accept without reservation the brotherhood of man under the fatherhood of God. If men are not creatures of soul, as well as of body, they are not better than the field mule." He acknowledged that some people defined human welfare in material terms, but it was really the "things of the spirit" like justice, freedom, and equality that satisfied people's creative needs.[29]

In his 1954 State of the Union Address, President Eisenhower mentioned that the American people "have always reserved their first allegiance to the kingdom of the spirit." He told the young people assembled at the World Christian Endeavor Convention in July 1954, that a "spiritual base" underlay all free government. As long as we recognized "the spiritual values in man" and "the dependency of free government upon these spiritual values," then everything the administration was trying to do would make sense.[30] Even further, he informed the Washington Hebrew Congregation that the United States was "a spiritual organism" and the president was the official head of a nation which was "religious in its background" and stood on "a spiritual foundation."[31]

The second component was his assumption that American democracy in particular rested on a spiritual foundation. In December 1946, the general declared that he was "a fanatical devotee of the American system of democracy." It possessed "two fundamentals"—a deep and abiding religious faith among the people and a system of freedoms and rights for the individual that generally would be called "free enterprise." In 1948, he asserted that "a democracy cannot exist without a religious base" and that "I believe in democracy."[32] In 1952, he asserted that "free government is the political expression of a deeply felt religious faith," and that it could not be explained "in any other terms than religious." He insisted that the Founders

> had to refer to the Creator in order to make their revolutionary experiment make sense: it was because "all men are endowed by their Creator with certain inalienable rights: that men could dare to be free."[33]

He underscored this strongly at the first Presidential Prayer Breakfast in 1953 where he interpreted the statement in the Declaration of Independence about our rights having come from the Creator: "In one sentence we established that every free government is imbedded soundly in a deeply felt religious faith or it makes no sense." That was why prayer was so important; it was an effort to get in touch with the Infinite.[34] In his remarks for the 1953 "Back to God" program, the president maintained that the human rights we cherish so sincerely "are God-given" and "belong to the people who have been created in His image." Two years later, he said in the same context that "without God, there could be no American form of Government, nor an American way of life." The recognition of the Supreme Being was the first and most basic "expression of Americanism." Again, at a news conference in 1957, he repeated his stance:

> I believe that all forms of free government are based either knowingly or unknowingly on deeply held religious convictions, and that religious conviction is the equality of man that is acknowledged nowhere except that all men are the sons of a Creator, a common Creator.[35]

The third aspect of Eisenhower's civil religion was its crusading character. In his 1952 campaign pronouncements, he portrayed America as a chosen nation with a "continuing purpose." The "forefathers" demonstrated that only "a people strong in Godliness" could overcome tyranny and liberate themselves and others. Now it was up to America to prove that its perpetually renewed faith was equal to the challenge of today's tyrants. In his statement to the Episcopalian press, Eisenhower polemicized:

> What is our battle against communism if it is not a fight between anti-God and a belief in the Almighty? Communists know this. They have to eliminate God from their system. When God comes in, communism has to go.

A few days later, he told a rally in Billings, Montana, that a strong America was the only hope for peace in the world and the country needed a leadership imbued with the idea that the "Almighty takes a definite and direct interest, day by day, in the progress of this nation."[36]

On election eve he spoke of "organized evil challenging free men in their quest of peace." He said he knew the evil well—it was "Godless communism." It was "not a political nor a military enemy, but a moral enemy" that was challenging our security and fortune, and above all, "our very definition of life itself." The weapons required for the struggle were guns, international compacts, sound trade policies, and a firm currency, but more than anything else, "we must be armed with devotion to the morality of freedom." Then he quoted the familiar "America is great because she is good" passage from Alexis de Tocqueville's *Democracy in America*, and challenged his hearers to take up the righteous struggle.[37]

Repeatedly during his years in office, the president returned to the theme of the global struggle "between a civilization that is firmly based in a religious faith, and atheism or materialism." At the Christian Endeavor Convention, he referred to "the great conflict that is going on in the world today." In this, one side upheld the freedom and dignity of humanity and thereby recognized its spiritual character. The other lived by the materialistic dialectic and denied all of the values that the young people present supported. He concluded that:

only a great moral crusade, determined that men shall rise
above this conception of materialism, rise above it and live
as people who attempt to express in some faint and feeble
way their conceptions of what the Almighty would have
us do—that is the force that will win through to victory.
Then the world will have prosperity and peace.[38]

In a televised speech to the nation prior to his departure
to the Geneva Summit Conference in 1955, Eisenhower
maintained that the world was divided by an iron curtain.
The world's free population lived under one religion or
another and believed in a divine power and Supreme Being.
In this crucial moment it would be only natural for a people
steeped in a religious civilization to turn to the divine power
which all have in their own hearts for guidance, wisdom,
and help in order to do that which was right. He then called
on the 165 million religious Americans to crowd into their
places of worship on their next sabbaths, ask God for help,
and demonstrate to all the world their country's aspirations
for peace.[39]

In a commencement address at Mount St. Mary's
College in Emmitsburg, Maryland, in 1958, the president
called attention to the "global struggle" between "atheistic
communism and every kind of free government which has
its true roots in a deeply felt religious faith." He challenged
the graduates that, if they believed in human dignity, the
value of the individual's soul, and every right which "our
founders said was given to us by our Creator," they should
then hold fast to the conviction that the struggle was truly "a
combat with this atheistic doctrine." The mission of the
United States was to carry freedom and liberty to the
emerging peoples of the world, so that they would not "fall
into immense dislocations and strange misunderstandings."[40]

The general, who once told a group of chaplains from
the NATO forces at a meeting in The Hague in 1952 that he
was a "convinced, nearly fanatic Protestant,"[41] espoused a
civil theology that in reality far exceeded particularistic
bounds. It emphasized God as the wellspring of individual
and national strength, government as resting on a spiritual
foundation, faith as a public virtue, and the utilitarian nature
of religion in the apocalyptic struggle against communism.
Eisenhower's admirers saw him as a man of great faith who
drew upon the resources of divine power in energizing the

nation to carry out its spiritual tasks. He was spearheading "America's spiritual recovery" and contributing to an "unparalleled" religious awakening in the land.[42]

Critics of his public faith were less sanguine. Most noteworthy was William Lee Miller, who penned a number of articles collected into a book entitled *Piety Along the Potomac*. He suggested that President Eisenhower, like many Americans, was a "fervent believer in a very vague religion." Eisenhower talked about "believing" or "faith" independent of its object ("the devoted people meeting here believe, first of all, always in faith," so he told the Evanston assembly of the World Council of Churches); he stressed feeling rather than content or meaning ("our form of government has no sense unless it is founded in a deeply felt religious faith, and I don't care what it is"); he recommended religion for its utility ("faith is the mightiest force that man has at his command"); he connected this generalized religion with the nation's "foundation"; and he distinguished the United States from the communist world on the grounds that our country was religious while the Soviets' was atheistic. Religion appeared to be little more than an endorsement of the aims and purposes of America, "the mightiest power which God has yet seen fit to put upon his footstool." In essence, the values which sprang from this commitment to religion-in-general were values in general, or as Eisenhower once put it: "Honesty, decency, fairness, service—all that sort of thing."[43]

THE PRESIDENT AS THE NATION'S PASTOR

Whether or not he fully understood the ramifications of his civil theology, Eisenhower took his pastoral duties very seriously. For example, he established cordial relationships with clergy from various religious traditions, regularly gave speeches at the meetings of Protestant (both ecumenical and evangelical), Roman Catholic, and Jewish bodies, and included two devout churchmen in his cabinet, John Foster Dulles, Secretary of State, and Ezra Taft Benson, Secretary of Agriculture. Christian ideas permeated the thinking of Dulles, a prominent international lawyer and leader in Presbyterian and ecumenical circles, who shared Eisenhower's conviction that the cold war had to be fought on the spiritual as well as the material and military level.[44] Benson belonged to the Council of Twelve Apostles, the central administrative organ of the Latter-Day Saints church. In the interview with Eisenhower, Benson questioned whether his appointment would be a liability, given his close tie with the Mormon church. The president-elect responded firmly that, because of the need to restore public confidence in government, "We've got to deal with spiritual matters. I feel your church connection is a distinct asset."[45]

When the new cabinet convened on January 12, 1953, Eisenhower asked Benson to begin the session in prayer, and the practice of an opening silent prayer at cabinet meetings persisted throughout his administration. This action gained the approval of Catholics as well as Protestants. The Jesuit weekly *America* praised him for his forthrightness in testifying to the "realization of our dependence on God's providence" and thanked him for reminding us to pray "for the welfare of the country and for the guidance of those who are charged to labor for the common good."[46] Of crucial significance to his pastoral function were Eisenhower's actions on his first inauguration day. In the morning, he and his entourage (Vice President Nixon, cabinet members, White House staff, and their families—some 176 people according to the press report) attended a private service at the National Presbyterian Church in order to "seek strength in prayer and in the Word of God for his overwhelming new responsibilities," as its pastor, Dr. Edward L. R. Elson, later stated. "The mood of the service was that of placing the destiny of the nation in God's hands." During the previous month, Elson had courted the president-elect in New York, and he released a statement that the Eisenhowers had chosen his church as their place of worship and that there would be a pre-inaugural service. Being a former army chaplain, he could relate to Eisenhower, and even Billy Graham personally recommended the congregation as a church home to him.[47]

Eisenhower said in his memoirs that he had been mulling over religion for several weeks. He did not want the inaugural address to be a sermon, but he wished to make clear his "deep faith in the beneficence of the Almighty" without creating the impression that he intended to avoid his own responsibilities by passing them on to the Deity. "I was seeking a way to point out that we were getting too secular." Thinking on this as he was returning from church to his suite at the Statler Hotel, he decided to write a brief prayer to read before beginning the inaugural message. Mamie agreed enthusiastically, and he jotted it down in five or ten minutes. He had it typed and read it to those in the room; they thought it was most fitting for the occasion. This reflected the great anxiety he had about the inaugural speech in general, and he continued to rework it almost to the last minute. As he rode to the Capitol with retiring President Truman, the sun broke through the heavy clouds that overshadowed the city, and God seemed to be smiling on the events transpiring below.[48]

He took the presidential oath with his left hand resting on two Bibles. One, which had been used by George Washington in 1789, was open to Psalm 127:1: "Except the Lord build the house, they labour in vain that build it: except the Lord keep the city, the watchman waketh but in vain." The other had been given to him by his mother when he graduated from West Point and was open to 2 Chronicles 7:14, the proof text par excellence of American civil religion:

> If my people, which are called by my name, shall humble themselves, and pray, and seek my face, and turn from their wicked ways: then will I hear from heaven, and will forgive their sin, and will heal their land.[49]

After receiving the oath, he asked people "to bow your heads" and offered "the little private prayer" he had written. This was an action unique in the annals of presidential inaugurations, and the prayer is a landmark document in American civil religion:

> Almighty God, as we stand here at this moment my future associates in the executive branch of government join me in beseeching that Thou will make full and complete our dedication to the service of the people in this throng, and their fellow citizens everywhere.

> Give us, we pray, the power to discern clearly right from wrong, and allow all our words and actions to be governed thereby, and by the laws of this land. Especially we pray that our concern shall be for all the people regardless of station, race, or calling.

> May cooperation be permitted and be the mutual aim of those who, under the concepts of our Constitution, hold to differing political faith; so that all may work for the good of our beloved country and Thy glory. Amen.

The address which followed was an affirmation of faith in free government under God and a call for spiritual rededication and moral renewal. "Whatever America hopes to bring to pass in the world must first come to pass in the heart of America," averred the new president. The peace the country was seeking was "the practice and fulfillment of our whole faith among ourselves and in our dealings with others." It would be a way of life, a hope for the brave, and the work that awaits us all, and it must be done with bravery, charity, and prayer to Almighty God.[50]

On February 1, Eisenhower took a step that was fraught with controversy as well as deep meaning—he presented himself for baptism and membership in the National Presbyterian Church. (Mamie was already a Presbyterian.) Before the election he had been urged to join a church, but he refused to do so just to court votes and told a banker friend, "I have always sort of treasured my independence." But, after the inaugural he discussed the matter with Elson, and they decided that he would receive baptism in the presence of the elders prior to the morning worship and then in the public service he and Mamie would be taken into the church. This was the first time in American history that a chief of state had been baptized while in office.[51]

Immediately, the story was picked up by the press, which resulted in strained relations between the president and his pastor. That day, Eisenhower wrote in his diary:

> Mamie and I joined a Presbyterian church. We were scarcely home before the pact was being publicized, by the pastor, to the hilt. I had been promised, by him, that there would be no publicity. I feel like changing at once to another church of the same denomination. I shall if he breaks out again.[52]

Elson quickly promised Eisenhower in a letter that he would try to be a good pastor and be available to render spiritual service. He would not use or permit anyone else to use the pastoral relationship for any but religious purposes, and he would not disclose anything discussed with the president in private.[53] The troubled waters were quickly calmed. The president regularly attended worship there, contributed money to the church, assisted in its building program, and occasionally passed copies of Elson's sermons along to his staff. A tempest in a teapot arose in 1955 when Senator

Matthew Neely of West Virginia accused Eisenhower of making political capital out of his church attendance. The solon declared that he joined only after becoming president and pictures of him leaving church were in the newspapers every Monday morning. This evoked such a storm of protest that Neely had to beat a hasty retreat. The incident underscored the point that a church relationship was an important element of the president's civil role, and any criticism of this would be viewed by the public with extreme disfavor.[54]

It goes without saying that President Eisenhower occupied a central position in the flowering of public religiosity in the 1950s.[55] He gave his full blessing to the most significant symbolic events of the decade—the adoption of "In God We Trust" as the national motto and the addition of the words "under God" to the Pledge of Allegiance. In fact, when he signed the latter into law, he expressed pleasure that:

> from this day forward, the millions of our school children will daily proclaim in every city and town, every village and rural schoolhouse, the dedication of our Nation and our people to the Almighty. To anyone who truly loves America, nothing could be more inspiring than to contemplate this rededication of our youth, on each school morning, to our country's true meaning. . . .In this way we are reaffirming the transcendence of religious faith in America's heritage and future; in this way we shall constantly strengthen those spiritual weapons which forever will be our country's most powerful resource, in peace or in war.[56]

Eisenhower took part in the annual Presidential (now National) Prayer Breakfasts, a custom that was inaugurated with his blessing in 1953 and that became one of the centerpieces of civil religion in the subsequent years.[57] He also lent his name to the Foundation for Religious Action in the Social and Civic Order and maintained complex and ever-expanding relationships with church and religious bodies. In July 1956, he authorized the creation of a White House staff position to coordinate religious affairs, to which Congregationalist minister Frederic E. Fox was appointed. His tasks were to answer correspondence from groups and individuals with religious concerns, help write the president's speeches to religious bodies, and assist in resolving church-state controversies. Fox sensed that the president's duties were essentially pastoral"; that is, the chief executive was expected to encourage worthy pursuits, promote charity, and strengthen the moral fiber.[58]

A NATION UNDER GOD

The gentle and sincere President Eisenhower celebrated the rites of the civil faith in a manner that endeared him even to those who did not share his political persuasion. In fact, the Republican National Committee adopted a statement saying that he was "not only the political leader but the spiritual leader of our times."[59] He gave homage to the Deity in his inaugural addresses, proclaimed the annual day of prayer, expressed his public theology before religious and secular groups alike, and worshipped regularly, both in his home church and with other congregations. He linked spiritual renewal and national renewal, and spurred his fellow-citizens to higher spiritual and moral achievements. Under his pastoral care, the nation formally acknowledged its position in God's providence and its humble dependence upon the Deity. The Judeo-Christian consensus was expanded and intensified, and the great majority of Americans were brought under its benevolent wings. Finally, he employed the civil faith in the ideological struggle between Western liberal democracy and Soviet communism, thus helping to strengthen the resolve of many Americans whose enthusiasm for the cold war had begun to wane.

However, storm clouds lay on the horizon. As the cold war wound down, new nations were emerging in the non-Western world that rejected the American idea of liberal democracy and benevolent global hegemony. At home, the race issue was becoming more and more intense. Many young people felt alienated from their elders and were looking for something more meaningful than economic prosperity and physical comfort. Their idealism was channeled into the election of John F. Kennedy, but their dreams were shattered by his cruel death and the escalating conflict in Southeast Asia. American civil religion was about to enter a time of severe testing, and the result would be the emergence of a virile priestly form under Richard M. Nixon.

9

RICHARD M. NIXON AND PRIESTLY CIVIL RELIGION

Speaking to a delegation from the National Council of Churches on September 9, 1959, President Eisenhower reiterated his familiar stance that free government was the political expression of some form of religious belief and called this the strongest link among the countries of the West. But then, he went one step further:

> Indeed I think this even includes the Mohammedans, the Buddhists, and the rest; because they, too, strongly believe that they achieve a right to human dignity because of their relationship to the Supreme Being. We must remember always that there are others that can have this same feeling of unity, because of their recognition of a religious destiny.[1]

Was he giving civil religion a global dimension, or was this an implicit move in the direction of deism-in-general, where just the acknowledgement of a "Supreme Being" was sufficient? Could American pluralism be confined merely within Judeo-Christian bounds?

FROM WHITTIER TO WATERGATE

The answer lay in the election of Richard M. Nixon, the quintessential high priest of American civil religion in its vaguest form. At long last, the "religious issue" which had so poisoned electoral politics in 1928 and had reared its ugly head again in 1960 could be laid to rest, and the great broadening of public religion that had occurred during the Roosevelt and Eisenhower years was confirmed. The election of Roman Catholic John F. Kennedy to the nation's highest office, the serious bid which Edmund Muskie made for the Democratic nomination in 1972, and the nomination of Catholics for vice president by one of the two major parties in 1964, 1968, 1972, and 1984 were proof of this. Moreover, the Christian Barry Goldwater, who was of Jewish background, was the 1964 Republican candidate. The Judeo-Christian consensus was now solidly established, and the man whom most American evangelicals believed was truly a Christian president took upon himself the responsibility of affirming it.

Richard Milhous Nixon came from old American stock— the first Milhous, a Quaker, had arrived in Pennsylvania in 1729, while the first Nixon had arrived from Ireland in 1753. Both families followed the westward movement across the United States, picking up along the way the spiritual and cultural values fostered by evangelicalism and the revivalist tradition. The Nixons found a spiritual home in frontier Methodism, while the Quaker faith of the Milhouses underwent modification under the impact of revivalism.

In the nineteenth century, Quakers were torn between two influences. The "meetinghouse" approach of their origins stressed plainness of speech, simple lifestyle, nonviolence, compassion for the needy of the world, and the Inner Light of the Holy Spirit in every person; the "steeple house" religiosity of the West was marked by professional ministers and evangelical sermons. The Friends living in the Midwest and on the Pacific Coast adopted much of the theology and practice of evangelical Protestantism, although they still retained the ethical and the Inner Light emphasis of traditional Quakerism and in some cases continued to have "silent" meetings in addition to structured worship services. The town where Nixon's parents spent much of their lives, Whittier, California, had been founded in 1887 as a "Quaker city" by a Chicago businessman and eventually became the center of a Quaker-style revivalism. The California Yearly Meeting of Friends even had tent meetings, sermons, hymn singing, and spoken prayers.

It was in Whittier that Frank Nixon, who hailed from a conservative Methodist background, met and married the Quaker Hannah Milhous. Their faiths had become so much alike that he joined her congregation, became an active worker there, and saw to it that their children received a common religious upbringing in the Friends Sunday school. Born in Ohio in 1878, Francis Anthony Nixon held various odd jobs before relocating in southern California in 1907. There he worked as an electric railway motorman, a citrus farmer, a carpenter, and finally as the proprietor of a combination grocery store and filling station. Hannah Milhous, born into a fairly prosperous Quaker family in Indiana, had moved to California with her parents in 1897 at the age of twelve. After their marriage in 1908, the couple lived in various places, eventually settling down in Whittier in 1922 where Frank operated his market. Their son Richard was born in Yorba Linda on January 9, 1913, the second of five boys, two of whom died at relatively young ages.

The elder Nixons were two very different personalities. Hannah was patient, long-suffering, hard-working, peaceful, and extremely pious. Frank was of a sultry disposition, rigid, uncompromising, hot-tempered, and combative. The contrast between Hannah's Quaker pacifism and Frank's Methodistic crusading mentality undoubtedly helped to shape their son's character, for he manifested both sets of traits in his religious and political life in the years to come.

In 1930, Richard entered Whittier College, a small Friends-related liberal arts college in his hometown, where he excelled in his studies and demonstrated considerable skill as an orator and organizer. He graduated near the top of his class, received a scholarship to Duke University law school in North Carolina, and earned his law degree in 1937. He returned to Whittier and joined a local law firm. There Nixon met Pat Ryan, an attractive high school teacher, and they were married in 1940. They had two daughters, one of whom eventually married the grandson of General Eisenhower.

When World War II broke out, Nixon volunteered to work for the Office of Price Administration in Washington. As a Quaker, he had a religious exemption from military service, but after a few months behind a desk he waived it and accepted a commission in the navy. He served in the South Pacific, eventually attaining the rank of lieutenant commander. He returned home after the war to what was a humdrum existence as a small-town barrister. Then came the break that was to change his life. Although he had been a rather diffident Republican, he was recruited to run for Congress in 1946 against a popular and seemingly well-entrenched Democrat, Jerry Voorhis. What followed was a hard-hitting campaign from which Nixon emerged victorious. His political career had been launched.

From this point on, his rise was meteoric. During the next four years, he attracted attention by his work on the House Un-American Activities Committee and was transformed into a national figure by his dogged pursuit of the alleged communist spy Alger Hiss. In another slashing campaign in 1950, Nixon ousted the incumbent U.S. Senator Helen Gahagan Douglas, and in 1952 he was selected as Eisenhower's running mate to balance the ticket. He was almost forced out of the race by a campaign fund scandal, but he succeeded in weathering the storm through the dramatic "Checkers Speech" on national television and was elected in November.

Nixon was now vice president, the second youngest in American history, and almost became president when Eisenhower was struck down by a heart attack in 1955. Events then took a turn for the worse when the president considered dropping him from the ticket in 1956 and when he was humiliated in anti-American riots while visiting Venezuela in 1958. He regained some stature through the "kitchen debate" with Nikita Khrushchev in Moscow in 1959, did his best to maintain good relations with both the conservative and liberal wings of the party, and finally received Eisenhower's blessing to run as his successor in 1960. However, Nixon lost to John F. Kennedy by a razor-thin margin in a hard-fought struggle, and his political fortunes plummeted.

He returned to private life as a corporate lawyer with one foot each in California and New York City, but he failed in a bid at a political comeback in 1962 in the governor's race in his home state. Although Nixon now practiced law to make a living, the be-all and end-all of his existence continued to be politics, and he engaged in a grueling schedule of speech making and campaigning for other candidates which kept him in the public eye. Thus, when he made the fateful decision to seek the presidency in 1968, it was the culmination of lengthy effort. Because so many

Republican politicians were obligated to him for assistance he had rendered, obtaining the nomination was never seriously in doubt.

After scoring a narrow victory over Hubert Humphrey and third-party contestant George Wallace, Nixon set out to remake the country in a somewhat more conservative mold and to extricate the United States from the quagmire in Southeast Asia. He entered the White House during a stormy period in American history—in the midst of revulsion against the Vietnam War, urban violence, and social unrest. Still, his accomplishments were noteworthy—the first humans on the moon, progress toward arms limitation with the Soviet Union, the establishment of formal ties with the People's Republic of China and East Germany, and a negotiated end to the Vietnam conflict. Nixon buried his Democratic opponent George McGovern in 1972, only to have everything swept away in the ensuing Watergate scandal. He was forced to resign the presidency in August 1974, and his political career came to an ignominious end, or so it seemed. However, since 1980 he has gradually begun to win back respect and assume the character of an "elder statesman."

WHO IS RICHARD NIXON?

What kind of a man is Richard Nixon? It is difficult to tell from his early political autobiography, *Six Crises* (1962), or his post-Watergate works, *RN: the Memoirs of Richard Nixon* (1978), *The Real War* (1980), and *Leaders* (1982). The various biographical accounts are all either out-dated or so colored by the polemics surrounding his presidency and the Watergate affair as to be of limited value. The first substantial scholarly biography only appeared in 1987, although a listing of specialized studies, first-person accounts by those associated with his administration in some way, and journalistic narratives of the period would run to several pages.[2]

Nixon was undoubtedly one of the most complex personalities ever to occupy the nation's highest office. This is why many commentators try to explain his behavior by utilizing psychohistorical methodology;[3] yet so few of them have ever succeeded in capturing the essence of the man. An observation by *New York Times* writer Robert Semple in 1968 underscores just how little people actually knew about the "real Nixon." He said the man about to enter the White House was:

> moody, detached, standing alone without any plain inherited ideology or natural allies, offering only himself and his hopes that he could "do better"; a conditional figure, inscrutable and puzzling, a man without a political address, a lifetime politician whose true values and bedrock political philosophy would be known only when the nation asked him what his answers to the problems were.[4]

From his youth Nixon had been an introverted but a highly active, aggressive, and disciplined person. His ability to maintain a grueling work schedule was legendary, and he demonstrated a mastery of facts and understanding of complex political situations. At the same time, he was subject to periods of depression, anxiety, and agonizing grief. He developed a combative style—one characterized by rhetorical excess and a strategy of destroying his opponents by whatever means necessary—but still he possessed ideological flexibility. He lacked clear ideals and beliefs and was not wedded to a rigid framework of principles, whether they be political, moral, or religious in nature. The American public sadly learned this as they watched the sordid Watergate affair unfold.

His overriding concern was with himself and the achievement of "self-management," as James Barber puts it. For example, Nixon portrayed the struggle with Soviet communism in such terms as determination, will, stamina, and willingness to risk all for victory. "How can we instill in our children not only a faith greater than theirs but the physical, mental, and moral stamina to outlast the enemies of freedom in this century of crisis?" Victory in a great cause like this or any other one required will power, personal mobilization, effort, and struggle.[5] Self-discipline and self-management were the keys to getting and exercising power. This motivated Nixon more than any other single factor, but the passion for power would be his undoing in the end.

Also striking about Nixon was the way in which he was, in the words of Fawn Brodie, "the man of paradox." As the presidential candidate in 1968, he promised to bring truth in government but instead built an administration on lies. He identified with a historic peace church, yet he ordered more bombs dropped than any other man in history. He possessed the feeling of omnipotence but suffered from a fatalistic instinct that nothing he did would ever be crowned with ultimate success. He was the supreme anticommunist but established friendly relations with the largest bloc of communists in the world. He promised to return power to the people but threatened the Constitution with his own usurpations of power. He talked about law and order but said that if the president chose to do something, that made it legal. He professed to have no interest in wealth but revealed an exaggerated fondness for the trappings and pageantry of royalty once he set foot in the White House. Although he manifested tendencies toward self-destruction, he is the symbol of the supreme survivor.[6]

Who is the "real Nixon"? The answer is that nobody knows for certain because the complexity of the man defies friends and foes alike. And the ambiguities that cloud his personality are similar to those obscuring his religious beliefs.

RICHARD NIXON'S RELIGIOUS FAITH

As strange as this may seem, the Quaker experience had a profound impact on the shaping of Nixon's personality.[7] Religious observance was a central feature of his youth. His family attended services at the East Whittier Friends Church four times on Sunday—Sunday school, morning worship, late afternoon Christian Endeavor, and evening service— and Wednesday prayer meeting and Thursday choir practice as well. Young Nixon frequently played the piano at these services, before retiring at night regularly read from a Bible his mother had given him, and taught a high school Sunday school class. From his Quaker upbringing he learned tolerance of other peoples and races, the importance of peace and international understanding, and the idea that God helps those who help themselves. However, he also acquired a distaste for showing emotions or physically expressing feelings, since in Quakerism one's religious sensitivities were directed inward. At the same time, he was encouraged to stand up, speak out, and pray before the congregation as the Spirit led him, though these actions usually were devoid of emotion and more rational than religious. It is fair to say that his experience as a Quaker was a blending of private reserve and public confidence.[8]

There was an evangelical dimension as well. His Friends congregation placed great emphasis on the importance of accepting Jesus as the sacrifice for sins and on repenting of everything that was wrong in one's life, in other words, being "born again." In the smaller Christian Endeavor youth meeting he would testify openly about his religious experience and even lead the gathering. Moreover, Frank Nixon took the boys into Los Angeles to hear the popular revivalists of the day like Billy Sunday, Aimee Semple McPherson, and Robert "Fighting Bob" Shuler, and his son vividly recalled (in an article in Billy Graham's *Decision* magazine) attending a Paul Rader meeting in 1926 where "we joined hundreds of others in making our personal commitment to Christ and Christian service."[9]

Still, although religion and prayer were very much a part of his family life, these were essentially personal and private matters. As the presidential aspirant told journalist Garry Wills in 1968, Quakerism with its emphasis on privacy strengthened his own temperament and made him "an introvert in an extrovert profession." Also, Nixon did not publicly display his religion and claimed this was the reason that he did not engage in the common practice of quoting the Bible in his speeches. He later mentioned in his memoirs that President Eisenhower had urged him "to refer to God from time to time in my speeches, but I did not feel comfortable doing so."[10]

What this evangelical faith really meant to the mature Nixon is quite enigmatic. Commentators often point out that the personalized, internalized Quakerism of his mother and the more aggressive, outgoing revivalistic evangelicalism of his father were sources of tension in the young man.[11] His own statements of faith merely add to the confusion. For example, in a paper written for a class at Whittier College in the 1930s, which Nixon included in his memoirs as a "clearer picture" of his beliefs than anything he could reconstruct today, he maintained that he had given up many of the ideas he had learned in his youth about the infallibility and inerrancy of the Bible but still believed that God was the Creator, the First Cause of all that exists, who directed the cosmos in some unknown way. Jesus was the Son of God but not in the physical sense of the term. Yet, "he reached the highest conception of God and of value that the world had ever seen," and he lived and taught "a philosophy which revealed these values to men." In effect, "Jesus and God are one, because Jesus set the great example which is forever pulling men upward to the ideal life. His life was so perfect that he "mingled' his soul with God's." With respect to the resurrection, Nixon asserted that "the literal accuracy" of the story was "not as important as its profound symbolism." The significant fact was that Jesus lived and grew after his death in the hearts of men. "It may be true that the resurrection story is a myth, but symbolically it teaches the great lesson that men who achieve the highest values in their lives may gain immortality." Down playing the physical resurrection, he suggested that "the modern world will find a real resurrection in the life and teachings of Jesus."[12]

In the 1962 *Decision* article, however, Nixon claimed he was "old-fashioned" when it came to the matter of personal religious commitment,and he believed America needed "more preaching from the Bible, rather than just about the Bible" or about "religion in the abstract." In this age of crisis, "there is desperate need for strength and character and spirit if we are to survive." He went on to express in vintage civil religion terminology his "profound conviction" that the national experience "is evidence of the interdependence of a widely shared religious faith and the vigorous health of a free American society." He referred to the American people's "ultimate commitments and duties" and the "faith of their fathers," concluding that "in the deepest and richest sense, we are a people of faith," one which "has evoked out of diversity a unity of basic purpose and single-minded pursuit of essential goals" and "elicits a spontaneous consensus and a natural harmony out of fifty states and tens of thousands of local self-governing communities." It enables resting social order on an "inborn respect for law rather than on an omnipresent national police." The American people are a religious people whose faith "ultimately goes back to the fundamental truths of the Bible."[13]

The confusing character of Nixon's faith was perceived by the dean of evangelical theologians, Carl F. H. Henry. In 1968, when he was editor of *Christianity Today*, he interviewed the candidate and found him to be "remarkably imprecise about spiritual realities and enduring ethical concerns." Henry characterized Nixon as "the confident champion of a free world where divine Providence benevolently guarantees America's ongoing global leadership rather than, as in the Bill of Rights, towers as Supreme Source, Sanction, and Stipulator of universal human rights."[14] In short, Henry recognized that the core of Nixon's faith was civil religion.

It seems reasonable to conclude that the young Richard Nixon had an evangelical experience whose residual effects could be seen throughout his life. Although by the time of his college days he had adopted a much more liberal faith, one whose doctrinal formulation would be unacceptable to those very evangelicals who most admired him as a "truly Christian president," he would evoke the Quaker elements of his upbringing when it served his purposes. Almost effortlessly, he channeled the broad, humanitarian faith of the Friends into a highly generalized civil religion whose primary focus was on spirit and determination.

Thus, it is noteworthy that even though Nixon identified with his Quaker background, as a mature adult he seldom set foot inside the East Whittier Friends Church, nor did he worship in the Washington meetinghouse where Herbert Hoover, the only other Quaker president, had attended regularly. This did not seem to be much of a problem to the Religious Society of Friends, since they did not have very precise standards for communicant status, and the "discontinuance of membership" or "disownment" could only result when a congregation by consensus action determined that an erring member was incapable of restoration. Only when the Vietnam War intensified in 1973 did the president's critics seriously demand that he be disowned by the East Whittier congregation. However, the pastor, T. Eugene Coffin, reported that the church's ministry and counsel committee reviewed the matter and concluded it would be an "unchristian act" to cancel his membership. Indeed, Coffin said, the role of the meeting should be one of prayerful support and counsel. This did not mean condoning the wayward member's sin but providing the kind of spiritual climate in which the person could repent and start life anew. In this way, the lines of communication to Nixon could be kept open and the church's concerns regarding his decisions could be shared with him. As far as can be determined, Nixon was never excommunicated, but he did not resume attending the Friends meetings either.[15]

Actually, his chief source of spiritual counsel was Evangelist Billy Graham, who established a pastoral relationship that lasted even after he had been swept out of the White House. Graham had met Nixon's parents during a Youth for Christ rally in Whittier in 1948 and their son two years later. After the Washington crusade of 1952, Graham and Nixon became warm friends and the relationship deepened during the vice-presidential years. They often played golf together and Nixon addressed Graham's New York crusade on July 20, 1957. The correspondence between the two contained in the recently released vice-presidential papers reveals that they were on a first-name basis and that Graham functioned as a behind-the-scenes adviser to the Nixon campaign in 1960, particularly with regard to handling the sticky religious issue. He urged Eisenhower to support Nixon's candidacy and even decided to come out publicly for the Republican hopeful in an article that was to be published in *Life* on the eve of the election, but the magazine's editor decided to pull it at the last moment.[16]

After the California debacle in 1962, Graham looked toward the future and consoled Nixon with the words: "You will have another major opportunity in the next few years to serve the American people," and "In due season you will be called upon to bear heavy responsibilities for this nation."[17] After the death of John Kennedy, Graham became an intimate of President Johnson but at the same time kept his relationship with Nixon intact. Not only did they spend time together on the links, but Graham also assisted in Hannah Nixon's funeral (September 1967) and advised Nixon about running for the presidency. He invited the evangelist to spend three days with him at Key Biscayne, Florida, at the end of December to discuss the matter, engaging him in long talks about theology, politics, and sports. Then, as they parted, Graham told him: "Dick, I think you should run. If you don't, you will always wonder whether you should have run and whether you could have won or not. You are the best prepared man in the United States. . . . I think it is your destiny to be President."[18]

After receiving the nomination, Nixon requested (but did not follow) the evangelist's advice on a running mate, and Graham all but endorsed him during the campaign. Graham was already at the executive mansion (as Johnson's guest) when Nixon moved in on January 20, 1969, offered a major prayer at the inaugural ceremony, preached at the first White House religious service, and was a regular participant in the annual National Prayer Breakfasts. The chief executive frequently contacted the evangelist by telephone for spiritual counsel or just a friendly chat; he also gave talks at the East Tennessee crusade in Knoxville in 1970 and at the Billy Graham Day celebration in Charlotte, North Carolina in 1971. During the 1972 campaign, the preacher came out publicly for Nixon's reelection and even relayed a message from Lyndon Johnson advising the president simply to ignore McGovern. As in the 1960s, Graham did not criticize the president's handling of the Vietnam imbroglio, and his continuing silence provoked a storm of criticism.[19]

Graham's position as the president's pastor became even more precarious as the Watergate scandal deepened. Critics now called him the "White House chaplain," spoke of the "Nixon-Graham doctrine" (all problems are at their root spiritual ones, all religion is virtuous and will guarantee public justice), suggested he was more a politician than a preacher, and accused him of promoting civil religion. Graham had become so caught in the web of Nixon's priestly civil religion that many doubted his ministry could survive, and even some of his evangelical well-wishers urged him to cut the tie with the White House.[20]

NIXON'S CIVIL THEOLOGY

As the high priest of American public religion, Richard M. Nixon articulated a coherent civil theology. The first and central idea was that of *spirit*. Opening his presidential campaign in New Hampshire in February 1968, Nixon announced that America was facing "a crisis of the spirit," and he responded dramatically: "To a crisis of the spirit, we need an answer of the spirit." This line reappeared in his inaugural address a year later and was trumpeted abroad by his religious partisans. In his view, the nation was lacking a spirit of justice, law, and reconciliation and was torn by discord, division, and unfulfilled aspirations. But within ourselves lay the answer to that crisis:

> When we listen to "the better angels of our nature," we find that they celebrate the simple things, the basic things—such as goodness, decency, love, kindness.

Thus, America could "heal its spirit and find its soul again," by drawing on "that something more" which our nation has meant to the world.[21]

The new president then called on his people to join together to "build a great cathedral of the spirit—each of us raising one stone at a time, as he reaches out to his neighbor, helping, caring, doing." It would not be a life of "grim sacrifice" but of high adventure—one "as rich as humanity itself, and as exciting as the times we live in." By engaging in this cause higher than themselves, Americans would find fulfillment in the use of their talents and "achieve nobility in the spirit that inspires that use."[22]

How a solution to the problems of the spirit could be found was demonstrated by the voyage of the Apollo astronauts to the moon. According to Nixon, they told the people back home: "Our destiny lies not in the stars but on Earth itself, in our hands and our own hearts." He then concluded:

> We have endured a long night of the American spirit. But as our eyes catch the dimness of the first rays of dawn, let us not curse the remaining dark. Let us gather the light.
>
> Our destiny offers, not the cup of despair, but the chalice of opportunity. So let us seize it, not in fear, but in gladness—and, "riders on the earth together," let us go forward, firm in our faith, steadfast in our purpose, cautious of the dangers; but sustained by our confidence in the will of God and the promise of man. [23]

For him, the concept of "spirit" was a pragmatic matter, one that emphasized self-confidence, individual achievement, and the overcoming of obstacles. On numerous occasions he employed this term in his public addresses:

• *Kansas City, Missouri, July 6, 1971*: America's spirit would enable it to overcome the moral decadence that caused other great civilizations of the past to fall.

• *Catoosa, Oklahoma, June 5, 1971*: It was the same spirit that forged the Union in 1776, bought Louisiana in 1803, bridged the continent with rails in 1869, settled the Oklahoma Territory in 1889, developed the Tennessee Valley in the 1930s, put men on the moon in 1969, and made the Arkansas River navigable in 1971.

• *Salt Lake City, Utah, July 24, 1970*: The "kind of spirit" that brought the pioneers to Utah in 1846 and took men to the moon "has built the greatest country on the earth" and "blessed us with the greatest ability that the world has ever seen" to solve our national problems.

- *Colorado Springs, Colorado, June 4, 1969*: Our current exploration of space "is a reaching-out of the human spirit. . . .Every man achieves his own greatness by reaching out beyond himself, and so it is with nations." When a nation "believes in itself," as the Athenians and Renaissance Italians did, it "can perform miracles."
- *Washington, D.C., April 19, 1971*: Our nation had such a deep-rooted tradition of greatness that "the flame of the American spirit" could not be extinguished even by so dark a nightmare as the Vietnam War.[24]

Nixon was utilizing a religious term, spirit, to express a very secular understanding of America. He portrayed it as the animating force in American achievement, one which was in need of reaffirmation and renewal because of the assaults on the nation's way of life from within and without that were then occurring. Moreover, the spirit of America was transcendent and universal, as he pointed out about the quest for world peace in the inaugural address in 1969:

> The peace we seek to win is not victory over any other people, but the peace that comes "with healing in its wings"; with compassion for those who have suffered; with understanding for those who have opposed us; with the opportunity for all the peoples of this earth to choose their own destiny.

As Presbyterian theologian Charles Henderson aptly observes, the attributes which Nixon applied to the beneficent American spirit were precisely those of the Christian deity— healing power, compassion for the helpless, forgiveness for the sinner, and the granting of freedom to all persons to choose their own ultimate destiny.[25]

The second element in Nixon's civil theology is his belief in *the innate goodness of America*. In the first inaugural address he asserted: "I know America. I know the heart of America is good." In the second inaugural he boasted that "America's record in this century has been unparalleled for its responsibility, for its generosity, for its creativity, and for its progress." Then, he intoned three times, "let us be proud," about things the nation had achieved—it produced more freedom and abundance than any other system in history, fought four wars this century to help others resist aggression, and made a breakthrough in creating a lasting structure of peace.[26] In the speech accepting the presidential nomination in 1968, Nixon maintained that America "is a great nation" because "her people are great." The country was in trouble only because "her leaders have failed," and it needed leaders to "match the greatness of her people." In the 1972 acceptance speech he declared: "I believe in the American system [and] realize how fortunate we are to live in this great and good country." In the Alfred M. Landon lecture at Kansas State University in 1970 he told his listeners that "the heart of America" was "strong," "good," and "sound," while at the dedication of the Arkansas River Navigation system in 1971 he reminded the audience of some "fundamental truths," especially that "America is a beautiful country, and the American people are a good people, they are a strong people, with faith in God and faith in themselves."[27]

Perhaps on no other occasion did President Nixon wax so eloquent about American goodness than he did at the National Prayer Breakfast on February 2, 1971. At its founding, "America was a good country" which "stood for spiritual and moral values that far transcended the strength and the wealth of the nations of the old world." As the Bicentennial approached, his aspiration was that it would continue to be "a good country in every sense of the word: Good at home, good in our relations with other nations in the world." The prayer breakfasts taking place around the country were reminders that, despite what the cynics were saying, "there is a great deal of goodness in this country, a great deal of moral strength and fiber still left. . . .In the end, that's what really matters." His prayer was that America would continue to "be truly a good country and the hope of the world still."[28]

This leads to the third feature of the president's civil theology, his utopian *vision of American mission*. In his 1968 acceptance speech, Nixon held up the prospect that after eight years of his presidency, "everyone on earth—those who hope, those who aspire, those who crave liberty—will look to America as the shining example of hopes realized and dreams achieved." In the 1970 State of the Union address he expressed the wish that "it not be recorded that we lack the moral and spiritual idealism which made us the hope of the world at the time of our birth" and set forth the exemplary vision of an America that had solved its social and economic problems and was at peace with all lands.[29]

At the National Prayer Breakfast in 1970 the president talked about the "spiritual strength" that united Americans and gave them "an extra power" to look beyond the seemingly overwhelming material problems in order to "see the promise of a better life for us and all the peoples in the world." Recognizing that America "is a nation under God," he declared that it had a destiny:

> not . . . to conquer the world or to exploit the world, but a destiny to give something more to the world simply than an example which other nations in the past have been able to give—a great military strength and great economic worth—to give to other nations of the world an example of spiritual leadership and idealism which no material strength or military power can provide.[30]

Speaking before the same group two years later, Nixon reminded his hearers that, because "it was right to do so," America helped both its allies and former enemies to get back on their feet after World War II and did the same for underdeveloped countries as well. He went on to express himself emphatically in the first person. This was how we showed our dedication to what the nation had stood for from its very beginning, namely, liberty and justice for all throughout the world. The task now before America was to work for global peace. "Let us remember that as a Christian nation, but also as a nation enriched by other faiths as well, that we have a charge and a destiny." The great asset which the United States had in playing the role of peacemaker was that it neither wanted anything from nor wished to impose its will on any other nation. We desired that they would have what we have, one nation with liberty and justice for all. Thus, "our role may be to help build a new structure of peace in the world," where people with great differences could live together rather than fight about them. He then asked people to pray that "this Nation, under God, in the person of its President, will, to the best of our ability, be on God's side."[31]

These three ideas surfaced repeatedly in Richard Nixon's speeches —the stress on spirit, American goodness, and national mission—and that prompted one of his critics, Charles Henderson, to issue a sharp indictment:

> Nixon systematically appropriates the vocabulary of the church—faith, trust, hope, belief, spirit—and applies these words not to a transcendent God but to his own nation, and worse, to his personal vision of what that nation should be. . . .Lacking a transcendent God, he seems to make patriotism his religion, the American dream his deity. Far from returning to the "spiritual sources" that made this nation great, he accomplishes a macabre reversal of those traditions, selling the mirror image as the original.[32]

However, this highly optimistic and positive priestly civil faith was precisely what made Nixon so appealing. Although his ideas were hardly new, no other twentieth century president had spoken with quite the intensity and conviction as he had, and the war-weary populace welcomed his words of comfort and reassurance. Few realized that he had essentially detached his views from the Deity and reattached them to national transcendence.

Yet, to be fair, Nixon did defer to a transcendent deity on one significant occasion. In his second inaugural address, where he called on his fellow-citizens to "renew the spirit and the promise of America as we enter our third century as a nation," he also acknowledged that "we shall answer to God, to history, and to our conscience for the way in which we use these [next four] years." He then asked his people for prayers that he might have "God's help in making decisions that are right for America" and requested their help "so that together we may be worthy of our challenge." His hope was that on its two-hundredth birthday America would be "as bright a beacon of hope for all the world" as when it began. He ended by linking faith in each other with that in God:

> Let us go forward from here confident in hope, strong in our faith in one another, sustained by our faith in God who created us, and striving always to serve His purpose.[33]

THE PRIESTLY PRESIDENT IN ACTION

Martin Marty's model of the priestly style of civil religion in the context of the self-transcendent nation perfectly fits

Richard Nixon. His speeches reveal how he took the vocabulary of transcendence and applied it to his personal vision of America. He functioned as a priest comforting his people, forgiving their sins, assuring them of their inherent goodness, enhancing their self-esteem, and sanctifying their national institutions. As he said so forcefully in the second inaugural, "The time has come for us to renew our faith in ourselves and in America."[34] Thus, Nixon's sporadic religiosity can best be understood when viewed against the backdrop of his priestly role.

The drama opened on January 20, 1969. Before the new president proceeded to the Capitol to be sworn in, 750 people crowded into the State Department auditorium for a prayer service. The inaugural ceremony itself included, as Congressman Frank Horton put it, "a full-scale worship service."[35] Prayers were offered by five clerics—Protestant (Billy Graham), Roman Catholic (Archbishop Terence Cooke), Greek Orthodox (Archbishop Iakovos), Jewish (Rabbi Edgar F. Magnin), and a black churchman, Bishop Charles Ewbank Tucker—while the Mormon Tabernacle Choir sang a patriotic song and the Marine Corps Band played "God Bless America." The ceremony lasted a full hour, and in the stenographic text published in the *Congressional Record*, the prayers took up thirty-five column inches of space while the president's inaugural address required only twenty-nine inches.[36]

On the following Sunday, President Nixon initiated a practice that captured the heart of middle America but produced uneasiness among more thoughtful church leaders and theologians—he began sponsoring worship services in the White House. He personally chose the ministers and his staff selected the individuals who would receive invitations to attend. The preacher on that first occasion, January 26, was Billy Graham, who opened with a typical civil religion prayer:

> We thank thee that we are a nation under God and that our forefathers handed us this torch of faith. . . .Along with millions of Americans who are in churches throughout the nation, we are honoring thee and worshiping thee as the only true God in sovereign law.

Then he used as his text the president's phrase, "To a crisis of the spirit, we need an answer of the spirit," and preached one of his customary evangelistic sermons. However, because the occasion was so public in character, Graham omitted a verbal call to make one's commitment to Christ.[37]

Nixon justified his White House services on strictly civil religion grounds. He said he wanted to convert the great East Room into a "church" on Sunday mornings so that it might serve as a reminder that "we feel God's presence here, and that we seek His guidance here," and that we are "one nation, under God, indivisible." Americans, he added, "still are basically a religious people," and he "wanted to do something" to encourage attendance at services and thereby accent the country's "basic faith in a Supreme Being. What better example could there be than to bring the worship service, with all its solemn meaning, right into the White House?" He also claimed that he disliked "going to church for show" because worship was a very private matter.[38] The president hoped to lead in the revival of moral values by making a dramatic public emphasis on worship, and in so doing he created an extraordinary syncretism of church religion and civil religion.

There were twenty-six services during the first two years of his administration, and then they became rather infrequent as criticism of them mounted. Various commentators noted that the preachers were "safe" types, that is, none were extremists of the right or left or "mainline" church figures who were openly critical of his handling of the Vietnam War. The detractors called attention to the bland and even deferential quality of the sermons, such as that of Rabbi Louis Finkelstein who suggested "the 'future historian'" might look back on this generation and say "that in a period of great trials and great tribulations, the finger of God pointed to Richard Milhous Nixon, giving him the vision and the wisdom to save the world and civilization." Reinhold Niebuhr caustically remarked about this one: "It is wonderful what a simple White House invitation will do to dull the critical faculties."[39]

Referring to the guest list—an invitation was one of the most sought-after items in Washington—Michael Novak pointed out that none of the poor, weak, or "little" people of America were to be found in the services. It was "interest-group religion" pure and simple, a "combination of religion and private presidential politics" since only the wealthy and powerful were ever allowed in.[40] Edward Fiske argued that the services enabled the identification of organized religion with national values and, to a lesser extent, with the policies of the Nixon administration; it was religion divorced from coherent ritual and a sense of the transcendent.[41] In short, the services constituted a "conforming" or "established" religion, and they must be seen as a serious attempt to institutionalize priestly civil religion.

Throughout his first term, Richard Nixon exuded the image of a great man of faith. Besides his well-publicized White House services, he attended and gave eloquent talks at the National Prayer Breakfasts and sponsored a special breakfast on the occasion of the annual National Day of Prayer on October 22, 1969. There he affirmed "the spiritual heritage of America" and talked about how all lawmakers recognized that there were times when they needed "help beyond ourselves" to make the right decisions for the nation.[42] He appealed to Roman Catholics by calling on Pope Paul VI at the Vatican in 1969 and 1970, praising the pontiff's "moral and spiritual leadership," and endorsing the idea of diplomatic ties with the Holy See.[43] Moreover, speaking before the Knights of Columbus in 1971 and the National Catholic Education Association in 1972, he commended parochial schools for providing children "with the moral and spiritual values so necessary to a great people in great times," and declared himself to be "irrevocably committed" to helping "non-public schools."[44]

President Nixon also tied America's space exploits to civil religion. When he greeted the Apollo 11 astronauts aboard the USS *Hornet* on July 24, 1969, after they had returned from the first landing on the moon, he exuberantly exclaimed that "this is the greatest week in the history of the world since the Creation" and directed the ship's chaplain to offer a prayer of thanksgiving. One line from Commander John A. Piirto's prayer was especially noteworthy: "May our country, afire with inventive leadership and backed by a committed followership, blaze new trails into all areas of human care."[45] At a dinner in their honor three weeks later Nixon thanked the astronauts for raising "the sights of men and women throughout the world to a new dimension—the sky is no longer the limit." In a speech to the nation he evoked "the spirit of Apollo 11"—a "spirit of peace and brotherhood and adventure," where "man" had dreamed, dared, and done the impossible, and proposed that in this spirit America could abolish poverty and put an end to dependency.[46]

When the Apollo 13 mission was aborted as it neared the moon and the crew barely succeeded in returning to earth, the president proclaimed Sunday, April 19, 1970, as a National Day of Prayer and Thanksgiving for the Safe Return of the Astronauts. He praised the men as a "great inspiration to all of us" and said they demonstrated "that the American character is sound and strong and capable of taking a very difficult situation and turning it into really a very successful venture." He also mentioned that "never have so many people on this earth" prayed so much for the success of their mission, and "whatever our religious faith may be. . . , we know that through our prayers we helped to participate in this successful recovery." Moreover, the mission reminded us "of our proud heritage as a nation" and that "in a crisis, the character of a man or men will make the difference."[47]

Nixon traveled to Hawaii to welcome them back and attended a church service in Honolulu on the Sunday he had designated as the National Day of Prayer. Before the pastor's sermon, the president told the congregation about the "men and women of great character and strength" in the United States and how the incident reminded us "of the true brotherhood of man." He said that "more people prayed last week than perhaps have prayed in many years" and this indicated the "religious strength" of America. The fact that people turned to spiritual help and prayed for the assistance of God when faced with this potential tragedy reflected that "we have come a long way in this country because we have had faith in God." The "future will be better if we continue that faith" and develop it in our churches Sunday after Sunday, day after day.[48]

It is no wonder that Nixon was widely regarded as a man of faith, and his efforts to promote civic piety were recognized by Religious Heritage of America, which named him as "Churchman of the Year" in 1970 for "creating an atmosphere for a return to the spiritual, moral, and ethical values of the Founding Fathers."[49] evangelicals adopted him as one of their own, and he in turn seized the opportunity to enlist them in his cause.[50] One example was his appearance at the Billy Graham crusade in Knoxville in 1970 where he lauded America's religious faith and told young people how much he was dedicated to the cause of peace, environmental protection, education, and racial justice. Another was the 1971 celebration in Charlotte honoring Graham where he expounded on the greatness of America, the spiritual and moral character of its people, and his efforts to end the Vietnam War.[51]

By far the most important festival of civil religion, exploiting evangelical sentiment but stage-managed by the White House, was Honor America Day which took place in Washington on July 4, 1970. The idea for it allegedly arose out of a conversation between Nixon and Graham in which the latter said: "Mr. President, everyone talks about what's wrong with America. Why doesn't someone talk about what's *right* with America?" Thereupon Graham, comedian Bob Hope, Hobart Lewis of the *Reader's Digest*, and hotel magnate J. Willard Marriott organized a celebration where ordinary citizens could speak out for the country. The White House assigned Jeb Magruder as the "liaison person" to insure "the event was run the way Haldeman and the President wanted it run." For most people it was merely a patriotic Fourth of July ceremony, featuring Graham in a morning interfaith religious service and big-name entertainment in the evening. In fact, the evangelist delivered his finest civil religion sermon where he called on his hearers to honor America, rededicate themselves "to God and the American dream," and "never give in" to those who were critical of old-fashioned virtues and, by implication, of the president's Vietnam initiative. Columnist David Lawrence called it "a day of celebration unique in history," but he did not know that for the administration clique it was, as Magruder revealed in his memoirs, "a political event, one in which honoring America was closely intertwined with supporting Richard Nixon, and in particular with supporting his policy in Vietnam at a time when a great many people were opposing it with rallies of their own."[52]

In the 1972 campaign, both candidates pulled out all the religious stops. The reelection committee even recruited evangelical stalwart Harold Ockenga to form a Clergy-for-Nixon organization to counter the small but pesky Evangelicals for McGovern group, a move that was simply electoral overkill.[53] Nixon claimed the civil religion "high ground" and easily elbowed his Democratic rival aside. He affirmed the symbols of priestly transcendence which gave a subliminal message of political and religious righteousness. These symbols, as Richard Scammon and Ben Wattenberg put it, appealed to the "unyoung, unpoor, and unblack" voters, those who were "middle-aged, middle-class, middle-minded."[54] McGovern's prophetic civil religion with its accent on guilt, prodigality, and the need for America to "come home" alienated much of the populace. Nixon's message was one of comfort and national affirmation, while McGovern challenged people to recognize they had sinned and were in need of redemption. The only "return" that Nixon considered was to the public religion of an earlier era which, as Henderson puts it, "sees a perfect harmony between faith in God and in the nation and which identifies the will of God with the welfare of the state." This was the civil religion which most Americans accepted, and the Democratic candidate had no hope of dislodging it.[55] There was no place for the prophetic faith of Abraham Lincoln in Nixon's America.[56]

NIXON'S FALL

The presidency is a sacred office. In recent times, as presidents have increasingly emphasized their priestly functions, they have conducted the rituals and repeated the creeds which serve to keep alive the "sacred cosmos" and define the collective existence of the American people. Thus, the erosion of trust that followed in the wake of the Watergate revelations left Nixon vulnerable to the consequences of his own misdeeds. In the famous address of April 30, 1973, the day of the major Watergate resignations, he tried to separate himself from the dirty work of his underlings and to portray himself as having been too busy to concern himself with their doings. He called for reforms to keep such things from happening again, but he would not accept any responsibility for them. Instead, he reiterated how much he loved America and believed it was the hope of the world: "I know that in the quality and wisdom of the leadership America gives lies the only hope for millions of people all over the world that they can live their lives in peace and freedom." In fact, he saw his office as the hope of the world, and knew that if he were to be exposed as unworthy of the sacred trust placed in him, he would quickly be toppled from power.[57]

As the months passed, Nixon's position steadily eroded.

Cracks in the evangelical bulwark began to show when on February 1, 1973 Senator Mark Hatfield electrified the audience (which included the president) at the National Prayer Breakfast with his prophetic remarks about the idolatry of the "god of civil religion" and his summons to "repentance from the sin that has scarred our national soul." Then, as more and more revelations were made and Nixon aides fell from power, the chief executive almost in desperation summoned Graham from Switzerland to lead a White House worship service on December 16 and provide him with reassuring words. But now even the evangelist was starting to have doubts, which he expressed in a *Christianity Today* interview.[58]

From here on it was all downhill. At the National Prayer Breakfast on January 31, 1974 the president gave a rambling, almost incoherent talk identifying with his Quaker heritage and Lincoln. Observers left wondering if he had lost contact with reality. Then, Hatfield proposed a National Day for Humiliation, Fasting, and Prayer modeled after the one proclaimed by Lincoln. The idea obtained Senate approval, and the speech making and religious activities in the capital and around the country on that day, April 30, reflected the fact that the chief priest of the public faith was no longer functioning.[59]

The release of the transcripts of the Oval Office tapes sealed Nixon's doom. Graham confessed that the revelations were "a profoundly disturbing and disappointing experience" and that "one cannot but deplore the moral tone" implied in them. He still continued to offer spiritual help to the president, but his overtures were rejected.[60] However, the evangelist emerged from the Nixon experience considerably chastened and in subsequent years not only sought to maintain some distance between himself and the president but also spoke out against the nuclear arms race and for better relations with communist-bloc countries. Civil religion themes were no longer noticeable in his sermons except on patriotic holidays and his evangelistic ministry assumed a distinctly global orientation.

During the last night in the White House with his world collapsing around him, Nixon wept and implored Henry Kissinger, not widely known as a man of faith, to kneel with him in prayer. The next morning, August 9, he closed out his presidential career by signing the resignation document and delivering a brief farewell address to his staff which contained a most remarkable comment: "We come from many faiths, we pray perhaps to different gods—but really the same God in a sense," and "always you will be in our hearts and you will be in our prayers." With that, he departed for his California home, and left the priestly mantle for his successor, Gerald Ford, who proceeded to rally the country around himself by appealing to civil religion.[61]

In the midst of this turbulent period, theologian Richard Neuhaus wrote that Christianity and Judaism were "in symbiotic relationship to the civil religion. Each supports the other; each lends plausibility to the other." In America organized Christianity succeeded because of "the assumption that membership in a church is supportive of true Americanism." Similarly, American public values "depend on the belief commitments that are nurtured by church and synagogue."[62] Richard Nixon, however, had taken civil religion beyond this more limited basis. Under his presidency, the national God had become so generalized that any faith would suffice. Moreover, he so identified the welfare of the nation with his welfare and survival that whatever was necessary to keep him in power was justifiable, and illegal actions, regardless of their nature, if they were performed in the name of national security, were acceptable. In the end, Nixon lost touch with the Judeo-Christian Deity that was so much a fixture in civil religion, and the new god he had created was unable to save him.

10

JIMMY CARTER AND THAT OLD-TIME (CIVIL) RELIGION

In July 1986, *Time* magazine reported an incident involving a presidential tape and Watergate conspirator Charles Colson. However, this time the president was Jimmy Carter, the tape was the type used in carpentry measurement, and the place was not Washington but an apartment building in Chicago. The two "born-again" politicos were working together on a project sponsored by Habitat for Humanity, a Christian organization that provided low-cost housing for the poor. Carter had done previous Habitat stints in New York City, but this was the first outing for Colson, who after turning to Christ had founded Prison Fellowship Ministries. He commented that the ex-president was similar to his old boss Richard Nixon in one respect— both were "slave drivers," but for two altogether different causes. Besides, quipped Colson, "this one doesn't end us up in jail—just at hard labor!"[1]

The shadow of the Nixon presidency has been long and dark. This is true in terms of religion as well as in terms of scandal and foreign affairs—as the anecdote illustrates. Recalling the religious aura of the Nixon administration, a Los Angeles Times reporter during the 1976 campaign asked the Democratic candidate, who openly proclaimed his Christian faith, if he intended to hold worship services in the

White House. Carter responded that he had no plans to do so because of his belief in the separation of church and state, and he added: "I would expect to worship in a nearby Baptist church on Sunday morning with as little fanfare as possible and, hopefully, after the first few Sundays I would be accepted as a member of the church."[2] He did just that, and no religious services took place in the presidential mansion during the Carter years.

A BORN-AGAIN POLITICIAN

David Awbrey, a young newspaper reporter with previous training in both history and theology, was fascinated by the former governor of Georgia who was gradually pulling ahead of the pack in 1976. One day, the skeptical newsman jumped into the back seat of Carter's limousine as it headed for the airport after a campaign stop in Baltimore. As the car sped on its way, Awbrey and others present fired questions about religion at the presidential aspirant. His replies revealed that he had immersed himself in the Bible, had read many major Christian thinkers and was conversant with theology, and had himself known those "dark nights of the soul" which galvanized faith. "By the end of the trip," Awbrey wrote later, "I was convinced that Jimmy Carter was one of the most sincere, true-believing Christians I had ever met."[3] Before the race was over, many others would agree.

The one thing which almost everyone recalls about the 1976 election was Carter's willingness to identify himself as a born-again Christian. But before he established himself as a viable candidate, the press often ridiculed his lack of name recognition by referring to him as "Jimmy Who?"[4] What in fact then was the background of this intensely religious man who seemed to come out of nowhere to capture first the nomination and then the presidency itself?[5]

James Earl Carter, Jr. was born on October 1, 1924, in the rural community of Plains, Georgia. His father, James Earl, Sr., was a farmer and businessman, and his mother, Lillian Gordy Carter, a nurse. He grew up in a world dominated by the extended family, the immediate community, the local congregation, and traditional values. Even though they were only occasional church-goers, the elder Carters saw to it that their children from earliest youth attended worship. The Plains Baptist Church became the core of young Jimmy's daily life. It steeped him in the Bible and, along with his family, gave him a sense of love, assurance, warmth, and security. At age eleven, he professed faith in Christ, was baptized, and joined the church. Before long, he had become a Sunday school teacher.

After graduating from high school in 1942, Carter chose a career in the navy. He received an appointment to the U.S. Naval Academy and eventually was commissioned in 1946. During his Annapolis years, he wooed a hometown girl (Rosalynn Smith, whom he married after graduation), taught a Sunday school class, and witnessed to his Christian experience in student discussions. He continued to practice his faith as a young naval officer, first on a battleship and later aboard submarines, and often taught Bible classes at sea.

An ambitious person, Carter in 1950 requested assignment to the new atomic submarine program. The selection interview brought him face-to-face with the "father of America's nuclear sub fleet" and head of the project, Admiral Hyman Rickover. The admiral's steely stare and unsmiling countenance made the younger man uncomfortable and unsure. After a rough interview, Rickover posed a question which Carter thought he could answer to his advantage: "How did you stand in your class at the Naval Academy?" Swelling with pride, he replied: "Sir, I stood fifty-ninth in a class of 820!" But instead of congratulating him, Rickover shot back: "Did you do your best?" Carter paused, gulped, and confessed: "No, sir, I didn't always do my best." A long pause followed and finally he asked Carter one final question: "Why not?" The young officer sat there for a while, shaken, and then slowly left the room in silence.[6]

Carter was accepted into the program but never forgot the incident. Those words and Rickover's personal example—"he was unbelievably hardworking and competent, and he demanded total dedication from his subordinates"—made the admiral a hero in the young Georgian's eyes. He had been a maverick outsider and an engineering genius who was shunted aside by the Navy bureaucracy until President Harry Truman discovered and empowered him. Carter used the admiral's question as the title of his political autobiography, and in it wrote that "Rickover had a profound effect on my life—perhaps more than anyone except my own parents."[7] Clearly, this drive for excellence, growing out of his Christian mindset and his experience with Rickover, was a vital aspect of his character.

His father's premature death in 1953 forced Carter to choose between a promising naval career and the family peanut business. Although Rosalynn did not like the action, he resigned, returned to Plains, and resettled his young family there. It was a difficult decision, but according to Carter, "I had only one life to live, and I wanted to live it as a civilian, with a potentially fuller opportunity for varied public service."[8]

In addition to working his own spread, Carter operated his late father's farm supply business. He did the manual labor while his wife kept the books, and the peanut warehouse soon grew into a profitable operation. At the same time, the Carters were active workers in the Plains church, both as teachers and lay leaders. He was superintendent of the junior high department and a deacon—the latter a leadership position in Baptist churches reserved for only serious and mature Christians. He also took part in civic affairs by serving on the county school board, hospital authority, and library board, and as director of the Georgia Crop Improvement Association. Carter's involvement in the religious and political life of south Georgia occurred during the height of the civil rights movement, the late 1950s and early 1960s. In those days, he did not hide his belief that segregation was wrong. He sincerely wished to see injustice halted and spoke out courageously in favor of civil rights when hard decisions faced the community. He admitted his fears but did not hesitate to stand against nearly everyone, whether they were friends, relatives, customers, neighbors, or fellow deacons. For example, during this period the Billy Graham Association decided to present an evangelistic film at a theater in nearby Americus, which the local ministers welcomed. Then they learned that the Graham organization intended to adhere to its policy that meetings must not be segregated, and none of them were willing to chair the event. Carter, however, volunteered to do so, and it was the first integrated audience in Sumter County, Georgia, in this century. Although Carter took a stand, he did not "lead" as such. In other words, he was not a "civil rights activist."[9]

Even though the rough style of southern politics was not inviting to a young "moderate" like Carter, public service did appeal to him. A reapportionment of the Georgia senate made it a more effective and responsive body, and he considered making a bid for a seat. He talked over the matter with a minister whose counsel he respected, and they reviewed the various forms of public service, including elected office. When Carter said that he might run for the state senate, the minister expressed dismay and strongly advised him not to become involved in such a "discredited profession." After some heated discussion, the preacher exclaimed in exasperation: "If you want to be of service to other people, why don't you go into the ministry or into some honorable social work?" Carter snapped back: "How would you like to be the pastor of a church with 80,000 members?" His spiritual adviser then conceded that it might be possible to stay honest and at the same time minister to the 80,000 citizens of Georgia's fourteenth senate district.[10]

With only an embryonic theology of public service, Carter announced his candidacy in 1962. He was elected after a bruising campaign, and a second term followed in 1964. Through intelligence and hard work he became a leader in the senate and won the admiration of his colleagues. Four years as a legislator whetted his appetite for higher office, and he entered the Democratic primary for governor in 1966. In a hard-fought race, he finished in third place.[11]

Exhausted by the torturous campaign and demoralized by its outcome, the forty-two-year-old Carter now faced a spiritual crisis. Just as his political career seemed to have ended, a series of experiences rejuvenated his Christian commitment and outlook on public service. Between fall 1966 and early spring 1967, he seriously rethought his original commitment to Christ. What resulted was a spiritual renewal or, in Baptist parlance, a "rededication" of his life to Christ.

First, during a visit with his sister, Ruth Carter Stapleton, he shared his trauma and despair. Although Ruth was four years younger than he, they were close friends. She had gone through a spiritual crisis of her own in 1959 and then became an evangelist and religious counselor. She later recalled the moment when they were sitting in the woods. As she put it:

> Jimmy's whole life went before him, as he held his face up, tears were just falling, and he said "Ruth, I don't know how I hesitated. I'll give up everything. I would

> rather have what you have than to even be President of
> the United States."
>
> Jimmy was having a series of awarenesses of some lacks
> in his life; maybe motivation, a sense of direction. It was a
> time of self-analysis. . . .He was wondering if he was
> doing enough, caring enough for mankind. Then he
> moved into a new dimension. . .a deeper commitment. I
> don't know that he had ever made a complete commit-
> ment of his political life before. After that, Christ came
> first because his ambitions were very fervent at the time.
> So it was a whole new phase of life he was moving into. It
> was to serve Christ in his work.[12]

A speaking engagement at a nearby church further
challenged him spiritually. He had been invited to talk on
"Christian witnessing," and proud of his service to the
church, he prepared his address in a mood of smug self-
satisfaction. But then he compared his own record of
witnessing for Christ with his activities in the recent
gubernatorial race. He realized that in crisscrossing the state
he had met more than 300,000 Georgians, while by contrast,
since returning home from the navy, he had visited for the
church around two families per year or a total of 140 people,
assuming an average of five people per family. As he later
told the story: "The comparison struck me—300,000 visits
for myself in three months, and 140 visits for God in fourteen
years!" He then opened the Bible and read in Luke 18:10–14
about the Pharisee, one of "the churchmen" of Jesus' day,
who took great pride and satisfaction because he was not an
extortioner, adulterer, or tax collector, and Jesus' response,
that those who humbled themselves would be exalted. ""For
the first time I saw that I was the Pharisee."[13]

About that time, he heard a sermon entitled "If You
Were Arrested For Being a Christian, Would There Be
Enough Evidence To Convict You?" at the Plains church. It
made an indelible impression on him.

> I was then a member of the largest and most prestigious
> church in town, a Sunday School teacher and a deacon,
> and I professed to be quite concerned about my religious
> duties. But when asked that question I finally decided that
> if arrested and charged with being a committed follower
> of God, I could probably talk my way out of it! It was a
> sobering thought.

In a 1976 interview with Bill Moyers, he elaborated on the incident:

> I had never really committed myself totally to God—my Christian beliefs were superficial. Based primarily on pride, and—I'd never done much for other people. I was always thinking about myself, and I changed somewhat for the better.I formed a much more intimate relationship with Christ.[14]

The upshot of this dark night of the soul was Carter's decision to "surrender to serve," made in much the same way that other Baptists would "surrender to preach." It was both a rededication of his life to Christ and an affirmation of his God-given vocation as a public servant. It deeply affected how he would campaign for higher offices and carry out the duties that came with those positions.

In 1967 and 1968, Carter went on two short-term lay mission trips under the auspices of the Southern Baptist Home Mission Board to cities in Pennsylvania and Massachusetts. He was part of a team which went door to door witnessing and helping people with special needs. In this way Carter learned firsthand about the plight of the big-city poor and the value of Christlike humaneness in dealing with their problems.[15]

Later, after prowling Georgia with his broad smile and delivering hundreds of speeches filled with populist rhetoric and agrarian values to civic, political, and religious groups, Carter entered the governor's race in 1970, and this time was victorious. He was a tireless worker and reasonably effective state executive, but being essentially conservative in matters of finance and liberal on questions of civil rights and social justice meant his relations with the legislature were stormy. The politics of contention during his four years in office earned him the nickname of "Jungle Jimmy." His tumultuous term also was exemplified by the occasion when he hung a portrait of fellow Baptist Martin Luther King, Jr., in the capitol building while the Ku Klux Klan paraded outside and a racially mixed choir sang "We Shall Overcome" inside.

Carter now was ready to seek the Democratic nomination for president in 1976. He believed that he could provide the country with strong moral leadership at a time of national uncertainty, and from the outset of his campaign, he promised "to restore in our country what has been lost." He said he would bring to the presidency a sense of integrity, excellence, boldness, inspiration, and commitment to social justice. Or, as a neighbor from Plains put it in homespun fashion, "He loves the Lord and wants to bring the country back to where it was."[16]

Thus, it is not surprising that Carter's religion was a campaign issue. From the outset he was open about his beliefs, and he fascinated the media with his knowledge of the Bible, desire to apply its tenets to government, and admission that he prayed daily. One columnist, Richard Reeves, even speculated that Carter's successes in the early primaries could be attributed to a spiritual connection he had made with the American people. Journalists pressed him to explain the meaning of "born again," and he acceded to their wishes just before the North Carolina primary. Newsman Jerry terHorst described the scene:

> An awkward hush fell over the room. Listeners squirmed and reporters lowered their eyes to their note pads. Everyone was embarrassed—except the candidate. Quietly, unblinkingly, he provided answers. Then the subject changed, and everyone was relieved. Frontrunner Jimmy Carter had just explained his religious faith in a way seldom heard from the lips of a politician.[17]

The media responded frenetically to this simple confession of faith in Jesus Christ. Reporters plowed through theological dictionaries in public libraries and telephoned church historian Martin Marty in Chicago, and one TV network anchorman assured his viewers:

> Incidentally, we have checked this out. Being "born again" is not a bizarre experience or the voice of God from a mountaintop. It's a fairly common experience known to millions of Americans—especially if you're a Baptist.

The awkwardness of the press in handling the story of Carter's faith was especially clear in the confusing religious terminology which most major newspapers and newsmagazines used during the campaign.[18]

THE FAITH OF PRESIDENT CARTER

Carter was the seventh occupant of the nation's highest office who openly professed to be a born-again Christian.

The others were Rutherford B. Hayes, James A. Garfield, Benjamin Harrison, William McKinley, Woodrow Wilson, and Gerald Ford. As presidential scholar Dan F. Hahn confirms: "The most obvious characteristic of Jimmy Carter, revealed in his rhetoric as well as other ways, was that he was a deeply religious person."[19]

There were three factors that shaped Carter's mature presidential faith—his Baptist heritage, wide reading in theology and literature, and the crucible of his own experiences.[20] The years of church attendance and exposure to Baptist preaching and Sunday school materials had a profound impact on him. Southern Baptist leader Foy Valentine pointed this out in an opinion piece he contributed to the *New York Times* in 1976 that was intended to alleviate misunderstandings about Baptists in general and explain who Jimmy Carter was. Valentine underscored that Southern Baptists were sinners saved by grace and people who accepted the Bible as their "guide in faith and practice." From biblical belief flowed the other Baptist doctrines, all of which Carter freely embraced—voluntary religion, the worth of every individual, the necessity for evangelism, a high code of personal ethics, congregational church government, and the separation of church and state as the best guarantee of religious liberty.[21]

The president possessed a great reverence for and knowledge of the Bible. UPI reporter Wesley Pippert, who covered the White House during these years, observed: "Carter had a mastery of Scripture that was revealed by his Sunday school lessons and dog-eared Bible."[22] In the campaign, reporters often quizzed him about the Bible, and his responses revealed that he was no right-wing fundamentalist. At the same time, they failed to trip him up with contradictions or to get him to compromise his belief in biblical authority. On one occasion he wrote to the *Atlanta Constitution* correcting a story which claimed that he did not believe the biblical accounts of miracles. Carter clearly qualified as an evangelical in his commitment to biblical infallibility, and he could have signed the statement which the Evangelical Theological Society requires of its members: "The Bible alone, and the Bible in its entirety, is the Word of God written and is therefore inerrant in the autographs."[23]

His prayer life as president was legendary. Only Washington and Lincoln were more known for prayer than he was. In his memoirs Carter revealed that the loneliness of making major decisions drove him to prayer, and he delineated how it helped him in his political duties:

> And I prayed a lot—more than ever before in my life— asking God to give me a clear mind, sound judgment, and wisdom in dealing with affairs that could affect the lives of so many people in our own country and around the world. Although I cannot claim that my decisions were always the best ones, prayer was a great help to me. At least, it removed any possibility of timidity or despair as I faced my daily responsibilities.[24]

Private family worship was another part of his life. Frequently he mentioned that he and his wife read the Bible together and prayed each day, usually in the evening. However, Carter was stingy with details about his personal life and did not say much about what part these private devotions played in his presidency. One reference in his memoirs does throw a little light on this. As the time of the 1980 Democratic National Convention neared and stories about his brother Billy's dealings with Libyans filled the press, Rosalynn became quite agitated. Jimmy calmed her by telling "her to reread the words of Jesus from our previous night's chapter, which happened to be John 14 ('Let not your heart be troubled: ye believe in God, believe also in me.')"[25]

Carter also bore witness to his faith in conversations with foreign leaders, but this was done privately. Among those to whom he spoke were Chung Hee Park of South Korea, Polish Communist Party Secretary Eduard Gierek, and Chinese Vice Premier Deng Xiaoping. His most fruitful effort in evangelical diplomacy was with Deng who promised that he would grant Carter's request to permit the distribution of Bibles and more religious freedom and would think about allowing Western Christian missionaries to return to China.[26]

Responsible political behavior was a further outgrowth of Carter's Baptist upbringing. Journalist-theologian James Wall points out that "service to others" is precisely what Carter "learned was his duty as a small boy in the Plains Baptist Church. We have been put on earth to serve others."[27] As president he visualized himself as the "First Servant" of the nation, just as a Baptist minister was supposed to be the "First Servant" of his congregation.[28]

Moreover, politics was a "high calling" which should result in a life of honesty, integrity, and sensitivity in dealing with people. Carter was particularly concerned with the proper use of power, and his restraint in employing force—seen in his handling of the Iranian hostage crisis and his being the first president in fifty years not to send American troops into combat—grew out of his biblical conviction that power is to be utilized to serve. During the 1980 campaign he said forthrightly: "I have always tried to use America's strength with great caution and care and tolerance and thoughtfulness and prayer."[29]

Carter's belief in social justice and his willingness to embrace civil rights were undoubtedly shaped by his Sunday School experience. The teacher's guides were written by some of the most enlightened Southern Baptist leaders of the times, including George W. Truett, Herschel H. Hobbs, Jimmy Allen, Foy Valentine, William Pinson, and, most importantly, the ethicists T. B. Maston of Southwestern Baptist Seminary and Henlee Barnette of Southern Baptist Seminary. These men passed on to young teachers their own progressive insights on the social issues of the day and the views of important theologians from other traditions. In short, there was much in the materials published by the Sunday School Board which sensitized Baptists to the social dimension of the gospel. The result was that many of them acted on what they professed, and this was certainly the case with Jimmy Carter.[30]

His unshakeable commitment to the separation of church and state also came from his Baptist roots. Although some Baptists in the 1980s who lusted after political power repudiated this doctrine which was such a vital part of their heritage, their forebears would have defended it to the death. The same Carter, who freely confessed that faith in Christ played a large role in his political life, stressed that the Constitution and his Baptist beliefs prohibited him from formulating public policy on the basis of his personal religious preferences. Being a strict separationist, that is, one who believed there should be the greatest distance possible between the institutional forms of the state and the church, Carter consistently opposed state aid to church-related institutions of learning, refused to support a constitutional amendment allowing government-sponsored prayer in the public schools, favored taxation of church properties not used directly for religious purposes, and declined to hold worship services in the White House. Only in his appointment of an envoy to the Vatican did he significantly deviate from strict separation.[31]

Carter's wide reading in theology and literature added an important dimension to his faith. In the White House he devoured political works, especially those dealing with the administration of his favorite president, Harry S. Truman, as he believed so many of the problems he faced were similar to those of that era.[32] By his own count, he had read works by theologians Reinhold Niebuhr, Karl Barth, Dietrich Bonhoeffer, Paul Tillich, and Soren Kierkegaard; sociologist Robert Bellah; philosophers Will Durant and Martin Buber; historian Barbara Tuchman; novelist James Agee; social critics William J. Lederer and Eugene Burdick; and poet Dylan Thomas. He also drew inspiration from Lincoln, Truman, Gandhi, and Martin Luther King, Jr.[33]

Carter often cited a paraphrase of Niebuhr's thought during the 1976 campaign and in presidential speeches: "The sad duty of politics is to establish justice in a sinful world."[34] At other times when he wanted to stress the need for balance between possibilities and limitations in the American experiment, Carter quoted Niebuhr's well-known words: "Man's capacity for justice makes democracy possible, but man's capacity for injustice makes democracy necessary."[35] Thus, Carter drew upon Niebuhr's ideas while struggling to adapt liberal political goals to the realities of human nature—a kind of sophisticated "Christian Realism," as some have called it. Don Winter points out that Niebuhr recommended a "blend of the realism of the conservative creed and the idealism of the liberal spirit. . .as the best contemporary expression of the pragmatic approach to politics required by Christian insight into the human situation." Niebuhr's concept of Christian Realism, with its emphasis on establishing a relatively just order through a pragmatic balance of forces, seems to have deeply influenced Carter's politics, making him a liberal on some issues and a conservative on others.[36]

The two also agreed about the effect on political conduct of the biblical concept of "dying to self," while a Niebuhrian flavor was manifested in Carter's insistence that faith in Christ enabled him to do the best he could, permitted him not to worry about defeat, and gave him in inner calm. Thus, after explaining his religious views to the press during an interview in 1976, he calmly ended with: "If there are those who don't want to vote for me because I'm a deeply committed Christian, I believe they should vote for someone else." Likewise, when the defeated Carter returned to Plains in 1981, his faith sustained and invigorated him as he adjusted to his new life.[37] Carter's views, thus, reflected those expressed by Niebuhr:

> Perhaps the most important relevance of Christian faith. . .is a sense of serenity and a freedom from hysteria in an insecure world full of moral frustrations. We have to do our duty for a long time in a world in which there will be no guarantees of security and in which no duty can be assured the reward of success. . . .We must sow without promising whether we can reap. We must come to terms with the fragmentary character of all human achievements and the uncertain character of historic destinies.[38]

There is also a Niebuhrian base for Carter's role as a prophet in politics. The theologian argued, "It is a fact that those who hold great economic and political power are more guilty of pride against God and of injustice against the weak than those who lack power and prestige." However, all was not lost, since any oligarchy, group, or individual could see the light, repent, and change their ways. Religion held out the possibility that "old forms of life may be renewed, rather than destroyed by the vicissitudes of history." The ¨condemnation which Carter heaped upon the "Washington establishment" clearly bore Niebuhr's imprint, and the prophetic element in his political rhetoric grew more evident as time passed.[39]

Carter was influenced by Robert Bellah as well. To be sure, the president did not directly quote the sociologist from California, but Bellah was one of the "religious leaders" whom he invited to the "domestic summit conference" at Camp David in July 1979, to advise him about how to cope with the "moral and spiritual crisis" which was eroding the nation's self-confidence. Bellah certainly concurred with this view of a nation in crisis and wrote eloquently about it, especially in the *Broken Covenant* (1975) which Edwin Gaustad called a "jeremiad with footnotes." Many of Bellah's concerns were echoed in Carter's energy speech later that month—for instance, the need to reestablish a sense of national purpose and unity on the basis of sacrifice and the call to renounce self-centeredness and excessive individualism.[40]

The third factor shaping Carter's White House faith was the crucible of experience. The crisis of soul in 1966–67 was part of this; also important were the adverse reactions to his religious expressions during the campaign. Carter's beliefs were criticized or called into question by both secularists and Christians, the media, and the so-called intellectual elite. Perhaps most painful were the slings and arrows of his fellow evangelicals. One spokesperson for the evangelical left charged him with duplicity and failure to apply his biblical profession of faith to the "real" political issues of the day—Vietnam, racism, and economic justice—and judgmentally concluded:

> Carter feels sincerely his commitment to Christ. . . .And he will tell Christians that it comes first, because that is what any Christian is to believe. But in reality, the campaign, the presidency, the oath of office, and the nation come first.

On the other end of the spectrum, the editor of a fundamentalist paper would not even concede the genuineness of his commitment to Christ and categorically asserted: "To Carter, the Bible offers no concrete decrees on right and wrong."[41] The attacks became increasingly savage as the term neared its end. His presidency had bogged down politically and the novelty of his Baptist words and ways had worn off. His religion was now fair game for his enemies.[42]

Carter's response to the assaults on the integrity of his faith was to pursue an independent course. This hurt his standing with the evangelicals, since he seldom was seen with Billy Graham and turned down invitations to address the meetings of such powerful organizations as the National Religious Broadcasters. When he finally did agree to speak to the NRB in 1980, it was too late to mend fences there. Also, in January 1980, he invited several NRB figures to a consultation at the White House, but afterwards one of their number circulated a false report that Carter freely admitted the presence of homosexuals on his staff.[43] In spite of this increasing hostility from his fellow believers, the president persevered in his devotional life, witnessing, and involvement in the First Baptist Church of Washington as a part-time Sunday school teacher. In short, his experiences nudged him in the direction of relying on his own private spiritual resources and avoiding intimacy with the evangelicals, his largest natural constituency.

Thus, the three shaping influences produced a chief executive who was deeply religious, thoughtful, intense, complex, and a Christian realist, and he translated his personal faith into what properly may be called a "moral presidency." The resulting presidential style reflected his religious temperament, and this got him into political trouble. As Charles O. Jones observes:

> Jimmy Carter was a missionary as president—bound and determined to make the changes he judged necessary. If it was the right thing to do, then it was the right thing to do. To the extent that changes in political style accomplished the goal, then he would concede that changes were in order (though his instinct often led him initially to inept modifications). Where changes in style led to significant compromises in substantive goals, however, Carter was opposed.[44]

But it was more than a matter of style. Carter's election symbolized America's longing for purity and a restoration of older values in the wake of Vietnam and Watergate, and he had a mandate to make morality the basis for government. Obviously, this did not preclude pragmatism, and the reality sometimes fell far short of the ideal; but he seriously tried to make morality a meaningful factor in the implementation of public policy.

Carter's philosophy of the restraint of power, principle of servant leadership, bold stand for human rights, and peace initiatives (especially in the Middle East) exemplified the highest ideals of Christianity. Yet, conservative critics condemned him as "immoral" because he would not submit to Congress constitutional amendments prohibiting abortion and permitting officially sanctioned prayer in public schools. Evangelist James Robison even went so far as to charge that Carter "doesn't really understand what it is to have convictions."[45]

His belief that power should be used to serve rather than to destroy or coerce was best illustrated in the Iranian hostage crisis, when he could have obliterated Tehran with the flick of a switch and substantially raised his popularity rating in the polls at home. (A derisive piece constantly heard on pop music radio stations at the time was a takeoff on the Beach Boys' hit song "Barbara Ann" that went, "Bomb, bomb, bomb, bomb Iran.") Unfortunately, most Americans interpreted Carter's practice of "prayerful restraint" as a lack of forcefulness and rejected his idea of a moral presidency. Many allegedly moral people abandoned him to pursue "single issue politics," while others turned their back on his call for sacrifice, believing that the day of economic reckoning could be postponed indefinitely. Throughout 1976 Carter had called for a "government as good as the American people"—the underlying assumption being that they were capable of wanting and sustaining "goodness" in government. Perhaps he was wrong. Maybe, as Richard Hutcheson suggests, the Watergate crowd *was* that government as good as the American people.[46]

CARTER AS A CIVIL RELIGIONIST

Given his background, Carter naturally employed civil religion terminology in his presidential campaign. However, the force of his born-again rhetoric ruffled many feathers during the race. For example, media pundit Harriet Van Horne scolded him for offending people with his "down-home, born-again Christianity." She attributed his civil abrasiveness to a lack of religious tact and declared that "in this ecumenical age, it might be more tactful for Governor Carter to cite the Judeo-Christian ethic rather than attributing all his talk of love and humility to the teachings of Jesus."[47]

Carter did not modify his language to satisfy critics, but he did embrace the main thrust of traditional American civil religion and integrated it into his own personal faith. Although he claimed not to view the presidency as a pastorate, like others before him, he sounded a pastoral note in his campaign speeches. He talked of his desire to bring "healing" to the spiritual wounds of America and affirmed there was "no reason why government should not represent the highest possible common ideals and characteristics of the people who form and support it. Its example should be inspirational and not embarrassing."[48]

More conspicuous were the priestly elements in his preelection rhetoric. Sometimes Carter blended the pastoral with the priestly, as when he said that the chief of state should emulate Christ because he is the one who "can speak with a clear voice, who can set a standard of morals, decency, and openness." But the priestly element usually surfaced as a rhetorical stroking of the collective ego of the public. Appealing to the electorate's basic goodness, the candidate declared: "Let us always put our faith in the American people and in their courage, for as long as we do, as long as they are with us, no power on earth can prevail against us or our nation."[49]

Carter's message also contained a prophetic element. He pronounced "prophetic judgment" on the Washington establishment, set forth the vision of a new America where order and prosperity would replace the chaos and economic disparity of the early 1970s, and proclaimed the current crisis to be a spiritual as well as a political one. His discourse brought a sense of transcendence to politics in general and civil religion in particular. Thus, Carter served notice:

> Our nation now has no understandable national purpose, no clearly defined goals, and no organizational mechanism to develop or achieve such purposes or goals. . . .It is time for us to reaffirm and to strengthen our ethical and spiritual and political beliefs.[50]

The candidate's most forthright prophetic statement was in his acceptance speech at the Democratic convention on July 14, 1976. Mixing Wilsonian moralism with traditional public faith, he quoted from civil scripture (the Declaration of Independence) and reaffirmed America's sense of world mission:

> America's birth opened a new chapter in mankind's history. Ours was the first nation to dedicate itself so clearly to basic moral and philosophical principles: That all people are created equal and endowed with inalienable rights to life, liberty, and the pursuit of happiness; and that the power of the government is derived from the consent of the governed.

> This national commitment was a singular act of wisdom and courage, and it brought the best and the bravest to our shores. It was a revolutionary development that captured the imagination of mankind. It created the basis for a unique world role for America—that of pioneer in shaping more decent and just relations among people and societies. Today, 200 years later, we must address our-

selves to that role, both in what we do at home and in how we act abroad.[51]

Although Carter may not have had a clear intellectual conception of civil religion as defined by scholars, he exploited it in the 1976 campaign. After the victory over Ford, he followed the example of his predecessors by celebrating it at the inauguration. Of course, he did not refer to Christ—in fact, the word God or its equivalent appeared only twice in his address. However, he deviated from the use of clerics from the four major expressions of the Judeo-Christian faith to perform the inaugural prayer rites, choosing instead to utilize only Methodist Bishop William Cannon of Atlanta and Roman Catholic Archbishop John Roach from the home state of Vice President Walter Mondale. Jewish involvement was restricted to a cantor from Atlanta, Isaac Goodfriend, who sang the national anthem at the close of the ceremony, and some Jewish observers regarded this as a slight.[52]

The address itself was reminiscent of Wilson's first inaugural, since the return to first principles and the establishment of justice were prominent themes in both.[53] There was also an implicit moralism, but Carter decided not to issue a plea for national repentance because he "feared that a modern audience might not understand a similar call from me." In most regards, however, it was a civil religion speech similar to those he had given on the campaign trail— a mixture of priestly and prophetic elements laced with and modified by his own evangelical piety and idealism. The "city upon a hill" theme appeared when he intoned, "We know that the best way to enhance freedom in other lands is to demonstrate here that our democratic system is worthy of emulation." He linked the spiritual dimension of civil religion with evangelical humanitarianism by asserting that:

> Two centuries ago our nation's birth was a milestone in the long quest for freedom, but the bold and brilliant dream which excited the founders of our nation still awaits its consummation. I have no new dream to set forth today, but rather urge a fresh faith in the old dream. Ours was the first society openly to define itself in terms of both spirituality and of human liberty. It is that unique self-definition which has given us an exceptional appeal; but it also imposes on us a special obligation—to take on

those moral duties which, when assumed, seem invariably to be our own best interests.

He assumed a priestly position by asserting faith in the American people and stroking them: "You have given me a great responsibility—to stay close to you, to be worthy of you and to exemplify what you are. . . .Your strength can compensate for my weakness, and your wisdom can help minimize my mistakes." The powerful Bible passage with which he began his address, Micah 6:8 ("He hath showed thee, O man, what is good; and what doth the Lord require of thee, but to do justly, and to love mercy, and to walk humbly with thy God"), was thus converted into a muted plea to renew "our search for humility, mercy, and justice," not a call for national repentance.[54]

A prophetic strain, nevertheless, was detectable in the speech. In one place, he proclaimed the need for an "absolute" commitment to wars against poverty, ignorance, and injustice, and in another, he declared there were limits to American resources and power and appealed for discipline and sacrifice. Having grounded his remarks in religious and patriotic hopefulness, Carter reminded the nation that a day of reckoning lay in the future: "We have learned that 'more' is not necessarily 'better,' that even our great nation has its recognized limits, and that we can neither answer all questions nor solve all problems."

Following the inauguration, Carter participated in various civil religion activities, of which the most important was the annual National Prayer Breakfast. His remarks about the public faith at these events gradually became less priestly and more prophetic in tone. The theme of the prayer breakfast address in 1977 was "the need for national humility," and here the president developed his evangelically oriented servant theology. He stressed Jesus' servanthood as a counterpoint to pride, both personal and national, and referring to the glib phrase "public servant," pointed out how hard it was to visualize the president of the United States as a genuine servant. He then suggested that pride could only be overcome and justice established when leader-servants were "strong enough and sure enough to admit our sinfulness and our mistakes." Moreover, he was concerned that the model of the "city upon the hill" not be compromised by national arrogance and a failure to live up to the

Founders' ideals. He wanted to see those people who looked
to America for inspiration continue to have respect for our
nation "because of the same vision of our forefathers who
inspired us." In order to do this, an admission of sinfulness
and true national humility was required.[55]

Carter's prayer breakfast address in 1978 had a flavor of
ecumenical civil religion. He shared his own faith, albeit
remarkably generalized, with the audience and then related
it to his recent experiences with Hindu, Muslim, and Jewish
political leaders around the world. Finally, he turned to the
American scene, noting that the Constitution prohibited the
establishment of religion, but:

> that did not mean that leaders of our nation and the
> people of our nation are not called upon to worship,
> because those who wrote the Declaration of Indepen-
> dence and the Bill of Rights in our Constitution did it
> under the aegis of, the guidance of, and with a full belief
> in God.[56]

The president returned to a prophetic theme at the 1979
gathering. In an address informed by his evangelical outlook, he admonished people to be careful about going along
with corrupt and misguided policies, as so often had been
the case in the past, and warned that:

> we must avoid a distortion or rationalization because of
> materialistic inclinations in our own hearts, of our own
> religious faith and its beliefs. When any religion impacts
> adversely on those whom Christ described as the "least of
> these," it can have no firm foundation in God's sight.[57]

In 1980 he dealt with personal and national "spiritual
growth" in a tone that was more like a pastoral homily. The
Iranian hostage crisis was much on his mind, and he testified
that he had developed spiritually because of it. He closed
with an observation rather than an admonition, but it was
one fraught with religious meaning:

> Well, growth in a person's life, growth for a nation,
> growth spiritually, all depend on our relationship with
> God. And the basis for that growth is an understanding of
> God's purpose, and a sharing of difficult responsibilities
> with God through prayer.[58]

Thus, Carter's prayer breakfast addresses reveal a development away from the priestly themes of the campaign to more prophetic ones, with the Iranian crisis in the last year of his administration diverting his attention to pastoral concerns.

Another manifestation of his public religion was his human rights policy, again a prophetic approach tempered by evangelical faith. He believed that such rights originated in the Judeo-Christian tradition, and he announced at the inaugural that they would be central to his administration's foreign policy. Carter wanted to export American morality, but in a noninterventionist form. He declared in classic nineteenth-century civil religion terms: "Promoting human rights, or freedom, or democracy, is a proper element of the foreign policy of a great nation."[59] This flowed from his scriptural sense of morality and civil religion understanding of national mission—and was more in the prophetic than in the priestly tradition.

The climactic formulation of Jimmy Carter's mature public faith was his energy speech in 1979, when he donned the mantle of a civil religion prophet. By this time his presidency was in deep trouble, as its accomplishments— civil service reform, industrial deregulation, the Panama Canal treaties, a modest reduction in foreign oil imports, improved relations with China, and the Egyptian-Israeli Peace Treaty—were overshadowed by the problems of White House estrangement from Congress, inflation, unemployment, Soviet adventurism, and an uneasy, ill-defined feeling that American power was on the wane. Most irritating of all were the nation's unresolved energy difficulties.

Carter had pledged to bring the energy crisis under control and called on Americans to see it as "the moral equivalent of war." But after two years, he had realized only meager results, and critics uncharitably abbreviated his martial declaration as MEOW. Enveloped in gloom, Carter retired to Camp David in July 1979, to ponder why Congress and the American people had so easily forgotten the oil panic of 1973–74. Were they too soft morally to make the necessary sacrifices in order to allow the country to free itself from dependence on foreign oil?

As mentioned above, Carter brought 130 national leaders to his Maryland retreat to consult about "the crisis of the American spirit." Included were ten religious figures, and given the president's propensity to frame problems and solutions in spiritual constructs, they may well have been the most influential of all those summoned to the mountain hideaway. Ecumenical but not all-inclusive (no fundamentalists were present), they helped to set the tone for his upcoming energy address. They told him that the problem went deeper than the frustrations of filling station lines and oil shortages. It was a spiritual crisis, and Americans must repudiate the ethics of materialism sold to them by the consumer society. He should provide bold leadership, tell the truth about the limitations of material progress, and ask for sacrifice. Most importantly, he must challenge the current materialistic value system and call upon the people to pledge themselves to national renewal based on nonmaterialistic assumptions.[60]

Strengthened by these consultations, Carter framed his energy speech of July 15 in terms of "a moral and spiritual crisis" and "a crisis of confidence" in national values and institutions. Actually two speeches in one, the first half addressed the underlying spiritual malaise plaguing the nation, while the second half laid out a six-point program for solving the energy crisis.[61] The first part was a major affirmation of presidential civil religion in which he wove together a plea for personal and national renewal in a twentieth-century version of Lincoln's prophetic faith. He deftly linked the spiritual state of the individual with national purpose as he described the situation:

> It is a crisis that strikes at the very heart and soul and spirit of our national will. We can see this crisis in the growing doubt about the meaning of our own lives and in the loss of a unity of purpose for our nation. The erosion of our confidence in the future is threatening to destroy the social and the political fabric of America. The confidence that we have always had as a people is not simply some romantic dream or a proverb in a dusty book that we read just on the Fourth of July. It is the idea which founded our nation and which has guided our development as a people. Confidence in the future has supported everything else—public institutions and private enterprise, our own families, and the very Constitution of the United States.

In a prophetic fashion, the president confessed that "too many of us now tend to worship self-indulgence and consumption. Human identity is no longer defined by what one does but by what one owns." Then he lamented, "there is growing disrespect for Government and for churches and for schools, the news media and other institutions. This is not a message of happiness or reassurance but it is the truth. . . .There is simply no way to avoid sacrifice." With great vigor, he challenged the American people to choose which path they would take:

> One is the path I've warned about tonight—the path that leads to fragmentation and self-interest. . . .It is a certain road to failure.

> All the traditions of our past, all the lessons of our heritage, all the promises of our future point to another path: the path of common purpose and the restoration of American values. That path leads to true freedom for our nation and ourselves. We can take the first steps down that path as we begin to solve our energy problem. . . .On the battlefield of energy we can win for our nation a new confidence, and we can seize control again of our common destiny.

The reporting of the president's address was as pious and civil religious as the speech itself. In *Newsweek*, the lead sentence was cast in Mosaic language (with an accompanying illustration featuring Carter as Moses):

> In an atmosphere of high political drama, Jimmy Carter came down from Catoctin mountaintop last week with his proposed new declaration of independence of foreign oil—and a very nearly missionary sense of calling to unite America behind it.

The speech was described as "a sermon" in which Carter reached back to "the psaltery rhetoric of his nomination" to rekindle the spirit of concern once characteristic of the American nation during a time of emergency, and in the process sought to "resurrect his own faltering Presidency" by using a "kind of sawdust-trail revivalism." His "Sunday night witness for America" was a "save-the-nation circuit ride" where he delivered "a homily" on how to "save the nation" from the "spiritual exhaustion" which he saw as the real basis of the current energy problem. Other spiritual buzz words crowded the report: "faith," "message," "renewal," "cosmic gloom," "sacrifice," "soul," "peace-in-the-valley politics," "communion with the people," and "doom-cryers." Following this orgy of religious descriptology, the article concluded:

> Carter's Sunday evening sermon was at least a begin-ning—a return to the strains of civic and religious faith that suffused his 1976 campaign. He chose in his speech to run against that exhaustion of hope and purpose he sees as "a fundamental threat to American democracy"— and, as he saw so clearly on the mountaintop, to his own future.[62]

With this speech, Carter's pilgrim's regress in civil religion was complete. He had started out as a generalist, instinctively practicing the public faith, informing it with his personal evangelical beliefs, and preaching an upbeat form of mildly priestly civil religion. Then, he gradually moved toward a modern-day prophetic variety, albeit one strongly affected by his own biblical faith. He realized that long-term sacrifice rather than short-term serenity was needed to solve the intractable problems facing the nation. He entered the presidency standing on the backs of two horses—priestly and prophetic civil religion—but the crises he encountered made it clear that prophetic preaching and not priestly stroking was needed if he were to restore the traditional values and national goals to which he was committed. Thus, he eventually firmly planted both feet on the horse of old-fashioned prophetic civil religion.

James Barber believes Carter was elected because "he expressed the moral theme people wanted to hear in 1976."[63] This was no doubt true, but that refrain could not carry his presidency for long. Thus, as he analyzed the spiritual dimensions of national problems and struggled to translate this moral theme into public policy, the prophetic note entered his civic preaching, especially in the appeals for nuclear weapons control and energy conservation. More-over, unlike his mentor Lincoln, Carter tried to arouse people about crises they had not yet experienced. His situation was analogous to that of Roosevelt prior to Pearl Harbor, not Lincoln during the Civil War, despite what he said about the moral equivalent of war.

The change in the president's personal Christian life paralleled that in his civil religion. Unlike Lincoln, Carter had been a confirmed believer before entering the White House, but like Lincoln, he underwent significant spiritual growth there, one which went hand in hand with the shift in civil religion emphasis. Both expert observer Wes Pippert and Carter himself agreed that spiritual maturation had occurred.[64] The irony is that this growth failed to prevent his repudiation by the electorate in 1980.

THEY WANTED A PRIEST, NOT A PROPHET

Carter's failure as a political leader was, in part, public rejection of his civil religion. He told the American people what they did not want to hear—that they would have to renounce their profligate lifestyles. They spit out the medicine of sacrifice which he offered them in favor of the priestly sugar pill administered by Ronald Reagan. They turned away from Carter's prophetic view of power to Reagan's politics of nostalgia for the bygone America of limitless plenty and power. Further, his moralizing rhetoric, often overbearing piety, and civic religiosity gained him the enmity of the media and party professionals, and he was caricatured and abandoned by those he needed most to make his presidency succeed.[65]

Further, large numbers of evangelicals joined their fellow Americans in repudiating Carter's prophetic civil religion. Mobilized against Carter by the New Religious Right in 1979–80, their disavowal of his civil religion of restraint and international good will was translated into votes for Reagan. They were drawn by the voice of a high priest who promised to preside over restored national power and prestige. As historian James A. Patterson assesses the situation:

> In 1976, many evangelicals were drawn to Jimmy Carter because of his openly professed born-again faith, whereas NCR support of Reagan in 1980 seemed to relate more to his political conservatism than to his personal spirituality.[66]

They longed for a priestly style civil faith, and Carter's opponent offered that. Many evangelicals wanted to hear words of joy about America's power and plenty, not the pious homilies of a Baptist lay preacher or the calls to sacrifice and repentance of a civil prophet.

As for Carter, during his White House years he grew in both his personal and public faith. The Georgian moved from a priestly to a prophetic view of the religious dimensions of his office, and in a manner reminiscent of southern evangelical Christianity, his basic theme became "give me that old-time (civil) religion." When his term began, his civil faith resembled that of his immediate predecessors; when he left office, it sounded more Lincolnian. During his tenure, he checked the development of both the "imperial presidency" and priestly civil religion with his "moral presidency" and increasingly prophetic faith.

Why Carter would in the end be spurned by the American people was foreseen by columnist James Reston. In a perceptive analysis of the inaugural address he suggested that it raised two vital questions: (1) Was the president's appeal to the noble principles of the American past relevant? and (2) Were the American people ready to respond to his call for austerity, discipline, and sacrifice for the common good?[67] The answers were given in 1980. The modern civil religion prophet was clearly without honor in own country.

11

RONALD REAGAN AND THE EXALTATION OF AMERICAN CIVIL RELIGION

The scene at the Mayport Naval Station in Jacksonville, Florida, was one of deep mourning. The speaker on that sad morning, May 22, 1987, eulogized the three dozen victims of the Iraqi missile attack on the USS *Stark* which had occurred in the Persian Gulf five days earlier. Then, he consigned them to the care of the Almighty:

> Let us remember. . .to understand that these men made themselves immortal by dying for something immortal, that theirs is the best to be asked of any life—a sharing of the human heart, a sharing in the infinite. In giving themselves for others, they made themselves special, not just to us but to their God. "Greater love than this has no man than to lay down his life for his friends." And because God is love, we know He was there with them when they died and that He is with them still. We know they live again, not just in our hearts but in His arms. And we know they've gone before to prepare a way for us.
>
> So, today we remember them in sorrow and in love. We say goodbye. And as we submit to the will of Him who made us, we pray together the words of scripture: "Lord, now let thy servants go in peace, Thy word has been fulfilled."[1]

These solemn phrases were not uttered by any minister of religion or ordained clergy, but by the President of the United States, Ronald Reagan. Probably no other statement reveals so clearly how civil religion in his administration had been elevated to such a high level that it stood on an equal basis to the particular religion practiced by millions of Americans in their churches, synagogues, and temples. Here he was acting in his capacity as the high priest of American civil religion, albeit more unabashedly, forcefully, compellingly, and with greater national acceptance than any previous president. Civil religion had now become so polished and rapacious that for the first time it was in direct competition with genuine religion. Never had it occupied such an exalted place in the national experience.

FROM THE SILVER SCREEN TO THE WHITE HOUSE

Ronald Reagan will undoubtedly go down in history as one of the most controversial personalities ever to reside in the executive mansion. During his years in office, Reagan's admirers saw him as a man of vision who sparked a rebirth of hope in the future and faith in America. He halted the inflationary spiral, cut taxes, relaxed the controls that were strangling business enterprise, and brought about economic recovery. He renewed people's awareness of the evils of communism and rebuilt the nation's defenses, enabling the country to negotiate with the Soviet Union from a position of strength and making it once again respected in the world. His supporters in the evangelical Protestant and Roman Catholic communities, the overwhelming majority in the former and a large, influential group in the latter, saw him as God's man of the hour, the person who almost single-handedly stemmed the tide of liberalism and secularism, renewed constitutional government, and restored the traditional values of the family, home, school, and church to their rightful place in American life.

However, in the view of his critics, Reagan pandered to the wish-fantasies of the American people and pursued policies which, although highly popular, were destined to be catastrophic. They said that he surrounded himself with corrupt, self-serving advisers; made the skies unsafe by firing striking air traffic controllers and by unwisely deregulating the airline industry; followed an economic program of

massive tax cuts, free trade, and increased defense spending
that produced both unprecedented budget deficits and a
stock market crash; and achieved little of substance in foreign
relations, either in the Middle East or Central America, the
two areas with which he was most concerned. Detractors
also argued that his reductions in social programs had led to
a deterioration in the quality of life for racial minorities,
while the promotion of "traditional values" had eroded the
gains made by women and breached the barrier between
church and state. Even the most cursory review of the
literature will reveal just how great the differences in opinion
are.[2]

The future president was born in Tampico, Illinois on
February 6, 1911, into humble circumstances. His father,
John Edward Reagan (1883–1941), was the son of Irish
immigrants who came to America in 1856 and settled in
northwestern Illinois. Orphaned at age 6, Jack Reagan, as he
was called, was raised by relatives and became a footloose
shoe salesman. His mother, Nellie Clyde Wilson (1883–
1962), was the granddaughter of Scottish and English
immigrants. She later shortened her name to Nelle. Her
family was of rural origins and not especially religious, and a
priest officiated at her marriage with the hard-drinking Irish
Catholic in November, 1904. Their first child, John Neil, born
in 1908, was baptized a Roman Catholic and remained close
to his father. Such was not the case with the second son,
Ronald Wilson, who was born two and one-half years later.
Since, in the interim, Nelle had joined the Christian Church
(Disciples of Christ) which required a personal confession of
faith and baptism by immersion, the infant was not christened. The family lived in various places in Illinois as Jack
Reagan bounced around from job to job, until they finally
settled in Dixon in 1920, the city that the future president
would always regard as his hometown.

Although Nelle disliked her husband's lifestyle, she was
faithful to him, and she concentrated on rearing the boys in
the Christian Church, into which both of them were baptized
on June 21, 1922. Neil apparently went along with this to
please his mother but eventually returned to the Catholic
fold, while Ronald became involved in the life of the Dixon
congregation. He attended Sunday school and all the church
services, occasionally taught a Bible class, acted in his
mother's dramatic skits, and dated the pastor's daughter.

He did well in high school, worked in the summer as a lifeguard at the local beach, and then enrolled in Eureka College, a Disciples school, where he majored in economics and engaged in all the campus activities he could. He graduated in 1932 and eventually landed a job as a sports broadcaster at a radio station in Davenport, Iowa. He also got involved in New Deal politics alongside his father, who campaigned for Franklin Roosevelt and consequently was put in charge of the new Federal Emergency Relief Administration office in Dixon. The younger Reagan voted for Roosevelt that year and identified with the Democratic party, even to the point of imitating FDR's style and rhetoric.

Early in 1933, he moved to a larger station, WHO in Des Moines, where he gained a reputation as an effective sportscaster and radio announcer. During a visit to California in 1937, he took a screen test and was given a contract by Warner Brothers. He became a successful actor, moved his parents to Los Angeles, and even helped set up his brother in the advertising business. Although Nelle was active in a Christian church there, her son was by this time largely indifferent about such matters. Still, he maintained the image of a clean-cut, all-American boy by playing "good guy" parts and marrying the twenty-three-year-old divorced actress Jane Wyman in 1940. With his attractive wife and two small children, he fit in well with the basic conservatism that then characterized the motion picture industry. In 1938, he joined the Screen Actors Guild, a Democratic and fully Rooseveltian union organization that did battle with the movie moguls, and in 1947 he became its president.

Reagan had just reached "star" status when America entered World War II. He obtained a commission in the air corps, but bad eyesight made him ineligible for combat duty, and he was assigned to the Hal Roach studios at Culver City to make training and propaganda films. After the war, he went through a period of severe adversity. He had huge tax debts, few good parts came his way, his Warner contract was cancelled, and his choice of roles so deteriorated that he had to play opposite a chimpanzee. Even as his career and marriage distintegrated (he and Jane Wyman divorced in 1949), he grew more involved in union politics and labor strife. At the time, Reagan was regarded as a radical, but he severed his left-wing ties and freely cooperated with the FBI and the House Committee on Un-American Activities in their probes of Hollywood in the late 1940s. This enabled him to emerge unscathed from the controversies over alleged communist infiltration of the film industry. As Garry Wills puts it: "Though Reagan did not change his party registration until 1962, his world and his views were conservative, business-oriented, and actively anti-Communist from 1947 on."[3]

Then, a new love came into his life, actress Nancy Davis. Born in 1921, she was the daughter of Edith Luckett, an actress whose husband left her when Nancy was an infant.[4] In 1929, Edith remarried a well-to-do neurosurgeon, Dr. Loyal Davis, who adopted Nancy, thus insuring that she would have a comfortable life even in the depths of the depression. She attended a private school and Smith College and then embarked upon an acting career, making several films with Metro-Goldwyn-Mayer. Nancy married Ronald Reagan in 1952 and they had two children, though she continued making films for a while. She brought to the marriage a fervent sense of loyalty and a desire to advance the interests of the man in her life. Nancy also courted rich socialites and cultivated her husband's growing political conservatism, and without a doubt she was the indispensable element in his later success.

After a disastrous Las Vegas night club stint, Reagan's career took a turn for the better when in 1954 he was employed as host of the *General Electric Theater* television show. He filmed the introductions, starred from time to time, and for three months each year toured GE plants as a "corporate ambassador," thereby gaining exposure around the country and "soaking up the mindset of men on the make in the Eisenhower years," as James Barber points out.[5] Although during the 1950s he continued the fiction of being a Democrat, he had in fact moved far to the right and had become one of the most ardent champions of big business. When the GE contract ran out in 1962, his brother Neil secured him the job of hosting TV's *Death Valley Days*.

The Goldwater campaign of 1964 marked Reagan's emergence on the national political stage. He was co-chair of the California Goldwater committee, and his nationally televised speech on October 27, "A Time for Change," made him an instant hit with conservatives. After the election debacle, Reagan presented himself as the agent of healing in the party and the voice of responsible conservatism. A group of wealthy businessmen coalesced behind him and provided him with the financial means to enter the California governor's race. He ran as "the candidate of the people" and won a smashing victory over the Democratic incumbent in 1966. He proved to be more moderate than his electoral rhetoric (under him state spending doubled and taxes increased dramatically), and his penchant for delegating governmental responsibility to his friends became well-known.

Reagan angled for the presidential nomination in 1968, but he was outmaneuvered by Nixon and decided to remain in the governor's chair. He made a second bid in 1976 but could not dislodge the incumbent, President Ford. However, after the Watergate disaster and Carter victory, the conservative forces cut themselves loose from their traditional party allegiances and regrouped as the "New Right." They saw Reagan as a man after their own heart and worked diligently to secure his nomination and election in 1980. Still, his triumph was hardly overwhelming, since he received just slightly over half of the votes cast in a presidential election marked by the lowest percentage voter turnout in history.

THE NEW RELIGIOUS RIGHT AND REAGAN'S VICTORIES

One of the most remarkable features of the Reagan campaigns in 1980 and 1984 was the mobilization of large numbers of evangelical Christian voters, many of whom had voted Democratic or not at all in previous presidential elections. The realization that modern evangelicals were susceptible to conservative appeals came as no surprise to historians, since many fundamentalist preachers had bitterly denounced the New Deal in the 1930s and aligned themselves with anticommunist movements in the 1950s and 1960s. Richard Nixon had actively courted evangelicals in 1960, 1968, and especially in the 1972 race against George McGovern. Then in 1975–76, Arizona Congressman John B. Conlan and Campus Crusade for Christ leader Bill Bright launched a low-key effort to elect conservative Christians to public office, but a piece of investigative journalism in *Sojourners* magazine blew the cover on the venture and effectively eliminated it as the Reagan campaign vanguard in the evangelical community.[6] Nevertheless, his aide Charles Hobbs prepared a campaign tract, *Ronald Reagan's Call to*

Action, which was published by a leading evangelical firm, while religious television talk-show host George Otis elicited his views on "spiritual and moral issues" in a lengthy interview that received wide publicity in the evangelical press and was designed to show that he was "one of them."[7] However, the conservatives' efforts could not overcome Jimmy Carter's appeal to the evangelical community in 1976.

Meanwhile, as already mentioned, the political right was building a disciplined, well-organized, and well-financed network of loosely knit affiliates existing outside the framework of the Republican party. Utilizing computerized fundraising techniques, these groups amassed a war chest totaling millions of dollars, much of which came in small donations from blue collar workers, housewives, and businessmen who were discontented, angry, and resentful about the changes taking place in American life and the perceived failure of the Carter administration to respond to their concerns. New Right figures also saw the potential of the "televangelists," preachers who had built large ministries by means of the electronic media, to influence evangelicals dissatisfied with lifestyle changes and the secularization of American society.

Thus, with the creation of such organizations as the Moral Majority, Christian Voice, and the Religious Roundtable, an alliance between the secular and religious right was forged, and the meshing of television and the computer took place. The fundamentalist ministers and TV evangelists eagerly jumped at the opportunity to promote their social views and exercise some real political muscle for the first time. "Born-again politics" was now a reality, as pastors and laypeople were urged to become involved in politics, inform their followers about the political and moral views of candidates, and get them registered and voting for those candidates who would "bring America back to God."

The story of the formation, composition, and activities of the "New Religious Right" is well known and does not require detailed recounting here.[8] The "newness" of the movement, that which made it different from the earlier Christian right, was, as Erling Jorstad succinctly shows, due to several factors. These included the participation of clergy in the day-to-day process of electioneering; the extensive use of television; the raising of massive sums of money for political purposes; the involvement of fundamentalists who laid aside their traditional separatism to work together with people of differing religious views to advance the higher cause of conservative political action; concentration on a sweeping sociomoral agenda rather than some single-issue reform; the exploitation of "secular humanism" as the overarching conspiracy on which to blame America's woes; and the existence of a national rather than a regional constituency of activists and supporters alike. Its strength caught the media and scholarly world by surprise, for they had been arguing that America was becoming a secular society and that organized religion was in decline.[9]

Like the secular right, the religious right was firmly anticommunist and rejected accommodation with the Soviet Union. Being on the conservative side of almost all public issues, it opposed labor unions, expansion of the federal government, affirmative action programs, busing school children to achieve racial integration, environmentalism, gun control, and any diminution of military strength. Added to this was a deep, emotional commitment to a package of social or "family" issues. The central demand was a constitutional amendment prohibiting abortion. Most of its adherents were also against the Equal Rights Amendment, pornography, state-supported day-care centers for working mothers and shelters for battered wives, child abuse legislation, and granting civil rights to homosexuals. Many advocated parental control over textbooks and the content of instruction in the public schools, including the teaching of free enterprise, patriotism, and creationism and an end to sex education, and of course, the restoration of classroom prayer and Bible reading. They favored the elimination of all state regulations governing private or parochial schools, and the provision of vouchers or tuition tax credits to assist parents who sent their children to them.

What is most significant was that the religious right groups and sympathizers threw themselves body and soul into the Reagan campaign, sincerely believing that he was a godly, evangelical Christian who would achieve the spiritual reclamation of America. They distributed tracts and books extolling his spiritual qualities, used mass mailings, media blitzes, and voter registration drives to rally conservative believers behind the Reagan standard, and did what they could to minimize the Christian faith of the two far more active churchmen who were candidates in 1980, President

Carter and third-party hopeful, independent Republican John B. Anderson. New Right evangelicals brought their influence to bear in writing the Republican platform, which came out against the ERA and abortion, while the Rev. Jerry Falwell edged his way into the circle of Reagan's advisers and was consulted about the selection of George Bush as his running mate. In turn, the candidate appeared before the premier New Religious Right gathering, the "National Affairs Briefing," and at the conservative Coral Ridge Presbyterian Church in Fort Lauderdale, Florida. In both places he courted evangelicals by endorsing their stance on the theory of evolution, abortion, and state interference in religious matters.[10]

To be sure, some analysts question whether the mobilized Christians had been the decisive factor in the Reagan victory. These pundits maintain that the pocketbook issues—unemployment, plant closings, inflation, rising interest rates, and energy shortages—coupled with the perception that America was losing its key role in world affairs were of greater concern to voters than the morality, social, and religious matters that the religious right had emphasized. Whether the New Right rode or created the anti-incumbent, anti-Democrat, anti-liberal wave in the 1980 election remains an open question, but it undoubtedly was now a political force to be reckoned with.[11]

In 1984, the New Religious Right worked hand in hand with the Reagan-Bush reelection committee to rally voters. For his part, the president appeared before major evangelical bodies—most notably the National Religious Broadcasters, National Association of Evangelicals, and Baptist Fundamentalism 1984 conferences—as well as some Roman Catholic and Jewish gatherings, but ignored the meetings of the "mainline" Protestant denominations and ecumenical organizations. With White House cooperation, three religious publishing houses produced books on or by Reagan which were designed for mass distribution.[12] The Rev. Tim LaHaye, whom the reelection committee assigned to keep the evangelicals in the chief executive's corner, formed the American Coalition for Traditional Values and enlisted many TV preachers and evangelical leaders in an endeavor to educate their followers to cast ballots for "pro-moral candidates." Campaign chairman Senator Paul Laxalt sent "Dear Christian Leader" letters to 45,000 selected ministers and priests urging them to organize registration drives in their churches and assure the reelection of President Reagan and Vice President Bush. Religious Right figures were given prominent places at the Republican National Convention, and a variety of things were done to woo Roman Catholic and Jewish voters as well. Probably in no election campaign in American history, not even 1928 or 1960, did religion receive a larger billing than in 1984.[13]

Again, as in 1980, this vote-hustling may not have been necessary. President Reagan's personal popularity was so great that he ran far ahead of New Right politicians who shared local tickets with him: he was able to carry some senatorial candidates on his coattails, such as Jesse Helms in North Carolina, but he could not bring along Roger Jepson in Iowa and Albert Lee Smith in Alabama. The election was a referendum on his performance as president, not an affirmation of his social policy. Heating up the religious question only diverted the attention of conservative Protestants and Catholics from other issues in the campaign. Reagan's own faith was never an issue, and the hoopla raised by the religious right only served to obscure how much the whole matter was really a question of civil religion, rather than personal belief.

IN GOD HE TRUSTS

Just what kind of faith did Ronald Reagan possess? Since he so often injected religious themes into his public addresses and met with and courted religious leaders and their organizations, few aspects of his presidency were fraught with more controversy and ambiguity than this. Evangelical admirers regarded him with fondness as a brother in Christ: "he is probably the most evangelical president we have had since the founding fathers" (Pat Robertson); "he is a godly leader; a man of spiritual understanding and knowledge" (Nashville businessman David Shepherd); "Ronald Reagan is a born again Christian" (Herb Ellingwood, lawyer and staff member).[14] In fact, the prominent Southern Baptist pastor Adrian Rogers asked him point-blank during the 1980 campaign whether he knew the Lord Jesus or if he only knew "about" him, and the candidate replied: "I *know* him."[15] On the other hand, critics regarded his faith as shallow, insipid, and politically motivated. Their feelings were best summed up in a pithy phrase coined by Martin Marty in an editorial on presidential piety in 1984: Mr. Reagan is "sincere but inauthentic."[16]

In spite of the strong differences of opinion concerning the nature of his faith, Reagan's personal beliefs were closely linked with his public religion.[17] Most importantly, it was the religious worldview that he acquired in his youth that would later make him acceptable to conservative evangelicals. This was shaped by his mother Nelle, who had undergone a conversion experience and thereafter had devoted her life to the congregations in the places where she lived, especially in Dixon where she taught Sunday school, presided over the women's missionary society, visited hospital patients and prisoners, staged religious dramas that she had composed herself, and was in every sense a pillar of the church.

Nelle saw to it that her son's life was centered in the church which he joined at age eleven, and she instilled in him the outlook of the Disciples with its emphasis that reason applied to Scripture could lead one to salvation. It was a piety that stressed personal study of the Word of God, hard work, and moral strictness but downplayed emotionalism and isolation from the world. After leaving Illinois, Reagan strayed from his Disciples' moorings, but he attended services from time to time. The mother and son transferred their memberships to the fashionable Hollywood-Beverly Christian Church, and apparently he gave money to the church.[18] He often mentioned Nelle and her impact on him, and the comment in his address to women leaders of Christian religious organizations on October 13, 1983, may be regarded as typical:

> Nelle Reagan, my mother, God rest her soul, had an unshakable faith in God's goodness. And while I may not have realized it in my youth, I know now that she planted that faith very deeply in me. She made the most difficult Christian message seem very easy. . . .Her way was forgiveness and goodness, and both began with love.[19]

Film star Reagan's connection with the church in the 1940s and 1950s was rather tenuous, and he was well-known as a "ladies' man" (during his bachelor periods), a light drinker, and a teller of off-color jokes. His second wife was not noted for her piety, the four children of his two marriages were scarcely examples of a model Christian family, and thirty years in Hollywood left him reasonably tolerant of aberrant sexual behavior. As governor, he endorsed the Equal Rights Amendment (but backed down later because of conservative opposition) and signed into law a therapeutic abortion bill. After he left office, he helped kill an initiative that would have barred homosexual teachers from California classrooms, and he was embarrassed by the release of his federal income tax return for 1979, which revealed he had donated less than one percent of his adjusted gross income to charitable and religious causes.[20]

Such a pattern of behavior would hardly have endeared him to evangelicals, but there was another side to his religious development. At some point in the 1950s, Reagan's mother-in-law introduced him to Billy Graham. As a result of this introduction, Reagan and Graham became warm friends. During the 1960s, he came to know several prominent evangelical charismatics, including Pat Boone, George Otis, Harald Bredesen, Herbert Ellingwood, and Demos Shakarian. Most importantly, in 1964 he began attending Bel Air Presbyterian Church and developed a close relationship with its evangelical pastor, the Rev. Donn Moomaw, although he did not move his membership there.

When he was elected governor of California, Reagan began to be much more outspoken about his faith. He declared during the inauguration week that he intended to conduct his office according to the teachings of Jesus and to seek God's help in the discharge of his duties. He occasionally met with Moomaw for prayer and twice asked Graham to address the state assembly. Once he invited the evangelist to speak to his cabinet about the second coming of Christ.[21] In his letters and speeches he frequently referred to the Bible and the power of prayer. Reagan's charismatic friends even held intercessory prayer meetings in his office, and in 1974 they allegedly secured the miraculous healing of his chronic ulcer condition.[22]

During his governorship occurred one of the most bizarre incidents in the history of political religiosity. On September 20, 1970, Ellingwood brought entertainer Pat Boone, his wife Shirley, and charismatic media personalities Otis and Bredesen to the executive mansion in Sacramento, where they had an intense conversation with the Reagans about biblical prophecy, the "signs of the times," and the "outpouring of the Holy Spirit" in the last days. Then, as they arose to leave, they decided to have prayer together. The seven formed a circle and held hands. Otis reported that he clasped Reagan's left hand and began praying audibly. Suddenly:

> "The Holy Spirit came upon me and I knew it. In fact, I was embarrassed. There was this pulsing in my arm. And my hand—the one holding Governor Reagan's hand—was shaking. I didn't know what to do. I just didn't want this thing to be happening. I can remember that even as I was speaking, I was working, you know, tensing my muscles and concentrating, and doing everything I could to stop the shaking.

> "It wasn't a wild swinging or anything like that. But it was a definite, pulsing shaking. And I made a great physical effort to stop it—but I couldn't."

> As this was going on, the content of Otis's prayer changed completely. His voice remained essentially the same, although the words came much more steadily and intently. They spoke specifically to Ronald Reagan and referred to him as "My son." They recognized his role as leader of the state that was indeed the size of many nations. His "labor" was described as "pleasing."

> The foyer was absolutely still and silent. The only sound was George's voice. Everyone's eyes were closed.

> "If you walk uprightly before Me, you will reside at 1600 Pennsylvania Avenue."

The session ended, the seven rather sheepishly let go of hands, and Reagan took a deep breath and said, "Well!" Years later, Otis recalled that his "prayer-turned-prophecy" had been precise about the future. "God had a plan," he said, "but it was conditional. It hinged on Reagan's actions." In the eyes of his charismatic admirers, he obviously had met the divine standard.[23]

Reagan's religious views crystallized during the gubernatorial years and were increasingly articulated after coming to Washington. For one thing, he placed strong emphasis on the efficacy of the Bible. In the 1976 Otis interview he observed that "in his entire history man has written about four billion laws" but with these "they haven't improved on the Ten Commandments."[24] At a news conference in 1985 he affirmed: "I've found that the Bible contains an answer to just about everything and every problem that confronts us. . . .[T]hat one book could solve a lot of problems for us." At the National Prayer Breakfast in 1983 and the National Religious Broadcasters' meetings in 1983 and 1984, the president declared that inside this book are "all the answers to all the problems" that man has ever known or that face us today.[25]

Further, Reagan had great confidence in the Bible's reliability. "Christ in His own words gave us reason to accept literally the miracle of His birth," and "I have never had any doubts about it [the Bible] being of divine origin," because no similar collection of writings has lasted so long and the Old Testament prophecies "predicted every single facet" of Christ's life, death, and messiahship hundreds of years before his birth.[26] He often quoted Scripture in his speeches, and among his favorite passages was "where two or three are gathered in my name, there I am in the midst of them" (Matt. 18:20). In fact, he once used the verse to counter the charge that he was attending too many public prayer breakfasts instead of praying in secret, as Jesus had directed in Matthew 6:5–6.[27]

Prayer was also very important to Reagan. He told Moomaw in 1966 that throughout his life he "received comfort and help from God" when he asked for it, and the two things he requested most in his prayers were "wisdom and strength." He was so convinced somebody was "listening up there" that he would "be scared to death" if this were not the case, and he said he got "answers" to his prayers.[28] On various occasions he compared his situation to that of Lincoln, "driven many times to my knees by the overwhelming conviction that I had nowhere else to go," and he quipped to people who said they were praying for him that if someone "got a busy signal, it was just me in there ahead of him." He believed in the efficacy of intercessory prayer because of what his mother Nelle had taught him, and this provided him with the "strength that I otherwise would not possess." Prayer has "power" and is "the greatest tool that we have."[29]

Reagan also often expressed a sense of divine calling and destiny. This was best exemplified by his reaction to Terence Cardinal Cooke, who visited him in the hospital two weeks after the assassination attempt on March 30, 1981. The cardinal told Reagan, "The hand of God was upon you," to which the president replied: "I know, and whatever time He's left for me is His." He then amplified this statement at the National Prayer Breakfast the following February:

> I've always believed that we were, each of us, put here for a reason. That there is a plan somehow—a divine plan for all of us. I know now that whatever days are left of me belong to Him.[30]

One aspect of the divine scheme that especially intrigued him was the future. During a visit with Billy Graham in 1967, Reagan engaged in a lengthy discussion about the return of Christ, and in the subsequent years he often talked about biblical prophecy with his evangelical friends. In 1971, he had invited Graham to address the California legislature on the topic, and that same year Reagan had a conversation with a state senator in which he identified Russia with Gog, who supposedly would invade Israel in the end-times, and intimated that a nuclear war (the Battle of Armageddon) would soon take place. Moreover, during the 1979–80 campaign and in his first presidential term, he made several off-the-cuff remarks about a possible nuclear apocalypse. The matter was raised in the 1984 campaign and put a scare into some non-evangelicals, but in fact it had little impact. Most evangelicals agreed with the general thrust of his eschatology, while his political supporters easily fended off the issue as a last-minute ploy by the Democrats to halt the Reagan steamroller.[31]

Thus, Reagan talked like an orthodox evangelical, but was he? His replies to queries as to whether he was "born again" contained a note of ambiguity. For example, he told George Otis in 1976:

> I can't remember a time in my life when I didn't call upon God and hopefully thank Him as often as I called upon Him. And yes, in my own experience there came a time when there developed a new relationship with God, and it grew out of need. So, yes, I have had an experience that could be described as "born again."

Four years later, at a press conference in Victorville, California, he was asked whether he considered himself a born-again Christian. After hesitating for a moment, he responded:

Well, I know what many of those who use that term mean by it. But in my own situation it was not in the religion, or the church that I was raised in, the Christian Church. But there you were baptized when you yourself decided that you were, as the Bible says, as the Bible puts it, that that is being born again. Within the context of the Bible, yes, by being baptized.[32]

Many evangelicals would not regard these as particularly profound statements of faith, but their very vagueness placed him squarely in the mainstream of general Protestantism and revealed that he was not a religious fanatic. Thus, he could carry out his functions as the presidential priest of civil religion with little difficulty.

Moreover, he held to a generalized view of all people as children of God, a doctrine that is anathema to fundamentalists, and he often expressed it before religiously inclined audiences in Washington:

- *National Prayer Breakfast, February 3, 1983*: [We should pray for] forgiveness for the resentment and the bitterness that we sometime feel toward someone. . . , forgetting that we are brothers and sisters and that each of them is loved equally by God as much as we feel that He loves us.
- *National Religious Broadcasters, January 30, 1984*: Under this roof, some four thousand of us are kindred spirits united by one burning belief: God is our Father; we are his children; together, brothers and sisters, we are one family. (Applause)
- *National Prayer Breakfast, January 31, 1985*: You see the heroism and goodness of men and know in a special way that we are all God's children. The clerk and the king and the communist were made in His image. . . .I'm convinced more than ever that man finds liberation only when he binds himself to God and commits himself to his fellow man.
- *Lighting the National Christmas Tree, December 12, 1985*: This season is rich in the meaning of our Judeo-Christian tradition. [And the] deepest truth of all [is] that there can be no prisons, no walls, no boundaries separating the members of God's family. [Let us] come together as one family under the fatherhood of God, binding ourselves in a communion of hearts.[33]

Ironically, then, the conservative evangelicals had thought Reagan to be like them, when in fact he had a liberal, broad-minded faith that facilitated his role in the civil religion. Although he frequently talked about religious matters and liberally sprinkled his speeches with "God words," he also claimed that he did not "wear his religion on his sleeve," and he chose not to attend a house of worship regularly. When he needed evangelicals' support, he could talk their language; but after becoming president, he functioned as a traditional conservative and more or less relegated their issues to the back burner.

In fact, as Garry Wills trenchantly observes, Reagan (and some of his conservative followers) departed from orthodoxy in an even more significant way. He and they put aside the "sick soul" aspect of traditional religion that stressed humanity's fall, original sin, and the need for repentance and humility. The new Reaganesque faith was "healthy-mindedness," and it replaced "sin" with "sadness" as the real enemy of human nature. The new virtues were optimism, success, prosperity, and assertiveness. To acknowledge limits and talk of self-denial, like Jimmy Carter did, was to "love misery" and have a "martyr complex."[34]

REAGAN'S CIVIL RELIGION

The themes that would distinguish President Reagan's civil religion appeared in his acceptance speech at the Republican convention in Detroit on July 17, 1980. He declared that the United States was a unique nation because it was founded on a "compact of freedom," the voluntary binding together of free people to live under the law of the community which they created. He went on to say that it was time to renew the compact and make "a new beginning," and he urged his listeners around the country to pledge

> to restore, in our time, the American spirit of voluntary service, of cooperation, of private and community initiative; a spirit that flows like a deep and mighty river through the history of our nation.

After listing the failures of the Carter administration and promising to repair the damage done to the national economy and defenses, he sang the praises of the land and its people:

It is impossible to capture in words the splendor of this vast continent which God has granted as our portion of His creation. There are no words to express the extraordinary strength and character of this breed of people we call Americans. . . .

They are the kind of men and women Tom Paine had in mind when he wrote, during the darkest days of the American Revolution, "We have it in our power to begin the world over again."

He asked people to "trust that American spirit which knows no ethnic, religious, social, political, regional, or economic boundaries." It was wrong to say this spirit no longer existed, as he had seen and felt it across the land, ready to blaze into life and do the practical things that should be done to put America back to work and make it great in the world again. He ended with an appeal to the public faith:

Can we doubt that only a Divine Providence placed this land, this island of freedom, here as a refuge for all those people in the world who yearn to breathe free? Jews and Christians enduring persecution behind the Iron Curtain; the boat people of Southeast Asia, Cuba, and of Haiti; the victims of drought and famine in Africa, the freedom fighters in Afghanistan, and our own countrymen held in savage captivity.

I'll confess that I've been a little afraid to suggest what I'm going to suggest. I'm more afraid not to. Can we begin our crusade joined together in a moment of silent prayer? [Pause] God bless America.[35]

At least four elements were evident in Reagan's civil faith. The first was American exceptionalism, the idea that America has a unique place in history. According to this view, America was chosen by God, its people are heroic, self-reliant, and freedom-loving, and it stands as a beacon to the world of the inestimable benefits of a society which is governed by consent and where the free individual under God can live in peace and happiness. Although government has now gotten out of hand, the American spirit is alive and well. To set things aright again, people need only to renew their original compact of freedom and civic virtue.[36]

Reagan repeatedly affirmed that a "divine plan" put the American continent here between the two oceans, where people who "had a special love for freedom" could come and create "something new in all the history of mankind—a country where man is not beholden to government; government is beholden to man." It was "set apart in a special way," and men and women from every corner of the world "came not for gold but mainly in search of God. They would be free people, living under the law, with faith in their Maker and in their future." The first settlers"asked that He would work His will in our daily lives, so America would be a land of fairness, morality, justice, and compassion."[37]

As a result, the president could say, "I believe in the goodness of the American people," and suggest that they were "blessed in so many ways [because] we're a nation under God, a living and loving God." At the same time, were they to turn away from the Deity in their everyday living, they could not expect him to protect them in a crisis. But if that should happen, "He told us what to do" in the "promise" contained in 2 Chronicles 7:14, the "if my people" passage. Reagan had no doubt that Americans qualified as the "my people" in this Scripture, and that is why he quoted it so often. Also, he took his oath of office both times with his hand resting on his mother's Bible open to the page containing it. By embracing the "John 3:16 of American civil religion," the president had reaffirmed Americans as God's chosen people.[38]

Moreover, God made America what it is today. Reagan said at the University of Notre Dame in 1981 that "our intellectual and spiritual values are rooted in the source of all strength, a belief in a Supreme Being, and law higher than our own." At Christmas time that year he observed "We Americans have always tried to follow a higher light, a star, if you will. . . .At times our footsteps may have faltered, but trusting in God's help, we've never lost our way." In his 1986 message to Congress he noted that the rights to life, liberty, and the pursuit of happiness were a gift from the Creator, not a grant from the government, and that Divine Providence imposed the duty on government to respect and secure these rights. Thus, he would "work to restore the legal protection of the unborn." Reagan made the same point in July 1987 when he told pro-life activists that we could "appeal to the goodness we know we can find in every American" and "call upon the power of His love" to secure anti-abortion legislation. In 1983, he said to an audience in South Carolina that "the loving God" who blessed this land

and "made us a good and caring people should never have been expelled from America's classrooms." He should be welcomed back, because we gain not only moral courage but also intellectual strength when we trust in him.[39]

God had specific tasks for his chosen nation to perform. As the president declared in a Constitution celebration in 1987:

> The guiding hand of providence did not create this new nation of America for ourselves alone, but for a higher cause: the preservation and extension of the sacred fire of human liberty. This is America's solemn duty.

At the Spirit of America Festival in Decatur, Alabama, on July 4, 1984, he pointed out that God made it "the land of limitless possibilities." As a nation, "we stand as a beacon" and like a "shining city for all the world upon the hill." Other countries see and try to emulate our entrepreneurial spirit, and recognize that "freedom is the one condition in which man can flourish." Humanity was meant to be free, and "democracy is just a political reading of the Bible." He told an American Legion convention two months later that "keeping alive the hope of human freedom is America's mission and we cannot shrink from the task or falter in the call to duty." America must not just be militarily strong but also morally powerful, and have "a creed, a cause, a vision of a future time when all people of the world will have the right to self-government and personal freedom." It must be "a beacon of hope, a shining city in a world grown weary of war and oppression."[40]

In his 1982 Landon Lecture at Kansas State University, Reagan joined American exceptionalism to civil religion. "We can be proud of the red, white, and blue, and believe in her mission," because in a world wracked by tensions, "America remains mankind's best hope." Everyone is counting on us to protect the peace, promote new prosperity, and provide a better world, and we can do this "if we remember the great gifts of our Revolution: that we are one Nation under God, believing in liberty and justice for all."[41]

A second feature of his public religion was an emphasis upon America as a spiritual nation. At the 1984 National Prayer Breakfast, Reagan echoed and endorsed the words first uttered by Philippine Ambassador Carlos Romulo:

Never forget, Americans, that yours is a spiritual country. . . . Underlying everything else is that fact that
America began as a God-loving, God-fearing, God-wor-
shipping people, knowing that there is a spark of the
Divine in each one of us. It is this respect for the human
spirit which keeps America invincible.[42]

In a 1982 speech in New Orleans, Reagan went further
to say that "the spirit of America is good. Her heart is strong
and true." We must never let anyone say that "America's
spirit is crushed. We've seen it triumph too often in our lives
to stop believing in it now." Moreover, the source of this
spiritual strength is God, and

standing up for America means standing up for the God
who has so blessed our land. We need God's help to
guide our nation through stormy seas. . . .Trusting in
Him, believing in each other, working together, we will
rebuild America—the land of our dreams and mankind's
last great hope.[43]

However, as he told a meeting of conservatives that
same year, "we live today in a time of climactic struggle for
the human spirit, a time that will tell whether the great
civilized ideas of individual liberty, representative government, and the rule of law under God will perish or endure."
Our need, he said in the 1981 inaugural address, is to "renew
ourselves here in our own land," and then we will again "be
the exemplar of freedom and a beacon of hope for those who
do not now have freedom."[44]

Reagan saw himself as the one who would lead this
revival of the spirit. He told a meeting of publishers in 1982,
his biographer in 1983, and a group of reporters in 1984, that
he believed the country was "hungry for a spiritual revival"
and "for people to believe again in things that they once
believed in." He agreed with Theodore Roosevelt's statement, "The Presidency is a bully pulpit," and said he would
keep working on those social issues that had to do with the
morals of the country and the standards that made it great.[45]

In his 1984 State of the Union address, Reagan declared
that "there was a hunger in the land for a spiritual revival, if
you will, a crusade for renewal." In fact, he informed the
cadets at West Point in 1981 that "a spiritual revival" was
going on in the country, and the National Association of
Evangelicals in 1983 that "America is in the midst of a

spiritual awakening and a moral renewal." To the NAE a year later, he explained that God gave us free will and the power to choose our own destiny: "The American people decided to put a stop to that long decline, and today our country is seeing a rebirth of freedom and faith—a great national renewal." But this is more than a material renewal; it is "a spiritual reawakening. Faith and hope are being restored. Americans are turning back to God." And with this restored spiritual power, based on a general but nevertheless real "faith and hope," they would be able to tackle the problems of keeping the country strong and restoring basic values to the land.[46]

The third element in his public faith was that religion-in-general is a requirement for a healthy national existence. Reagan said repeatedly that the answers to America's problems could be found in the Bible and even proclaimed 1983 as the Year of the Bible, and he said on dozens of occasions that prayer should be "restored" to the schools, although none of his prayer amendment proposals ever cleared the Senate. In his opinion, God was one of America's "decent" or "traditional" values, and the nation's laws were based upon religion.

The major affirmation of his understanding of the role of religion in American life was an address he delivered at an "Ecumenical Prayer Breakfast" during the Republican convention in Dallas on August 23, 1984. He led off by saying, "I believe that faith and religion play a critical role in the political life of our nation." All churches had a strong influence on the state and this benefited America as a nation. The Founders of the country understood that there was a divine order which transcended the human order and that the bedrock of moral order was religion. He went on to cite historical examples to show that religion played a strong and positive role in national life, but then in the 1960s, things changed. The Supreme Court rulings on school prayer and Bible reading and the rapid advance of secularism diminished the role of religion in national life. New forces abroad were intolerant of religion, and it now needed "defenders against those who care only for the interests of the state." Nevertheless:

> The truth is, politics and morality are inseparable. And as morality's foundation is religion, religion and politics are

necessarily related. We need religion as a guide. . .and our government needs the church, because only those humble enough to admit they're sinners can bring to democracy the tolerance it requires in order to survive.

However, he was not calling for any establishment of religion. The tolerant society actually was open to and encouraged all religions, which did not weaken the nation but instead made it strong. Looking back through time to the great civilizations that rose and declined, the thing they all had in common was that "one of the significant forerunners of their fall was their turning away from their God or gods." Thus, without God there is no civic virtue and "democracy will not and cannot long endure. If we ever forget that we're one nation under God, then we will be a nation gone under."[47]

A fourth motif in Reagan's civil religion was that America must be militarily and spiritually strong so it can resist the consummate foe, communism. Speaking to American troops in Korea in 1983, he insisted that the communist system was based on hatred and oppression, attacked every form of human liberty, and declared "those who worship God to be enemies of the people." He boasted in June 1987 that the road to peace was through unquestioned American strength and "our crusade" had turned the tide of history into a freedom tide, with the result that in the past six years, "not one square inch of ground has been lost to Communism and a small nation—Grenada—has been liberated."[48]

Reagan decried the evils of communism in numerous addresses, but by far the most famous one was given to the National Association of Evangelicals in Orlando, Florida, on March 8, 1983. Toward the end of the thirty-minute speech, which essentially was a litany of civil religion, he said that the only morality the Soviet leaders recognized was that which furthered world revolution and that they repudiated all morality that proceeded from supernatural ideas. He was willing to negotiate with them to reduce the nuclear threat, but they must be made to understand that we will never compromise our principles, give away our freedom, or "abandon our faith in God." After recounting a melodramatic anecdote about Pat Boone who preferred to see his daughters die rather than grow up under communism, he spoke in a pastoral voice: "Let us pray for the salvation of all those who live in that totalitarian darkness—pray they will discover the joy of knowing God."

Then the president dropped some of the most memorable lines of his career. He urged the listeners to be aware that while the Soviets preach the supremacy of the state and predict it will dominate all peoples on the earth, "they are the focus of evil in the modern world." He then criticized the folly of those who practiced "simple-minded appeasement or wishful thinking about our adversaries" and urged the evangelicals "to speak out against those who would place the United States in a position of military and moral inferiority." He aimed his barbed remarks specifically at those who supported a nuclear freeze, and urged them to beware of the temptation to declare both sides equally at fault and to call the arms race a giant misunderstanding. To do so would be to "ignore the facts of history and the aggressive impulses of an evil empire. . .and thereby remove yourself from the struggle between right and wrong, good and evil." He ended by saying, "I believe that Communism is another sad, bizarre chapter in human history whose last pages even now are being written." This is so because the source of American strength in the quest for human freedom is spiritual, not material.[49]

Two years later, he defended his defense build-up before the National Religious Broadcasters in yet another choice civil religion speech. After receiving a rousing "Amen" from the audience for saying he had not been reelected in November to turn back to the policies of the past, he invoked Scripture to justify a strong defense:

> I found myself wanting to remind you of what Jesus said in Luke 14:31: "Oh, what king, when he sets out to make [war]—or meet another king in battle will not first sit down and take counsel whether he is strong enough with 10,000 men to encounter the one coming against him with 20,000. Or else, while the other is still far away, sends a delegation and asks the terms of peace." I don't think the Lord that blessed this country, as no other country has ever been blessed, intends for us to have to someday negotiate because of our weakness.[50]

THE APOTHEOSIS OF CIVIL RELIGION

America had been adrift since the late 1960s, and Jimmy Carter's use of a prophetic civil religion did not meet the public's felt need for comfort, reassurance, and sense of direction. Thus, Ronald Reagan and the New Right came along at an opportune moment, and their program for the restoration of traditional common values and "spiritual revival" was seen as the answer to the malaise gripping the land. Although superficially this seemed to be a "Christian" emphasis, and millions of adherents to the religious right certainly perceived it as such, in reality Reagan was utilizing a highly generalized, albeit theistic, public faith as the basis for national moral renewal. This was best exemplified by his repeated calls for the "restoration" of prayer to the public schools. The Deity who would be honored by the daily devotions of school children would be none other than the one of civil religion, and certainly not the particular God worshipped by Christians, Jews, Muslims, or any other religious community.

Matters were complicated by the ongoing spectacle of politicized religiosity during the Reagan years. For the evangelicals, the president's men served up a feast of White House invitations, private briefings, speeches at evangelical gatherings, political appointments, social legislation, and promises. Reagan also courted Roman Catholics by meeting with luminaries like Pope John Paul II, Mother Teresa, Cardinal Cooke, and others. He assigned a staff person to be a religious liaison with Catholics, endorsed their stands on abortion and parochial school aid, appeared before their gatherings, and most importantly, established full diplomatic relations with the Holy See in 1984.[51] He also hoped to win Catholic backing for his foreign policy and military build-up, but this effort was only partially successful.[52] He tried to broaden his appeal to Jews by speaking to their religious bodies, appointing a liaison staff person for this community, and standing up firmly for Israel. However, the overtures achieved little because of unease about his social agenda and the 1985 Bitburg fiasco.

The Department of Education's crusade against secular humanism and for traditional values gained wide support in conservative Protestant and Catholic circles, but by 1987 it had begun to flag, thanks mostly to adverse court rulings on key cases. Furthermore, scandals involving several evangelical administration figures, the Iran-Contra affair, and severe economic problems weakened President Reagan's effectiveness. As his second term drew to a close, religious appeals no longer seemed to help in achieving his objectives.

Yet, during his administration civil religion reached new heights as he donned the vestments of high priest. He was at his best when he presided over national festivals like the Los Angeles Olympic Games in 1984 and the reopening of the Statute of Liberty in 1986 and officiated at the various memorial services for Americans killed in the line of duty. In the latter rites, he in effect prayed people into civil religion heaven and pronounced death in the service of the country to be ipso facto death in the service of America's god. The dead thus became part of a collective national soul. This could be seen in his remarks about the victims of the USS *Stark* incident, as well as when he told the nation about the 241 marines killed in the 1983 Beirut bomb attack: "I will not ask you to pray for the dead, because they're safe in God's loving arms and beyond need of our prayers" and "They're now part of the soul of this great country and will live as long as our liberty shines as a beacon of hope to all those who long for freedom and a better world."[53] Concerning the members of a paratroop unit who were killed in a plane crash in 1985, the president intoned:

> And so, we pray: Receive, O Lord, into your heavenly kingdom, the men and women of the 101st Airborne, the men and women of the great and fabled Screaming Eagles. They must be singing now, in their joy, flying higher than mere man can fly and as flights of angels take them to their rest. . . .They are now in the arms of God.[54]

Most significant was his eulogy for the astronauts killed in the Space Shuttle *Challenger* disaster in 1986: "We can find consolation only in faith, for we know in our hearts that you who flew so high and so proud now make your home beyond the stars, safe in God's promise of eternal life." Here, he functioned as both pastor and priest by comforting his people with the assurance that the seven tragic victims, whose personal faiths spanned the range from evangelical and mainline Protestant to Roman Catholic, Jewish, Buddhist, and nothing in particular, were at rest with God.[55]

Thus, under Ronald Reagan civil religion not only transcended all boundaries of particular religion, but also every American who "believes in God" now was included under its benevolent wings. Reagan renewed the theme that those who died in the service of their country were sacrificing their lives on behalf of America's Deity. Moreover, in an interesting new development, the president as high priest consigned people to civil religion heaven. The sacred dead became a part of the collective national soul as well. Finally, in Reagan's civil theology, the focus shifted from the prophetic emphasis on sin to a priestly stress on sadness as the real enemy of humankind.

The result of this renewal of America's holy destiny as the modern world's "city upon a hill" combined with the new developments in public theology was a civil religion which was highly useful in promoting the national purposes as viewed by the Reagan administration. Although like so many of his fellow citizens, the president possessed a personal faith that was genuine and meaningful to him, both he and they subsumed it under the higher public faith. Civil religion reached a new pinnacle in the American experience as it was exalted by a powerful, priestly president.

12

CIVIL RELIGION AND THE PRESIDENTS OF THE FUTURE

The public faith encapsulated in American civil religion underwent a complex development during the nation's history, and the president played the central role in the process. The core belief was that the United States was a chosen nation, whose divinely appointed responsibility was to be a model before all the world of the benefits of right religion, individual liberty, and political democracy. Under the benevolent, superintending hand of the Almighty, its people were to practice patriotism and alleviate ills within their own society. When the nation failed to live up to its calling, prophetic leaders would invoke the transcendent power to call it to repentance and return to the paths of righteousness. The American vision was that of a sacred-secular millennium in which, under God, democracy, personal freedom, economic prosperity, and fraternity would prevail. And, at least until the twentieth century, this civil millennial kingdom was perceived as essentially a Christian one. In it, former presidents were elevated to national sainthood, while the current chief executive leads his people in the cultic observances of the civil faith and through oratory and example inspires them to greater deeds. Noted columnist James Reston aptly appraised the situation when he declared: "The White House is the pulpit of the nation and the president is its chaplain."[1]

AN IDEOLOGICAL ISSUE?

As suggested in the opening chapter, there are two kinds of controversies surrounding civil religion, and no scholarly consensus is likely on either in the foreseeable future. One area of disagreement is over the validity of the concept itself; the other is whether it is basically beneficial or harmful. However, one thing is clear. Among those who believe there is such a thing as civil religion, the differences do not necessarily fall along ideological lines; it is not a liberal versus conservative issue. One finds proponents and critics of public religion on both ends of the religious and political spectrum, and in fact, some even distinguish between "good" and "bad" uses of it.

An example of this ambivalence toward civil religion in the evangelical Christian world is the case of Senator Mark Hatfield and Evangelist Billy Graham. In his widely acclaimed National Prayer Breakfast speech of 1973, Hatfield criticized the "god of civil religion" for being a "small and very exclusive deity, a loyal spiritual advisor to American power and American prestige, an exclusive defender of the American nation, and the object of a national folk religion that is devoid of moral content." But only a year later, he puzzled many people when he persuaded the Senate to set aside a "National Day for Humiliation, Fasting, and Prayer" in order to urge the nation to reconfirm its ideals.[2] Was this an affirmation of civil religion after all, but only in its prophetic rather than its priestly form?

In the case of Graham, he seemed first uncritically to embrace civil religion, then later to repudiate it. At the annual Southern Baptist Convention in 1964, he called for a "prayer amendment," insisting that moral influence was needed in the schools and that "nonsectarian" prayer could provide this. A reporter questioned him whether only through the God in Christ could one be assured of eternal salvation, and the response was yes. The individual then asked Graham if Jews had to believe in God as defined in the Christian faith, and again he answered affirmatively. If so, the reporter queried, how can you speak of nonsectarian prayer when there "is only one God and he can be known only in Jesus Christ? What God, by your definition, would be equally acceptable to Jew and Christian alike?" Now rather flustered, the evangelist retorted with a civil religion concept: "Do you mean the God up there or the God in Christ?" Nevertheless, a dozen years later, he flatly stated that civil religion is "nothing more than a combination of contradictory viewpoints fused into a soulless pattern of pragmatic opportunism." It appears that in the interim he had changed his mind about the positive value of civil faith.[3]

Among non-evangelicals, some have supported civil religion and others have criticized it. For example, Robert Bellah has been one of its leading advocates, claiming that its benefits outweighs its dangers, and that it would not entail the worship of the nation but provide "an understanding of the American experience in the light of ultimate and universal reality." Most importantly, it would supply Americans with a basis for self-criticism and an understanding of their mission in the world.[4] Sidney Mead agrees that there is little danger of idolatry in the American public faith. He believes that the "neutral" civil authority in America promotes pluralism to keep any one sect from imposing its "definition of truth" on the others, and in fact, uses the sects to communicate the universal verity of God's primacy over all human institutions. This, he maintains, is diametrically opposite to the worship of the state, nation, or "American way of life."[5]

It is also worth recalling that liberals like John Dewey were the ones who energetically promoted the "religion of democracy" during the early part of the twentieth century. This variety of civil religiosity was a prophetic faith that posited the spiritual oneness of Christianity and democracy. It was based on a democratic theology which maintained that the will of God was revealed in the life of the people. By compelling loyalty to the ideals of America, it achieved the task of uniting the nation to save the world from the onslaught of autocracy.[6]

On the other hand, Will Herberg refers to American civic faith as a "super-religion" which is the religious aspect of Americanism and embraces the three major faiths. He goes on to say that civic religion "has always meant the sanctification of the society and culture of which it is the reflection," something which Jewish-Christian faith regards as "incurably idolatrous." Civic religion, he argues, "validates culture and society, without in any sense bringing them under judgment," and it gives them "ultimate sanction." The social order and cultural values are "divinized by being identified with the divine purpose."[7] Martin Marty goes even further in criticizing civil religion by labelling it "religion-in-general." He suggests that it posits a "harmless little divinity who has almost nothing in common with the God of Christianity." This god is understandable and manageable, comforting, and an "American jolly good fellow."[8]

Richard John Neuhaus, a Lutheran social critic who is widely respected in both evangelical and non-evangelical circles, is more difficult to place on the religio-political spectrum. (In the 1960s he was a fervent civil rights activist and Vietnam War opponent while two decades later he had become a neoconservative.) In his recent works, he has eloquently defended a civil religion of sorts. To be sure, he rejects the term itself and speaks of a "common faith," "democratic faith," or "public philosophy," but still he insists that the Judeo-Christian religion should occupy the vital center of American existence. This "sacred canopy" brings all institutions and belief systems under judgment and is "describable in terms of the promises and judgments revealed in the biblical story." Furthermore, he insists that "on balance and considering the alternatives, the influence of the United States is a force for good in the world," and that "patriotism is a species of piety" which, when reflective, constitutes "a context within which political responsibilities can be examined."[9]

In summing up, two points need to be made. Although civil religion may seem to have become a focal point of ideological conflict in the late 1960s and early 1970s, it is really much more than this. Numerous thinkers, regardless of whether they are supportive of any particular regime in Washington, have expressed the need for a workable public philosophy that has a religious component or is religiously based. Many of those individuals feel this philosophy should be related in some manner to a vital public religion. Second, in spite of what some commentators may say to the contrary, civil religion is very much alive and an active force in contemporary America.

CIVIL RELIGION IN THE FUTURE

The continuing presence of civil religion raises a number of questions. One of these concerns the inherent tensions in American society between civil faith and particular faiths. These tensions have become more pronounced with the increasing pluralism resulting from the influx of new peoples from the non-European world after 1945. How will civil religion in the future promote national unity, especially in integrating these new citizens, many of whom are not Christians? In the nineteenth century, the civic religion had been a generalized evangelical Protestantism. Religious disestablishment and denominational diversity were accepted within the confines of a common evangelical belief system. Although maintaining a sensible piety among the populace was a public concern, the ever-present religious diversity precluded any possibility of a national consensus at the denominational level, and accordingly, the burden of fostering both national unity and civic piety fell upon the general Protestant public faith. By the twentieth century, however, such a plethora of churches and religions dotted the cultural landscape of America that the civil religion had to be enlarged to include all of them, if possible.[10]

This development has not been without tensions of its own. Many American evangelicals did not recognize how civil religion had changed and they continued to support it as if it were still some kind of general evangelical Protestantism. After all, the language of civil religion is by its very nature conducive to allowing each person, denomination, or sect to read into it whatever they choose. Moreover, the very reason for the existence of this kind of civil faith—namely, the multiplicity of sects, the pressures of denominations which insisted on religious freedom and separation of church and state, and in the end, the First Amendment itself— demanded the creation of a general public religion to help hold the young country together. The presence of a virile civil faith satisfied the various Protestants that their nation was, in fact, a godly one, and the First Amendment allowed them to go about their business of converting as many of their neighbors as possible.[11]

However, as civil religion in the twentieth century progressively embraced non-evangelical elements, many evangelicals grew uneasy that theirs was no longer the

"Christian nation" they believed it had been during the days of a general Protestant civil faith. Others continued to participate uncritically in the civil religion without giving much thought to its ideological base or the implications of their involvement. Still others began for the first time to think seriously about the nature and meaning of their adherence to the national civic faith. Consequently, some New Right evangelicals started talking about the need to restore the golden age of civil religion with its mythical base in a "Christian America." Whether the masses of "new Americans" will feel comfortable embracing the civil faith if it includes large numbers of fundamentalist Christians is an open question. In other words, civil religion is a fragile unity.

Still, many feel that some sort of a civil religion is required for American democracy to function properly. They contend it provides a set of transcendent values that constitute a standard of justice by which government actions may be measured. As the Declaration of Independence puts it, government deserves support only to the extent that it observes the rights bestowed on people by nature and nature's god. Historian Edwin Gaustad, a Baptist who is keenly aware that ecclesiastical authority cannot be counted on to foster a free and open society, argues that religion and democracy may not be segregated from one another and isolated into high-walled preserves. Unlike other political forms, democracy neither demands ultimate loyalty nor assumes total control, and as a result it respects the liberty of the soul and the sanctity of conscience. Gaustad points out that public religion, at least in a Judeo-Christian mold, is a bulwark of democratic society, and he concludes: "By insisting that absolute control is God's and that ultimate loyalties are heaven sent, religion keeps a limited democracy from becoming a prideful tyranny." And, by reserving worship to God alone, Judaism and Christianity resist the danger of a deified democracy. No state can endure godlike devotion without degenerating into demonic corruption.[12]

For those who accept the existence of a civil religion or its functional equivalent as a fact of American life, the question is not so much whether it is "good" or "bad" but rather how the tradition and symbols of a nation's civic faith can be utilized in a way that brings forth the most positive and constructive social results. Desirable results would include the enhancement of human freedom and dignity, social justice, the rule of law, and democratic norms. Moreover, if a democratic state is based on a transcendent reference point outside itself, it is in a better position to avoid the temptations of national arrogance and power. As political scientist James Fairbanks observes: "The American tradition of civil religion would seem to offer a way of giving a nation a sense of ultimate meaning while minimizing the dangers of political or religious absolutism."[13]

But, can civil religion deliver all that its advocates promise? The answer must be a qualified no. The ideals are there and they constitute a standard to which preachers and politicians alike regularly refer, but they are often neglected principles. In the very beginning, Native Americans (Indians) and people of African descent (slaves) were systematically excluded from participation in the American experiment in freedom. Although concepts originating in the public faith played an important role in the ending of slavery, blacks for many years were denied full rights as citizens. At the same time, immigrants from Europe and migrants from the countryside and small towns who streamed into the cities experienced exploitation by the new industrial system. Americans believed their "manifest destiny" was to bring freedom and democratic government to the whole world, but they betrayed their calling in the conquest of the Philippines, through the abandonment of internationalism after World War I, and by conducting a brutal war in Vietnam. The corruption that has plagued American political history— bribery, cover-ups, payoffs, rigged elections, and blatant defiance of the law by public officials, culminating in the great scandals of the late twentieth century, Watergate and the Iran-Contra Affair—reveals how civil religion lacked the power to establish justice or to deal with national arrogance, selfishness, pride, and folly. To quote the eminent Southern Baptist philosopher, Eric Rust:

> Somehow our civil religion never does save us. Nor does it maintain the system of justice, because once you put God up above as a vague something, sooner or later you can slide down into a secularity where God does not count at all. Then you have no sanction for a system of justice. It has no eternal foundations.[14]

THE PRESIDENT AS PRIEST

As has been shown, the president's role in the civil religion became increasingly priestly in nature, and Michael Novak correctly concludes that the president is now above all, "the high priest of the symbols and liturgies of the nation's self-understanding." The chief executives of the United States "perform priestly and prophetic roles, conduct high public liturgies, constantly reinterpret the nation's fundamental documents and traditions, [and] furnish the central terms of public discourse."[15] The priestly role which came to predominate in recent years was especially evident in the national ceremonials that conferred sacredness upon the country, such as Honor America Day in 1970 and the services for the victims of the *Challenger* and *Stark* disasters in l986-87.

Marty's model of civil religion helps to clarify how a distinct shift in the president's position in the public faith as prophet, pastor, and preacher to that of priest occurred during the course of the twentieth century. Roosevelt and Eisenhower functioned primarily as pastors (although there were occasional manifestations of the priest) within the variety of public faith that stressed the transcendent Deity. Nixon and Reagan, however, were much more priestly in character, and their faith was based on the self-transcendent nation. The pastoral civil religion talked about the nation being "under God," in other words, a fusion of the historic Judeo-Christian faith with indigenous national sentiment, while the national self-transcendent variety focused on the promise of America and declared God's work to be almost identical with that of the nation.[16]

It is one thing to see the president as prophet, summoning the nation to higher purposes and to fulfill its obligations, in the manner of a Lincoln, Wilson, or Carter; but for him to be a priest is a matter of a different order. Do Americans really want their president to be a high priest? Do they have any idea of what that really means? This is more than simply an academic question, as can be seen from Ray Price's memorandum recommending the strategy that should be used to sell candidate Nixon to the American public in 1968. His contention was that voters respond to the image and not the man, and the task before the campaign committee was to construct a Nixon who would correspond to the reverence with which the office was held. Price wrote:

> People identify with a President in a way they do with no other public figure. Potential presidents are measured against an ideal that's a combination of leading man, God, father, hero, pope, king, with maybe just a touch of the avenging Furies thrown in. They want him to be larger than life, a living legend, and yet quintessentially human; someone to be held up to their children as a model; someone to be cherished by themselves as a revered member of the family, in somewhat the same way in which peasant families pray to the icon in the corner. Reverence goes where power is; it's no coincidence that there's such persistent confusion between love and fear in the whole history of man's relationship to his gods. Awe enters into it. . . .
>
> Selection of a President has to be an act of faith. . . .This faith isn't achieved by reason; it's achieved by charisma, by a feeling of trust that can't be argued or reasoned, but that comes across in those silences that surround the words. The words are important—but less for what they actually say than for the sense they convey, for the impression they give of the man himself, his hopes, his standards, his competence, his intelligence, his essential humanness, and the directions of history he represents.[17]

The president as high priest possesses what amounts to a sacred character, and thus his actions may not be resisted in any meaningful fashion. In a civil religion sense he is, to use David's phrase, "the Lord's anointed," and "who can stretch forth his hand against [him], and be guiltless?" (1 Sam. 26:9). Senator Hatfield reports how he felt the brunt of this sort of thinking when he stood up against Nixon's Vietnam policy. One letter writer declared that Hatfield could not possibly be a Christian believer "because you won't support the boys in Vietnam and you're fighting President Nixon who has been placed there by God." Another constituent denounced the senator for making himself "more powerful than the president of the United States" and then added:

> Why do you think you have the right to interfere with our president? Have you forgotten that God's way is to respect and honor those in authority? What higher power is there than President Nixon? God put him there.

'Whosoever therefore resisteth the power, resisteth the ordinance of God.'[18]

Yet, the revelation of this same Nixon's moral failure led to his precipitous fall from power. Michael Novak accurately gauged the situation when he wrote that the force of the civil religion helped to drive Nixon from the White House. It was the office itself, not the particular individual occupying it at the time, that carried "the sacred seal," and "the public outrage confirmed the sanctity of the office."[19] The religious-mythic aura which surrounded the president was shattered when, through the taped conversations in the Oval Office and the revelations of the Watergate committee hearings, the American public became privy to the political chicanery and "ungodly" vulgarity of life in the innermost circle. The people discovered that their sacred leader had lied to them, used the language of the gutter, and engaged in the obstruction of justice. Besides losing the legal, political, and ethical supports for his presidency, Nixon no longer had the religious-mythic backing of the people whom he had betrayed. With a certain irony, he who had lived by priestly civil religion, perished by priestly civil religion.[20]

TOWARD A RESPONSE TO REVITALIZED CIVIL RELIGION

Since civil religion appears to be here to stay, it is important that people, especially those who call themselves biblical Christians, be sensitive to its manifestations and cautious in their commitments. For one thing, they need to recognize that, ironically, the erosion of the traditional Christian consensus in America contributed materially to the revival and extension of public religion. For another, they must see that the civic faith is not identical with their personal evangelical faith or even their general denominational beliefs. This confusion of personal faith with civil religion, for example, may help to explain the vehemence of the public outcry against the Supreme Court rulings on school prayer and Bible reading, the extraordinarily high opinion poll findings—as much as 80 to 90 percent of those questioned—in favor of "restoring" prayer in the public schools, and the vast number of people who profess "belief in God" to pollsters yet do not belong to a church or attend worship services with any kind of regularity.[21]

In the case of Christians, the public faith's deistic unitarianism ignores the scandal of the cross and the particularity of the religion which insists that God has shown humanity his face in Jesus Christ. Civil religion does stress belief in God and places value on the practice of religion in general, but the contemporary priestly variety has little or nothing to say about sin, guilt, judgment, punishment, and humility. When the cross and the flag arouse the same sentiment in an American Christian, then the faith has been drained of its vitality. What remains in the way of spiritual values are lowest common denominator generalities designed to offend no one and, insofar as possible, to please everyone.

Therefore, evangelicals in particular need clearly to understand that Christianity and civil religion are not the same thing. American Christians do the cause of Christ an enormous disservice when they communicate a contrary understanding to people elsewhere. In fact, civil religion simply becomes more intense and often dangerous to the survival of genuine Christianity when it is hitched to an evangelical bandwagon. The reality Christian believers must face is that there can be no Christian state as such, and it is not the job of the church to serve as the transcendent reference point for the state. Instead, like the prophet Amos who preached judgment on the surrounding peoples (Amos 1:3–2:3), the church coexists in a perpetual state of tension with the political order. Its responsibility is not to identify with the state but to remind it of the divine demand for justice.

Furthermore, Christians and peoples of other faiths need to keep in mind that presidents as a rule use religious language during civic functions in order to communicate more effectively with the citizenry. That has been a recurring theme throughout this book, and numerous studies of presidential statements have borne it out. For example, in his analysis of presidential inaugural addresses, James H. Smylie points out that in them the chief executives describe the purpose of the United States of America under God, dedicate themselves and the people to the fulfillment of the nation's just purposes which are consonant with the will of God, and legitimize the transfer of government authority from one president to another. Cynthia Toolin adds that the president addresses the people like a priest does his parish. He "comforts his citizens, telling them that we control our destiny." God "blesses this nation's superior form of government" and wants all nations to imitate it. He then reinforces these ideas by drawing upon America's religious heritage.[22]

It has been made abundantly clear that presidents borrow religious symbols and terminology and even exploit them for political purposes. Thus, people should fully recognize this state of affairs and not be misled by the use of "God words" into thinking that a man of intense personal piety has taken up residence at 1600 Pennsylvania Avenue. On the other hand, many if not most of the chief executives have had genuine and substantial personal faiths, and it would be grossly unfair to accuse them of hypocrisy simply because they confused their private and public faiths. Since only recently scholars have begun to pay serious attention to the matter and through their research bring to light the very real distinctions existing between the two dimensions of private and public piety, it is wrongheaded to expect that the presidents themselves would have been aware of the situation.

When it comes to civil religion itself, the prophetic variety is much to be preferred over the priestly. To be sure, as Foy Valentine points out, "as a homemade god, civil religion can neither judge us nor save us."[23] However, surely worthy of commendation are those presidents who gave the Deity first place in their thinking, held the nation accountable to God for its shortcomings, and affirmed a religious vision of the future which, in the words of James Wall, "sees a nation as a community of diverse persons, yet one wherein all in their diversity are under the care of a God who has shown his love for his entire creation."[24] Therefore, the prophetic presidents—Lincoln and Carter, and to a lesser extent, Wilson and Franklin Roosevelt—receive higher marks in this study than the more priestly ones.

The civil religion can draw upon a common fund of shared values like individual liberty, religious and cultural pluralism, civic responsibility, and a desire for social justice; but it is also open to manipulation by those who primarily have their own personal and national interests in mind. Thus, civil religion must be subjected to continuous judgment and critique in order to prevent it from becoming an idolatrous and demonic culture religion. Christians in particular must be biblically informed, eternally vigilant, and actively and responsibly involved in the modern world so they do not fall victim to "culture Christianity."[25]

A CONCLUDING WORD TO THE PRESIDENT AND HIS PEOPLE

The main argument of this book has been that the president has come to play the central role in American civil religion. This is a situation with which sincere believers, whether they be Christians, Jews, or adherents of any of the innumerable other religious communities that populate the land, will have to cope. Americans expect their chief executive to manifest a certain measure of religious faith, especially on public occasions, and this is not likely to change in the next few decades.[26] It is doubtful whether atheists, agnostics, and members of nontheistic faiths will be able to alter that situation in the foreseeable future, although Supreme Court rulings since the 1960s have acknowledged their full rights as citizens. At best, they simply will have to compete in the marketplace with people of theistic convictions to shape the public faith.

What then is the proper stance of the president of the United States with respect to religion in general and civil religion in particular? Robert L. Maddox, a Southern Baptist minister who was a speech writer and liaison person with religious groups in the Carter administration and later the executive director of Americans United for Separation of Church and State, provides some helpful suggestions. Maddox insists that the populace should not impose on the presidency any religious test as such, but the chief executive should nonetheless come to the office with some kind of moral and ethical values compatible with the ideals of the majority of Americans and by which he can be judged. He should appreciate the delicate balance between the Establishment and Free Exercise clauses of the First Amendment and do all in his power to uphold these principles. The president should also respect the distinctly spiritual and reconciling mission of religious communities and discourage all attempts to inject partisanship into the churches and synagogues and thereby divide congregants along political lines. He should feel free to attempt to sell his own views, even in the area of personal morality, while at the same time sincerely respecting diversity of opinion. He is at liberty to foster morality and to govern on the basis of biblical ethics, but at the same time he must avoid a sectarian religious agenda. Above all, he must provide vision and energy for the betterment of his people and encourage justice.[27] This kind of arrangement will help him avoid the pitfalls of civil religion and come closer to the ideal of serving as president of all the people.

Christians as well must face the civil religion question squarely. They must resist the tendency to blur public religion and genuine Christian faith, because this confuses outsiders about the United States and leads them to believe, erroneously to be sure, that America is a Christian nation.[28] The civil religion reading of American history with its emphasis on "special providence" and the "chosen nation" has done untold mischief, as it served first to justify the destruction of the indigenous Indian culture and then foreign intervention, war, and the imposition of American values, institutions, and commercial enterprises on other peoples. Americans are only now discovering how this outlook has engendered bitter animosity in other parts of the world. Moreover, Christians must recognize that the beliefs of American civil religion are not those of Christianity but of another faith. In fact, civil religion comes dangerously close to blasphemy when it identifies God with the national destiny and in essence reduces the universal God of the Bible to the tribal god of America.

The bottom line is that the premier biblical proof text of modern-day civil religion—2 Chronicles 7:14—simply does not apply to America. The "my people" in this passage refers to Israel and may not be transferred to any other national grouping. Christians from every country are included in the ranks of the new "holy nation" of redeemed men and women out of all the lands and peoples of the earth (1 Peter 2:9). To this the Apostle Paul adds:

> You are all sons of God through faith in Christ Jesus, for all of you who were baptized into Christ have clothed yourselves with Christ. There is neither Jew nor Greek, slave nor free, male nor female, for you are all one in Christ Jesus (Gal. 3:26–28 NIV).

American Christians cannot avoid the existence of civil religion, but they do not have to affirm it. They, along with their presidents, can love their country and work to make it a better place. By functioning as salt and light (Matt. 5:13–16), believers can bring biblical values to bear in the political process and encourage leaders to govern more responsibly. Finally, they can make their nation and the world a better place in which to live by reading their New Testament through the decultured eyes of faith and taking its message seriously in its entirety.

SUGGESTIONS FOR FURTHER READING

Readers who wish to explore the question of civil religion in greater depth will find the following works to be helpful. Most of them are currently in print, and all are readily obtainable at larger libraries. Inclusion of an item does not necessarily imply our endorsement of its contents.

Ahlstrom, Sydney E. *A Religious History of the American People*. New Haven: Yale University Press, 1972.

Albanese, Catherine L. *Sons of the Fathers: The Civil Religion of the American Revolution*. Philadelphia: Temple University Press, 1976.

Bellah, Robert N. *The Broken Covenant: American Civil Religion in Time of Trial*. New York: Seabury Press, 1975.

Bellah, Robert N., et. al. *Habits of the Heart: Individualism and Commitment in American Life*. Berkeley: University of California Press, 1985.

Bellah, Robert N. and Phillip E. Hammond. *Varieties of Civil Religion*. San Francisco: Harper & Row, 1980.

Bellah, Robert N. and William G. McLoughlin, eds. *Religion in America*. Boston: Houghton Mifflin, 1968.

Benson, Peter L. and Dorothy L. Williams. *Religion on Capitol Hill: Myths and Realities*. San Francisco: Harper & Row, 1982.

Cherry, Conrad. *God's New Israel: Religious Interpretations of American Destiny*. Englewood Cliffs, N.J.: Prentice-Hall, 1971.

Cuddihy, John Murray. *No Offense: Civil Religion and Protestant Taste*. New York: Seabury Press, 1978.

Dunn, Charles W., ed. *American Political Theology: Historical Perspective and Theoretical Analysis*. New York: Praeger, 1984.

Ellul, Jacques. *The Subversion of Christianity*. Grand Rapids: Wm. B. Eerdmans, 1986.

Gehrig, Gail. *American Civil Religion: An Assessment*. Storrs, Conn.: The Society for the Scientific Study of Religion, 1979.

Handy, Robert T. *A Christian America: Protestant Hopes and Historical Realities*, 2d ed. New York: Oxford University Press, 1984.

Henry, Maureen. *The Intoxication of Power: An Analysis of Civil Religion in Relation to Ideology*. Dordrecht and Boston: D. Riedel, 1979.

Herberg, Will. *Protestant-Catholic-Jew*, rev. ed. Garden City, N.Y.: Doubleday, 1960.

Herbert, Jerry S., ed. *America, Christian or Secular? Readings in American Christian History and Civil Religion*. Portland, Ore: Multnomah Press, 1984.

Hughey, Michael W. *Civil Religion and Moral Order: Theoretical and Historical Dimensions*. Westport, Conn.: Greenwood Press, 1983.

Hutcheson, Robert G., Jr. *God in the White House: How Religion Has Changed the Modern Presidency*. New York: Macmillan, 1988.

Kelly, George Armstrong. *Politics and Religious Consciousness in America*. New Brunswick, N.J.: Transaction Books, 1984.

Lipset, Seymour M. *The First New Nation*. New York: W. W. Norton, 1979.

Marty, Martin E. *A Nation of Behavers*. Chicago: University of Chicago Press, 1976.

McBrien, Richard P. *Caesar's Coin: Religion and Politics in America*. New York: Macmillan, 1987.

Mead, Sidney E. *The Nation with the Soul of a Church*. New York: Harper & Row, 1975.

Mead, Sidney E. *The Old Religion in the Brave New World: Reflections on the Relation Between Christendom and the Republic*. Berkeley: University of California Press, 1977.

Menendez, Albert J. *Religion and the U. S. Presidency: A Bibliography*. New York: Garland, 1986

Neuhaus, Richard John. *The Naked Public Square*. Grand Rapids: Wm. B. Eerdmans, 1984.

Noll, Mark A., Nathan O. Hatch, and George M. Marsden. *The Search for Christian America*. Westchester, Ill.: Crossway Books, 1983.

Reichley, A. James. *Religion in American Public Life*. Washington, D. C.: Brookings Institution, 1985.

Richey, Russell E. and Donald G. Jones, eds. *American Civil Religion*. New York: Harper & Row, 1974.

Rouner, Leroy S., ed. *Civil Religion and Political Theology*. Notre Dame: University of Notre Dame Press, 1986.

Silk, Mark. *Spiritual Politics: Religion and America Since World War II*. New York: Simon and Schuster, 1988.

Skillen, James W., ed. *Confessing Christ and Doing Politics*. Washington, D.C.: APJ Education Fund, 1982.

Smart, James D. *The Cultural Subversion of the Biblical Faith: Life in the 20th Century under the Sign of the Cross*. Philadelphia: Westminster Press, 1977.

Stringfellow, William. *An Ethic for Christians and Other Aliens in a Strange Land*. Waco: Word Books, 1973.

Tuveson, Ernest L. *Redeemer Nation: The Idea of America's Millennial Role*. Chicago: University of Chicago Press, 1968.

Wald, Kenneth D. *Religion and Politics in the United States*. New York: St. Martin's Press, 1987.

Wilson, John F. *Public Religion in American Culture*. Philadelphia: Temple University Press, 1979.

ABBREVIATIONS IN THE NOTES

Cong. Rec.

Congressional Record. Washington, D.C.: Government Printing Office, 1874–. (All references are to volume number and date of entry)

Inaugural Addresses

Inaugural Addresses of the Presidents of the United States from George Washington 1789 to Richard Milhous Nixon 1973. Washington, D.C.: Government Printing Office, 1974.

Messages and Papers

James D. Richardson, ed., *A Compilation of the Messages and Papers of the Presidents.* New York: Bureau of National Literature, 1925.

Papers WW

Arthur S. Link, ed., *The Papers of Woodrow Wilson.* Princeton: Princeton University Press, 1966–. (All references are to volume number)

PPAFDR

Samuel I. Rosenman, ed., *The Public Papers and Addresses of Franklin D. Roosevelt.* New York: Random House, Harper, 1938–50. (All references are to volume number)

Public Papers

Public Papers of the Presidents of the United States. Washington, D.C.: Government Printing Office, 1957–. (All references are to the year of the particular president's administration)

WCPD

Weekly Compilation of Presidential Documents. Washington, D.C.: Government Printing Office, 1965–. (All references are to the year of the particular president's administration)

NOTES

PREFACE

[1] The recent use of the concept and the ensuing debate over its utility was inaugurated by the publication of Robert N. Bellah's "Civil Religion in America," *Daedalus* 96 (Winter 1967): 1-21.

[2] *Zorach v. Clauson* 343 U.S. 306 (1952).

CHAPTER ONE

[1] *New York Times*, Nov.26, 1963, pp. 1, 8.

[2] Ibid., Jan. 21 1961, p. 8.

[3] Ibid., p. 12.

[4] *Inaugural Addresses of the Presidents of the United States from George Washington 1789 to Richard Milhous Nixon 1973* (Washington, D.C.: Government Printing Office, 1974), 267–70 (hereafter cited as *Inaugural Addresses*).

[5] Sidney Verba, "The Kennedy Assassination and the Nature of Political Commitment," in *The Kennedy Assassination and the American Public*, ed. Bradley S. Greenberg and Edwin B. Parker (Stanford: Stanford University Press, 1965), 352.

[6] *New York Times*, Nov. 26, 1963, pp. 1, 8–9, 12.

[7] Clinton Rossiter, *The American Presidency* (New York: Harcourt, Brace and World, 1960), 74–108; and Alfred H. Kelly, Winfred A. Harbison, and Herman Belz, *The American Constitution: Its Origins and Development*, 6th ed. (New York: Norton, 1983), 100–102.

[8] Rossiter, *American Presidency*, 18. The three-hundred pound Taft was big enough to mean this both literally and figuratively.

[9] The problem of definition is a knotty one. Four terms central to the discussion defy precise definition: (1) evangelical, (2) fundamentalist, (3) the New Political Right, and (4) the New Religious Right. "evangelical" may best be understood in the context of "evangelical Christianity," which some writers also refer to as "evangelicalism." We prefer the terms "evangelical" and "evangelical Christianity" because they have greater historical meaning and clarity than the more recently coined expression "evangelicalism." The problem is compounded when one tries to differentiate evangelical from fundamentalist because, as political scientist James Reichley notes, the distinction between the two was and remains "somewhat hazy." And, after devoting eighty-six pages to a survey of "The evangelical Tradition in America" in his book of the same title, church historian Leonard Sweet could only conclude that "more study" was needed before any consensus might be reached on a working definition of either evangelicalism or fundamentalism.

Given these difficulties, we choose to use the terms without precise definition. Close scholars of evangelical Christianity and political religion may wish to take issue with this, but we see no alternative. Thus, when we speak of "evangelicals," we refer to those adherents to the Christian faith who hold the following theological beliefs in common: (1) the Bible is the ultimate authority for faith and practice in the religious life; (2) Jesus of Nazareth was God incarnate; and (3) eternal salvation comes through personal faith in Jesus Christ and his work on the cross and leads to a spiritually transformed life (many call this being "born again"). evangelicals are considered theological conservatives because they perceive of themselves as custodians of biblical orthodoxy. Fundamentalists can best be seen as the "right wing" of evangelical Christianity. In 1984 Martin Marty estimated that some 10 to 20 million out of a total of 40 to 50 million adult Americans claiming to be evangelicals were fundamentalists.

The New Political Right is equally difficult to define. We use it to describe the heirs of the Taft-McCarthy Republicanism of the 1950s and the Goldwater-Reagan Republicanism of the l960s, who reject the New Deal social and economic philosophy and the internationalist outlook of the traditional "Eastern establishment" in their party. It is in essence right-wing conservatism, embodied in the 1980s primarily in the Reagan-controlled Republican party but also practiced by many Democrats and "independents." The New Religious Right is a coalition of fundamentalist Protestants, pro-life Roman Catholics, conservative Jews, and Mormons who banded together in a variety of organizations (such as the Moral Majority) to support the New Political Right, especially its social programs.

For more information on these topics see Carl F. H. Henry, *Evangelicals in Search of Identity* (Waco: Word Books, 1976); Robert D. Linder and Richard V. Pierard, *Twilight of the Saints: Biblical Christianity and Civil Religion in America* (Downers Grove, Ill.: InterVarsity Press, 1978), 189-90; Jackson W. Carroll, Douglas W. Johnson, and Martin E. Marty, *Religion in America: 1950 to the Present* (San Franciso: Harper & Row, 1979), 96-99, 113-18; Martin E. Marty, "Twelve Points to Consider about the New Christian Right," *Context* 15 (July 1980): 1; "An Interview with Donald W. Dayton," *Faith and Thought* 1 (Spring 1983): 24-34; James D. Hunter, *American Evangelicalism: Conservative Religion and the Quandary of Modernity* (New Brunswick, N.J.: Rutgers University Press, 1983), 50-54; Robert C. Wuthnow, "The Political Rebirth of American Evangelicals," in *The New Christian Right: Mobilization and Legitimation,* ed. Robert C. Liebman and Robert C. Wuthnow (New York: Aldine, 1983), 168-85; George M. Marsden, "The Evangelical Denomination," in *Evangelicalism and Modern America,* ed. Marsden (Grand Rapids: Eerdmans, 1984), vii-xix; Martin E. Marty, "Fundamentalism as a Social Phenomenon," in ibid., 56-68; John S. Saloma III, *Ominous Politics: The New Conservative Labyrinth* (New York: Hill and Wang, 1984), xvii-xxii, 3-23; Leonard I. Sweet, "The Evangelical Tradition in America," in *The Evangelical Tradition in America,* ed. Sweet (Macon, Ga.: Mercer University Press, 1984), 1-86; and A. James Reichley, *Religion in American Public Life* (Washington, D.C.: Brookings Institution, 1985), 312-13, 319-31.

[10]S. Robert Lichter and Stanley Rothman, "Media and Business Elites," *Public Opinion* 4 (November 1981): 42-46, 59-60; and Wesley E. Miller, "The New Christian Right and the News Media," in *New Christian Politics,* ed. David G. Bromley and Anson Shupe (Macon, Ga.: Mercer University Press, 1984), 139-49.

[11]Paul F. Boller, Jr., "Religion and the U. S. Presidency," *Journal of Church and State* 21 (Winter 1979): 5-21.

[12]Senator Hatfield was bitterly attacked by many evangelicals for his opposition to the Vietnam War. Strong criticism also came from this quarter when he voted in favor of relinquishing U. S. ownership of the Panama Canal and when, as chair of the Senate Appropriations Committee, he opposed some of President Reagan's defense spending requests. On the

treatment he received for his Vietnam stance, see Hatfield, *Between a Rock and a Hard Place* (Waco: Word Books, 1975); and Robert Eells and Bartell Nyberg, *Lonely Walk: The Life of Senator Mark Hatfield* (Chappaqua, N.Y.: Christian Herald, 1979). Hatfield told the authors about the other matters in a personal communication on March 10, 1987.

[13] Michael Novak, *Choosing Our King: Powerful Symbols in Presidential Politics* (New York: Macmillan, 1974), 3–5; Charles P. Henderson, Jr., "Civil Religion and the American Presidency," *Religious Education* 70 (September–October 1975): 473–85; Robert N. Bellah, "Civil Religion in America," 1–21; and Lewis Lipsitz, "If, as Verba Says, the State Functions as a Religion, What Are We to Do Then to Save Our Souls?" *American Political Science Review* 62 (1968): 530.

[14] Bellah, "Civil Religion in America." This piece provoked so much discussion in the scholarly world that he later commented: "In 1967 I published an essay I have never been allowed to forget." Bellah and Phillip E. Hammond, *Varieties of Civil Religion* (San Francisco: Harper & Row, 1980), 3.

[15] Bellah, "Civil Religion in America," 1, 18–19.

[16] For example, Charles P. Henderson and Robert S. Alley take this position. See Henderson, "Civil Religion and the American Presidency," 477–78; and Alley, *So Help Me God: Religion and the Presidency: Wilson to Nixon* (Richmond, Va.: John Knox Press, 1972), 13–19.

[17] We strongly subscribe to the separation of the institutions of church and state but recognize that the separation of religion and politics not only is impossible but also in the main undesirable. As Leonard Sweet (*The Evangelical Tradition*, 15) observes: "Clearly politics and religion do mix in American history, though in complex and surprising ways, and the mixing can sometimes be seen in the relationship between religious values and voting behavior both in Peoria and on the Potomac."

Moreover, all political entities by definition need some moral parameters and, from the Judeo-Christian perspective, some transcendent reference point by which they may be judged. Vital religion can provide these. See Linder and Pierard, *Twilight of the Saints*, 173–86; and Linder, "Church and State," in *Evangelical Dictionary of Theology*, ed. Walter A. Elwell (Grand Rapids: Baker, 1984), 233–38.

[18] Emile Durkheim, *The Elementary Forms of the Religious Life* (New York: Macmillan, 1915), 415–47; Robin M. Williams, Jr., *American Society: A Sociological Interpretation* (New York: Knopf, 1951), 312; Clifford Geertz, "Ethos, World-View and the Analysis of Sacred Symbols," *Antioch Review* 17 (December 1957): 421–37; Peter Berger, *The Sacred Canopy: Elements of a Sociological Theory of Religion* (Garden City, N.Y.: Doubleday, 1967), 22–26; Robert N. Bellah, *The Broken Covenant: American Civil Religion in Time of Trial* (New York: Seabury, 1975), ix–x; and Bryan S. Turner, *Religion and Social Theory* (London: Heinemann, 1983), 38–62.

[19] Novak, *Choosing Our King*, 302–3; and Bellah, "Civil Religion in America," 8.

[20] Robert N. Bellah, "American Civil Religion in the 1970s," *Anglican Theological Review*, supp. ser., no. 1 (July 1973): 9.

[21] The Bill Klem anecdote is courtesy of Martin E. Marty, *A Nation of Behavers* (Chicago: University of Chicago Press, 1976), 225.

[22] Despite historian John F. Wilson's effort to channel the debate in "a more positive direction" by substituting the term "public religion" for "civil

religion," the existing expression is still the most useful. See Wilson, *Public Religion in American Culture* (Philadelphia: Temple University Press, 1979), 3–22; idem, "The Status of 'Civil Religion' in America," in *The Religion of the Republic*, ed. Elwyn Smith (Philadelphia: Fortress, 1971), 1–21; Bellah, "Civil Religion in America," 1; idem, "American Civil Religion in the 1970's," 8–20; Russell E. Richey and Donald G. Jones, "The Civil Religion Debate," in *American Civil Religion*, ed. Richey and Jones (New York: Harper & Row, 1974), 3–18; Marty, *Nation of Behavers*, 180–203; and Reichley, *Religion in American Public Life*, 47–52.

Catherine L. Albanese, *America: Religion and Religions* (Belmont, Calif.: Wadsworth, 1981), 283–309, has contributed the analytical tool of dividing the loose system described as American civil religion into creed, code, and cultus. Unfortunately, she drew her conclusions about the current state of the public faith before the beginning of the Reagan presidency, and this skewed her final assessment, wrongly we believe, in the direction of its decline.

[23] Bellah, "Civil Religion in America," 1–21; Will Herberg, *Protestant–Catholic–Jew: An Essay in American Religious Sociology* (Garden City, N.Y.: Doubleday, 1960), 72–98; and Conrad Cherry, *God's New Israel: Religious Interpretations of American Destiny* (Englewood Cliffs, N.J.: Prentice–Hall, 1971), 1–24.

[24] This possibility is raised by Bellah, "Civil Religion in America," 15.

[25] J. Paul Williams, *What Americans Believe and How They Worship* (New York: Harper & Row, 1962), 484; Charles P. Henderson, Jr., *The Nixon Theology* (New York: Harper & Row, 1972), 174–93; Martin E. Marty, "Two Kinds of Two Kinds of Civil Religion," in *American Civil Religion*, ed. Richey and Jones, 139–57; and Marty, *Nation of Behavers*, 180–203.

[26] W. Lloyd Warner, *American Life: Dream and Reality* (Chicago: University of Chicago Press, 1962), 5–34; Conrad Cherry, "Two American Sacred Ceremonies: Their Implications for the Study of Religion in America," *American Quarterly* 21 (Winter 1969): 739–54; Kalmin D. Smith, "The Politics of Civil Religion," *American Benedictine Review* 26 (March 1975): 89–106; and Linder and Pierard, *Twilight of the Saints*, 15–21.

[27] *Inaugural Addresses*, 2.

[28] Ibid., 257.

[29] Paul A. Carter, "The Pastoral Office of the President," *Theology Today* 25 (April 1968): 52.

[30] *New York Times*, July 18, 1980, p. 8.

[31] "I am charged with being a preacher. Well, I suppose I am. I have such a bully pulpit." Quoted in Christian F. Reisner, *Roosevelt's Religion* (New York: Abingdon, 1922), 204.

[32] Quoted in Marty, "Two Kinds of Two Kinds of Civil Religion," 147. See also Carter, "The Pastoral Office of the President," 52–63; and Thomas A. Bailey, *Presidential Greatness: The Image and the Man, from George Washington to the Present* (New York: Appleton-Century-Crofts, 1966), 200–201.

[33] "National Prayer Breakfast," *Congressional Record* 123 (Feb. 10, 1977): 4343–44 (hereafter cited as *Cong. Rec.*); "To Lift a Nation's Spirit," *Newsweek* 95 (July 23, 1979): 20–26; Arthur Schlesinger, Jr., "Pretension in the Presidential Pulpit," *Wall Street Journal*, March 17, 1983, p. 26; Hugh Sidey, "The Right Rev. Ronald Reagan," *Time* 121 (March 21, 1983): 18; Richard V. Pierard, "Reagan and the Evangelicals: The Making of a Love Affair,"

Christian Century 100 (Dec. 21–28, 1983): 1182–84; and Raymond Coffey and Storer Rowley, "Reagan and Religion," *Chicago Tribune*, March 11, 1984, sec. 5, pp. 1, 4.

[34] Alley, *So Help Me God*, 16–19.

[35] Rossiter, *American Presidency*, 41.

CHAPTER TWO

[1] Jeffrey Hadden, "Televangelism and the Future of American Politics," in *New Christian Politics*, ed. Bromley and Shupe, 151–56.

[2] Jerry Falwell, for example, has repeatedly emphasized that his Moral Majority is not a fundamentalist Christian religious organization but a religiously diverse political movement. He declared publicly in a major news magazine, "We are made up of fundamentalists, evangelicals, Roman Catholics, conservative Jews, Mormons, and even persons of no religious belief who share our concerns about the issues we address." *Newsweek* 97 (Sept. 21, 1981): 17.

[3] Bill Keller, "Lobbying for Christ: evangelical Conservatives Move from Pews to Polls, But Can They Sway Congress?" *Congressional Quarterly Weekly Report*, Sept. 6, 1980, p. 2634.

[4] "Bill Moyers' Journal," transcript, broadcast of Sep. 26, 1980, p. 12. On this documentary, Moyers queried James Robison, a Baptist evangelist and Dallas organizer, concerning the purpose of the Roundtable briefing. He raised the pluralism issue and questioned whether a "moral majority" was possible or even desirable in modern America. Robison replied, "We've had Catholics, Jews, all denominations, people that don't wave a cross or a Christian flag at all; but they're people of principle who love this country, and they're sick and tired of the poor people and the minorities getting all the lying liberal politician promises for the government handouts," ibid., p. 6. Thus, by affirming the religious pluralism of their movement, Robison and other New Religious Right leaders clearly placed the main thrust of their activities under the banner of civil religion.

[5] See above chapter one. Falwell and other New Religious Right luminaries subsequently apologized for Smith's remarks and assured Jewish leaders that their goal was not to make America a "Christian society." Moreover, in the months that followed, evangelical Christians across the country repudiated the preacher's statement, and eventually Smith himself held conciliation meetings with Jewish figures where an amicable understanding was reached concerning the matter. A study of religiously conservative, evangelical Protestants commissioned by B'nai B'rith in 1986 revealed an overwhelming rejection of the view about God's response to Jewish prayers which Smith had so carelessly enunciated. *Newsweek* 96 (Nov. 10, 1980): 76; *Christianity Today* 25 (Jan. 23, 1981): 40–41; *New York Times*, Jan. 9, 1987, p. 14; and "Nationwide Attitudes Survey, September 1986," report presented to the Anti-Defamation League of B'nai B'rith by Tarrance, Hill, Newport, and Ryan, Houston, Tex., copy in possession of the authors.

[6] Robert D. Linder, "Civil Religion in Historical Perspective: The Reality That Underlies the Concept," *Journal of Church and State* 17 (Autumn 1975): 399–421.

[7] Ronald Grimsley, *Rousseau and the Religious Quest* (Oxford: Clarendon Press, 1968), 76–86.

[8] For various views on Rousseau and his consistency or lack thereof, see *The Political Writings of Jean-Jacques Rousseau*, ed. C.E. Vaughan, 2 vols. (Cambridge: University Press, 1935), especially the introduction by the editor; David Cameron, "Rousseau, Professor Derathe, and Natural Law," *Political Studies* 20 (June 1972): 195–201; Maurice W. Cranston and Richard S. Peters, eds., *Hobbes and Rousseau: A Collection of Critical Essays* (Garden City, N.Y.: Doubleday, 1972); and Maurice W. Cranston, *Jean Jacques: The Early Life and Work of Jean-Jacques Rousseau, 1712-1754* (New York: Norton, 1983). For Locke, see John M. Dunn, *The Political Thought of John Locke* (Cambridge: Cambridge University Press, 1969), 27–40, 262–67.

[9] Jean-Jacques Rousseau, *The Social Contract and Discourses*, ed. G. D. H. Cole (New York: Dutton, 1950), 139. Also see Jean-Jacques Rousseau, *Oeuvres Completes, Du Contrat Social*, ed. Bernard Gagnebin and Marcel Raymond (Paris: Gallimard, 1964), 3:468.

[10] In Rousseau's conception of the social contract, each individual voluntarily forms part of what he calls "the general will." Because each person is a part of the whole, he or she continues to be free. However, the majority, which always knows what is best for the group, is the custodian of the general will. The individual must obey the general will, for the majority is a better judge than the individual of what is best. On this topic, see Rousseau, *Du Contrat Social*, 3:368–75.

[11] Louis J. Voskuil, "Jean-Jacques Rousseau: Secular Salvation and Civil Religion," *Fides et Historia* 7 (Spring 1975): 11–26.

[12] This brief summary of Rousseau's concept of civil religion and its relation to the totality of his discussion of the social contract does not do full justice to the French thinker. There has been a great deal of debate over why he developed the idea and whether or not its implementation would lead to a more altruistic, public-spirited civil society or to a political order in which the state becomes the transcendent point of reference for both politics and religion. See Waldemar Gurian, "Totalitarianism as Political Religion," in *Totalitarianism*, ed. Carl J. Friedrich (Cambridge: Harvard University Press, 1954), 119–29; and Reinhold Niebuhr, *Christianity and Power Politics* (New York: Scribner's, 1940), 117–30.

[13] Rousseau, *Du Contrat Social*, 3:464–68.

[14] Durkheim, *Elementary Forms of the Religious Life*, 474–75.

[15] Rousseau, *Du Contrat Social*, 3:468; and Plato, *The Dialogues*, ed. Benjamin Jowett (Oxford: Oxford University Press, 1892), 2:109–29.

[16] Plato, *The Republic*, ed. Benjamin Jowett (Oxford: Oxford University Press, 1892), 1:621–82. Also see Ellis Sandoz, "The Civil Theology of Liberal Democracy: Locke and His Predecessors," *Journal of Politics* 34 (February 1972): 2–7.

[17] Ernest Barker, *Church, State, and Education* (Ann Arbor: University of Michigan Press, 1957), 133–36; and Michael A. Smith, *From Christ to Constantine* (London: InterVarsity Press, 1971), 74–91.

[18] *The History of the Decline and Fall of the Roman Empire*, ed. J. B.Bury (New York: F. De Fau, 1906), 1:35–6.

[19] Eusebius of Caesarea, *The Ecclesiastical History* (Cambridge: Harvard University Press, 1953–57), 1:405–37; N. H. Baynes, "The Great Persecution," in *The Cambridge Ancient History*, ed. J. B. Bury, S. A. Cook, F. E. Adcock, M. P. Charlesworth, and N. H. Baynes, 12 vols. (Cambridge: Cambridge University Press, 1923–39), 12:646–77; and W. H. C. Frend,

Martyrdom and Persecution in the Early Church, rev. ed. (Grand Rapids: Baker, 1981), 477–535.

[20]Kenneth S. Latourette, *A History of Christianity* (New York: Harper & Row, 1953), 92; N. H. Baynes, *Constantine the Great and the Christian Church*, 2d ed., preface by Henry Chadwick (New York: Oxford University Press, 1972), 1–9; and Andras Alfoldi, *The Conversion of Constantine and Pagan Rome*, trans. Harold Mattingly (Oxford: Clarendon, 1948), 21–35.

[21]W. H. C. Frend, *The Rise of Christianity* (Philadelphia: Fortress Press, 1984), 484–88. The discussion of Constantine is based on pp. 473–505.

[22]Cited in ibid., 486. Italics added.

[23]J. W. C. Wand, *A History of the Early Church to A.D. 500* (London: Methuen, 1937), 131; and Guglielmo Ferrero and Corrado Barbagallo, *A Short History of Rome*, 2 vols. (New York: Putnam's, 1918–19), 2:418.

[24]Barker, *Church, State, and Education*, 131–35.

[25]Ernst H. Kantorowicz, "*Pro Patria Mori* in Medieval Political Thought," *American Historical Review* 56 (April 1951): 472–92.

[26]Joseph R. Strayer, "Problems of State-Building," in *Medieval Statecraft and the Perspectives of History*, ed. Strayer (Princeton: Princeton University Press, 1971), 251–348.

[27]J. E. J. Quicherat, *Proces de condemnation et de rehabilitation de Jeanne d'Arc*, 5 vols. (Paris: Renouard, 1841–49), 5:127.

[28]Gerhart B. Ladner, "Aspects of Medieval Thought on Church and State," *Review of Politics* 9 (October 1947): 403–22.

[29]Kantorowicz, "*Pro Patria Mori*," 491.

[30]G. R. Cragg, *The Church and the Age of Reason, 1648-1789* (Baltimore: Penguin, 1970), 209–33.

[31]Ronald J. VanderMolen, "Western Secularization as a Continuing Process: Ironic Origins and Puzzling Results," *Fides et Historia* 8 (Fall 1975): 50–51.

[32]Robert N. Bellah, "The Five Religions of Modern Italy," in *Varieties of Civil Religion*, ed. Bellah and Hammond, 86–118.

[33]David J. Diephouse, "The 'German Catastrophe' Revisited: Civil Religion in the Third Reich," *Fides et Historia* 7 (Spring 1975): 55.

[34]Reinhold Niebuhr, *Christianity and Power Politics* (New York: Scribner's, 1940), 117–30; and Jacques Ellul, "Les religions seculieres," *Foi et Vie* 69 (1970): 73.

[35]John Aylmer, *An Harborowe for Faithfull and Trewe Subjects* (Strassburg: n.p., 1559), [Sig. P4, margin; Sig. R].

[36]John Foxe, *The Acts and Monuments*, ed. S. R. Cattley, 8 vols. (1837–41; reprint, New York: AMS Press, 1965), 1:vi–viii, 305–86, and passim.

[37]William Haller, *Foxe's Book of Martyrs and the Elect Nation* (London: Jonathan Cape, 1963), 224–50; and William M. Lamont, *Godly Rule: Politics and Religion, 1603-1660* (New York: St. Martin's, 1969).

[38]Bruce Murphy, "Christianity and Civil Religion in Cromwellian England," *Fides et Historia* 7 (Spring 1975): 27–39.

[39]John Owen, "Christ's Kingdom and the Magistrate's Power," sermon published in *The Works of John Owen*, 24 vols. (Edinburgh: T. & T. Clark, 1850–53), 8:381. The scriptural basis for Owen's allusion is Jeremiah 8:20.

[40]Sandoz, "The Civil Theology of Liberal Democracy," 9–14, 34–35; Dunn, *The Political Thought of John Locke*, 222–28; and Michael P. Zuckert, "Locke and the Problem of Civil Religion," in *The Moral Foundations of the*

American Republic, ed. Robert H. Horwitz (Charlottesville: University Press of Virginia, 1986), 181–203.

[41] Robert D. Linder, "Ronald Reagan at Kansas State: Civil Religion in the Service of the New Right," *Reformed Journal* 32 (December 1982): 14.

[42] George F. Willison, *Saints and Strangers* (New York: Reynal and Hitchcock, 1945), 1–11, 121–68, and 408–22; and George Langdon, *Pilgrim Colony: A History of New Plymouth, 1620–1691* (New Haven: Yale University Press, 1966), 12–37.

[43] B. P. Poore, ed., *The Federal and State Constitutions*, 2 vols. (Washington, D.C.: Government Printing Office, 1878), 1:931.

[44] William Bradford, *Of Plymouth Plantation, 1620-1647*, ed. S. E. Morison (New York: Knopf, 1952).

[45] John Winthrop, *Papers*, ed. A. B. Forbes, 5 vols. (Boston: Massachusetts Historical Society, 1929–47), 2:29; and Loren Baritz, *City on a Hill: A History of Ideas and Myths in America* (New York: Wiley, 1964), 3–45.

[46] For example, see John Adams to Hezekiah Niles, Feb. 13, 1818, in *The Selected Writings of John and John Quincy Adams*, ed. Adrienne Koch and William Peden (New York: Knopf, 1946), 203; Catherine L. Albanese, *Sons of the Fathers: The Civil Religion of the American Revolution* (Philadelphia: Temple University Press, 1976), 19–45; and Sydney E. Ahlstrom, "Religion, Revolution and the Rise of Modern Nationalism: Reflections on the American Experience," *Church History* 44 (December 1975): 499–500.

[47] *Inaugural Addresses*, 21.

[48] Bellah, "Civil Religion in America," 7–9; and D. Elton Trueblood, *The Future of the Christian* (New York: Harper & Row, 1971), 89–92.

[49] Cherry, "Two American Sacred Ceremonies," 741.

[50] Ibid.; Warner, *American Life: Dream and Reality*; and John H. Westerhoff III, *McGuffey and His Readers* (Nashville: Abingdon, 1978), 18–24.

[51] Cherry, "Two American Sacred Ceremonies," 739–54; Bellah, "Civil Religion in America," 11; and Trueblood, *Future of the Christian*, 98–99. It is noteworthy that the Lincoln Memorial provided the setting for both Martin Luther King, Jr.'s "I Have a Dream" speech in 1963 and Billy Graham's Honor America Day address in 1970.

[52] Oliver Wendell Holmes, *The Poetical Works of Oliver Wendell Holmes* (Boston: Houghton Mifflin, 1975), 194.

[53] *Minersville School District v. Gobitis*, 310 U.S. 596 (1940). He was citing a 1907 case, *Halter v. Nebraska*. The Gobitis ruling, which had to do with the refusal of Jehovah's Witnesses to salute the flag, was overturned three years later.

[54] Nathan O. Hatch, "The Origins of Civil Millennialism in America: New England Clergymen, War with France, and the Revolution," *William and Mary Quarterly* 31 (July 1974): 429. Also see Hatch, *The Sacred Cause of Liberty: Millennial Thought in Revolutionary New England* (New Haven: Yale University Press, 1977), 21–74; and Robert N. Bellah, "Religion and the Legitimation of the American Republic," in *Varieties of Civil Religion*, ed. Bellah and Hammond, 10–13.

[55] Patricia U. Bonomi, *Under the Cope of Heaven: Religion, Society, and Politics in Colonial America* (New York: Oxford University Press, 1986), 161–216.

[56] John E. Smylie, "National Ethos and the Church," *Theology Today* 20 (October 1963): 314.

[57] *New York Morning News*, Dec. 27, 1845, p. 1.

[58] Matthew Simpson, "Indiana Conference," *The Methodist*, 2 (Oct. 12, 1861): 313.

[59] William G. McLoughlin, ed., *The American Evangelicals, 1800-1900* (New York: Harper & Row, 1974), 1.

[60] Carlton J. H. Hayes, *Essays on Nationalism* (New York: Macmillan, 1926), 6, and passim.

[61] Ralph H. Gabriel, *The Course of American Democratic Thought*, 2d ed. (New York: Ronald Press, 1956), chap. 3; and Ahlstrom, "Religion, Revolution and the Rise of Modern Nationalism."

[62] Westerhoff, *McGuffey and His Readers*, 13–26, and 91–110; and Robert W. Lynn, "Civil Catechetics in Mid-Victorian America: Some Notes About American Civil Religion, Past and Present," *Religious Education* 48 (January–February 1973): 5–27.

[63] George M. Marsden, "America's 'Christian' Origins: Puritan New England as a Case Study," in *John Calvin: His Influence in the Western World*, ed. W. Stanford Reid (Grand Rapids: Zondervan, 1982), 250–53.

[64] Henry May, *The Enlightenment in America* (New York: Oxford University Press, 1977).

[65] Gabriel, *American Democratic Thought*, 14–25; Ahlstrom, "Religion, Revolution and the Rise of Modern Nationalism," 502–3; Sidney E. Mead, *The Nation With the Soul of a Church* (New York: Harper & Row, 1975), 56–57; and Seymour M. Lipset, *The First New Nation*, (New York: Basic Books, 1963), 61–98.

[66] *Inaugural Addresses*, 21.

[67] Sydney E. Ahlstrom, "Requiem for Patriotic Piety," *Worldview* 18 (August 1972): 9–11; and Trueblood, *The Future of the Christian*, 88–89. The comment attributed to Bismarck is in Thomas A. Bailey, *The American Pageant* (Lexington, Mass.: D. C. Heath, 1971), 668.

[68] See John Dewey, *A Common Faith* (New Haven: Yale University Press, 1934), 43–51, 87.

[69] Aaron I. Abell, *The Urban Impact on American Protestantism, 1865-1900* (Cambridge: Harvard University Press, 1943); Sidney E. Mead, *The Lively Experiment: The Shaping of Christianity in America* (New York: Harper & Row, 1963), 134–55; Sydney E. Ahlstrom, *A Religious History of the American People* (New Haven: Yale University Press, 1972), 842–56; and Don S. Ross, "The 'Civil Religion' in America," *Religion in Life* 44 (Spring 1975): 24–35.

CHAPTER THREE

[1] Daniel J. Boorstin, *The Americans: The National Experience* (New York: Vintage Books, 1965), 349.

[2] Ibid., 349–51; Horatio Hasting Weld, *Pictorial Life of George Washington* (Philadelphia: Lindsay and Blakiston, 1845), 219–20.

[3] Catherine L. Albanese, *Sons of the Fathers: The Civil Religion of the American Revolution* (Philadelphia: Temple University Press, 1976), 143–81.

[4] The standard biography is Douglas Southall Freeman, *George Washington*, 7 vols. (New York: Scribners, 1948–57). Also first-rate and more up-to-date are James T. Flexner, *George Washington*, 4 vols. (Boston: Little Brown, 1965–72), and John Alden, *George Washington: A Biography* (Baton Rouge: Louisiana State University Press, 1984). The biographical information concerning Washington is drawn from these works. For a slightly different view of the first president as a rather ordinary, noncharismatic person

whom American necessity made into a manufactured hero, see Barry Schwartz, *George Washington: The Making of an American Symbol* (New York: Free Press, 1987).

[5] B. F. Morris, *Christian Life and Character of the Civil Institutions of the United States* (Philadelphia: G. W. Childs, 1864), 11, 166; Philip Slaughter, *Christianity the Key to the Character and Career of Washington* (Washington, D.C.: Judd & Detweiler, 1886), 2; Willam Meade, *Old Churches, Ministers, and Families of Virginia*, 2 vols. (Philadelphia: J. B. Lippincott, 1857), 2:243; and Norman Vincent Peale, *One Nation Under God* (Pawling, N.Y.: Foundation for Christian Living, 1972), 14.

[6] J. V. Nash, "The Religion and Philosophy of Washington," *Open Court* 43 (February 1932): 73; and Pat Robertson, *America's Dates with Destiny* (Nashville: Thomas Nelson, 1986), 107–8.

[7] Paul F. Boller, Jr., *George Washington and Religion* (Dallas: Southern Methodist University Press, 1963), 5.

[8] Ibid., 3–23. On Washington's religious beliefs, see also Vernon B. Hampton, *Religious Background of the White House* (Boston: Christopher Publishing House, 1932), 196–99, 330–37.

[9] For the full story of the famous legend-maker, see the Marcus Cunliffe edition of Mason Locke Weems, *The Life of Washington* (Cambridge: Cambridge University Press, 1962), ix–lxii.

[10] Weems, *The Life of George Washington*, 29th ed. (Frankford, Pa.: J. Allen, 1826), 184; Boller, *George Washington and Religion*, 8–10; and Edmund Fuller and David E. Green, *God in the White House: The Faiths of American Presidents* (New York: Crown Publishers, 1968), 10–11.

[11] Martin E. Marty, "Legends in Stained Glass," *Christian Century* 93 (May 5, 1976): 447; and Boller, *George Washington and Religion*, 10.

[12] Ibid., 24–44; Freeman, *Washington*, 1:194, 196; 2:387–88, 397; and Fuller and Green, *God in the White House*, 9–12.

[13] Washington to Joseph Reed, March 7, 1776, in *The Writings of George Washington*, ed. John C. Fitzpatrick, 39 vols. (Washington, D.C.: Government Printing Office, 1931–44), 4:380. See also ibid., 26:449–50, 27:24–25, 37:284; and James T. Flexner, *Washington: The Indispensable Man* (Boston: Little Brown, 1974), 74.

[14] Washington to James Anderson, Dec. 24, 1795, in *Writings*, ed. Fitzpatrick, 34:407.

[15] Freeman, *Washington*, 5:92.

[16] *The Basic Writings of George Washington*, ed. Saxe Commins (New York: Random House, 1948), 504.

[17] Boller, *George Washington and Religion*, 92–115.

[18] Fuller and Green, *God in the White House*, 12–14.

[19] Albanese, *Sons of the Fathers*, 146–47.

[20] Albanese, *America: Religion and Religions*, 295–97, 308–9.

[21] *Inaugural Addresses*, 2.

[22] Ibid., 4.

[23] *Writings*, ed. Commins, 616.

[24] Anson Phelps Stokes and Leo Pfeffer, *Church and State in the United States*, rev. ed. (New York: Harper & Row, 1964), 87. The Revolutionary era was a crucial period for the development of civil religion in the new nation. Sidney Mead insists that the denominational pluralism of America interacted with the cosmopolitan Enlightenment assumptions of the Revolutionary leadership to form a "religion of the republic." This civil religion, like those

which rely on revelation, was essentially prophetic in that it called the
nation back from its waywardness. Washington's presidential thanksgiving
proclamations, beginning in 1789, are clear examples of this prophetic type
of civil religion. *The Nation with the Soul of a Church* (New York: Harper &
Row, 1975), 65–67, 114–20.

25 *Writings*, ed. Commins, 651–52.

26 *The Writings of George Washington*, ed. Jared Sparks, 12 vols. (Boston:
John B. Russell, 1834–37), 12:227. A good indication that Washington was
referring here to religion in general and not specifically to Christianity was
the treaty that was being negotiated at the same time with the Muslim Bey of
Tripoli. The document was signed on November 4, 1796, and the following
year it was approved by President John Adams and ratified by the Senate.
Particularly significant was Article 11: "As the government of the United
States of America is not in any sense founded upon the Christian Religion—
as it has in itself no character of enmity against the laws, religion or
tranquility of Musselmen [Muslims]. . . , it is declared by the parties that no
pretext arising from religious opinions shall ever produce an interruption of
the harmony existing between the two countries." *Treaties and Other
International Acts of the United States of America*, ed. Hunter Miller (Washington, D.C.: Government Printing Office, 1931), 2:365.

27 The material on the development of Washington as a totem of
American civil religion is taken from Dixon Wector, *The Hero in America*
(New York: Scribners, 1941); Bernard Mayo, *Myths and Men: Patrick Henry,
George Washington, Thomas Jefferson* (Athens: University of Georgia Press,
1959); Boorstin, *The Americans*, 337–56; and Albanese, *Sons of the Fathers*,
143–81. Also important is the discussion in Edwin S. Gaustad, *Faith of Our
Fathers: Religion and the New Nation* (San Francisco: Harper & Row, 1987), 71–
84.

28 Marcus Cunliffe, *George Washington: Man and Monument* (Boston:
Little, Brown, 1958), 213.

29 Cited in ibid., 13.

30 William A. Bryan, *George Washington in American Literature, 1775-1865*
(New York: Columbia University Press, 1952), 118.

31 The development of the popular notion of Washington as Moses is
insightfully discussed in Robert P. Hay, "George Washington: American
Moses," *American Quarterly* 21 (Winter 1969): 780–91.

32 Thaddeus Fiske, *A Sermon, Delivered Dec. 29, 1799, At the Second Parish
in Cambridge, Being the Lord's Day Immediately Following the Melancholy
Intelligence of the Death of General George Washington, Late President of the United
States of America* (Boston: James Cutler, 1800), 10.

33 Francis D. Quash, *An Oration Delivered on the Fourth of July, 1820, Before
the Cincinnati and Revolution Societies* (Charleston, S.C.: W. P. Young, 1820),
8.

34 *Maryland Journal and Baltimore Advertiser*, July 8, 1777, p. 1; and
Pennsylvania Mercury and Universal Advertiser, July 8, 1785, p. 1.

35 Elias Boudinot, *An Oration, Delivered at Elizabeth-Town, New Jersey,
Agreeably to a Resolution of the State Society of Cincinnati, on the Fourth of July,
MDCCXCIII; Being the Seventeenth Anniversary of the Independence of America*
(Elizabethtown, N.J.: Shepard Kollock, 1793), 7; Samuel Miller, *A Sermon,
Delivered in the New Presbyterian Church, New York, July Fourth, 1795* (New
York: T. Greenleaf, 1795), 6; and Cyprian Strong, *A Discourse, Delivered at*

Hebron, at the Celebration of the Anniversary of American Independence, July 4th 1799 (Hartford: Hudson and Goodwin, 1799), 6.

[36] Fiske, *A Sermon*, 19.

[37] Margaret B. Stillwell cites 440 published eulogies of Washington immediately following his death, the overwhelming majority of which utilize the Moses analogy. "Checklist of Eulogies and Funeral Orations on the Death of George Washington, December, 1799–February, 1800," *Bulletin of the New York Public Library* 20 (May 1916): 403–441. See also Mark A. Noll, "The Image of the United States As a Biblical Nation,"in *The Bible in America: Essays in Cultural History*, ed. Nathan O. Hatch and Noll (New York: Oxford University Press, 1982), 41, 45, 53–54.

[38] Isaac Braman, *An Eulogy on the Late General George Washington, Who Died, Saturday, 14th December, 1799* (Haverhill, Mass.: Seth H. Moore, 1800), 5.

[39] This point was made among others by Jonathan Huse, a Congregationalist minister in Maine, but he was partially in error. Although George's father considered a naval career for him, the younger Washington never did become a midshipman in the British navy. *Discourse. . .Delivered in Warren* (Wiscasset, Me.: Henry Hoskins, 1800), 5–6. See Flexner, *George Washington*, 1:30–31.

[40] Peter Folsom, *An Eulogy on Geo. Washington, Late Commander in Chief of the Armies of the United States of America* (Gilmanton, N.H.: E. Russell, 1800), 6.

[41] John I. Carle, *A Funeral Sermon, Preached at Rockaway, December 29, 1799, on the Much Lamented Death of General George Washington, Who Departed This Life December 14, 1799, at Mount Vernon, in the Sixty-Eighth Year of His Age* (Morristown, N.J., Jacob Mann, 1800), 10.

[42] Braman, *An Eulogy*, 13.

[43] Huse, *Discourse*, 11. The entire Old Testament book of Deuteronomy was, of course, Moses' valedictory address. One Washington eulogist approvingly quoted the appraisal of the president's "Farewell Address" which appeared in the *British Analytical Review* for January 1797: "There is nothing in profane history to which this sublime address can be compared. In our Sacred Scriptures we find a parallel in that recapitulation of the divine instructions and commands, which the legislator of the Jews made in the hearing of Israel, when they were about to pass the Jordan." Thaddeus Mason Harris, *A Discourse, Delivered at Dorchester, Dec. 29, 1799* (Charlestown, Mass.: Samuel Etheridge, 1800), 13.

[44] Ebenezer Gay, *Oration* (Suffield, Conn.: Edward Gray, 1800), 14–15.

[45] Jedidiah Morse, sermon recorded in the *Proceedings of the Town of Charlestown, in the County of Middlesex and Commonwealth of Massachusetts; In Respectful Testimony of the Distinguished Talents and Pre-eminent Virtues of the Late George Washington* (Charlestown: Samuel Etheridge, 1800), 35. See also Huse, *Discouse*, 7–9.

[46] Carle, *A Funeral Sermon*, 8–12.

[47] Joseph Buckminster, *Religion and Righteousness the Basis of National Honor and Prosperity: A Sermon, Preached to the North and South Parishes in Portsmouth, Fraternally United in Observances of the 22d February, 1800* (Portsmouth, N.H.: Charles Pierce, 1800), 8–10; and Fiske, *A Sermon*, 10–11. It should be noted that after all the analogies had been drawn, patriotic orators admitted that there were at least two significant differences between the ancient and modern Moses. First, the original one was directly inspired

by God, while Washington was not. Second, the Hebrew leader beheld but
did not enter the Promised Land, while the American Moses both entered
and enjoyed the new land and saw his country's glory fulfilled.

⁴⁸Eli Forbes, *An Eulogy Moralized, on the Illustrious Character of the Late
General George Washington, Who Died on Saturday, the 14th Day of December,
1799* (Newburyport, Mass.: Edmund M. Blunt, 1800), 14.

⁴⁹Weems, *Life of Washington*, Cunliffe ed., 166. (The text is that of the
9th edition, published in 1809.) Boller points out that all of this occurred in
Weems' imagination and not in reality. In fact, Washington's secretary,
Tobias Lear, was present and left an account of the deathbed scene. The
former president neither called for an Episcopalian clergyman nor uttered
any words of a religious nature. He died simply and peacefully. Boller,
George Washington and Religion, 113; and Lear, *Letters and Recollections of
George Washington* (New York: Doubleday, Page, 1906), 133.

⁵⁰Weems, *Life of Washington*, Cunliffe ed., 167–68.

⁵¹Mary Antin, *The Promised Land* (Boston: Houghton Mifflin, 1912), 222–
23.

CHAPTER FOUR

¹William L. Gaylord, *The Soldier God's Minister, A Discourse Delivered in
the Congregational Church, Fitzwilliam, N.H., Sabbath Afternoon, October 5,
1862, on the Occasion of the Departure of a Company of Volunteers for the Seat of
War* (Fitchburg, Mass.: Rollston, 1862), 19–20.

²Robert Penn Warren, *The Legacy of the Civil War* (New York: Random
House, 1961), 3.

³William J. Wolf, *Lincoln's Religion* (Boston: Pilgrim Press, 1970), 24, 192;
and D. Elton Trueblood, *Abraham Lincoln: Theologian of American Anguish*
(New York: Harper & Row, 1973). Historians generally consider Wolf the
best study of Lincoln's religion. It was originally published in 1959 as *The
Almost Chosen People*, and then in slightly revised form in 1963 as *The Religion
of Abraham Lincoln*. The 1970 edition is yet another revision. Trueblood's
volume is more a study of Lincoln's religious thinking than his religion per
se. Also of merit is William E. Barton, *The Soul of Abraham Lincoln* (New York:
Doran, 1920).

⁴Richard Hofstadter, *The American Political Tradition* (New York: Knopf,
1948), 92.

⁵Ibid., 92–134; Lloyd Lewis, *Myths After Lincoln* (New York: Harcourt,
Brace, 1929); Stephen B. Oates, *Abraham Lincoln: The Man Behind the Myth*
(New York: Harper & Row, 1984); and *Inaugural Addresses*, 128. The best
discussion of the religious dimensions of the conflict is Ronald D. Rietveld,
"The American Civil War: Millennial Hope, Political Chaos," and a "Two-
Sided 'Just War,'" in *The Wars of America: Christian Views*, ed. Ronald A.
Wells (Grand Rapids: Eerdmans, 1981), 67–90.

⁶Walt Whitman, *The Best of Walt Whitman*, ed. Harold W. Bodgett (New
York: Ronald Press, 1953), 264–65; and *Life* 46 (Feb. 9, 1959): 60.

⁷John Hay, *Letters*, 5 vols. (New York: Gordian Press, 1969), 3:328.

⁸Albert J. Menendez, *Religion and the U.S. Presidency: A Bibliography*
(New York: Garland, 1986), 67; and Earl C. Kubicek, "Abraham Lincoln's
Faith," *Lincoln Herald* 85 (Fall 1983): 188.

⁹The biographical materials are taken from James G. Randall, *Lincoln,
the President*, 2 vols. (New York: Dodd, Mead, 1945–55); Benjamin P.

Thomas, *Abraham Lincoln* (New York: Knopf, 1952); and Stephen B. Oates, *With Malice Toward None: The Life of Abraham Lincoln* (New York: Harper & Row, 1977). Also worth reading is the beautifully-written work by Carl Sandburg, *Abraham Lincoln: The Prairie Years, The War Years*, 6 vols. (New York: Harcourt, Brace, 1929–36), but it must be used with care since the author did not document his sources.

[10] Allan Nevins, *The Emergence of Lincoln*, 2 vols. (New York: Scribners, 1950), 1:188.

[11] As Wolf points out, "The conflicting evidence on Lincoln's religion is incredibly complex. One could 'prove' almost anything by selecting what he wanted from the sources." *Lincoln's Religion*, 26. For a summary of the claims of the various denominations on Lincoln, see ibid., 201–3. His friends Simpson and Gurley were evangelicals, and there is some evidence that he embraced an evangelical faith in Christ at some point during his presidency, but this cannot be proven conclusively. Ibid., 193, 203, 213; Trueblood, *Lincoln*, 95–117; and David Hein, "The Calvinistic Tenor of Abraham Lincoln's Religious Thought," *Lincoln Herald* 85 (Winter 1983): 212–20.

[12] For an excellent summary of the historical background of Lincoln's faith, see Mark Noll, "The Perplexing Faith of Abraham Lincoln," *Christianity Today* 29 (Feb. 15, 1985): 12–14.

[13] Most students of Lincoln's faith hold this position, for example, Wolf, *Lincoln's Religion*, 9, 82–87. For a dissenting view, see David Hein, "Abraham Lincoln's Theological Outlook," in *Essays on Lincoln's Faith and Politics*, ed. Kenneth W. Thompson (Lanham, Md.: University Press of America, 1983), 105–79.

[14] One of the authors' great-grandfathers, Andrew Hynes Linder, who knew Lincoln personally during his young manhood, thought so, and in imitative admiration changed his own religion to Universalist. See Wolf, *Lincoln's Religion*, 7–9, 42–51, 69–79, 89–114, who rejects the charge that Lincoln was once an "infidel."

[15] Ibid., 51, 67–68. Also see Trueblood, *Lincoln*, 3–25; and Ronald D. Rietveld, "Lincoln and the Politics of Morality," *Journal of the Illinois State Historical Society* 68 (1975): 33–35.

[16] Sandburg, *The Prairie Years*, 1:336–37.

[17] *The Collected Works of Abraham Lincoln*, ed. Roy Basler, 9 vols. (New Brunswick, N.J.: Rutgers University Press, 1953), 1:382. As Wolf warns, it would be a mistake to conclude that Lincoln believed nothing beyond the points which he made in this statement. He was a politician refuting a local libel, not a theologian delivering a testament of faith to all the world. He provided just enough of his own religious orientation to make the required refutation, but the document is significant because it reveals a man who clearly felt that religion was important and should be respected. Wolf, *Lincoln's Religion*, 72–73. In the same handbill, Lincoln declared: "I do not think I could myself, be brought to support a man for office, whom I knew to be an open enemy of, and scoffer at, religion."

[18] Wolf, *Lincoln's Religion*, 113; and Lincoln, *Works* 4:190–91.

[19] On Lincoln and the Bible, see S. Trevena Jackson, *Lincoln's Use of the Bible* (New York: Eaton and Maine, 1909); and Clarence Macartney, *Lincoln and the Bible* (New York: Abingdon, 1949). Henderson told the anecdote to Vice President Adlai E. Stevenson who recounted it in his memoirs, *Something of Men I Have Known* (Chicago: A. C. McClurg, 1909), 352.

[20] Lincoln, *Works* 7:524; and Wolf, *Lincoln's Religion*, 39, 131.

[21] Noll, "Perplexing Faith of Abraham Lincoln," 14.

[22] Trueblood, *Lincoln*, 33.

[23] Ida Tarbell, *The Life of Abraham Lincoln*, 4 vols; (New York: Lincoln Historical Society, 1902), 2:92. Also see Charles L. Woodall, "Lincoln's Religion and the Denominations," *Lincoln Herald* 84 (Fall 1982): 171.

[24] Wolf, *Lincoln's Religion*, 126. Dr. Phineas Gurley, the president's pastor at the New York Avenue Presbyterian Church, claimed that the death of Willie Lincoln in 1862 and the visit to the Gettysburg battlefield in 1863 finally led Lincoln to personal faith in Christ. Gurley also indicated that Lincoln planned to make a public profession of his faith at some opportune time in the near future—a future which never came. Ibid., 213.

[25] Sidney E. Mead, *The Lively Experiment*, 73; idem., *The Nation with the Soul of a Church*, 68; Wolf, *Lincoln's Religion*, 24; Trueblood, *Lincoln*, 118–19; and Bellah, "Civil Religion in America," 9–10.

[26] Garry Wills, *Inventing America: Jefferson's Declaration of Independence* (New York: Vintage, 1979), xxi–xxii; and Anson Phelps Stokes, *Church and State in the United States*, 3 vols. (New York: Harper & Row, 1950), 3:113.

[27] Wolf, *Lincoln's Religion*, 58; Hofstadter, *American Political Tradition*, 101; and Robertson, *America's Dates With Destiny*, 147, 151–52.

[28] For example, Lincoln said at Trenton, New Jersey, on the way to his inauguration that this mission was "something that held out a great promise to all the people of the world to all time to come." Lincoln, *Works* 4:236.

[29] Ibid., 4:193–94. Chesterton's observation is cited in his essay, "What I Saw in America," in *The Man Who Was Chesterton*, ed. Raymond T. Bond (New York: Dodd, Mead, 1946), 192.

[30] Lincoln, *Works* 4:236; Wolf, *Lincoln's Religion*, 152; and Trueblood, *Lincoln*, 119–21.

[31] Lincoln, *Works* 5:532–37.

[32] Ibid., 4:426. Much of this analysis of the "Last, Best Hope Speech" is based on the treatment in Mead, *The Lively Experiment*, 72–89. Whereas Mead refers to "the democratic way," we prefer the term "the American Democratic Faith" because it more accurately describes the ideology which Lincoln developed.

[33] Ibid., 80–83.

[34] *Inaugural Addresses*, 123.

[35] Ibid., 125; and Lincoln, *Works* 4:426, 439.

[36] Edmund Wilson, *Eight Essays* (Garden City, N.Y.: Doubleday, 1954), 189.

[37] Lincoln, *Works* 7:23.

[38] Wolf, *Lincoln's Religion*, 169–70.

[39] "The old man of sin" is used in the generic sense here, as it is in the New Testament. However, the national dedication would be extended only later to "all people" — meaning women as well as men—without a civil war, but in much the same manner as it was extended to all black men in the later nineteenth century. Some would argue that, in a Lincolnian theological sense, the process is still going on in the late twentieth century.

[40] Roy P. Basler, *Abraham Lincoln, His Speeches and Writings* (Cleveland: World Publishing Co., 1946), 42.

[41] Wolf, *Lincoln's Religion*, 170–71.

[42] The extemporaneous nature of this phrase is discussed in Trueblood, *Lincoln*, 133–35. He calls it an "inspired interpolation." Interestingly, the motto "In God We Trust" was placed on the nation's coinage for the first

time in 1864. Richard V. Pierard, "One Nation Under God: Judgment or Jingoism?" in *Christian Social Ethics*, ed. Perry C. Cotham (Grand Rapids: Baker, 1979), 93–94.

43 Francis B. Carpenter, *Six Months at the White House* (New York: Hurd and Houghton, 1866), 282.

44 Lincoln, *Works* 6:155–56; and Reinhold Niebuhr, "The Religion of Abraham Lincoln," in *Lincoln and the Gettysburg Address*, ed. Allan Nevins (Urbana: University of Illinois Press, 1964), 75.

45 *Inaugural Addresses*, 127–28.

46 The address contains fourteen references to God, several scriptural allusions, and four direct quotations from the Bible: Gen. 3:19, Matt. 7:1, Matt. 18:7, and Ps. 19:9. As Trueblood observes: "It is difficult to think of another state paper so steeped in Scripture and so devoted to theological reflection." *Lincoln*, 136. The debate over Lincoln's use of political religion, especially in the second inaugural address, is detailed in Glen E. Thurow, *Abraham Lincoln and American Political Religion* (Albany: State University of New York Press, 1976); and William S. Corlett, Jr., "The Availability of Lincoln's Political Religion," *Political Theory* 10 (November 1982): 520–40.

47 We reject the notion that Lincoln was a civil religion priest, as claimed by Melvin B. Endy, Jr. in "Abraham Lincoln and American Civil Religion: A Reinterpretation," *Church History* 44 (June 1975): 229–41. Although there is some indication of a priestly role on Lincoln's part, it seems to us that the evidence of the preponderance of his prophetic office is overwhelming. He functioned as a civil religion "clergyman," facing his people with a word *from* God rather than with his back to them speaking a word *to* God on their behalf.

48 Woodall, "Lincoln's Religion and the Denominations," 171.

49 Donald Capps, "The Death of Father Abraham: The Assassination of Lincoln and Its Effect on Frontier Mythology," in *Religious Encounters with Death*, ed. Frank E. Reynolds and Earle H. Waugh (University Park: Pennsylvania State University Press, 1977), 233.

50 David Donald, *Lincoln Reconsidered: Essays on the Civil War Era*, 2d ed. (New York: Vintage, 1961), 145–46, 154.

51 Roy P. Basler, *The Lincoln Legend: A Study in Changing Conceptions* (New York: Octagon Books, 1969), 125–26; and Capps, "The Death of Father Abraham," 241–44.

52 Ralph Woods, "A Candid View of Honest Abe," *This Week*, Feb. 11, 1968, p. 18; W. Lloyd Warner, *American Life: Dream and Reality*, rev. ed. (Chicago: University of Chicago Press, 1962), 20–23; and John G. Nicolay and John Hay, *Abraham Lincoln: A History*, 10 vols. (New York: Century, 1914), 10:347.

53 Gilbert Haven, *National Sermons* (Boston: Lee and Shepherd, 1869), 552–80. Other parallels mentioned were their humble births, the fact that their fathers had been carpenters by trade, and their practice of speaking in parables and homey sayings.

54 Joel Bingham, *National Disappointment, A Discourse Occasioned by the Assassination of President Lincoln* (Buffalo, N.Y.: Breed, Butler, and Co., 1865), 35–36.

55 Edmund Wilson, *Patriotic Gore* (New York: Oxford University Press, 1962), 130.

56 Wolf, *Lincoln's Religion*, 180; Hofstadter, *American Political Tradition*, 92; Vachel Lindsay, "Abraham Lincoln Walks at Midnight," in *The Congo and*

Other Poems (New York: Macmillan, 1914), 146; and Mike Fargo, "Lincoln's Legacy: A Nation Under God," in *A Nation Under God?* ed. C. E. Gallivan (Waco: Word Books, 1976), 13.

[57] Warner, *American Life*, 23.

[58] Wilson, "The State of Civil Religion," 4.

[59] Warner, *American Life*, 14.

[60] An interesting variant of public religiosity developed in the territories of the old Confederacy after the Northern victory which sustained the regional identity for at least two generations. See Charles Reagan Wilson, *Baptized in Blood: The Religion of the Lost Cause, 1865-1920* (Athens: University of Georgia Press, 1980); and idem, "The Religion of the Lost Cause: Ritual and Organization of the Southern Civil Religion, 1865-1920," *Journal of Southern History* 46 (May 1980): 219-38.

CHAPTER FIVE

[1] James F. Rusling, "Interview with President McKinley," *Christian Advocate* 78 (Jan. 22, 1903): 137.

[2] The best biographical treatment is H. Wayne Morgan, *William McKinley and His America* (Syracuse: Syracuse University Press, 1963). The first substantial biography, Charles S. Olcott, *The Life of William McKinley*, 2 vols. (Boston: Houghton Mifflin, 1916), is quite dated. Margaret Leech, *In the Days of McKinley* (New York: Harper, 1959), is a respected popular treatment. Lewis L. Gould, *The Presidency of William McKinley* (Lawrence: University Press of Kansas, 1980), is a careful study of his administration and the best introduction to the bibliography on him. Of the many scholarly articles, John S. Latcham, "President McKinley's Active-Positive Character: A Comparative Revision with Barber's Typology," *Presidential Studies Quarterly* 12 (Fall 1982): 491–521, is especially noteworthy.

For impressionistic discussions of McKinley's religious faith see William Judson Hampton, *The Religion of the Presidents* (Somerville, N.J.: Unionist-Gazette Press, 1925), 76–79; Vernon Hampton, *Religious Background of the White House*, 311–12, 356–59; Bliss Isely, *The Presidents: Men of Faith* (Boston: W. A. Wilder, 1953), 186–93; Fuller and Green, *God in the White House*, 157–61; and John Sutherland Bonnell, *Presidential Profiles: Religion in the Life of American Presidents* (Philadelphia: Westminster, 1971), 158–63.

[3] H. Wayne Morgan, ed., "A Civil War Diary of William McKinley," *Ohio History* 69 (July 1960): 283.

[4] Morgan, *William McKinley*, 34–36.

[5] Ibid., 188–89.

[6] W. J. Hampton, *Religion of the Presidents*, 77–78.

[7] "Address at the Dedication of the Y.M.C.A. Building in Youngstown, Ohio, 6 September 1892," in *Speeches and Addresses of William McKinley* (New York: D. Appleton, 1894), 607.

[8] *Inaugural Addresses*, 169–77, 179–80.

[9] James D. Richardson, ed., *A Compilation of the Messages and Papers of the Presidents* (New York: Bureau of National Literature, 1925), 13:6251 (hereafter cited as *Messages and Papers*).

[10] Ibid., 6470–71.

[11] A concise, informative account of the Cuban problems and the road to war that incorporates the most recent scholarly interpretations and insights

is Gould, *Presidency of McKinley*, 59–90. See also Lester D. Langley, *The Cuban Policy of the United States: A Brief History* (New York: Wiley, 1968).

¹²*Messages and Papers* 13:6292.

¹³The support of clerics and the religious press for the Spanish-American War and expansionism is detailed in Julius W. Pratt, *Expansionists of 1898: The Acquisition of Hawaii and the Spanish Islands* (Baltimore: Johns Hopkins Press), 279–313; and John E. Smylie, "Protestant Clergymen and America's World Role 1865–1900: A Study of Christianity, Nationality, and International Relations" (Th.D. diss., Princeton Theological Seminary, 1959), 389–556.

¹⁴Quoted in Pratt, *Expansionists*, 280.

¹⁵*New York Times*, March 14, 1898, p. 2.

¹⁶Ibid., April 18, 1898, p. 10.

¹⁷Joseph B. Bishop, *Theodore Roosevelt and His Time Shown in His Own Letters* (New York: Scribners, 1920), 1:106.

¹⁸Quoted in Lewis L. Gould, *The Spanish-American War and President McKinley* (Lawrence: University Press of Kansas, 1982), 55.

¹⁹Among the most recent accounts of the conflict are Gould, *Spanish-American War* (1982); George O'Toole, *The Spanish War: An American Epic* (New York: Norton, 1984); David F. Trask, *The War with Spain in 1898* (New York: Macmillan, 1981); and Gerald F. Linderman, *The Mirror of War: American Society and the Spanish-American War* (Ann Arbor: University of Michigan Press, 1974). The widely varying treatment of the war and its origins by historians is ably examined in Joseph A. Fry, "William McKinley and the Coming of the Spanish-American War: A Study of the Besmirching and Redemption of an Historical Image," *Diplomatic History* 3 (1979): 77–97. By far the best treatment of the moral issues surrounding the conflict and U. S. foreign policy in the 1890s is Augustus Cerillo, Jr., "The Spanish-American War," in *The Wars of America*, ed. Wells, 91–125.

²⁰The information on troop strength and casualties is taken from O'Toole, *Spanish War*, 375.

²¹The three clerics are quoted in Smylie, "Clergymen," 431–32.

²²*New York Times*, May 2, 1898, p. 12.

²³*Messages and Papers* 13:6470–71, 6491–92, 6518–19, 6544.

²⁴*New York Times*, July 7, 1898, p. 1.

²⁵Ibid., July 11, 1898, p. 10.

²⁶Ibid.

²⁷*Messages and Papers* 13:6320.

²⁸Ibid., 6581–82.

²⁹There is considerable literature on the Philippine insurrection and its impact on American politics and life. A good introduction to the question is Richard E. Welch, Jr., *Response to Imperialism: The United States and the Philippine War, 1899-1902* (Chapel Hill: University of North Carolina Press, 1979).

³⁰The alternatives facing McKinley are excellently presented in ibid., 6–10.

³¹Rusling, "Interview with President McKinley," 137. The interview is also reprinted in Olcott, *William McKinley*, 2:109–11. An insightful commentary on this is contained in Morgan, *William McKinley*, 411–13.

³²The citations are in Smylie, "Clergymen," 489–90, 493, 505–6.

³³*New York Times*, Oct. 16, 1898, p. 3; Oct. 19, 1898, p. 3; Oct. 20, 1898, p. 3; Oct. 22, 1898, p. 1. These and the following speeches were also

published in the *Speeches and Addresses of William McKinley from March 1, 1897 to May 30, 1900* (New York: Doubleday & McClure, 1900).

[34] *New York Times*, Dec. 16, 1898, p. 1.

[35] Ibid., Feb. 17, 1899, p. 1.

[36] Important works dealing with this complex problem include Albert K. Weinberg, *Manifest Destiny: A Study of Nationalist Expansion in American History* (Baltimore: Johns Hopkins Press, 1935); Frederick Merk, *Manifest Destiny and Mission in American History: A Reinterpretation* (New York: Vintage, 1973); Russel B. Nye, *The Almost Chosen People* (East Lansing: Michigan State University Press, 1966); and David Healy, *U. S. Expansionism: The Imperialist Urge in the 1890s* (Madison: University of Wisconsin Press, 1970).

[37] William H. Davis, quoted in Weinberg, *Manifest Destiny*, 290.

[38] Robert Ellis Thompson, *The Hand of God in American History: A Study of National Politics* (New York: Thomas Y. Crowell, 1902).

[39] Reinhold Niebuhr, *Moral Man and Immoral Society* (New York: Scribners, 1932), 99–103.

[40] Olcott, *William McKinley*, 2:324–25.

CHAPTER SIX

[1] *New York Times*, July 11, 1919, pp. 1–2; *The Public Papers of Woodrow Wilson*, ed. Ray Stannard Baker and William E. Dodd, 6 vols. (New York: Harper, 1925–27), 5:538, 550–51; and Thomas A. Bailey, *Woodrow Wilson and the Great Betrayal* (New York: Macmillan, 1945), 4–6.

[2] The biographical literature on Wilson is overwhelming. The classic works are Ray Stannard Baker, *Woodrow Wilson: Life and Letters*, 8 vols. (Garden City, N.Y.: Doubleday, Page, 1927–39); and William Allen White, *Woodrow Wilson: The Man, His Times, and His Task* (Boston: Houghton Mifflin, 1924). Among the important modern treatments are Arthur Walworth, *Woodrow Wilson* (1st ed., New York: Longmans Green, 1958; 2d ed., Boston: Houghton Mifflin, 1965; 3d ed., New York: Norton, 1978); the double biography by John Milton Cooper, Jr., *The Warrior and the Priest: Woodrow Wilson and Theodore Roosevelt* (Cambridge: Harvard University Press, 1983); the magisterial but unfinished work by Arthur S. Link, *Wilson*, 5 vols. (Princeton: Princeton University Press, 1947–65); and Kendrick A. Clements, *Woodrow Wilson: World Statesman* (Boston: Twayne, 1988). Link's scattered writings on Wilson have been collected in *The Higher Realism of Woodrow Wilson and Other Essays* (Nashville: Vanderbilt University Press, 1971). He is also the general editor of *The Papers of Woodrow Wilson* (Princeton: Princeton University Press, 1966). By 1988 this massive series had reached 57 volumes and covered his life to April 1919 (hereafter cited as *Papers WW*).

Studies which focus on more limited aspects of his career include John M. Mulder, *Woodrow Wilson: The Years of Preparation* (Princeton: Princeton University Press, 1978), a book which excellently analyzes the future president's religious background; Henry W. Bragdon, *Woodrow Wilson: The Academic Years* (Cambridge: Harvard University Press, 1967); Arthur S. Link, *Woodrow Wilson and the Progressive Era, 1910–1917* (New York: Harper & Row, 1954); Patrick Devlin, *Too Proud to Fight: Woodrow Wilson's Neutrality* (New York: Oxford University Press, 1975); Robert H. Ferrell, *Woodrow Wilson and World War I, 1917–1921* (New York: Harper & Row, 1985); and N.

Gordon Levin, Jr., *Woodrow Wilson and World Politics* (New York: Oxford University Press, 1968).

[3]The impact of his Presbyterian upbringing is spelled out in Link, "Woodrow Wilson and His Presbyterian Inheritance," *Higher Realism*, 3–20; and Mulder, *Wilson: Years of Preparation*, 33–38.

[4]Thomas Jefferson did not found the University of Virginia until after he left office. James A. Garfield, who was a teacher at and president of small Hiram College while he was only in his twenties, then became a lawyer, fought in the Civil War, and served in Congress for eighteen years before his elevation to the presidency.

[5]*Papers WW* 12:421.

[6]Link, *Higher Realism*, 131–32; Mulder, *Wilson: Years of Preparation*, 227; and *Papers WW* 20:159–61.

[7]Walworth, *Wilson*, 2d ed., 1:251.

[8]Louis B. Weeks III, "Racism, World War I, and the Christian Life: Francis J. Grimke in the Nation's Capital," *Journal of Presbyterian History* 51 (Winter 1973): 480–84. Mulder shows that he also manifested racist attitudes while serving as president of Princeton. *Wilson: Years of Preparation*, 174–75.

[9]Link, *Wilson and the Progressive Era*, 81–82. Arthur Link popularized the term "missionary diplomacy" in his many works on Wilson.

[10]For an insightful discussion of the influence Christian leaders and missionaries had on Wilson's China policy, see Eugene P. Trani, "Woodrow Wilson, China, and the Missionaries, 1913–1921," *Journal of Presbyterian History* 49 (Winter 1971): 328–51. He had recognized the new Chinese Republic and tried to persuade the ecumenical missionary leader, John R. Mott, to accept the appointment as the first United States minister to China. *Addresses and Papers of John R. Mott*, 6 vols. (New York: Association Press, 1946–47), 6:534–35.

[11]*Papers WW* 30:394.

[12]Cooper, *Warrior and Priest*, 274–75.

[13]*Papers WW* 40:534–39.

[14]Cooper, *Warrior and Priest*, 295–96, 410.

[15]Link refers to this period in March 1917 as "the time of Wilson's Gethsemane." *Wilson and the Progressive Era*, 275.

[16]Cooper, *Warrior and Priest*, 318.

[17]Baker and Dodd, *Public Papers of Wilson*, 5:286–88. It asked voters to express their approval of him by returning Democratic majorities to both houses of Congress. If they did not, the country's leadership would be divided and people in Europe would interpret the action "as a repudiation of my leadership."

[18]Almost every writer on Wilson calls attention to his religious dimension. Besides the works mentioned in note 3, see Arthur S. Link, "Woodrow Wilson: Presbyterian in Government," in *Calvinism and the Political Order*, ed. George L. Hunt (Philadelphia: Westminster, 1965), 157–74; Hampton, *Religious Background of the White House*, 90–101; and Fuller and Green, *God in the White House*, 174–83.

[19]*Papers WW* 31:222.

[20]Ibid., 53:534.

[21]Link, *Wilson*, 1:94.

[22]Baker, *Wilson: Life and Letters*, 1:66–67. When Wilson visited Columbia in 1916, he paused in the chapel doorway and said: "I feel as though I ought to take off my shoes. This is holy ground," ibid., 67.

[23] Journal entry, May 3, 1874. *Papers WW* 6:693.

[24] Baker, *Wilson: Life and Letters*, 1:68.

[25] Letter to Ellen Wilson, Aug. 10, 1913, *Papers WW* 28:132; letter to Mary Allen Hulbert, Aug. 10, 1913, ibid., 28:135; remarks at cornerstone laying, Dec. 19, 1913, ibid., 29:44–45. Cary T. Grayson, pointed out that the president not only regularly worshiped at Central Presbyterian, but also usually attended church services while traveling on vacation. *Woodrow Wilson: An Intimate Memoir* (New York: Holt, Rinehart and Winston, 1960), 14–15. His pastor, James H. Taylor, privately published an anecdotal account, *Woodrow Wilson in Church* (Charleston, S.C., 1952).

[26] Baker, *Wilson: Life and Letters*, 1:68; and Diary of Nancy Saunders Toy, entry on Jan. 3, 1915, *Papers WW* 32:8–9.

[27] Letter to M. A. Hulbert, Sep. 6, 1914, ibid., 31:3; and Grayson, *Woodrow Wilson*, 106.

[28] *Papers WW* 10:20; 14:184; 15:111. Walworth entitled chapter six of his Wilson biography, "University Pastor."

[29] For a perceptive content analysis of these sermons, see John M. Mulder, "Wilson the Preacher: The 1905 Baccalaureate Sermon," *Journal of Presbyterian History* 51 (Fall 1973): 267–84.

[30] *Papers WW* 1:188; Mulder, *Wilson: Years of Preparation*, 50–51.

[31] Ibid., 128–29, 145, 148–50; Address, "Religion and Patriotism," *Papers WW* 12:474–78.

[32] Ibid., 15:518; 16:349; 19:472; 20:333.

[33] Ibid., 19:218, 221.

[34] Ibid., 20:330–31.

[35] Ibid., 31:221, 227.

[36] White, *Woodrow Wilson*, 463; Mulder, *Wilson: Years of Preparation*, 177; Dragan R. Zivojinovic, *The United States and the Vatican Policies 1914-1918* (Boulder: Colorado Associated University Press, 1978); and Joseph P. Tumulty, *Woodrow Wilson As I Know Him* (Garden City, N.Y.: Doubleday, 1921), 64. Tumulty said Wilson interceded on behalf of the German Catholic missions at the peace conference. Ibid., 482–84.

[37] Mulder, *Wilson: Years of Preparation*, 180; *Papers WW* 20:523.

[38] Ibid., 19:107.

[39] *Inaugural Addresses*, 200.

[40] Address to the Federal Council of Churches, Columbus, Dec. 10, 1915, *Papers WW* 35:334; Fourth of July Address, Philadelphia, 1914, ibid., 30:254.

[41] Ibid., 12:475–76; 20:333 28:352; 31:221; 35:333.

[42] He said this in the Federal Council speech in 1915, ibid., 35:335. He expressed similar ideas in a talk, "Religion and Patriotism," at the Northfield (Mass.) Student Conference in 1902, ibid., 12:474–78.

[43] Speech in Indianapolis, Jan. 8, 1915, ibid., 32:41.

[44] Ibid., 20:332; 35:333.

[45] Ibid., 23:12–20. Link describes the curious situation where Wilson spent only one hour preparing what was to be "the ultimate in political addresses," one in which he identified Christianity with progressive democracy and found the moral authority for the progressive movement in orthodox Protestantism. *Wilson*, 1:320–22.

[46] *Papers WW* 23:378.

[47] William F. McCombs, *Making Woodrow Wilson President* (New York: Fairview, 1921), 208. He was the Democratic National Chairman.

[48] *Inaugural Addresses*, 202.

[49] Samuel F. Wells, Jr., "New Perspectives on Wilsonian Diplomacy: The Secular Evangelism of American Political Economy," *Perspectives in American History* 6 (1972): 419; Ross Gregory, "To Do Good in the World: Woodrow Wilson and America's Mission," in *Makers of American Diplomacy: From Benjamin Franklin to Henry Kissinger*, ed. Frank J. Merli and Theodore A. Wilson (New York: Scribners, 1974), 364–67; John Morton Blum, *Woodrow Wilson and the Politics of Morality* (Boston: Little, Brown, 1956), 84–85; and Arthur S. Link, *Wilson the Diplomatist* (Baltimore: Johns Hopkins University Press, 1957), 14–16.

[50] Samuel C. Blythe, "Mexico: The Record of a Conversation with President Wilson," *Saturday Evening Post* 186 (May 23, 1914): 4; and *Papers WW* 32:39.

[51] Wilson advanced the idea of a "universal association of nations" in an address on May 27, 1916, ibid., 37:114–16. He tried to pave the way for mediating a settlement in a note to the belligerents on Dec. 18,1916, ibid., 40:273–76.

[52] Ibid., 40:533–39.

[53] Ibid., 41:519–27.

[54] Wilson's reluctant decision to take the United States into the conflict reflected misgivings about the direction it might take. The often-cited conversation with Frank Cobb of the New York *World* on the night before the speech, in which the president lamented that war would "overturn the world we had known," require "illiberalism at home to reinforce the man at the front," and destroy tolerance and constitutional liberties, is as apocryphal as Washington's Valley Forge prayer. Baker, however, insists Wilson did tell Navy Secretary Daniels that "every reform we have won will be lost if we go into this war" and Democratic congressional leader William C. Adamson that war would cause a "general disorganization" and "legal and moral restraints" would be so relaxed that "it would require a generation to restore normal conditions." Baker, *Wilson: Life and Letters*, 6:506; and Jerold S. Auerbach, "Woodrow Wilson's 'Prediction' to Frank Cobb: Words Historians Should Doubt Ever Got Spoken," *Journal of American History* 54 (December 1967): 608–17.

[55] Ray S. Abrams, *Preachers Present Arms* (New York: Round Table Press, 1933); Michael Williams, *American Catholics and the War* (New York: Macmillan, 1921); John F. Piper, Jr., *The American Churches in World War I* (Athens: Ohio University Press, 1985); and Robert Bolt, "American Involvement in World War I," in *The Wars of America*, ed. Wells, 127–46.

[56] *Inaugural Addresses*, 204–5; *Papers WW* 45:536–38; 46:322–23; 51:131.

[57] Ibid., 48:517.

[58] Link, *Wilson the Diplomatist*, 104.

[59] *Papers WW* 53:541, 303.

[60] Ibid., 55:117; and White, *Woodrow Wilson*, 384.

[61] Baker and Dodd, *Public Papers of Wilson*, 6:262, 276–77, 292, 324–25, 415–16.

[62] Psychological insights are utilized in Sigmund Freud and William C. Bullitt, *Thomas Woodrow Wilson: A Psychological Study* (Boston: Houghton Mifflin, 1967); Alexander L. and Juliette L. George, *Woodrow Wilson and Colonel House: A Personality Study* (New York: John Day, 1956); and Edwin A. Weinstein, *Woodrow Wilson: A Medical and Psychological Biography* (Princeton: Princeton University Press, 1981).

⁶³Bert Edward Park, *The Impact of Illness on World Leaders* (Philadelphia: University of Pennsylvania Press, 1986), 4–5. He stresses that physicians no longer use dementia as a term for insanity, but rather to denote "an organic loss of intellectual functions." The argument for this thesis about Wilson's physiologically induced mental problems is defended in chapter 1 and appendix 1. See the debate over it in Juliette L. George, Michael F. Marmor, and Alexander L. George, "Issues in Wilson Scholarship: References to Early 'Strokes' in *The Papers of Woodrow Wilson*," *Journal of American History* 70 (March 1984): 845–53; and Arthur Link, Edwin A. Weinstein, et. al., "Communications to the Editor," ibid., 945–55.

⁶⁴On this see Lawrence E. Gelfand, *The Inquiry: America's Preparation for Peace, 1917-1919* (New Haven: Yale University Press, 1963).

⁶⁵Park, *Impact of Illness*, 32–33. He adds: "From the medical perspective," the factors of obstinacy, intransigence, increasing isolation, and a predisposition to secrecy, "frequently characterize patients suffering from an evolving dementia or organic brain syndrome."

CHAPTER SEVEN

¹*The Public Papers and Addresses of Franklin D. Roosevelt*, ed. Samuel I. Rosenman, 13 vols. (New York: Random House, Harper, 1938–50), 13:152–53 (hereafter cited as *PPAFDR*). One of the authors remembers his mother calling her two young boys to her side that day and praying for the soldiers in Normandy.

²There are several substantial biographies of Roosevelt. The most noteworthy are Frank B. Freidel, *Franklin D. Roosevelt*, 4 vols. (Boston: Little Brown, 1952–73), which carries the story to mid-1933; Geoffrey C. Ward, *Before the Trumpet: Young Franklin Roosevelt 1882-1905* (New York: Harper & Row, 1985), which deals with his youth; Arthur M. Schlesinger, Jr., *The Age of Roosevelt*, 3 vols. (Boston: Houghton Mifflin, 1957–60), which covers the period 1919 to 1936; Kenneth S. Davis, *FDR: The Beckoning of Destiny 1882-1928* (New York: Putnam, 1971), *The New York Years 1928-33*, and *The New Deal Years 1933-37* (New York: Random House, 1985, 1986); James MacGregor Burns, *Roosevelt*, vol. 1, *The Lion and the Fox*; vol. 2, *The Soldier of Freedom* (New York: Harcourt Brace Jovanovich, 1956, 1970); Rexford G. Tugwell, *The Democratic Roosevelt* (Garden City, N.Y.: Doubleday, 1957); Nathan Miller, *F.D.R.: An Intimate History* (Garden City, N.Y.: Doubleday, 1983); and Ted Morgan, *FDR: A Biography* (New York: Simon and Schuster, 1985). A major scholarly symposium is Herbert D. Rosenbaum and Elizabeth Bartelme, *Franklin D. Roosevelt: The Man, the Myth, the Era, 1882-1945* (Westport, Conn.: Greenwood Press, 1987).

³Burns, *The Lion and the Fox*, 12, 26. Peabody's impact on his religious development is detailed in Richard Thayer Goldberg, *The Making of Franklin D. Roosevelt: Triumph over Disability* (Cambridge, Mass.: Abt Books, 1981), 9–10. Goldberg suggests that Peabody may have influenced Roosevelt's decision to use a prayer on D-Day.

⁴Ibid, 12.

⁵FDR to Peabody, Jan. 11, 1941, in Frank D. Ashburn, *Peabody of Groton* (New York: Coward McCann, 1944), 349.

⁶Miller, *F.D.R.*, 141; James David Barber, *The Presidential Character: Predicting Performance in the White House*, 3d ed. (Englewood Cliffs, N.J.: Prentice-Hall, 1985), 193–99. (All references will be to this edition.)

⁷Burns, *The Lion and the Fox*, 117.

⁸Impressionistic treatments of Roosevelt's religion are Isely, *Presidents: Men of Faith*, 242–49; Fuller and Green, *God in the White House*, 201–6; Alley, *So Help Me God*, 58–69; and Bonnell, *Presidential Profiles*, 205–9. The most detailed study is by Merlin Gustafson in the Winter 1988 issue of the *Presidential Studies Quarterly*.

⁹*Inaugural Addresses*, 236, 239, 243, 247. The religious content of Roosevelt's inaugurals is examined in Charles V. La Fontaine, "God and Nation in Selected U.S. Presidential Inaugural Addresses, 1789–1945," *Journal of Church and State* 18 (Autumn 1976): 515–18.

¹⁰*Inaugural Addresses*, 248–49.

¹¹James Roosevelt, *My Parents: A Differing View* (Chicago: Playboy Press, 1976), 48–49; Burns, *The Lion and the Fox*, 237; Isely, *Presidents: Men of Faith*, 243–45; and *New York Times*, Sept. 16, 1936, p. 1; Jan. 21, 1937, p. 16.

¹²Ibid., March 5, 1933, p. 3; Jan. 21, 1937, p. 15; Jan. 21, 1941, p. 1; Jan. 21, 1945, p. 26.

¹³Burns, *Soldier of Fortune*, 447–48.

¹⁴Ashburn, *Peabody of Groton*, 295, 343–44.

¹⁵Now and then, critics referred to his infrequent attendance at a house of worship, as two examples from the year 1936 indicate. A noted Methodist, Dr. I. M. Hargett of Kansas City, claimed he went to services less than any other recent president and expressed the wish that he "instead of political powwows, fishing trips, and sailboat rides, would attend church every Sunday and set a good example for the nation's youth."Norman Vincent Peale of New York condemned his "indifferent attitude toward the church" and accused him of being "flippant toward religion." His many Sunday outings and faith in human intelligence acting without communion with God were the cause of "so many vital mistakes in the New Deal." *New York Times*, July 15, 1936, p. 2; Aug. 19, 1936, p. 2.

¹⁶Eleanor Roosevelt, *This I Remember* (New York: Harper, 1949), 67–69, 346; Davis, *FDR: Beckoning of Destiny*, 83; and Frances Perkins, *The Roosevelt I Knew* (New York: Viking, 1946), 141. The latter work by his Secretary of Labor contains a poignant account of his faith.

¹⁷Tugwell, *Democratic Roosevelt*, 32.

¹⁸Grace Tully, *F.D.R. My Boss* (New York: Scribners, 1949), 295–96; and Samuel I. Rosenman, *Working with Roosevelt* (New York: Harper, 1952), 433.

¹⁹Eleanor Roosevelt, *This Is My Story* (New York: Harper, 1937), 149–50.

²⁰Idem, *This I Remember*, 346–47. According to Perkins, in his last years Roosevelt became quite interested in Kierkegaard. *The Roosevelt I Knew*, 147–48.

²¹*The Secret Diary of Harold L. Ickes* (New York: Simon and Schuster, 1954), 2:290–91.

²²Rosenman, *Working with Roosevelt*, 20. The extent to which religious bigotry was a factor in the campaign is detailed in Edmund A. Moore, *A Catholic Runs for President: The Campaign of 1928* (New York: Ronald Press, 1928); and Allan J. Lichtman, *Prejudice and the Old Politics: The Presidential Election of 1928* (Chapel Hill: University of North Carolina Press, 1979).

²³Rosenman, *Working with Roosevelt*, 24.

²⁴"Religion and Liberty," *Commonweal* 25 (April 16, 1937): 680; also in *PPAFDR* 4:96.

²⁵*New York Times*, Jan. 21, 1937, p. 15. Before this time, the practice had been that the oath of office was administered to the new vice president by

the outgoing one in the Senate chamber and the Senate chaplain (always a Protestant clergyman) would offer a prayer. Then the president went to a temporary platform on the east side of the Capitol where, surrounded by friends, legislators, and government officials and before an audience of thousands, he took his oath from the chief justice of the Supreme Court. His hand rested upon an open Bible which he might kiss at the conclusion (Roosevelt chose not to do so), and then he delivered the inaugural address. No inaugural prayer had been given since the first inauguration in 1789. However, Washington had initiated the custom of adding "so help me God" to the oath and kissing the Bible, two things which were part of the English coronation ritual. Milton J. Medhurst, "From Duche to Provoost: The Birth of Inaugural Prayer," *Journal of Church and State* 24 (Autumn 1982): 582–86. Another innovation in 1937 was that the vice president took his oath in public on the inaugural platform immediately preceding that of the president.

[26] The priest's relations with Roosevelt are detailed in Charles J. Tull, *Father Coughlin and the New Deal* (Syracuse: Syracuse University Press, 1965). See also James Roosevelt, *My Parents*, 241. Father Ryan's ties with the Roosevelt administration are detailed in Francis L. Broderick, *Right Reverend New Dealer, John A. Ryan* (New York: Macmillan, 1963).

[27] This matter is examined in Henry L. Feingold, *The Politics of Rescue: The Roosevelt Administration and the Holocaust, 1938-1945* (New Brunswick, N.J.: Rutgers University Press, 1970); and Saul S. Friedman, *No Haven for the Oppressed* (Detroit: Wayne State University Press, 1973).

[28] *New York Times*, July 1, 1937, p. 13.

[29] Ibid., Nov. 5, 1944, p. 38; Rosenman, *Working with Roosevelt*, 502–3.

[30] James Roosevelt, *My Parents*, 241–42; *PPAFDR* 4:96.

[31] *PPAFDR* 3:97; 5:18; *New York Times*, Feb. 26, 1935, p. 9.

[32] *PPAFDR* 2:517–20.

[33] Ibid., 2:379–82.

[34] Ibid., 5:85–87. Two years later he said the same thing in a letter to the United Methodist Council. He also called for a "return to religion as exemplified in the Sermon on the Mount." *New York Times*, Feb. 4, 1938, p. 18.

[35] *PPAFDR* 5:85.

[36] Ibid., 5:609–10.

[37] A introduction to the moral and religious aspects of U.S. actions prior to and during the Second World War is provided in Richard V. Pierard, "World War II," in *The Wars of America*, ed., Wells, 147–74.

[38] *PPAFDR* 8:1–3; and Rosenman, *Working with Roosevelt*, 182.

[39] *PPAFDR* 9:550–53. In a speech in Brooklyn the day before, he said that the dictators and their supporters "hate democracy and Christianity as two phases of the same civilization." They oppose democracy because it is Christian and Christianity because it preaches democracy. Ibid., 532.

[40] Ibid., 10:672. His close adviser Harry Hopkins declared: "You can see the real Roosevelt when he comes out with something like the Four Freedoms." These are not catch phrases. *"He believes them!* He believes they can be practically attained." Robert E. Sherwood, *Roosevelt and Hopkins: An Intimate History* (New York: Harper, 1948), 266.

[41] *PPAFDR* 10:439–41; and Rosenman, *Working with Roosevelt*, 296–97.

[42] FDR to Pius XII, Dec. 23, 1939, in *PPAFDR* 8:606–8; FDR to Pius XII, Feb. 14, 1940, in Elliott Roosevelt, ed., *F.D.R.: His Personal Letters, 1928-1945*

(New York: Duell, Sloan, and Pearce, 1950), 4:1000–1. See also Myron Taylor, ed., *Wartime Correspondence Between President Roosevelt and Pope Pius XII* (New York: Macmillan, 1947). On the same date in 1939, Roosevelt sent substantially identical letters to the presidents of the Federal Council of Churches and the Jewish Theological Seminary of America asking them to come to Washington from time to time to discuss with him how peace and alleviation of suffering might be furthered. *PPAFDR* 8:608–9.

[43]FDR to Pius XII, Sep. 3, 1943, in *FDR: Personal Letters* 4:1204–5; *PPAFDR* 9:101–2.

[44]*PPAFDR* 0:514–15; 11:35, 41–42.

[45]*PPAFDR* 11:288–89; *New York Times*, Nov. 13, 1942, p. 25.

[46]*PPAFDR* 13:152–53. Rosenman said Roosevelt composed the prayer the weekend before D-Day with the help of his daughter Anna and her husband. He watched the president read it over the air and noted that "deep religious faith was apparent in his voice and in his countenance." *Working with Roosevelt*, 433.

[47]*New York Times*, March 27, 1943, p. 7; *Time* 44 (Dec. 12, 1944): 73.

[48]Edward L. R. Elson, *America's Spiritual Recovery* (Westwood, N.J.: Revell, 1954), 44. The work of the chaplains and the simple faith of American servicemen and women are portrayed in a collection of essays and first person accounts intended for popular consumption, Ellwood C. Nance, ed., *Faith of Our Fighters* (St. Louis: Bethany Press, 1944).

[49]*New York Times*, May 22, 1944, p. 9; Frances Brentano, ed., *Nation under God* (Great Neck, N.Y.: Channel Press, 1957), 92.

CHAPTER EIGHT

[1]*New York Times*, Dec. 23, 1952, p. 16.

[2]Statement made in a press conference at Columbia University. Ibid., May 4, 1948, p. 43.

[3]The most useful biographical works on Eisenhower are Marquis Childs, *Eisenhower: Captive Hero* (New York: Harcourt, Brace, 1958); Herbert S. Parmet, *Eisenhower and the American Crusades* (New York: Macmillan, 1972); Peter Lyon, *Eisenhower: A Portrait of the Hero* (Boston: Little, Brown, 1974; Elmo Richardson, *The Presidency of Dwight D. Eisenhower* (Lawrence: Regents Press of Kansas, 1979); R. Alton Lee, *Dwight D. Eisenhower: Soldier and Statesman* (Chicago: Nelson-Hall, 1981); Robert A. Divine, *Eisenhower and the Cold War* (New York: Oxford University Press, 1981); William B. Ewald, Jr., *Eisenhower the President: Crucial Days, 1951–60* (Englewood Cliffs, N.J.: Prentice-Hall, 1981); Fred I. Greenstein, *The Hidden-Hand Presidency: Eisenhower as Leader* (New York: Basic Books, 1982); Robert F. Burk, *Dwight D. Eisenhower: Hero and Politician* (Boston: Twayne, 1986); and above all, Stephen E. Ambrose, *Eisenhower: Soldier, General of the Army, President-Elect, 1890–1952*, and *The President* (New York: Simon and Schuster, 1983, 1984). The reevaluation of his presidency by historians in recent years is explored in Anthony James Joes, "Eisenhower Revisionism: The Tide Comes In," *Presidential Studies Quarterly* 15 (Summer 1985): 561–71. On the other hand, Piers Brendon, *Ike: His Life and Times* (New York: Harper & Row, 1986), sharply rejects the revisionist view and insists that he was a paradoxical person and a weak, negative, and unimaginative president. See also Joann P. Krieg, ed., *Dwight D. Eisenhower: Soldier, President, Statesman* (Westport, Conn.: Greenwood Press, 1987).

⁴The River Brethren was a Mennonite offshoot that originated shortly after 1775 along the Susquehanna River (hence the name). It incorporated the Anabaptist view of the church and discipleship, pietistic experiential religion, and Wesleyan perfectionism. Today the group is known as the Brethren in Christ. See Carlton O. Wittlinger, *Quest for Piety and Obedience: The Story of the Brethren in Christ* (Nappanee, Ind.: Evangel Press, 1978); and Martin H. Schrag, "The Impact of Pietism upon the Mennonites in Early American Christianity," in *Continental Pietism and Early American Christianity*, ed. F. Ernest Stoeffler (Grand Rapids: Eerdmans, 1976), 74–122.

⁵The most complete discussions of Eisenhower's religious background are Paul Hutchinson, "The President's Religious Faith," *Christian Century* 71 (March 24, 1954): 362–69, also in *Life* 36 (March 22, 1954): 150–70; Isely, *Presidents: Men of Faith*, 258–67; Fuller and Green, *God in the White House*, 212–18; Kenneth S. Davis, "The Abilene Factor in Eisenhower," *New York Times Magazine*, Dec. 9, 1951, pp. 12–13, 26; Bela Kornitzer, *The Great American Heritage: The Story of the Five Eisenhower Brothers* (New York: Farrar, Straus and Cudahy, 1955), 14–17, 133–44; Merlin Gustafson, "The Religion of a President," *Christian Century* 86 (April 30,1969): 610–13; and James C. Juhnke, "'One Nation under God': Religion and the American Dream," *Mennonite Life* 38 (December 1983): 23–26.

⁶Ambrose, *Eisenhower*, 1:24.

⁷Ibid., 1:36.

⁸On the campaign see John R. Greene, *The Crusade: The Presidential Election of 1952* (Lanham, Md.: University Press of America, 1985).

⁹See Merlin Gustafson, "Church, State, and the Cold War, 1945–1952," *Journal of Church and State* 8 (Winter 1966): 49–63.

¹⁰*Inaugural Addresses*, 252–56.

¹¹*Public Papers of the Presidents of the United States, Harry S. Truman* (Washington, D.C.: Government Printing Office, 1957–), 1950: 463; 1951: 212–13. This ongoing series produced by the National Archives contains in chronological order all the public addresses and statements of every chief executive from Hoover to the present, with the exception of Roosevelt who was covered by the privately published Rosenman compilation (hereafter cited as *Public Papers*, followed by the year of the particular president's administration and page number).

¹²Douglas A. MacArthur, *Revitalizing a Nation* (Chicago: The Heritage Foundation, 1952), 20–21.

¹³These and numerous other examples are quoted and documented in the articles by Richard V. Pierard: "Billy Graham and the U.S. Presidency," *Journal of Church and State* 22 (Winter 1980): 109–11; "Billy Graham and Vietnam: From Cold Warrior to Peacemaker," *Christian Scholar's Review* 10 (1980): 39–40; "From Evangelical Exclusivism to Ecumenical Openness: Billy Graham and Sociopolitical Issues," *Journal of Ecumenical Studies* 20 (Summer 1983): 433–34, 438–39; and "Billy Graham: Will He Stay the Course for Peace?" *Covenant Quarterly* 42 (Feb. 1984): 17–19.

¹⁴Frederic Fox, "The National Day of Prayer," *Theology Today* 30 (July 1973): 258–80.

¹⁵*New York Times*, Feb. 8, 1954, p. 11; "'Back to God' Movement," *America* 90 (Feb. 20, 1954): 526.

¹⁶Pierard, "One Nation Under God," in *Christian Social Ethics*, ed. Cotham, 85.

NOTES   **329**

17 *New York Times*, May 3, 1952, p. 16; and Pierard, "One Nation Under God," 85–86.

18 Eisenhower's friend William Clark related to Stewart Alsop on March 3, 1954 that General MacArthur had chided his staff officer for not attending a place of worship. Eisenhower replied that he had "gone to the West Point Chapel so g.d. often" that he was never going inside a church again. Quoted in Brendon, *Ike*, 9.

19 William L. Stidger, "General Eisenhower—His 'Little Service,' " in *Faith of Our Fighters*, ed. Nance, 198–200. See also Dwight D. Eisenhower, *Crusade in Europe* (Garden City, N.Y.: Doubleday, 1948), 172.

20 Eisenhower statement prepared for the *Episcopal Churchnews*, Sept. 21, 1952; text printed in the *New York Times*, Sep. 15, 1952, pp. 1, 16. He discussed the postponement in *Crusade*, 249–50.

21 *Public Papers* 1953:792.

22 Ibid., 1954:103–4.

23 *New York Times*, Dec. 23, 1952, p. 16; Eisenhower, *Crusade*, 471–72. The general expressed a Wilson-like view of the war in his memoirs:

> Daily as it progressed there grew within me the conviction that as never before in a war between nations the forces that stood for human good and men's rights were this time confronted by a completely evil conspiracy with which no compromise could be tolerated. Because only by the utter destruction of the Axis was a decent world possible, the war became for me a crusade in the traditional sense of that often misused word. *Crusade*, 157.

24 *New York Times*, Dec. 23, 1952, p. 16. See the discussion by Patrick Henry, "'And I Don't Care What It Is': The Tradition History of a Civil Religion Proof-Text," *Journal of the American Academy of Religion* 49 (March 1981): 35–49.

25 *New York Times*, May 20, 1947, p. 22; Kornitzer, *Great American Heritage*, 143.

26 *New York Times*, June 5, 1952, p. 16.

27 Ibid., July 12, 1952, p. 4.

28 Ibid., Nov. 4, 1952, p. 23.

29 Ibid., March 24, 1950, p. 18.

30 *Public Papers* 1954:22–23, 653.

31 Ibid., 1955:477.

32 Kornitzer, *Great American Heritage*, p. 143; *New York Times*, Dec. 4, 1946, p. 28; ibid., May 4, 1948, p. 43.

33 *New York Times*, June 5, 1952, p. 16; Sept. 15, 1952, p. 1.

34 *Public Papers* 1953:37–38.

35 Ibid., 1953:11; 1955:274; 1957:713.

36 *New York Times*, Sept. 15, 1952, pp. 1, 16; Oct. 6, 1952, p. 14.

37 Ibid., Nov. 4, 1952, p. 23.

38 *Public Papers* 1954:1067, 654–55.

39 Ibid., 1955:704–5.

40 Ibid., 1958:447.

41 Ibid., 1954:460; Hutchinson, *Christian Century*, 369.

42 Edward L. R. Elson asserted that "we are living today in what is destined to be the greatest religious awakening in the history of our nation." It is "a moral resurgence and spiritual awakening of national proportions," and the president's "inspiring leadership" is an "all-important stimulus"

behind it. "Through his personal conduct and expression he has become, in a very real sense, the focal point" of this revival. *America's Spiritual Recovery* (Westwood, N.J.: Revell, 1953), 33, 53. In 1958, after meeting with Eisenhower, Billy Graham told reporters that he had praised the president for his contribution to the unparalleled spiritual awakening that had taken place. *New York Times*, March 7, 1958, p. 15.

Actually, Graham's admiration for him knew no bounds, as his private correspondence reveals. For example, in one letter he even compared Eisenhower to Lincoln because "you have put a spiritual emphasis in the White House" and "have manifested sincerity, integrity and dedication." Then he added: "In my humble opinion you will go down in history as one of the greatest of our presidents." Graham to Eisenhower, Nov. 18, 1959, PPF 1052, Box 966, Eisenhower Library, Abilene, Kan.

[43] William Lee Miller, *Piety along the Potomac: Notes on Politics and Morals in the Fifties* (Boston: Houghton Mifflin, 1964), 19–20, 34; *Public Papers* 1954:737; *New York Times*, Dec. 23, 1952, p. 16.

[44] Michael A. Guhin, *John Foster Dulles: A Statesman and His Times* (New York: Columbia University Press, 1972); Henry P. Van Dusen, ed., *The Spiritual Legacy of John Foster Dulles* (Philadelphia: Westminster, 1960); Ronald W. Pruessen, *John Foster Dulles: The Road to Power* (New York: Free Press, 1982); and Mark G. Toulouse, *The Transformation of John Foster Dulles: From Prophet of Realism to Priest of Nationalism* (Macon, Ga.: Mercer University Press, 1985).

[45] Ezra Taft Benson, *Crossfire: The Eight Years with Eisenhower* (Garden City, N.Y.: Doubleday, 1962), 12; and Edward L. and Frederick H. Schapsmeier, *Ezra Taft Benson and the Politics of Agriculture: The Eisenhower Years, 1953-1961* (Danville, Ill.: Interstate Printers, 1975), 15–30.

[46] *America* 88 (March 9, 1953): 612. Appointments Secretary Thomas E. Stephens recalled that one day Eisenhower said after the end of a cabinet meeting: "Jesus Christ, we forgot the prayer!" Ewald, *Eisenhower the President*, 13.

[47] Elson, *America's Spiritual Recovery*, 53–55; idem, *Wide Was His Parish* (Wheaton, Ill.: Tyndale House, 1986), 110–12, 133; Childs, *Eisenhower*, 161; and *New York Times*, Jan 21, 1953, p. 18; Dec. 19, 1952, p. 24. Elson had been the 21st Army Corps and acting 7th Army chaplain in the European Theater of Operations. He saw considerable combat and held the rank of colonel. As he had been a military person and had the reputation of being highly disciplined and thorough, Eisenhower was naturally attracted to him. From 1969 to 1981, Elson served as chaplain of the U.S. Senate.

[48] Dwight D. Eisenhower, *The White House Years: Mandate for Change 1953-1956* (Garden City, N.Y.: Doubleday, 1963), 100–101; Emmet John Hughes, *The Ordeal of Power: A Political Memoir of the Eisenhower Years* (New York: Atheneum, 1963), 53, 55–56. Hotel owner Conrad Hilton formally presented to Eisenhower the desk on which he wrote the "little prayer" in a ceremony at the Presidential Prayer Breakfast three years later. *Public Papers* 1956:221.

[49] *New York Times*, Jan. 21, 1953, p. 19; J. W. Storer, *The Presidents and the Bible* (Nashville: Broadman, 1976), 141. Billy Graham, who at this stage in his career was a fervent promoter of American civil religion, apparently suggested the 2 Chronicles passage. Pierard, *Journal of Church and State*, 116.

[50] *Inaugural Addresses*, 257–62. His 1957 address also contained the customary references to the Deity and invoked divine blessing upon "our

common labor as a nation." Moreover, it expressed the exemplary quality of American life and the hope for peace, freedom, and international brotherhood. Ibid., 263–66.

⁵¹Brendon, *Ike*, 28; and Elson, *Wide Was His Parish*, 114–18.

⁵²*The Eisenhower Diaries*, ed. Robert H. Ferrell (New York: Norton, 1981), 226.

⁵³Forrest Boyd, *Instant Analysis: Confessions of a White House Correspondent* (Atlanta: John Knox, 1974), 63–64.

⁵⁴Ibid., 64–65; Elson, *Wide Was His Parish*, 132; Caspar Nannes, "The President and His Pastor," *Collier's* 136 (Nov. 11, 1955): 29–31; "The President and His Church," *U.S. News & World Report* 38 (April 8,1955): 50–52.

⁵⁵For details on public religiosity in the period see Pierard, "One Nation Under God," 85–98; J. Ronald Oakley, *God's Country: America in the Fifties* (New York: Dembner Books, 1986), 319–27; and Gerard Kaye and Ferenc M. Szasz, "Adding 'Under God' to the Pledge of Allegiance," *Encounter* 34 (1973): 52–56.

⁵⁶*Public Papers* 1954:563.

⁵⁷For the historical background of the National Prayer Breakfast and the prayer breakfast movement in general, see Richard V. Pierard, "On Praying with the President," *Christian Century* 99 (March 10, 1982): 262–64; and Norman P. Grubb, *Modern Viking: The Story of Abram Vereide, Pioneer in Christian Leadership* (Grand Rapids: Zondervan, 1961).

⁵⁸Merlin Gustafson, "The Religious Role of the President," *Midwest Journal of Political Science* 14 (November 1970): 708–22, is a detailed and insightful discussion of Eisenhower's priestly and pastoral roles.

⁵⁹Text of the statement in the *New York Times*, Feb. 18, 1955, p. 28.

CHAPTER NINE

¹*Public Papers* 1959:645.

²Stephen E. Ambrose, *Nixon: The Education of a Politician, 1913–1962* (New York: Simon and Schuster, 1987). The earlier biographical treatments of Nixon are numerous, and the most highly regarded ones are Bela Kornitzer, *The Real Nixon: An Intimate Biography* (Chicago: Rand-McNally, 1960); William Costello, *The Facts About Nixon: An Unauthorized Biography* (New York: Viking, 1960); Earl Mazo and Stephen Hess, *Nixon: A Political Portrait* (New York: Harper & Row, 1968); and Garry Wills, *Nixon Agonistes: The Crisis of the Self-Made Man* (Boston: Houghton Mifflin, 1970). Among the more helpful scholarly discussions of his presidency are A. James Reichley, *Conservatives in an Age of Change: The Nixon and Ford Administrations* (Washington: Brookings Institution, 1981), and Barber, *The Presidential Character*, 299–363.

³Bruce Mazlish, *In Search of Nixon: A Psychohistorical Inquiry* (New York: Basic Books, 1972); Arthur Woodstone, *Nixon's Head* (New York: St. Martin's, 1972); Eli S. Chesen, *Nixon's Psychiatric Profile: A Psychodynamic-Genetic Interpretation* (New York: Peter H. Wyden, 1973); David Abrahamsen, *Nixon Vs. Nixon: An Emotional Tragedy* (New York: Farrar, Straus and Giroux, 1977); and Fawn M. Brodie, *Richard Nixon: The Shaping of His Character* (New York: Norton, 1981).

⁴*New York Times*, Nov. 17, 1968, sec. 4, p. 1.

[5] Barber, *The Presidential Character*, 325; and Richard M. Nixon, *Six Crises* (Garden City, N.Y.: Doubleday, 1962), 282–83.

[6] Brodie, *Richard Nixon*, 23–24.

[7] Ambrose suggests that the impact of his Quaker heritage on his personality has been underestimated. *Nixon*, 31.

[8] Richard M. Nixon, "A Nation's Faith in God," *Decision* 3 (Nov. 1962): 3; idem, *RN: The Memoirs of Richard M. Nixon* (New York: Grosset & Dunlap, 1978), 13–14; Kornitzer, *The Real Nixon*, 239; and Wills, *Nixon Agonistes*, 32.

[9] Nixon, *RN*, 14; idem, "A Nation's Faith in God," 3; Renee K.Schulte, ed., *The Young Nixon: An Oral Inquiry* (Fullerton: California State University, Fullerton, Oral History Program, Richard M. Nixon Project, 1978): 60–63; and Brodie, *Richard Nixon*, 524, n. 21.

[10] Wills, *Nixon Agonistes*, 32; and Nixon, *RN*, 14.

[11] Mazlish, *In Search of Nixon*, 30–34; Brodie, *Richard Nixon*, 91; and Ambrose, *Nixon*, 30–31.

[12] Nixon, *RN*, 16.

[13] Nixon, "A Nation's Faith in God," 3.

[14] Carl F. H. Henry, "Reflections on a Nation in Transition," *Interpretation* 30 (Jan. 1976): 56.

[15] See Milton Mayer, "Disownment: The Quakers and Their President," *Christian Century* 90 (Oct. 10, 1973): 1000–3; T. Eugene Coffin, "Richard Nixon and the Quaker Fellowship," ibid., 91 (Jan. 2–9, 1974): 5–6; and Letters to the Editor, ibid. 90 (Dec. 12, 1973): 1237–38, and 91 (Feb. 13, 1974): 187.

[16] The Nixon-Graham relationship is explored in Richard V. Pierard, "Billy Graham and the U.S. Presidency," *Journal of Church and State* 22 (Spring 1980): 119–21, 125; idem, "Can Billy Graham Survive Richard Nixon?" *Reformed Journal* 24 (April 1974): 7–13; and idem, "Billy Graham: A Study in Survival," *Reformed Journal* 30 (April 1980): 8–9. The relevant correspondence is contained in the Richard M. Nixon Pre-presidential Material Project, Series 320, Vice Presidential General Correspondence Box 299, Federal Archives and Records Center, Laguna Niguel, Calif. Excerpts from this are published in Richard V. Pierard, "Cacophony on Capitol Hill: Evangelical Voices in Politics," in *The Political Role of Religion in the United States*, ed. Stephen D. Johnson and Joseph B. Tamney (Boulder: Westview Press, 1986), 83–84. The manuscript of the unpublished *Life* essay is also in the file.

[17] Graham to Nixon, Nov. 17, 1959; Graham to Nixon, Nov. 11, 1962, Nixon Pre-presidential Materials, Box 299.

[18] Nixon, *RN*, 292–93.

[19] Ibid., 673–74; and Pierard, "Can Billy Graham Survive Richard Nixon?" 10–12.

[20] Noteworthy contemporary critiques of the Graham-Nixon nexus include Edward B. Fiske, "The Closest Thing to a White House Chaplain," *New York Times Magazine*, June 8, 1969, pp. 27, 106–16; Reinhold Niebuhr, "The King's Chapel and the King's Court," *Christianity and Crisis* 29 (Aug. 4, 1969): 211–12; "The Preaching and the Power," *Newsweek* 76 (July 20, 1970): 50–55; Wesley Pippert, "Billy Graham: Prophet or Politician?" *Christian Life* 32 (May 1971): 28–29, 54–58; Charles P. Henderson, *The Nixon Theology* (New York: Harper & Row, 1972); Lowell D. Streiker and Gerald S. Strober, *Religion and the New Majority: Billy Graham, Middle America, and the Politics of the 70s* (New York: Association, 1972); Joe E. Barnhart, *The Billy Graham*

Religion (New York: Pilgrim, 1972); Ralph L. Moellering, "Civil Religion, the Nixon Theology, and the Watergate Scandal," *Christian Century* 90 (Sept. 26,1973): 947–51; and Pierard, "Can Billy Graham Survive Richard Nixon?"

[21] Richard M. Nixon, "A New Beginning," *Vital Speeches of the Day* 34 (March 1, 1968): 299–300; and *Inaugural Addresses*, 276.

[22] Ibid., 277–78.

[23] Ibid., 279.

[24] *Public Papers* 1969:434; 1970:434; 1971:562–63; 1971:811–12, 718.

[25] *Inaugural Addresses*, 279; and Charles P. Henderson, Jr., "Richard Nixon, Theologian," *Nation* 211 (Sept. 21, 1970): 235.

[26] *Inaugural Addresses*, 279, 283.

[27] Richard M. Nixon, "Acceptance Speech," *Vital Speeches of the Day* 34 (Sept. 1, 1968): 675; *Public Papers* 1970:763; 1971:719; 1972:789.

[28] Ibid., 1971:103.

[29] Nixon, "Acceptance Speech," 677; *Public Papers* 1970:15.

[30] Ibid., 1970:82–83.

[31] Ibid., 1972:124–26.

[32] Henderson, *Nixon Theology*, 193; and "Richard Nixon, Theologian," 235–36.

[33] *Inaugural Addresses*, 283. Robert Bellah maintains that this statement revealed Nixon to be in tension with the civil religion heritage but it did not repudiate the heritage as such. "American Civil Religion in the 1970's," 10–14.

[34] Marty, "Two Kinds of Civil Religion," 151–52; and *Inaugural Addresses*, 283.

[35] *Cong. Rec.* 115 (June 18, 1969): 16347.

[36] Ibid., 115 (Jan. 20, 1969): 1289–92. The level of religiosity subsided somewhat in the second inauguration. The number of prayers was reduced to four (only one Protestant, a black clergyman); the prayers took up twenty column inches while the president's address filled thirty-three inches in the *Congressional Record*. Ibid., 119 (Jan. 20, 1973): 1658–61.

[37] Ben Hibbs, ed., *White House Sermons* (New York: Harper & Row, 1972), 1–9.

[38] Ibid., v–vii.

[39] Ibid., 68; and Niebuhr, "King's Chapel and the King's Court," 211.

[40] Michael Novak, "White House Religion: A Tricky Business," *Christian Century* 87 (Sept. 23, 1970): 1112. Novak's instincts were correct. Two presidential aides later admitted the services were used for "stroking," that is, invitations were handed out to reward or appease friends and fulfill social obligations. Jeb Magruder in an interview with Studs Terkel, "Reflections on a Course in Ethics," *Harpers* 247 (Oct. 1973): 70; and Wallace Henley, *The White House Mystique* (Old Tappan, N.J.: Revell, 1976), 66–67.

[41] Edward B. Fiske, "Praying with the President in the White House," *New York Times Magazine*, Aug. 8, 1971, pp. 14–27, is the best critique of the services.

[42] *Public Papers* 1969:827–28; *Weekly Compilation of Presidential Documents* (Washington: Government Printing Office, 1965–), 1969: 1453–54. (Hereafter cited as *WCPD*.)

[43] *Public Papers* 1969:173, 182; 1970:778–79; *WCPD* 1970:733, 1131.

[44] *Public Papers* 1971:896; 1972:521. The ramifications of his "Catholic strategy," which also included opposing divorce and seeking the support of

high prelates for his Vietnam effort, is explored in John M. Swomley, Jr., "Church, State, and Mr. Nixon," *Nation* 215 (Sept. 11, 1972): 168–71.

[45]*Public Papers* 1969:542–43. A few days later Billy Graham told the president that he knew how he felt and understood what he meant, "but, even so, I think you may have been a little excessive." Nixon, *RN*, 429–30.

[46]*Public Papers* 1969:673; *WCPD* 5 (1969): 1112.

[47]*Public Papers* 1970:365–67.

[48]Ibid., 1970:371–72.

[49]*Newsweek* 75 (May 29, 1970): 96.

[50]Nixon staff member Wallace Henley, an evangelical, sadly admitted this after the Watergate debacle. *White House Mystique*, 74.

[51]*Public Papers* 1970:467–70; 1971:1047–50. A group of critics who were ejected from the hall in Charlotte filed a class action law suit, and the subsequent testimony revealed how Nixon's people had manipulated the event to discredit the Vietnam War opposition.

[52]*Group Research Report*, July 15, 1970, p. 50; Billy Graham, "The Unfinished Dream," *Christianity Today* 14 (July 31, 1970): 20–21; *Cong. Rec.* 116 (July 6, 1970): 22786–87; and Jeb Stuart Magruder, *An American Life: One Man's Road to Watergate* (New York: Atheneum, 1974), 119–21.

[53]Henley, *White House Mystique*, 64–65.

[54]Richard Scammon and Ben Wattenberg, *The Real Majority* (New York: Coward-McCann, 1970), 21.

[55]Henderson, *Nixon Theology*, 13. The use of religious symbolism by the two candidates and its role in the Nixon victory is explained clearly by Bernard F. Donahue, "The Political Use of Religious Symbols: A Case Study of the 1972 Presidential Campaign," *Review of Politics* 37 (Jan. 1975): 48–65. On religion and the 1972 election, see also Charles P. Henderson, Jr., "The [Social] Gospel According to 1. Richard Nixon 2. George McGovern," *Commonweal* 96 (Sept. 29, 1972): 518–25; and Ronald C. Wimberley, "Civil Religion and the Choice for President: Nixon in '72," *Social Forces* 59 (March 1980): 44–61.

[56]A work had been commissioned for the inaugural concert at the Kennedy Center which used a narrator and chorus with Lincoln's second inaugural address as its theme, but it was withdrawn by order of the Inaugural Committee "because the text might embarrass Mr. Nixon." *New York Times*, Jan. 20, 1973, p. 16.

[57]*Public Papers* 1973:328–33; James D. Fairbanks, "Priestly Functions of the Presidency," *Presidential Studies Quarterly* 11 (Spring 1981): 230; and "On Seeing the Presidency as Sacred," *Christian Century* 90 (May 16, 1973): 555–56.

[58]*Cong. Rec.* 119 (Feb. 8, 1973): 4176; (Dec. 22, 1973): 43589–91; and Billy Graham, "Watergate," *Christianity Today* 18 (Jan. 4, 1974): 8–19.

[59]*New York Times*, Feb. 1, 1974, p. 10. On the National Day for Humiliation, Fasting, and Prayer see *Cong. Rec.* 120 (April 30, 1974): 12270–81; and Linder and Pierard, *Twilight of the Saints*, 118–22.

[60]*New York Times*, May 29, 1974, p. 24.

[61]Bob Woodward and Carl Bernstein, *The Final Days* (New York: Simon and Schuster, 1976): 423; *Public Papers*, 1974:632; and Linder and Pierard, *Twilight of the Saints*, 111–12.

[62]Richard John Neuhaus, "The War, the Churches, and Civil Religion," *Annals of the American Academy of Political and Social Science* 387 (Jan. 1970): 138.

CHAPTER TEN

¹*Time* 128 (July 21, 1986): 57. Carter joined the Board of Directors of Habitat for Humanity in 1984. The work of the organization is detailed in Millard Fuller, *No More Shacks* (Waco: Word, 1986).

²*The Presidential Campaign, 1976*, 3 vols. (Washington: Government Printing Office, 1978–79), 1:561.

³David Awbrey, "Faithful to Faith: Belief Is Jeopardized When Religion Falls Prey to Politics," *Wichita Eagle-Beacon*, Oct.19, 1986, p. 3C.

⁴Leslie Wheeler, *Jimmy Who?* (Woodbury, N.Y.: Barrons, 1976).

⁵The biographical works that best treat the religious dimension of Carter's life are David Kucharsky, *The Man from Plains: The Mind and Spirit of Jimmy Carter* (New York: Harper & Row, 1976); James T. Baker, *A Southern Baptist in the White House* (Philadelphia: Westminster, 1977); and Wesley G. Pippert, ed., *The Spiritual Journey of Jimmy Carter in His Own Words* (New York: Macmillan, 1978). Carter's autobiographical accounts are *Why Not the Best?* (Nashville: Broadman, 1975); and *Keeping Faith: Memoirs of a President* (New York: Bantam Books, 1982). Rosalynn Carter's memoir is *First Lady from Plains* (Boston: Houghton Mifflin, 1984). Also important is the chapter, "A President Named Jimmy," in Barber, *The Presidential Character*, 401–37; and Betty Glad, *Jimmy Carter: In Search of the Great White House* (New York: Norton, 1980).

⁶Carter, *Why Not the Best*, 59.

⁷Ibid., 57.

⁸Ibid., 60.

⁹ Ibid., 417–18; and Robert L. Maddox, *Preacher at the White House* (Nashville: Broadman, 1984), 141–42.

¹⁰Carter, *Why Not the Best*, 79–80.

¹¹Because of Georgia's election laws at the time, second-place finisher Lester Maddox, an avowed segregationist, was able to win the run off primary with first-place finisher Ellis Arnall, and then go on to win the governorship in a bizarre general election. Barber, *The Presidential Character*, 427.

¹²William Greider, "A Carter Family Album," *Washington Post*, Oct. 24, 1976, p. A16; and Pippert, *Spiritual Journey of Jimmy Carter*, 7–8.

¹³Carter, *Why Not the Best*, 133.

¹⁴Ibid., 132; Moyers Interview in *The Presidential Campaign*, 1:176.

¹⁵Carter, *Why Not the Best*, 130–31; and Pippert, *Spiritual Journey of Jimmy Carter*, 6.

¹⁶Garry Wills, "The Plains Truth: An Inquiring into the Shaping of Jimmy Carter," *Atlantic* 237 (June 1976): 51. Also see "Jimmy Carter Explains His Faith," *Eternity* 27 (Sept. 1976): 80; and Carter, *Why Not the Best*, 27.

¹⁷Jerry F. terHorst, "Carter's Old-Time Religion in a New World," *Los Angeles Times*, April 2, 1976, II, 13. Also see Kenneth A. Briggs, "Carter's Evangelism Putting Religion into Politics for the First Time since '60," *New York Times*, April 11, 1976, pp. 1, 41; and Peter Goldman, "Sizing up Carter," *Newsweek* 88 (Sept. 13, 1976): 34–35, 48.

¹⁸An egregious example is the section entitled "Born Again" in the lead story on Carter in the September 13, 1976 issue of *Newsweek*, where Roman Catholic terminology was used to depict his faith and converts to Christ were described as belonging to Carter. See further Pippert, *Spiritual Journey of Jimmy Carter*, 2–3; and idem, "Jimmy Carter: My Personal Faith in God,"

Christianity Today 27 (March 4, 1983): 18. A useful analysis of the attacks on his religion is James M. Wall, "Words of Faith from Jimmy Carter," *Christian Century* 96 (Jan. 17, 1979): 38–39.

[19]Dan F. Hahn, "The Rhetoric of Jimmy Carter, 1976–1980," *Presidential Studies Quarterly* 14 (Spring 1984): 280.

[20]These are suggested by, but are by no means identical with, the sources listed by E. Brooks Holifield in "The Three Strands of Jimmy Carter's Religion," *New Republic* 174 (June 5, 1976): 15–17.

[21]Foy Valentine, "The Southern Baptists," *New York Times*, Nov. 21,1976, sec. IV, p. 17.

[22]Pippert, "Jimmy Carter," 21.

[23]Idem, *Spiritual Journey of Jimmy Carter*, 16–17; and Kucharsky, *The Man from Plains*, 23. Although he had no formal theological training, Carter was remarkably well-informed about Christian thought and biblical matters. When asked in 1983 to describe himself in the context of the theologically embattled Southern Baptist Convention, he ruled out "liberal" and placed himself in "the conservative, or moderate wing." Pippert, "Jimmy Carter," 21. According to Pippert, the Bible passages Carter quoted most frequently as a Sunday school teacher while he was president were Romans 3:23 and Luke 18:10–14. Ibid., 16.

[24]Carter, *Keeping Faith*, 62. Also see Kucharsky, *The Man from Plains*, 68–69, 83; and Pippert, "Jimmy Carter," 17, 20.

[25]Carter, *Keeping Faith*, 544. His relationship with Rosalynn was special and deep. As he comments: "We had been ridiculed at times for allowing our love to be apparent to others. It was not an affectation, but was as natural as breathing." Ibid., 18. In this respect, the media missed the point of Carter's much-publicized *Playboy* interview, where he admitted occasionally lusting after certain attractive women "in his heart." Reporters pounced on his confession and earthy language—actually, he was making a biblical point about love, sin and pride. Also, he claims it was an attempt to witness to people who seldom heard about Christian beliefs and moral standards, and that he was glad to share his religious views with *Playboy* readers. Robert Scheer, "Jimmy Carter: A Candid Conversation with the Democratic Candidate for the Presidency," *Playboy* 23 (Nov. 1976): 86; *Newsweek* 88 (Oct. 4, 1976): 70–71; and Pippert, *Spiritual Journey of Jimmy Carter*, 13.

[26]The secular press criticized his conversation with Park as "seeming to proselytize," while the evangelical papers were largely silent. However, the *Christian Century*'s James M. Wall came to his defense in an editorial, "When Religious Prejudice Dulls Judgment," ibid. 96 (Aug. 29–Sept. 5, 1979): 811–12. See also Pippert, "Jimmy Carter," 16–17, 19; and *The Baptist Digest*, July 9, 1984, p. 8.

[27]James M. Wall, "Jimmy Carter, Religion, and Public Service," *Christian Century* 102 (May 8, 1985): 459.

[28]Early in his administration Carter told a group of federal employees that he came to them not as the "First Boss" but as the "First Servant." He later revealed that he had been criticized for this remark because it was "lacking in macho." Pippert, "Jimmy Carter," 16.

[29]Cited in ibid. Also see Pippert, *Spiritual Journey of Jimmy Carter*, 14–15.

[30]Richard G. Hutcheson, Jr., "Jimmy Carter's Moral Presidency," *Christian Century* 96 (Nov. 21, 1979): 1156; Pippert, *Spiritual Journey of Jimmy Carter*, 10–11; and idem, "Jimmy Carter," 16.

31 *Public Papers* 1978:1115; and Ronald B. Flowers, "President Jimmy Carter, Evangelicalism, Church-State Relations, and Civil Religion," *Journal of Church and State* 25 (Winter 1983): 117–18.

32 Barber, *The Presidential Character*, 401; and Dotson Rader, "Living with Defeat," *Parade*, July 19, 1981, p. 8.

33 For examples see "Jimmy Carter Explains His Faith," 80; Goldman, "Sizing up Carter," 48; Pippert, *Spiritual Journey of Jimmy Carter*, 25, 37, 90, 104, 107, 127, 162, 171, 191, 214–5, 233, 242, 244–45, 253, 256; Hutcheson, "Jimmy Carter's Moral Presidency," 1156; Pippert, "Jimmy Carter," 16; *Public Papers* 1979:60; and Claire Randall, "Carter at Camp David: An Experience of Renewal," *Christian Century* 96 (August 1–8, 1979): 750–51. In his 1983 interview with Wes Pippert, the former president declared: "I've got a very good library on theology, including Niebuhr, Barth, Bonhoeffer, Tillich, and others." He was clearly the most theologically literate president in American history to date.

34 Goldman, "Sizing up Carter," 48–49. William Gunter, an attorney and later a state supreme court justice, introduced Carter to the theologian's work in the early 1960s by giving him a copy of *Reinhold Niebuhr on Politics*, a melange of excerpts from his voluminous writings that touched on political themes. According to Gunter, he and Carter discussed the book's contents and it became a veritable "political bible"for his fellow Georgian. Thereafter, Carter began including Niebuhr quotes in his political talks. Kucharsky, *The Man from Plains*, 19. However, as Don Winter points out, Carter's version of the "sad duty of politics" quotation was really a paraphrase which he used in two or three variants, and the actual words of Niebuhr were: "To establish justice in a sinful world is the whole sad duty of the political order." Harry R. Davis and Robert C. Good, ed., *Reinhold Niebuhr on Politics: His Political Philosophy and Its Application to Our Age as Expressed in His Writings* (New York: Scribners, 1960), 180; and Don Winter, "The Carter-Niebuhr Connection—the Politician as Philosopher," *National Journal* 10 (Feb. 4, 1978): 188–92.

35 Reinhold Niebuhr, *The Children of Light and the Children of Darkness* (New York: Scribners, 1944), viii.

36 Winter, "Carter-Niebuhr Connection," 188; Barber, *The Presidential Character*, 428–33; and Peter Goldman, "Carter up Close," *Newsweek* 89 (May 2, 1977): 32–38, 40, 45, 48, 50. The definitive biography is Richard W. Fox, *Reinhold Niebuhr* (New York: Pantheon, 1986). An unusually strong critique of his Christian Realism is Bill Kellermann, "Apologist of Power," *Sojourners* 16 (March 1987): 14–20.

37 Briggs, "Carter's Evangelism," 41; "Carter Says Faith Helped Him in Return to Private Life," *Wichita Eagle-Beacon*, March 12, 1983, p. 14Z.

38 Davis and Good, *Niebuhr on Politics*, 341.

39 Winter, "Carter-Niebuhr Connection," 191–92.

40 Hutcheson, "Jimmy Carter's Moral Presidency," ll56; and Randall, "Carter at Camp David," 750–51. Gaustad's review of Bellah's book appeared in *Church History* 45 (September 1976): 399.

41 Wes Michaelson, "The Piety and Ambition of Jimmy Carter," *Sojourners* 5 (October 1976): 18; and *The Sword of the Lord*, Aug. 13, 1976, p. 16.

42 For examples see Wall, "When Religious Prejudice Dulls Judgment," 811–12; Garry Wills, "Carter and His Religious Zeal," *Wichita Eagle-Beacon*,

June 6, 1980, p. 2C; and Hugh Sidey, "Assessing a Presidency," *Time* 116 (August 18, 1980): 13–14.

[43] Edward E. Plowman, "Carter's Presence Confirms Clout of Evangelical Broadcasters," *Christianity Today* 24 (Feb. 22, 1980): 48–49; Maddox, *Preacher at the White House*, 161–66; and Carter, *Keeping Faith*, 561–62. Jerry Falwell was the source of the accusation that Carter admitted at the meeting homosexuals were on his staff and defended their presence there. A tape was released which showed that no such conversation had taken place.

[44] Charles O. Jones, "Keeping Faith and Losing Congress: The Carter Experience in Washington," *Presidential Studies Quarterly*, 14 (Summer 1984): 438.

[45] John Maust, "Evangelist James Robison: Making Waves—And a Name," *Christianity Today* 29 (March 21, 1980): 50. See also John B. Anderson, "Faith, Virtue, and Honor Are Not Enough," *Christianity Today* 22 (Nov. 3, 1978): 14–20; and Wesley G. Pippert, "Moral Leadership Is Essential," ibid., 15–21.

[46] Hutcheson, "Jimmy Carter's Moral Presidency," 1163.

[47] Harriet Van Horne, "Good Omens," *New York Post*, June 21, 1976, p. 21. Carter did embrace the concept of the Judeo-Christian ethic as the basis of American culture, but it was never a natural part of his campaign rhetoric. Depending on the context of his speech, he occasionally referred to non-Christian sources of the values which he considered a part of American life, and like all orthodox Christians, he cherished the Hebrew Scriptures (the Old Testament) as his own. Pippert, *Spiritual Journey of Jimmy Carter*, 93–96, 191, 248, 253, 261.

[48] Carter, *Why Not the Best*, 136. Also see Susan Fraker, "Carter and the God Issue," *Newsweek* 87 (April 5, 1976): 18–19; Howard Norton and Robert Slosser, *The Miracle of Jimmy Carter* (Plainfield, N.J.: Logos, 1976), 87–88; Pippert, *Spiritual Journey of Jimmy Carter*, 122–23; and Keith V. Erickson, "Jimmy Carter: The Rhetoric of Private and Civic Piety," *Western Journal of Speech Communication* 44 (Summer 1980): 233.

[49] *Presidential Campaign, 1976*, 1:92. Christopher L. Johnstone, "Electing Ourselves in 1976: Jimmy Carter and the American Faith," *Western Journal of Speech Communication* 42 (Fall 1978): 242, argues the election turned on the broader theme of the faith that Americans had in themselves and their government.

[50] Carter, *Why Not the Best*, 149, 154. Also see Richard Reeves, "Carter's Secret," *New York Times*, March 22, 1976, p. 28; and John H. Patton, "A Government as Good as Its People: Jimmy Carter and the Restoration of Transcendence to Politics," *Quarterly Journal of Speech* 63 (October 1977): 249–57.

[51] Jimmy Carter, "Democratic National Convention: Acceptance Speech," *Vital Speeches of the Day* 42 (Aug. 15, 1976): 644.

[52] *Christianity Today* 21 (Feb. 4, 1977): 50. Goodfriend's role was criticized as "a sop to Jews" by Rabbi Marc Tanenbaum, and as mixing religion and patriotism by Greek Orthodox priest John Tavliridas.

[53] All quotations are from the text in *Public Papers* 1977:1–4.

[54] Carter said at the 1977 prayer breakfast and in his memoirs that he had considered using the stock civil religion passage 2 Chronicles 7:14 (like Eisenhower had done), but he had "second thoughts about how those who did not share my beliefs would misunderstand and react to the words 'wicked' and 'sin.'" *Public Papers* 1977:24; and Carter, *Keeping Faith*, 19–20. It

is ironic that many evangelicals had used this verse with unbounded enthusiasm during the 1975–76 Bicentennial observance, which for them was an unending festival of civil religion. Richard V. Pierard, "Evangelicals and the Bicentennial," *Reformed Journal* 26 (October 1976): 19–23.

⁵⁵*Public Papers* 1977:24–26.

⁵⁶Ibid., 1978:263–64.

⁵⁷Ibid., 1979:60.

⁵⁸Ibid., 1980:275–77.

⁵⁹Jimmy Carter, "Agape, Justice, and American Foreign Policy," *Reformed Journal* 36 (April 1986): 20. The article (pp. 15–20) is a thoughtful exposition of the themes of justice, human rights, and foreign policy from a decidedly Christian perspective but with civil religion overtones. Also see Pippert, *Spiritual Journey of Jimmy Carter*, 29–30, 93–95; and Flowers, "President Jimmy Carter," 125, 127–31.

⁶⁰Peter Goldman, "To Lift a Nation's Spirit," *Newsweek* 94 (July 23, 1979): 23, 25; and Randall, "Carter at Camp David," 750–51. The General Secretary of the National Council of Churches reported that Carter asked the religious leaders if the American people were ready to hear the hard message they were proposing and to grapple with problems that went to the very core of the value system which dominated society. Those present agreed that the people would respond if they were told the truth and given strong leadership. Ibid., 751.

⁶¹Quotations are from the text of the speech, entitled "Energy Problems: The Erosion of Confidence," in *Public Papers* 1979:1235–41.

⁶²Goldman, "To Lift a Nation's Spirit," 20–26. For a more scholarly analysis of the speech, see Dan F. Hahn, "Flailing the Profligates: Carter's Energy Sermon of 1979," *Presidential Studies Quarterly* 10 (Fall 1980): 583–86. Hahn shows the prophetic civil religion nature of the address, but his analysis is only of limited usefulness because he relied on pentecostal/charismatic sources instead of Baptist ones to illuminate Carter's speech.

⁶³Barber, *The Presidential Character*, 458.

⁶⁴Pippert, "Moral Leadership Is Essential," 15; and idem, "Jimmy Carter," 21.

⁶⁵Hahn, "The Rhetoric of Jimmy Carter," 268–69.

⁶⁶James A. Patterson, "Evangelicals and the Presidential Elections of 1972, 1976, and 1980," *Fides et Historia* 18 (June 1986): 55.

⁶⁷James Reston, "Revival Meeting," *New York Times*, Jan. 24, 1977, p. A23.

CHAPTER ELEVEN

¹*WCPD* 1987:572–73.

²The literature on Ronald Reagan is extensive, although much of it is journalistic or polemical in nature. For Reagan's early life, see his autobiographical narrative (with Richard Hubler), *Where's the Rest of Me?* (New York: Duell, Sloan, and Pearce, 1965), and the portrayal of his pregovernment years by Anne Edwards, *Early Reagan* (New York: Morrow, 1987). His political career in California and drive for the presidency are portrayed in Bill Boyarsky, *Ronald Reagan: His Life and Rise to the Presidency* (New York: Random House, 1981); Frank van der Linden, *The Real Reagan: What He Believes, What He Has Accomplished, What We Can Expect from Him* (New York: Morrow, 1981); and Rowland Evans and Robert Novak, *The Reagan*

Revolution (New York: Dutton, 1981). Lee Edwards, *Ronald Reagan: A Political Biography* (San Diego: Viewpoint Books, 1967; rev. ed., Houston: Nordland, 1981) is a favorable treatment. For his political addresses see Alfred Balitzer, ed., *A Time for Choosing: The Speeches of Ronald Reagan* (Chicago: Regnery Gateway, 1982). His personal correspondence as governor was compiled by Helene von Damm, *Sincerely, Ronald Reagan* (Ottawa, Ill.: Green Hill Publishers, 1976).

Significant works that touch on the first term are Lou Cannon, *Reagan* (New York: Putnam, 1982); Ronnie Dugger, *On Reagan: The Man and His Presidency* (New York: McGraw-Hill, 1983); Peter Hannaford, *The Reagans: A Political Portrait* (New York: Coward-McCann, 1983); Lawrence I. Barrett, *Gambling with History: Ronald Reagan in the White House* (Garden City, N.Y.: Doubleday, 1983); Laurence Leamer, *Make-Believe: The Story of Nancy and Ronald Reagan* (New York: Harper & Row, 1983); Robert Dallek, *Ronald Reagan: The Politics of Symbolism* (Cambridge: Harvard University Press, 1984); and Paul D. Erickson, *Reagan Speaks: The Making of an American Myth* (New York: New York University Press, 1985). An amusing but fanciful account from a psychoanalytic perspective is Lloyd de Mause, *Reagan's America* (New York: Creative Roots, 1984); while his many bloopers are recounted in Mark Green and Gail MacColl, eds., *Ronald Reagan's Reign of Error* (New York: Pantheon, 1987). The most insightful accounts to date are Barber, *The Presidential Character*, 460–99; Garry Wills, *Reagan's America: Innocents at Home* (Garden City, N.Y.: Doubleday, 1987); and Robert Lekachman, *Visions and Nightmares: America after Reagan* (New York: Macmillan, 1987).

[3] Wills, *Reagan's America*, 257.

[4] Cannon, *Reagan*, 141; and Wills, *Reagan's America*, 181. In her later years, Nancy Regan claimed she had been born in 1923.

[5] Barber, *The Presidential Character*, 477.

[6] Jim Wallis and Wes Michaelson, "The Plan to Save America," *Sojourners* 5 (April 1976): 5–12.

[7] Charles Hobbs, *Ronald Reagan's Call to Action* (Nashville: Thomas Nelson, 1976); "Reagan on God and Morality," *Christianity Today* 20 (July 2, 1976): 1047–48; and Doug Wead and Bill Wead, *Reagan in Pursuit of the Presidency—1980* (Plainfield, N.J.: Logos, 1980), 165–90.

[8] Materials about and by figures on the religious right would fill a small library. For details see the bibliographical works by Richard V. Pierard, "The New Christian Right," *TSF Bulletin* 5 (Nov.–Dec. 1981): i–iv; "The New Religious Right: A Formidable Force in American Politics," *Choice* 19 (March 1982): 863–79; "The Christian Right: Suggestions for Further Reading," *Foundations* 25 (April–June 1982): 212–27; and *Bibliography on the Religious Right in America* (Monticello, Ill: Vance Bibliographies, 1986). Also worthy of mention is the substantial book by Erling Jorstad, *The New Christian Right 1981-1988: Prospects for the Post-Reagan Decade* (Lewiston, N.Y.: Edwin Mellen Press, 1987).

[9] Jorstad, *New Christian Right*, 4–5.

[10] These efforts are detailed in Richard V. Pierard, "Ronald Reagan and the Evangelicals," in *Fundamentalism Today*, ed. Marla J. Selvidge (Elgin, Ill: Brethren Press, 1984), 52–56.

[11] For documentation see Richard V. Pierard, "Religion and the New Right in Contemporary American Politics," in *Religion and Politics*, ed. James E. Wood, Jr. (Waco: Baylor University Press, 1983), 65–69.

¹²Ronald Reagan, *Abortion and the Conscience of the Nation* (Nashville: Thomas Nelson, 1984); Bob Slosser, *Reagan Inside Out* (Waco: Word Books, 1984); and David Shepherd, ed., *Ronald Reagan: In God I Trust* (Wheaton, Ill.: Tyndale House, 1984).

¹³These and numerous other actions are described in Richard V. Pierard, "Religion and the 1984 Election Campaign," *Review of Religious Research* 27 (December 1985): 101–11; and Jorstad, *New Christian Right*, 127–52.

¹⁴*Wall Street Journal*, Sept. 18, 1984, p. 1; Shepherd, *Ronald Reagan*, 146; and Herbert E. Ellingwood, "Ronald Reagan: 'God, Home, and Country,'" *Christian Life* 42 (November 1980): 50.

¹⁵Interview with Rogers in Van der Linden, *Real Reagan*, 26. Rogers served four terms as president of the Southern Baptist Convention, 1978–80 and 1986–88 and was a board member of ACTV.

¹⁶Martin E. Marty, "Presidential Piety: Must It Be Private?" *Christian Century* 101 (Feb. 22, 1984): 187–88. Jim Wallis in *Sojourners* (13 [September 1984]: 18–21) went even further to accuse the president of being "idolatrous" in his beliefs.

¹⁷Scholarly assessments of his religious faith include Lawrence Jones, "Reagan's Religion," *Journal of American Culture* 8 (Winter 1985): 59–70; James David Fairbanks, "Reagan, Religion, and the New Right," *Midwest Quarterly* 23 (Spring 1982): 327–45; Pierard, "Ronald Reagan and the Evangelicals," 47–61; and Garry Wills, "Nelle's Boy: Ronald Reagan and the Disciples of Christ," *Christian Century* 103 (Nov. 12, 1986): 1002–6. Other treatments which contain useful primary information about his religious experience are William Rose, "The Reagans and Their Pastor," *Christian Life* 30 (May 1968): 23–24, 44–48; Von Damm, *Sincerely, Ronald Reagan*, 82–88; Ellingwood, "Ronald Reagan: 'God, Home, and Country,'" 24–25, 50–54; Wead, *Reagan in Pursuit of the Presidency—1980*; and Slosser, *Reagan Inside Out*.

¹⁸One news report (*Christianity Today* 11 [Feb. 17, 1967]: 47) claims that he not only joined the church but also contributed regularly to it, but evidence is lacking to substantiate this.

¹⁹*Public Papers* 1983:1450.

²⁰Boyarsky, *Ronald Reagan*, 177–81, 121–24; Evans and Novak, *Reagan Revolution*, 211–12; Edwards, *Ronald Reagan*, 201; and *Los Angeles Times*, Aug. 1, 1980, pp. 1, 17.

²¹Slosser, *Reagan Inside Out*, 135.

²²*Los Angeles Times*, July 15, 1978, sec. 1, p. 28. Herb Ellingwood, his legal affairs secretary, described this event in a speech at a Full Gospel Business Men's Fellowship convention.

²³Slosser, *Reagan Inside Out*, 13–19. The quotation marks are in the original and are Otis' remarks. See also Jones, "Reagan's Religion," 62, 68.

²⁴Wead, *Reagan*, 168–69. Also see the NRB speech in 1984 where he said that "since the beginning of civilization millions and millions of laws have been written," but they "have not improved on the Ten Commandments one bit." *WCPD* 1984:125.

²⁵*WCPD* 1985:213; 1984:122; *Public Papers* 1983:152, 178.

²⁶Von Damm, *Sincerely, Ronald Reagan*, 83; Wead, *Reagan*, 180.

²⁷Jack Anderson, "Reagan as Devout, but not Publicized," *Washington Post*, July 20, 1980, p. E7; Wead, *Reagan*, 182.

²⁸Rose, "Reagans and Their Pastor," 23–24; Wead, *Reagan*, 183–85.

[29] *WCPD* 1985:129; *Public Papers* 1983:359, 1451; 1982:109; *WCPD* 1984:148.

[30] Slosser, *Reagan Inside Out*, 82; *Public Papers* 1982:109; Wills, *Reagan's America*, 197. The president recounted the story of Cooke's visit to his hospital room to his biographer and again in the film shown at the 1984 Republican National Convention.

[31] Slosser, *Reagan Inside Out*, 16; Rose, "Reagans and Their Pastor," 47; Jones, "Reagan's Religion," 63–69; James Mill, "The Serious Implications of a 1971 Conversation with Ronald Reagan," *San Diego Magazine* 37 (August 1985): 140–41, 258; Ronnie Dugger, "Does Reagan Expect a Nuclear Armageddon?" *Washington Post*, April 8, 1984, C1; and Richard V. Pierard, "Reagan's Foreign Policy: Religious and Moral Issues," in *Religion and Politics: Is the Relationship Changing?* ed. Thomas E. Scism (Charleston, Ill: Eastern Illinois University, 1987), 82–84. The revelation of the president's Armageddon statements by the Christic Institute, a religiously oriented think tank, at a press conference on October 24, 1984, and the question raised about this in the second Reagan-Mondale debate had considerable damage potential, but it came too late to make any difference in the outcome of the election.

[32] Wead, *Reagan*, 173; *New York Times*, May 27, 1980, p. B9; and Elizabeth Drew, *Portrait of an Election: The 1980 Presidential Campaign* (New York: Simon and Shuster, 1981), 172–73.

[33] *Public Papers* 1983:178; *WCPD* 1984:122; 1985:108–9, 1493.

[34] This idea is developed in Wills, *Reagan's America*, 197–98, 383–86.

[35] Ronald Reagan, "Acceptance Address," *Vital Speeches of the Day* 46 (Aug. 15, 1980): 642–46.

[36] W. Wayne Shannon, "Mr. Reagan Goes to Washington: Teaching Exceptional America," *Public Opinion* 4 (December 1981): 13–17, 58; and Tami R. Davis and Sean M. Lynn-Jones, "City upon a Hill," *Foreign Policy* 55 (Spring 1987): 20–38, are useful critical assessments of this.

[37] *Public Papers* 1983:152; 1982:158, 1121. Other citations: *WCPD* 1984:100, 212; 1987:1072.

[38] *Public Papers* 1983:1451, 880. Reagan pointed out that his mother had written by the verse in the margin, "A most wonderful verse for the healing of the nations." *Public Papers* 1983:179. Both Slosser, *Reagan Inside Out*, and Shepherd, *Ronald Reagan*, contain the official White House photograph of the Bible open to 2 Chronicles 7:14. Other speeches citing the passage in a civil religion context are *Public Papers* 1982:159; 1983:1698; and *WCPD* 1984:314.

[39] *Public Papers* 1981:434, 1185; *WCPD*. 1986:171; 1987:63, 882; *Public Papers* 1983:1309;

[40] *WCPD* 1987:1032; 1984:980, 1223.

[41] *Public Papers* 1982:1120.

[42] *WCPD* 1984:149.

[43] *Public Papers* 1982:1485.

[44] Ibid., 1981:3; 1982:229.

[45] *Public Papers* 1982:1214; Slosser, *Reagan Inside Out*, 166; *WCPD* 1984:212–13.

[46] *Public Papers* 1981:462; *WCPD* 1984:87; *Public Papers* 1983:362; *WCPD* 1984:314–16.

[47] *WCPD* 1984:1159–61.

[48] *Public Papers* 1983:1594; *WCPD* 1987:752–53.

⁴⁹*Public Papers* 1983:362–64. For an eyewitness assessment of the speech, see Richard V. Pierard, "Mending the Fence: Reagan and the Evangelicals," *Reformed Journal* 33 (June 1983): 18–21.

⁵⁰*WCPD* 1985:130. The president rendered the text somewhat freely.

⁵¹He addressed the Knights of Columbus national convention and the New York State Federation of Catholic School Parents. *Public Papers* 1982:1009–14; *WCPD* 1984:487–90. For a sharp critique of the Knights of Columbus visit, see the editorial, "Holy Chief, We Praise Thy Name," *U.S. Catholic* 47 (Oct. 20, 1982): 2. The Reagan administration propounded the fiction that the relationship was with a political entity, the Vatican City, but Papal Nuncio Pio Laghi declared in no uncertain terms that the connection was with a spiritual body and most of the time would be taken up with spiritual, not political affairs. Pierard, "Reagan's Foreign Policy," 84–85.

⁵²Jim Castelli, "Religious Abuses in the Reagan Administration," *Christian Century* 102 (May 22, 1985): 527–28.

⁵³Television address, Oct. 23, 1983, *Public Papers* 1983:1522; Memorial service, Cherry Point, N.C., Nov. 4, 1983, ibid., 1541.

⁵⁴Memorial service, Fort Campbell, Ky., Dec. 16, 1985, *WCPD* 1985:1506.

⁵⁵Memorial service, Houston, Tex., Jan. 31, 1986, WCPD 1986:119. For biographical details on the astronauts, see the series "Seven Lives of the Last Crew of the *Challenger*," *New York Times*, Feb. 9–11, 1986. Christa McAuliffe was Catholic, Judith Resnick was Jewish, Ronald McNair belonged to black Methodist and Baptist churches, and Ellison Onizuka was an active Buddhist.

CHAPTER TWELVE

¹Quoted in a speech by Thomas E. Cronin, The Brookings Institution, printed in *Cong. Rec.* 116 (Oct. 5, 1970): 34919.

²Mark O. Hatfield, "Civil Religion," *Evangelical Visitor* 86 (Aug. 10, 1973): 4; idem, *Between a Rock and a Hard Place*, 94; and Linder and Pierard, *Twilight of the Saints*, 118–22.

³Alley, *So Help Me God*, 14–15; and Billy Graham, *Can the Tide Be Turned?* (Minneapolis: BGEA, 1976), 15.

⁴Bellah, "Civil Religion in America," 18.

⁵Mead, *Nation with the South of a Church*, 60–76.

⁶Jan C. Dawson, "The Religion of Democracy in Early Twentieth-Century America," *Journal of Church and State* 27 (Winter 1985): 47–63.

⁷Herberg, *Protestant–Catholic–Jew*, 263.

⁸Martin E. Marty, *The New Shape of American Religion* (New York: Harper & Row, 1959), 37–39.

⁹Richard John Neuhaus, *The Naked Public Square* (Grand Rapids: Eerdmans, 1984), 122–23, 72, 74; and "Religion, Secularism and the American Experiment," *This World* 11 (Spring–Summer 1985): 45. For incisive evaluations of Neuhaus's position, see the reviews of *The Naked Public Square* by Carl H. Esbeck, *Missouri Law Review* 50 (Winter 1985): 201–16; Richard V. Pierard, *New Oxford Review* 52 (July–August 1985): 26–28; Ronald A. Wells, *Reformed Journal* 34 (November 1984): 17–20; Harvey Cox, *New York Times Book Review*, Aug. 26, 1984, p. 11; and Arthur J. Moore, *Christianity and Crisis* 44 (Oct. 29. 1984): 406–7. Also noteworthy are George M. Marsden, "Secularism and the Public Square," *This World* 11 (Spring–Summer 1985): 48–62; the symposium *Religion in the Public Square*, ed. James

J. C. Cox (College Park, Md.: Washington Institute of Contemporary Issues, 1986); and Neuhaus's earlier book, *Time Toward Home: The American Experiment as Revelation* (New York: Seabury Press, 1975).

¹⁰R. Laurence Moore, *Religious Outsiders and the Making of Americans* (New York: Oxford University Press, 1986), 201–4.

¹¹This matter is developed further in Robert D. Linder, "Religion and the American Dream: A Study in Confusion and Tension," *Mennonite Life* 38 (December 1983): 17–22.

¹²Edwin S. Gaustad, *A Religious History of America* (New York: Harper & Row, 1966), 388–89.

¹³Fairbanks, "The Priestly Functions of the Presidency," 222–23. The entire article is an insightful discussion of the presidential role in civil religion. Also see Novak, *Choosing Our King*, 302–8.

¹⁴Eric Rust, "Limits of Civil Religion," *Baptist Peacemaker* 4 (October 1984): 8.

¹⁵Novak, *Choosing Our King*, 302, 309.

¹⁶Marty, "Two Kinds of Two Kinds of Civil Religion," 144–47, 151–52.

¹⁷A memorandum by Price written on November 28, 1967, published in Joe McGinniss, *The Selling of the President, 1968* (New York: Trident Press, 1969), 193–94. Price was a close friend of Nixon and his chief speech writer during the presidential years.

¹⁸Eells and Nyberg, *Lonely Walk*, 73; and Mark O. Hatfield, *Conflict and Conscience* (Waco: Word, 1971), 22.

¹⁹*New Republic* 173 (Nov. 22, 1975): 31.

²⁰Donahue, "Political Use of Religious Symbols," 60–61.

²¹Citing data published by Richard B. Dierenfeld in 1962 which revealed only 6.4% of the Midwestern and 2.4% of the West Coast schools surveyed had any sort of a homeroom devotional exercise, Martin E. Marty concludes that the American people "ritually 'took God out of the schools' before the Court did." "A Sort of Republican Banquet," *Journal of Religion* 59 (October 1979): 400.

²²James H. Smylie, "Providence and Presidents: Types of American Piety in Presidential Inaugurals," *Theology Today* 23 (Spring 1966): 282; and Cynthia Toolin, "American Civil Religion from 1789 to 1981: A Content Analysis of Presidential Inaugural Addresses," *Review of Religious Research* 25 (September 1983): 47. See also Fairbanks, "Priestly Functions of the Presidency," 214–32; Wilson, *Public Religion in American Culture*, 45–66; and Seymour H. Fersh, *The View from the White House* (Washington, D.C.: Public Affairs Press, 1961).

Actually, polls consistently show that Americans want their presidents to be religious. In most cases, voters place more importance on the fact that a candidate for the highest office believes in God than they do on whether he or she shares their political views.

²³Foy Valentine, "Civil Religion: A Biblical-Theological Assessment," *Search* 6 (Winter 1976): 50.

²⁴James M. Wall, "A Vision of the Future, Not a Tired Agenda," *Christian Century* 103 (Jan. 22, 1986): 60.

²⁵Robert E. Webber, *The Secular Saint: A Case for Evangelical Social Responsibility* (Grand Rapids: Zondervan, 1979), 127. This and an expanded version issued in 1986, *The Church in the World: Opposition, Tension, or Transformation?* (Grand Rapids: Zondervan), provide some models of church-state relationships and helpful guidance for Christians who wish to

work responsibly in the contemporary world. See also Robert D. Linder, "The Church and Politics: Some Considerations Concerning Christianity, Politics, and the Human Community," *Journal of the Irish Christian Study Centre* 3 (1986): 32–34.

[26] Marc H. Tanenbaum, "Civil Religion: Unifying Force or Idolatry?" *Religious Education* 70 (Sept.–Oct. 1975): 469–73.

[27] Robert L. Maddox, "Religion and U.S. Presidential Elections or Born Again Politics," in *Proceedings of the Second World Congress on Religious Liberty* (Washington, D.C.: International Religious Liberty Association, 1984), 72–73.

[28] This "holy history"—that makes America into a Christian nation which was founded on godly principles, was assigned the mission to model obedient Christian living and to spread the gospel to the ends of the earth, and thus was loved by God as no other nation in the world—is widely accepted among conservative Protestants and taught in their "Christian schools." The mythology of the view has been demonstrated in a concise and compelling fashion by three historians who are themselves committed Christians, Mark A. Noll, Nathan O. Hatch, and George M. Marsden, in a book specifically designed to reach the evangelical community, *The Search for Christian America* (Westchester, Ill: Crossway Books, 1983). A valuable commentary on their work is Ronald A. Wells, "The Demythologizing of Evangelical Civil Religion," *Christian Scholar's Review* 13 (1984): 254–58.

INDEX